THE BEGGING QUESTION

**Cultural Geographies
+ Rewriting the Earth**

Series Editors
Paul Kingsbury, Simon Fraser University
Arun Saldanha, University of Minnesota

THE BEGGING QUESTION

Sweden's Social Responses to the Roma Destitute

Erik Hansson
Foreword by Don Mitchell

University of Nebraska Press | Lincoln

The University of Nebraska Press is part of a land-grant institution with campuses and programs on the past, present, and future homelands of the Pawnee, Ponca, Otoe-Missouria, Omaha, Dakota, Lakota, Kaw, Cheyenne, and Arapaho Peoples, as well as those of the relocated Ho-Chunk, Sac and Fox, and Iowa Peoples.

Library of Congress Cataloging-in-Publication Data
Names: Hansson, Erik, author.
Title: The begging question : Sweden's social responses to the Roma destitute / Erik Hansson ; foreword by Don Mitchell.
Description: Lincoln : University of Nebraska Press, [2023] | Series: Cultural geographies + rewriting the earth | Includes bibliographical references and index.
Identifiers: LCCN 2022017262
ISBN 9781496225030 (hardback)
ISBN 9781496234575 (paperback)
ISBN 9781496234797 (epub)
ISBN 9781496234803 (pdf)
Subjects: LCSH: Begging—Sweden. | Marginality, Social—Sweden. | Romanies—Sweden—Social conditions.
Classification: LCC HV4583 .H435 2023 | DDC 305.5/6909485—dc23/eng/20220613
LC record available at https://lccn.loc.gov/2022017262

Designed and set in Minion Pro by L. Welch.

In memory of Gheorghe "Gica" Hortolomei-Lupu

Contents

Illustrations

Foreword

Don Mitchell

A decade ago the journal *Urban Geography* published a special issue under the title "The Americanization of Homelessness?"[1] The driving question was whether policies directed at managing homeless people in public spaces around the world were becoming increasingly like those pioneered in the United States: mean-spirited, aimed at pushing homeless people out more than accommodating their needs, rooted in a sense that homeless people were at best proto-criminals, but more typically simply criminal. The answer from the authors—reporting research from Sweden, South Korea, Japan, Germany, and Russia—was: sort of. These countries had adopted some policies bearing a family resemblance to America's revanchism, but given different welfare regimes, different articulations with global circuits of capital, and different criminal justice traditions, on the whole policies—and policing—tended not to be as harsh, homeless people not as thoroughly demonized, and support—from housing to job-seeking assistance and mental health care—a little more readily available.

In her outstanding article on Sweden, focusing on Gothenburg and its downtown redevelopment, Catharina Thörn explained that municipal authorities and private real estate interests most definitely worked to "exclude" homeless people from the city's public spaces—to make them as invisible as possible to residents, tourists, and investors—but did so in a way that was "soft."[2] By soft, she meant that authorities and private actors tended to deploy "a more elastic and fluid form of power" than did their American counterparts, even as they—like the Americans—tended to individualize homelessness, "focus[ing] on the rehabilitation of the homeless individual and access to temporary housing" rather than structural reforms of the housing market, which would address some of the root causes of homelessness. Programs of rehabilitation and the development of shelter were also most definitely accompanied by programs of "'sanitization' of public space for consumer-friendly purposes [in] Gothenburg just as in U.S. cities." It was only that this sanitation was achieved by different means. In particular, it involved the deployment of what Thörn (following the geographer John Allen) called "ambient power" in redeveloped and commodified public spaces. In Allen's words, ambient "power works . . . through the *experience* of space itself, through its *ambient* qualities. . . . Accessible yet closed, inclusive yet controlled, the very openness of this commercialized public space is precisely what allows consumers to be constructed through a logic of seduction."[3] One seductive strategy was to rebrand the center city as Gothenburg's "common living room" within which (white) citizens were depicted as "hosts" and made responsible for assuring that the space of the city was presentable when visitors came calling. Homeless people on benches, perhaps with cans of beer, were understood, implicitly at least, as out of place in such a living room. A kind of common sense, which homeless individuals often themselves bought into, was constructed. *Of course* the common living room should be neat and tidy. *Of course* that means that homeless people should not be there. Exclusion was not so much enforced as inevitable. For Thörn, exclusion was "revanchist" as it was in the USA, but such revanchism was softly applied.

A decade later, as Erik Hansson makes so clear in the pages that follow, it would be very hard to call Sweden's policies of exclusion "soft." Increasingly, homeless people—and especially their survival activities—are criminalized, and policies directed against them are increasingly more penal than persuasive. Across a great swath of the political spectrum, from the nationalist, racist, populist right of the Sweden Democrats to the squishy left of the Social Democrats there is significant support for banning begging, clearing out homeless encampments, and otherwise making homeless peoples' lives miserable. Private violence against the homeless is hardly absent as the very first pages of *The Begging Question* make clear. Such violence is usually publicly condemned, but it does not disappear. It remains a constant threat hanging over the heads of Sweden's homeless population.

What has changed?

One vital thing that has changed is that many, perhaps even most Swedish politicians and citizens would deny that those with whom Erik Hansson is concerned in this book are, in fact, "Sweden's homeless population." Instead, they are completely, ineluctably *Other*. They are, primarily, *not* the homeless of Catharina Thörn's Gothenburg, who were understood to be largely white, native-born, middle- and old-age alcoholic men, the so-called A-team that exists in just about every Swedish city and town. They are, instead, Roma (and other outcast) men and women, primarily from Romania and Bulgaria who began appearing on Swedish streets after these countries' ascension to the European Union in 2007—which, of course, was simultaneous with the global economic meltdown. Oppressed and discriminated against in their homeland,[4] barred or thrown out of work, often denied access to education, suffering from inadequate or absent housing, but now allowed to travel freely in Europe and to stay without a visa for up to three months in other countries, Roma beggars—referred to in policy as "vulnerable EU citizens"—found they could often make more money begging on Swedish streets, money necessary to support their children's schooling, their families' efforts to secure or build housing, and the universal need for food and clothing, than they could as casual, itinerant, or sometimes fully employed workers back "home."

As Erik Hansson so lucidly details in this book, the reaction to the sudden presence of this new, poor, different, vulnerable, *foreign* population was varied and complex. A not insignificant portion of the Swedish population met them with empathy, sympathy, and support, at least at first. But for many of these otherwise empathetic citizens, attitudes hardened, beginning around 2015, as the Swedish begging question became entangled in "the refugee crisis." In 2015 Sweden received proportionally more refugees and asylum-seekers from the Middle East and Africa than any other European country. At first Swedish politicians—again from a fairly wide spectrum, but this time from the Left Party to the neoconservative-populist Christian

Democrats—and much of society hailed Sweden's generosity and hospitality to this new, desperate population. By the end of November, however, the winds had shifted entirely, entrance of refugees and asylum-seekers into Sweden was halted, border guards were installed at key crossings, and the discourse transformed into one not of welcome, but of loss—the threat that immigrants posed to Swedes' sense of their own "Swedishness." In the process Roma beggars, already foreign, already Other, became *threateningly* foreign, *threateningly* Other, even to many who had previously been welcoming and sympathetic.

Some in Sweden, of course, had never been welcoming and sympathetic but had met the presence of Roma beggars with horror or hate right from the beginning. Their ideas, however subtly or unsubtly expressed, began to gain ground, to dominate the discourse. *The Begging Question* sets out to understand why—and how. Why and how did Sweden's heretofore "soft" policies—and discourses—of exclusion become so "hard"?

As Erik Hansson makes clear in the pages that follow, the sense that Roma beggars threatened the Swedish nation and (social) welfare state has much to do with their structural position within class society, a position that shifted, or evolved, with the arrival of asylum-seekers and refugees in 2015. But racism, both as a psychosocial discourse and a social or political-economic practice, also played a crucial role in Sweden's hardening attitudes toward the homeless. That the new homeless are Other, are foreign, are often darker-skinned, matters. But *The Begging Question* does not take that as given or for granted. Rather, Hansson seeks to explain both what constitutes racism, psychologically and materially, and how it has mattered socially and politically. His arguments are subtle and complex, though always expressed with an admirable clarity that makes them readily accessible even to those of us not familiar with some (or all) of his sources of theoretical inspiration. And they are made carefully. He shows that the hardening of Swedish attitudes toward homeless EU citizens cannot be explained *only* as racist. There is a lot more at work, both in regard to Sweden's self-image as a welfare state and Swedes' self-image as a generous, caring, and humanitarian people and in regard to the thorough neoliberal restructuring that self-same welfare state has undergone since the 1990s. In the pages that follow, Hansson insightfully blends historical-materialist and political-economic explanations, ideology-critique, and psychoanalytical theory to both describe and explain the complex social and political landscape of contemporary Swedish homelessness. The result is an incredibly deep, remarkably rich, and thoroughly enlightening analysis of the crisis of homelessness in Sweden.

I find myself somewhat surprised to be saying this. I have argued, quite starkly, that social, legal, political, policing, and violent actions aimed at homelessness and homeless people should *not* be understood as some kind of "sociopsychological" phenomenon, but should instead be seen as "a very material response to a very material set of processes" by which I mean that homelessness is rooted in and can be thoroughly explained through an understanding of the class dynamics and the political-economic structures, practices, and restructurings that define societies. These dynamics and practices are always situated within specific historical and geographical conditions, I argue, and thus what homelessness *is* constantly shifts in meaning and actuality, which in turn means that ideology and discourses of homelessness are vitally important. But these have explanations other than the psychological.[5] Erik Hansson begs to differ. He makes a compelling case here that these are *also* sociopsychological at base and can best be explained through psychoanalytic theory. The case is compelling (even as I disagree with aspects of it) precisely because of how he clarifies the ways in which psychological affects are fully and ineluctably *social* (not merely confined to individual psyches), and it is precisely in their sociality that they become causal. In turn that sociality is complexly, but invariably articulated within structuring, causal political-economic processes, not something external or separate from them. As a result, Erik Hansson provides a remarkably rich analysis of the present conjuncture and not just how Roma beggars exemplify it, but how the Swedish begging question constructs it.

In other words, there is much to be learned—I have learned a huge amount—about my newfound home of Sweden in the following pages, but not only about that. What Erik Hansson details here is not only about

Sweden. It is more broadly about our current, global, capitalist moment in which the Other is always already here, in our midst, and is not going away, no matter how desperately we think the solutions to "their" problems lie back in their "home," which in this case is to say Romania and Bulgaria. It is about Sweden's long history of racism, about the exclusive nature of its "people" (for whom the famous Swedish "People's Home"—*folkhem*— was built in the mid-twentieth century), and thus about the unavoidable exclusivity of "the people," wherever and whenever they are defined (as the agents of history, as the deserving citizens, and so forth). It is about what happens when whole classes of people fall between the humanitarianism of international law and the parochialism of national law. It is about the vital necessity of a lumpenproletariat to the functioning of capital and why radical politicians and activists on the left can no longer afford to be dismissive of this so-called parasitic class. It is about begging and home-lessness in Sweden, and it is important for the depth with which it tackles and the clarity with which it explains the problem, but mostly it is about how and why the dynamics of Othering are so exceptionally important in shaping the current global conjuncture.

Catharina Thörn was clear that the "soft policies of exclusion" she examined were never "soft" in the sense of easy or light or somehow not "revanchist." But compared to the policies-in-formation for excluding homeless Roma beggars from Sweden and Swedish society, they seem, in retrospect, to have been as soft as a welcoming couch had there been one in Gothen-burg's living room–like center city. They matched the political, social, and economic conjuncture of the moment. The harder line that Erik Hansson examines here matches the political, social, and economic conjuncture of our current moment. This book helps us understand the transition from one state of affairs to the other better than any other volume I know, and in doing so it sheds light on the broader *global* transition from the kind of liberal neoliberalism that marked the post–Cold War era to the illiberal, populist, authoritarian neoliberalism that marks the post–Great Recession world. That Sweden might be a central actor in this shift to a kind of authoritarian-populist neoliberalism will likely come as a surprise to many readers. In *The Begging Question*, Erik Hansson makes it starkly clear why it should not. Ambient power is still at work; it is just that the ambience is now strikingly different and so much harder. Even in Sweden. Especially in Sweden.

Acknowledgments

This book was made possible by a scholarship from Helge Ax:son Johnsons stiftelse. Aretousa Bloom, Ali Esbati, Mattias Gardell, Hanna Källebo Neikter, Joshua Levy, Patricia Lorenzoni, Irene Molina, Per-Erik Nilsson, Gunhild Setten, and Johanna Westeson read different chapters and excerpts of preceding drafts, giving important feedback that was crucial for steering the writing process. Maja Lagerqvist read through an entire manuscript early on and helped me in setting the tone. The reviews of Jesse Proudfoot, Catharina Thörn, and editors Arun Saldanha and Paul Kingsbury further helped in guiding my chaotic mind in the right direction—especially thanks to Catharina's generosity of time and insistence on the relevance of *Policing the Crisis*. Bridget Barry at UNP has been amazingly fast in responding and helping throughout this process. Effy Lindström, my copyeditor, has been the closest I've had to a "writer colleague" in writing this book, since her U.S. origin, knowledge of Sweden, and theoretical interests made her into the perfect conversation partner in making not only the English, but also the message, intelligible. Thank you, Don Mitchell, for your kind foreword—I look forward to discussing, and manipulating you into buying, the "sociopsychological" stuff you don't (yet) agree upon.

I wrote this book amid unique and rather alienating circumstances. After all, there was a global pandemic, and for the first time in my life, I was an immigrant (albeit one benefiting from the most luxurious edition of this subjectivity, as a Swedish academic visiting Norway). With that said, my newfound friendships in the Department of Geography in Trondheim— Hilde Nymoen Rørtveit, Gunhild Setten, Elizabeth Barron, Diana Vela Almeida, and Martina Calovi—have made the Otherness bearable. Especial thanks to my "godmothers" Hilde and Gunhild, who let me put so much time during my postdoc into writing this manuscript—without the freedom they granted me, this book would never have seen the daylight.

It goes without saying that I'm also indebted to my Swedish friends and family in inexhaustible ways. I want to give a shout-out to my former PhD candidate advisers David Jansson and Irene Molina back in Uppsala for their vital choice to trust my theoretical vision and letting me pursue it. Finally, I return to Maja. Let's represent the sublime by saying you're prettyyyy, prettyyyy good.

THE BEGGING QUESTION

The Problem

An Introduction

On August 8, 2018, Gheorghe "Gica" Hortolomei-Lupu was found beaten to death in a park in the town of Huskvarna, Sweden. Gica was a forty-eight-year-old divorced father of small children and an unemployed former typographer. A Romanian citizen, he had been homeless in the municipality for four years and begged for a living, though the local social service was unaware of his situation. Gica's assassins were a couple of teenage boys who had harassed him for two years and used to call him "the rat." That night they awoke him, filmed their deadly beatings, and then proudly spread the footage on Snapchat. It took more than a week for the police to start a criminal investigation, since the cause of death was initially labeled "natural causes." Although it was beyond reasonable doubt that the assault had led to Gica's death, it could not be proven that the teens *intended* to murder him, as the injuries they had inflicted are not typically fatal. In this regard Gica's otherwise poor health was thought to be a significant contributing factor; therefore, it could not be ruled out that he would have survived the attack under different circumstances.[1] Ultimately, two boys were convicted for serious assault, for which the elder, at seventeen, was sentenced to five months at a youth detention center, while the fourteen-year-old was considered too young for criminal liability. Meanwhile, Gica's relatives back home in Romania were not granted the right to compensation.[2]

This was the first acknowledged killing of an individual in Sweden commonly labeled as an "EU-migrant," "beggar," or, simply, "Roma." Notably, Gica himself was not Roma, but his social position in Sweden was equated with the Roma ethnicity. Although one man had died in 2014 due to suspected arson in an informal settlement in Stockholm, Gica's killing was the first case of deadly violence toward a member of this population leading to a guilty conviction.[3]

The prime minister and, in turn, leader of the Social Democratic Party (Sveriges socialdemokratiska arbetareparti—hereafter SAP), Stefan Löfven, commented on Gica's death. Löfven said he was "very distressed" and that "we need to discuss how to stop begging because that is no one's future."[4] This response, which frames the problem as the victim's livelihood, is symptomatic of Sweden's broader ideological stance toward what I call in this book *the Swedish begging question*. It was also politically strategic. With one month left until the national election, the remark signaled to the Swedish public that he would give them what they wanted: the nationwide *disappearance* of racialized individuals begging in urban spaces. Notably, this desire undergirded two levels of wishing. One level bore the egalitarian wish that no one should have to beg to survive. The other level represented the personal wish of eliminating the anxious encounter with the begging individual.

Löfven's statement could be read at both levels. Put into context, his latent message aimed to satisfy the personal desire of getting rid of "beggars," articulated as an egalitarian consideration. These "beggars" had been nationally present since the early 2010s, and in the national discourse the term signified foreign EU (European Union) citizens from Romania and Bulgaria, primarily of Roma origin. Due to severe poverty, these individuals and families had no choice but to travel to Sweden (and elsewhere) to find an income. No serious public efforts had been taken to combat their poverty. Instead, at the time of Gica's death, a social truth had been established: these poor people, who are vulnerable victims of racist discrimination in their home countries, require special protection, so what Sweden needs to do is to make sure these victims *return home*—in order for a magical "long-term solution" to be found. I say "magical" since there have been no serious suggestions from either politicians or experts explaining what this structural long-term solution would look like in practice.

This discursive strategy of naturalizing this social truth has been accompanied by state-biopolitical expulsion of Roma via a logic of something akin to "libertarian paternalism."[5] Since it is juridically impossible to deport EU citizens if they have not been severely unlawful, the directives of the state to its officials have been to foreclose these individuals' access to social rights: housing, education, sanitation, protection, and other social efforts that could fight poverty in Sweden (and elsewhere). This leads us to the curious thing about the Swedish case: the contradiction between this realpolitik and the discursive level. After all, Sweden is not unique in reproducing the structural discrimination, oppression, and persecution of Roma. What stands out is that, within this discursive framing and ideological belief system, Sweden's politics of foreclosure was seen as poverty alleviation rather than its antithesis.

Criminologist Vanessa Barker has called these Swedish state politics that target begging Roma "benevolent violence."[6] Indeed, this violent technology's desire-laden belief in doing something benevolent is a critical expression of what I call *the Swedish ideology*: the dominant nationalist ideology, or "social fantasy," of Sweden (and its Swedes) as morally exceptional.[7] The historical reflection of this ideology is the Swedish welfare state's exceptional socioeconomic success. In the twentieth century, Sweden was popularly interpreted as representing a "Third Way" somewhere between U.S. capitalism and Soviet socialism: a big intervening state apparatus with a Keynesian economic profile and institutionalized negotiations between capital and union interests, yet with a high degree of individualism. The expression "even in Sweden," popularized in academic discourse by geographer Allan Pred, represents the exceptional state of Sweden compared to the rest of the world.[8] Its exceptional characteristics are explicitly moralist: outstanding welfare, social equality, gender equality, humanitarianism, solidarity, and antiracism. One could also add to this list the perception of Sweden's erstwhile exceptional whiteness, with not only a "colorblind" antiracism, but also international public notions of Swedes being racially homogenous, blonde, blue-eyed, tall, and beautiful.[9] Within such an ideology, begging does not fit into established aesthetics—especially not if racialized.

When the issue originated in the 2010s, begging was depicted as something both "out-of-place" and "out-of-date." Thanks to the welfare state, poverty was supposed to have already been taken care of. At the same time, the moral character of the national ideology had rendered the prospect of *prohibiting* begging equally incompatible with the nation's self-image—Sweden, after all, had decriminalized begging once and for all in 1982. The most striking effect of this ideology was the delay in introducing anti-panhandling legislation into Swedish law. Until 2018 Sweden, with its lack of such regulations on both a national and local level, had been legislatively odd. Indeed, when the Swedish variant of allowing municipal zoning banning begging was finally adopted, the only EU countries without juridical space for criminalizing begging were Finland and Portugal.[10] In any case the former incompatibility of a moral intolerance of begging in Sweden and a moral intolerance of begging legislation in Sweden presented Swedish actors (political as well as private) with a *contradiction*, eventually culminating in the ideological solution represented by Löfven's comment.

What's more, this ideological contradiction has its own historical-material conditions, since what created the contradiction in the first place was the political conviction that Swedish authorities *could not* help the begging EU citizens by incorporating them into welfare schemes. This sentiment is informed by the present configurations of the capitalist and moral economy of Swedish society, with political institutions in a state of deadlock regarding the political fields relevant to the potential integration of the group: the labor market, the housing system, and the demarcation of the limits of social citizenship in-between national citizenship, the EU right of residence, and human rights conventions. Important, too, is the context in which begging arose: namely, a conjuncture of political, social, economic, and racial processes, which culminated in a general crisis on behalf of the state rulers—exemplified by the so-called refugee crisis of 2015 and the continuous rise in popular support of the radical-nationalist Sweden Democrats (SD). The latter, founded on an ash heap of Nazi, white power, populist, and fascist movements (including members who had served Waffen SS), entered the parliament in 2010.[11] Twelve years later, they had entered cooperation with right-wing parties and managed to receive 20 percent of the electoral support—thus becoming the second biggest party

THE PROBLEM

in Sweden. With a counter-ideology that depicted "mass immigration" as an existential threat to the nation and the welfare of the Swedes, SD also set themselves apart in the early 2010s by being the only party to demand the national prohibition of begging—at first.

Universal—Particular

THE UNIVERSAL IN THE PARTICULAR

This book is divided into two parts, since its aim is to answer two separate yet interrelated questions. The Swedish begging issue of the 2010s, and its fundamental moral contradiction as expressed in politics, discourse, and everyday street interactions, involve historical-geographical dimensions that were particular about the state of the nation for this era. However, it also involves dimensions that, I dare to say, are *universal*, both in the contextual sense of the current political economic order of the global capitalist system and in the almost perpetual anxiety the begging encounter appears to have induced throughout history and space since the dawn of recorded history. Understanding the Swedish begging question of the 2010s calls for an understanding of the dialectic between the particular and the universal. This dialectical method facilitates a better understanding of the Swedish political geography of today—a landscape of interest not only to Swedish residents but also to members of the international community. It is in this spirit that I invite readers to use the case of Sweden as a global reference point to investigate the international development of welfare politics and racism. It also helps us to reveal the universalities symptomatized in this story, regarding not only the reproduction of poverty and racial oppression in class society but also the disturbing *psychic* dimension underpinning this reproduction. This aspect pertains to the anxiety of the neighbor—the anxiety of encountering and handling human difference, a "difference" that is, in the end, nothing less than the universal trait of "humanity" itself.[12]

Without getting too ahead of myself, allow me to briefly touch on this bold and maybe controversial claim: in this book I contend that the sense of suffering stirred in people upon encountering the begging gesture—specifically, in class society (since without class differences, there would be no need for begging for survival in the first place), regardless of the time or place—relates to the unconscious handling of human finitude. This involves contending with the existential gap between, and within, human beings—in psychoanalyst Jacques Lacan's words, the desire of the Other. When we better appreciate this role of the unconscious in everyday life and in the politics reflecting and shaping it, we are, I believe, better prepared to try to resolve the global dialectics of poverty and racism. Nevertheless, the universal can only be glimpsed within the particular, which forces us to concretize the particularity in question as much as possible. As Marx said: "The concrete is concrete because it is the concentration of many determinations, hence unity of the diverse."[13] After all, without distinguishing the particularity of what appears to be a universal trait, we would entrap ourselves in dangerous ahistorical essentialism. If I dare to speak of "universality," "humanity," and "unconscious," this is because these properties are foremost understood as negations—negations of desires for these very abstractions, intended to help us escape the anxiety of human difference and suffering.

The book, then, attempts to perform this concrete abstraction of particularities and universalities by putting them in dialogue with each other. The first part addresses the universal in the particular, while the second deals with the particular in the universal. To begin, I aim to answer this question: *Why does begging constitute a social problem in the first place?* In this way I use the historical-geographical concrete, particular case of Swedish 2010s to unearth the universal kernel of relations of class society and the unconscious. Here, the particular is used to reveal the universal of begging itself. Abstracted, begging has historically been haunted by the moral ambivalence of its spectators. This historical continuity can be better understood if we introduce psychoanalytic theory into the analysis. To do this, we must also consider the evidence in the contemporary textual material that I've gathered, as it also points toward genuine moral agonies—considerations and benevolence alongside hatred, contempt, and sadism. The answer to this question, which, I argue, is "simply" that people feel bad about encountering begging because of their *empathetic capacity*, helps us better understand the development of the Swedish begging question in its particularity. It also helps us, as I demonstrate, gain a better grip on the power of racism in contemporary capitalist society, since this answer connotes the still understudied aspect of racism that philosopher Slavoj Žižek labels the unconscious fantasy of theft of Enjoyment.

In this book I present racism as a *dialectic* between unconsciously informed social fantasies and structural processes of racialization in which hierarchies of class exploitation take on racial appearances and consequences. These two parts mutually influence each other, constituting both stability and instability, contradiction and change. Here, it is helpful to understand the sometimes-needed analytical separation between poverty and racism, as well as the sometimes-needed analytical fusion between them. Just like a dialectic of universality and particularity ought not to reproduce ideological idealism on "human nature," a dialectic of racism, which in this book is also explicitly put in dialogue with psychoanalytic theory, ought not, as cultural theorist Stuart Hall warns us, to "ascribe racism-in-general to some universal functioning of individual psychology" or "a general psychology of prejudice": "The question is not whether men-in-general make perceptual distinctions between groups with different racial or ethnic characteristics, but rather, what are the specific conditions which make this form of distinction socially pertinent, historically active? What gives this abstract human potentiality its effectivity, as a concrete material force?"[14] Nevertheless, I believe it would be unfortunate to throw out the baby with the bathwater by leaving out altogether the "universal functioning of individual psychology" and "prejudice" from our theoretical investigations on why there is an "abstract human potentiality" for prejudice and racism in the first place.[15]

THE PARTICULAR IN THE UNIVERSAL

The Swedish begging question is a perfect example of how an issue of poverty becomes culturalized and racialized, even though the ideology performing this displacement of poverty as a social issue appears to be benevolent. This brings us to the question of the book's second part, where the particular of the universal is investigated. Here, the *universal* designates the well-documented tendency of begging under capitalism to increasingly transform from a social issue to one of order, with demands of criminalization and exclusion of the poor. Meanwhile, the *particular* relates, in this case, to the Swedish begging question of the 2010s and, what's more, its resolution of this universal tendency in a particular way and with a particular ideology. In order to appreciate this particularity, let us compare Sweden to other Nordic countries. In 2014 the Norwegian government made it possible for municipalities to outlaw begging.[16] The following year they planned to implement a national ban that would also criminalize the act of supporting "beggars" with housing, money, or food. This did not pass.[17] In Denmark, meanwhile, begging has been unlawful since the nineteenth century, and modern legislation has gone even further, forbidding NGOs (nongovernmental organizations) from assisting people without Danish security numbers. Plus, in 2017 it became possible to be sentenced to jail for *utryghedsskabende tiggeri* (insecurity-causing begging).[18] When the Danish social-democratic government supported a police effort in Copenhagen to crack down on "beggars," to avoid "making Denmark into a hotel" for foreign free riders, their legal spokesperson recommended the poor "choose another country, for example Sweden, because one knows there are better opportunities there."[19] Finally, in Finland, no change in legislation occurred in the decade in question, although there were two parliamentary propositions related to begging that gained recognition in 2010 and 2013.[20] It was in contrast to its neighbors, then, that Sweden's begging ban came "through the back door" in late 2018 through a legal reinterpretation of preexisting legislation in the Public Order Act, which "retroactively" made it possible to ban begging locally without the need for political decisions about new legislation. This unique maneuver reveals the aforestated particularity of the Swedish context, with its "benevolent violence" that ultimately accomplishes the universal tendency of waging war on the poor in capitalism.

But how was this particular road paved? This is what I answer in part 2, inquiring, *What happened in the Swedish begging question?* This question is articulated with both Sweden's ideology and imagined sense of moral exceptionalism in mind: How could, and did, the supposed "moral superpower" of Sweden go down the same road of racist-capitalist state oppression, while simultaneously upholding such a contradictory ideology of egalitarian and antiracist enlightenment? Part of the answer is, of course, found in the first part of this book, which investigates how the overdetermined anxiety revealed in the begging encounter plays an overlooked part in determining politics that reproduce poverty and racial hierarchies. But this partial answer begs its own follow-up question: if "everyone" feels bad about begging and wants it to vanish, it would lie in "everyone's" interest to make sure those begging do not have to beg for survival—in other words, fighting the disease of poverty rather than its symptom, begging. Here, the so-called easy way out would be to argue that poverty will never cease to exist so long as capitalism and class society continue to exist—and that is true. But it is here that the Swedish case becomes even more particular and therefore interesting. When Romanian Roma started begging on the streets following the financial crisis near the end of the first decade of the 2000s, begging was commonly interpreted as a novelty. Indeed, it has been a rather unusual sight in Nordic countries for the lion's share of the twentieth century due to welfare apparatuses and their attendant policies of preventing poverty. In other words, in the Swedish case, it *appeared* as though it was possible to neutralize poverty when it took the form of begging.

Nevertheless, the "old ways" were not applied to this poor population. Even here, there is an "easy way out" in which one attributes this change to the fact that "these beggars" were not Swedish citizens or formal residents—that if only the Romanian Roma were not foreigners (or Roma), they would have been saved by the Swedish authorities. Closely related to this reasoning is the idea that the welfare state is based upon a "paradoxical" distinction, with egalitarianism and equality for its "insiders" but penalism and elitism against "outsiders"—that it would be an essential logic of the welfare state in particular to insulate itself against poor immigrants in order to "protect" the social systems (as if this is not the moral idea of the post-feudalist state per se). This answer, I argue, plays too well into not only banal nationalist but also libertarian and social-chauvinist thinking to not arise suspicion.[21] Neither does it appear to be historically accurate if we examine the concrete. As late as 2013, the Swedish government gave undocumented children the right to health care and education and undocumented adults the right to acute health care. In 2015 the so-called refugee crisis emerged, making it political suicide to suggest such a proposal in Swedish parliament today. Even more interestingly, the rights afforded to undocumented children and adults in 2013 became interpreted as not applicable for "the beggars" and their children. Part of the reason for this lies in the continuation of anti-Roma racism in Sweden, but in order to make sense of racism in this particular story, it needs to be understood more as a dynamic structure than a cultural mentality. To quote Hall again: "It is only as the different racisms are historically specified—in their difference—that they can be properly understood as 'a product of historical relations.'"[22] In other words, we need to historicize and concretize the political development of the Swedish begging question of the 2010s in order to understand how the history of racisms "repeats itself"—though in different ways.

Notably, the begging question did not appear in a political vacuum; the politics, the welfare state apparatuses, the ideology, and the moral economy of the nation were in certain phases and relations to each other. What happened in Swedish politics was not isolated from what happened in the rest of the world in the 2010s; the Euro crisis, the Arab Spring, the Syrian war, the institutionalization of social medias, the global rise of racist and fascist movements, and the crisis of liberalism and social democracy all affected Swedish politics—not only in general but also regarding the begging question. Therefore, in part 2, I outline the political development of the Swedish begging question to explain how a *real* politics of poverty reduction for begging EU citizens became perceived as impossible. By explaining how political and institutional deadlocks of social policy fields intersected with not only the growing presence of begging but also of refugees and fascism, while decades of privatizations of the welfare systems took its toll, it becomes clearer how the politics of benevolent violence against "the beggars" emerged as a response to the crisis of the state rulers' *hegemony*. In this sense the "refugee crisis," which peaked in political discourse in late 2015 in Sweden, constituted a conjuncture of processes that made the dominating political class face a crisis of legitimacy, which culminated in them radically harshening Swedish refugee policy and the ideology on immigrants. This climax intersected with that of the begging question, which was relatively autonomous yet interrelated, as the politics against the "EU migrants" from then on became less "benevolent" and more violent. Though this correlation is no accident, it would be insufficient to blame this development on a vague, abstract, and noncontextual "racism." The fact that the politics concerning the EU citizens and the refugees *changed* implies that these politics were neither predestined nor unavoidable. From this perspective, racism here constitutes the question, not the answer.

THE CONCRETE

The concrete sources out of which I have here abstracted a "unity of the diverse" are primarily 1,329 media articles, most of which were published during the crucial years of 2014–16. Social media comment threads in connection to published articles also went into the data—likewise some relevant discussions on the infamous free-speech forum Flashback Forum. The data also contains interviews with fifty Swedish-speaking individuals, residing primarily in Stockholm and Gothenburg, on their thoughts on begging in Sweden. I use some of these informants' stories to "set the scene" in the next chapter. Additionally, I observed a Stockholm-based volunteer network that helps and communicates with begging homeless EU citizens. My own personal experiences with encountering the begging gesture in my everyday life in Stockholm and Uppsala has also, admittedly, influenced my analysis.

In terms of methodology, my textual analysis treats the media's reporting on relevant events as more or less an accurate reflection of how they occurred. This is also why I have chosen to ignore the wealth of "alternative" (that is, racist) media channels, which works as obvious distortive propaganda. In cases where certain depictions of events and reality have been challenged (by those not party to said propaganda networks), I have included these contentions. My analysis has focused primarily on the speech acts of social actors, on their truth claims, their rhetoric, and their arguments' coherence and interconnection with arguments of other actors. Put simply, I believe my analytical approach is most accurately labeled as a critique of ideology. Maybe it is even a *psychoanalytic critique of ideology*, since Lacanian psychoanalytic theory has been tremendously influential. My application of this "social" psychoanalysis is predominantly inspired by the corpus of Slavoj Žižek, who marries Lacanian theory with a "post-poststructuralist" Hegelianism and Marxian critique to create an eclectic political philosophy and social theory. There are, however, various other psychoanalytic thinkers and researchers from whom I have drawn inspiration, in order to clarify my reasoning as much as possible for those not familiar with psychoanalytic theory in a social scientific context. The presentation of the critique of the material and historical conditions under-pinning the ideology is in turn heavily inspired by Stuart Hall and acquain-tances' appropriation of Gramscian and Althusserian theory on hegemony, especially as applied in the seminal work *Policing the Crisis* from 1978.[23]

Some readers might become disappointed in the book's lack of gender analysis—both regarding the empirics and the theories—and I can only agree with the demur that many potential insights hereby become lost; unfortunately the enforced particularity of a book necessitates some down prioritizations, and I hope future publications on the subject matter will compensate this shortcoming.

The EU Déclassé Position

Before proceeding, a brief note about terminology: in this book, I analyti-cally term the social class position of the begging homeless individuals in Sweden relevant to this story as *the EU déclassé*. This term is my analytical elaboration of an anti-colonial Marxist term provided by Amílcar Cabral, which I theoretically develop in the next section.

The EU déclassé position is held by impoverished vulnerable people from primarily the European Union's poorest countries, Romania and

Bulgaria. What's more, the overwhelming majority are Romanian citizens and belong to the Roma minorities. Using their EU citizenship right of free movement, they travel to other EU states to find an income. Without formal employment or enrollment in school, they lack *the right of residence*. Instead, they are allowed to visit another country for three months as tourists. No border or ID control is regulating these visits. Most go back and forth between Sweden and their home country, monthly to annually, while some, like Gica did, stay for years. Notably, the EU right of residence affords one access to the same level of social security as host citizens. Without it, one does not have a right to social security or efforts on behalf of the host state under EU law. There is, however, *nothing hindering* the host country from interpreting EU laws more inclusively, or broadening the rights of visiting EU citizens with additional legislation of their own—which would also be more harmonious with the obligations of human rights conventions.

Since Swedish authorities have determined that EU déclassés lack the right to social welfare in Sweden, the norm is that EU déclassés are homeless while in Sweden. They sleep in informal settlements, in cars, under the bare sky, or if they're lucky, a few nights at shelters run by local NGOs. Typically they lack access to affordable health care, schooling, protection, sanitation, and public integration efforts, such as work training or education, though there are municipal exceptions. Significantly, there are no national rules on schooling or health care—it is up to the municipalities and regions to decide. The ages of EU déclassés range from children to ninety years old, but young children are rarely seen begging in Sweden. Among adult déclassés, both women and men beg and collect bottle deposits.

For this work, I have not interviewed begging people myself. There are, however, various reporters, NGO workers, and researchers who have. Drawing on this accumulation of research, I present an ideal-type description of the EU déclassé subject position below.

The majority of EU déclassés speak neither Swedish nor English, though many Romanians speak basic Latin languages, such as Spanish or Italian. This is because, before the global recession of 2007–9, some worked seasonally in these Mediterranean countries within the agricultural, construction, or cleaning sectors. Others have learned Spanish because they follow Spanish telenovelas. Many of those begging lack any kind of formal education, and some are illiterate. The majority have some kind of housing back home; however, the housing conditions are often of low or hazardous standards. As a rule, they are unemployed. This is also the usual stated reason when asked why they are in Sweden—they are looking for jobs but turn to begging for lack of options. If there are job opportunities back home, they are often so low paying that families cannot sustain themselves on those salaries. Consequently, begging abroad becomes a more rational option if one does not want to engage oneself in stealing, drug dealing, or prostitution—however, some of those begging have, of course, had to resort to undertaking these economic activities as well. Older generations had jobs before the fall of the dictatorships or when the financial crisis hit Southern and Eastern Europe, whereas some of the younger déclassés have never had any formal employment or a job-related income.[24]

The Roma, alongside Jewish people, have been treated as Europe's quintessential internal Other since medieval times. Indeed, in Romania, different groups of Roma were *slaves* until the 1850s. Their persecution continued in the twentieth century, during World War II. When, for example, the fascist National Legionary State sided with Hitler, Romanian authorities participated in the Holocaust of the Roma and others. After that, during Nicolae Ceaușescu's reign, from 1965 to 1989, "Roma" was ignored as an existing ethnic category in Romania. Instead, the Roma faced forced assimilation into the totalitarian-socialist industrial economy via universal labor duty. With the fall of Ceaușescu, Romania went through neoliberal shock doctrines, and the Roma category now became relevant once again for scapegoating. Institutional structural discrimination in work, education, housing, and health care intensified.[25] In fact, in 2014 it was estimated that roughly 90 percent of Romania's Roma households lived in poverty (in comparison with the national average of 32 percent).[26] There are no certainties regarding how many Roma live in Romania—it could be a half to two million individuals. Meanwhile, the majority of the Romanian population is poor, relative to other EU countries; therefore, since Romania's entry into the EU, roughly 3.5 million people (out of 23 million) have emigrated.[27]

The overwhelming majority of EU déclassés travel to Sweden and elsewhere voluntarily and organize traveling, begging, and sleeping among families or neighborhood groups. Some of them are kidnapped and forced into begging and prostitution by human traffickers, while others support themselves with illegal means besides begging. In 2015 the Swedish police presented its first—and so far only—national progress report on the presence of EU déclassés and their situation in Sweden. In the report the police acknowledged the existence of criminal activities within groups belonging to this population. However, the most significant crimes were pickpocketing and shoplifting, and trafficking was estimated to be very low. Although some trafficking cases were revealed, the conclusion was that the majority of déclassés come to Sweden voluntarily, with no illegal intent.[28] The number of "vulnerable EU citizens" (as they are named in official jargon) present in Sweden was estimated to be roughly 4,700 persons. While probably an underestimation, this number seems, at least until the pandemic, not to have changed.[29]

WHY "EU DÉCLASSÉ"?

Informing my choice of terminology is Amílcar Cabral, the revolutionary leader of the nationalist movement that eventually secured independence for Guinea-Bissau. He was also one of the most prominent postcolonial revolutionary thinkers of the twentieth century. Applying Marx's social class theory in a West African colonial context, Cabral categorized the exploited classes into different subgroups. Following Marx's problematic category of lumpenproletariat, Cabral termed one group *the déclassé*, which he argued constituted two subgroups: the "really déclassé people, such as beggars, prostitutes, and so on," which is the classic lumpenproletariat, and another group "not really made up of déclassé people, but we have not yet found the exact term for it": "It is mostly made up of young [people], who have recently arrived from the rural areas and generally do not work; they thus have close relations with the rural areas, as well as with the towns (and even with the Europeans). They sometimes live off one kind of work or another, but they generally live at the expense of their families."[30]

Since Cabral never "found the exact term," this subgroup remained sociologically ambiguous and never attained a clear specificity, since this class position of kinship networks was the reality for most young colonial Africans.[31] However, I argue the term "déclassé," provided as an analytical term for the relational class position of homeless and begging individuals of mainly Romanian citizenship and Roma origin in Sweden, works because of Cabral's nonspecificity of this "unnamable" subgroup. If "déclassé" here designates the life conditions of the people "not really made up of déclassé people," we escape the essentializing notion of "really déclassé people" as "unemployable," "beggars," "homeless," and so on. After all, the lived reality and life histories of people begging in Sweden are heterogeneous. Some find temporary jobs in Sweden, which does not necessarily mean they can stop begging. A majority are Roma, but not all of them. What's more, Roma ethnicity consists of many different social identities, including the heterogeneous Swedish Roma and Travelers who have lived in Sweden for five hundred years. From this perspective, the fuzziness of Cabral's term provides an accurate description of the heterogeneity and historical-geographical context of the begging population in this story.

The genealogical connection of "déclassé" to "lumpenproletariat" is significant too, as it illuminates the social and ideological status of the people it describes. Further, the word's meaning of someone "declassed" makes clear that people are declassed by others. Against Cabral, I argue there are no really déclassé people, since no one can be *outside* class within capitalist class society. However, people can be *deprived* of their class function vis-á-vis capital—facing long-term unemployment due to being fired, discriminated against, excluded, and so on. Within capitalism, this deprivation is more or less temporary. Consequently, I reject Cabral's distinction yet retain the undetermined character of the second group. I also note that his nondefinition bears a *geographical* aspect, which is of great importance to the class position of EU déclassés in Sweden. They migrate between Sweden, their home countries (mostly Romania and Bulgaria), and elsewhere. As a rule, they originate from rural areas and reside in urban areas while in Sweden. Here, the notion of traveling not only echoes the commonsensical perception of Roma people as "nomads," but it also highlights the EU déclassés' status as migrants *in-between* immigration and emigration, without attaching all the confusing various implications of the "immigrant" term. The prefix "EU," meanwhile, works as a scale demarcation, distinguishing them from other kinds of déclassés, such as ones born in Sweden or those from outside of Europe. It also highlights the structural role of EU membership as the legal enabler of the EU déclassés to come to Sweden in the first place without being immediately deported.

PART 1 Anxiety

The Universal in the Particular

1   Searching for Elucidations

I still vividly remember the occasion that made me decide to investigate the emotions that arise upon encountering people who beg. It went like this: On a gloomy and rainy autumn afternoon in Stockholm in late 2013, I entered a crowded subway car during rush hour. At that time brushes with begging had slowly become an everyday experience; indeed, my memory was still fresh with my first encounter with a person begging in the Swedish cityscape who was not a middle-aged, intoxicated, Swedish-speaking male (which was the typical profile of "beggars" before that time) but a non-white, non-Swedish-speaking, sober individual. It had been in Uppsala, in the late spring of 2012, and I had felt a combination of shock and a lump in my throat. Now, one and a half years later, the shock was absent when an elderly woman, speaking a foreign language, with a cane and an empty paper mug, entered the subway car. The lump, however, had lingered—in fact, it was probably even stronger than usual because of this woman's behavior. She moved slowly through the crowded car, continually crying and, with her gestures, insistently pleading with the passengers to help her by sparing some change. This stark emotional display on behalf of the begging person was unusual to me in these encounters—both before and after this occasion. However, what was probably most breathtaking about this woman's appearance was that, as she wailed, she refused to accept any fellow passenger's decision to feign ignorance to her and her plea. Indeed, as people averted their gaze and pretended not to hear her interpellation, she repeatedly made personal appeals to various individuals. Thank god she never tried this on me.

Within the car you could almost touch the condensed collective *anxiety*. In an ironic paradox, this woman—in spite of obviously being the least powerful individual present (in a material, socioeconomic sense)—was able to dominate the collective with her capacity to force all the passengers to react to her presence. Even the passenger's feigned ignorance was a response to the immense power of her actions. I remember imagining a collective sense of "us" being "held hostage" by her omnipotent presence in this enclosed space. All "we" who were not begging now shared an emotional community across class, age, race, and gender differences—united in being personally negatively affected. At least that was my sensation, as I watched how different individuals regarded one another with what I believed was a tacit understanding.

After a few minutes, in any case, this collective anxiety accumulated into an eruption of emotion, which took the form of a middle-aged man, all of a sudden, exclaiming to the rest of "us": "But she's faking! It's obvious that she's faking it!" I was shocked by my own immediate, overaggressive response, as I shouted back: "Well, doesn't that say a lot about her needs if she has to fake it?!" The man turned quiet, looked down, and mumbled something like, "Well, yeah, sure." This left me to contemplate my own reaction. It was so *angry*. Indeed, it made me think of my most recent Christmas dinner with family and relatives, where I also participated in a heated argument— this time, with a relative—on whether "beggars" were all criminal mafia or genuinely poor. My family member became as aggressive as I did. Back in the subway car, I reached the conclusion that this fellow passenger and I probably reacted out of a similar (if not the same) anxiety sensation, which had been collectively intensified. Through different meaning-making processes, guided by different values and experiences, we channeled this anxiety into aggression. Although I of course sympathized with the elderly woman, I would lie if I said her behavior did not cause me very negative emotions. At once it became obvious that my Christmas argument shared the same form: although there was no begging individual present, the experience of encountering begging made me and my yuletide opponent irrationally emotional, simply by debating the practice in the abstract.

But why did I become hostile on these occasions? Clearly, I almost instinctively treated my naysayers as the object of aggression, while they (initially) treated "the beggar" as the evil object in question. At the time interpretations of this *new* begging in Sweden had undergone a discursive change in the established media. In the phenomena's adolescence, the media had rather routinely treated it as the workings of some Eastern European "mafia" and human traffickers, with little in the way of proof, other than the word of a few police officers. Although the counternarrative emerged earlier, the discursive turning point occurred in March 2013, when a big investigative series was published in Sweden's most prominent morning paper, *Dagens Nyheter*, in which journalists had followed some begging people back to their home villages in Romania.[1] The story depicted remarkable poverty and horrendous deprivation among Romanian Roma and discrimination against them. Rather quickly this depiction was established as the dominant narrative in Swedish mainstream media. On this basis I found it outrageous that any "sane" people still could claim "they" were all part of a criminal conspiracy of human traffickers and charlatans. These people ought to know better! Nevertheless, the Christmas dinner and other occasions proved me wrong, and I started to become interested in what would later be (problematically) labeled as "alternative facts" or "fact resistance."

This antagonism between me as "enlightened" and those others was deepened by the political landscape at the time. Before the discursive (and ideological) shift, some representatives of the Moderate and Center parties had proposed begging prohibitions. But with the dominant interpretation now being antiracist and in solidarity with the racialized Other, the only parliamentary party in favor of a begging ban was SD, which had already proposed a nationwide ban in 2011.[2] Two years later, because SD was still commonsensically classified as a racist party and was the only party demanding criminalization, and because "the beggars" in question had now been labeled as "an oppressed ethnic minority," antipathy against begging was readily construed as racist sentiments. Besides, all the other parliamentary parties' leaders during these years wanted to distance themselves from SD as much as possible in the eyes of the voters (and used SD as a rhetorical tool against their opponents by playing association games); therefore, they avoided openly supporting repression of begging individuals, which discursively equaled supporting SD. From this perspective the malicious representation of begging Roma as deceptive criminals, articulated within this national-political context, made the one invoking this folklore (at least in my head, at the time) not only racist but also a tacit supporter of SD's fascist ideology.

On the whole my hostility against raising explicit suspicions regarding the déclassés could be partly explained by my discursive association of these statements with the racist ideology of SD. With the 2010 entrance of a radical-nationalist party to antiracist Sweden's parliament—in many ways constituting a trauma to the Swedish self-image—there was a strong national popular movement that aimed to dissociate and isolate SD and their ideology.[3] Nevertheless, my hostility was not only due to the racist Other; it was a condensed reaction following the emotional agony of the begging encounter. I managed to interpret this anguish as an encounter with poverty and structural racism, together with the identification of an *embodied* evil actor within this scene of injustice: my fellow man and his sentiments. Still, I could not ignore that my fellow man and I shared something: an emotional reaction to the presence of begging.

Having experienced a collectively shared anxiety of begging—one that could generate both antipathy and solidarity—I began to see that same ambivalence translated into the political debates and social practices of Swedish residents in relation to begging déclassés. Various private individuals were either engaging themselves in hate speech and hate crimes, abusing and terrorizing déclassés, or opening up their homes to them, initiating fundraisings for their sake or protesting evictions of their settlements. There seemed to be a shared kernel of passion between these political opposites, a shared kernel that I suspected had its origin partly in the common experience of initial anxiety in the physical encounter with begging in everyday spaces.

Four Ideal-Type Explanations

In the spring of 2014, I interviewed thirty Stockholmers on their experiences with and thoughts on encountering begging. In hindsight I believe the timing was ideal for the qualitative results of the interviews. The year

2014 was a "super election year," with both elections for the national as well as EU parliaments. Although SD was the only obvious representative of the desire to ban begging, it was not clear where the other parties stood on "the begging question"—what they believed to be the problem and how to solve it. Accordingly, it was a moment of ideological confusion on begging.

This confusion found expression not in the interviews' overall stance toward begging bans, as most opposed such bans. Their reasoning, however, varied widely. A national opinion poll from that same spring claimed the opposite: more than half the population supported prohibition, but the poll did not probe the moral reasoning behind people's stands.[4] We do not know, for example, whether individuals supported a ban because they wanted to punish "the beggars" for their economic activity—or save them from it. Those of my interviewees who opposed the ban believed it to be morally wrong (as an offense against the déclassés, or against Swedes themselves who maybe had dropped their wallet and wanted to buy a bus ticket—or as a matter of ethical principle) or pragmatically ineffective and a waste of policing resources. The identified problem with begging also differed: it was trafficking in disguise; an expression of an amoral work-shy cultural lifestyle; a threat to Swedish homeless people's livelihood; a public and aesthetic nuisance; an obstacle to pedestrian traffic; a sign of a failed welfare state; a sign of a failed European Union, globalization, neoliberalism, and so on. Interestingly, there was a small tension related to whether "the problem" came from outside of Sweden, or if it might be somehow linked to internal conditions. While quite clearly a majority identified begging as a foreign phenomenon, many of them nevertheless viewed the development as a consequence of the exceptional Swedish welfare society now in decline. Take, for example, this man in his late fifties, lamenting Sweden's heyday as one of the wealthiest and simultaneously most equal countries in the world: "And we were number one. That's not the case any longer. We have well and truly slipped down the scale. All these important basic functions of society [such as] a school for *everyone* that works. Healthcare. And childcare and . . . (*sighs*) the social services [that] are on their way to be razed. Well, that's the truth."

Almost everyone connected their interpretations to a relatively uniform depiction of Sweden: a moral, good place in an unjust world where no one had to beg for survival. As one twenty-five-year-old woman explained: "We've always been well-off in Sweden and in some way [there] have been different safety nets in society the whole time . . . We take *care* of each other." Likewise, a woman in her fifties said: "There were like no beggars in the world before. There just weren't. [I] was born . . . just during the time when all this kind of stuff was, taken care of. When people *had* a place to be . . . It was a completely different attitude in the sixties, seventies, and a good part of the eighties. And now, it's vanished."

One man in his seventies argued that, in encounters with "beggars," it was "as if the world has come to our doorsteps": "I have previously felt that we have been more, screened off, from the world's complications and we have had like . . . our *folkhem*, and our problems. But here comes, like, a screaming destitution that makes its entrance, which before now was really an exception, in Swedish society. It has really been an exception that there are people who have begged."

Curiously enough, few termed "the beggars" as "Roma," which later on would be the common label of the déclassés in the media and everyday life. However, almost everyone acknowledged that "the beggars" were "Roma." One such person, a woman in her eighties, told me: "I think humans are humans. We are all different beings, from different countries, yet we still are humans. But sometimes, I think . . . One especially sees Roma then. Roma, who are, nomads, one might say whom . . . are . . . [well,] maybe not criminals but maybe they are . . . thieves or whatever." A minority were blatantly racist in their identification of begging as being a "Gypsy problem," with "Gypsies" not wanting to hold themselves to ordinary societal norms of work and respectability. The following quote, from a man in his twenties, is broadly representative of this mindset: "Well, it is the case, that this is a Gypsy problem. [It's] largely only this group that has chosen to step outside the normal way, right? To live in a society, having an occupation, contributing, within the framework of the common. [. . .] In several ways, this is [*almost whispering*] a self-imposed role. To . . . do this. No one has forced them to do it, and there's no one [stopping them from] looking for real, simpler jobs if they wanted to."

On the opposing side, one woman in her fifties made a correlation between her memories of Swedish Roma in the countryside in her childhood and the present déclassés:

I see that it's exactly the same people, the ones who traveled around . . . I have pictures in my photo album that I saw a while ago, and it's exactly the same; nothing has changed. But now they're just herded around in a different way. And this was in the fifties and sixties. So that's what it makes me think of; it's the same. And when I see these camps in Högdalen [a Stockholm suburb], it's the same kind of camps that we had then. You start to see what this is—it's pure racism. It's gone on for so many years.

Many other interviewees, however, interpreted begging itself as something novel and unusual in Sweden in the early 2010s. One man in his twenties put it this way:

I think many people in Sweden, if you really think about it, are startled by such a radical change of . . . public space, that has occurred the past . . . yeah, say three, four, five years, that we . . . haven't seen at all in . . . cities like [Stockholm, Gothenburg, and Malmö]. Today I would say, if you travel out in the country, you see it in almost every larger town, and you see it even in suburbs with single-family housing, in . . . central places, squares and stores.

This perceived novelty, it must be stressed, is a partial truth. After all, in the aftermath of the Swedish financial crisis and cutbacks in public spending in the 1990s, there had been a resurgence of panhandling in the three conurbations of Stockholm, Gothenburg, and Malmö. This moral problem, however, was rather quickly neutralized, since the begging individuals were identified as lone, white, Swedish, male "homeless addicts."[5] In other words, they were deemed *undeserving poor* who could seek help from social authorities "if only they wanted to," and their need for money was interpreted as a desire for drugs. There were also, relative to the forthcoming Roma population, far fewer of them. Notably, these individuals still exist, though strangely enough, they were never labeled "beggars" by the informants: this etiquette was reserved for the EU déclassés. The latter differed from the former by being collectively organized, foreign, racialized, of both sexes, of all ages, and mostly able-bodied. And unlike the homeless white male population, whose presence was generally confined to the conurbations, the déclassés gradually showed up all over the country, in practically all towns and many rural localities. The interviewees interpreted them as either more or less "deserving" than their precursors. On the national scene of the 2010s, EU déclassés were subject to actions of hate and fear, as well as sympathy, kindness, and solidarity, to a completely different degree than the earlier cohort.

An interesting theme in the interviews was the perception of differing levels of *transparency* regarding "the beggars'" background and *intentions* with the begged money. Comparing the "Swedish" homeless population to the new "foreign" panhandlers, a man in his fifties explained: "When I was younger, then I knew that this, [spared] change would go to a pilsner. [. . .] I was one hundred percent sure [*laughing*]. And now, well I have no idea. [I think] that's why I don't give to them."

While the ideological strategy of making "the homeless addict" the exception that proves the rule (he begged because of sickness or laziness) allowed the social fantasy of Sweden as a place of moral exceptionalism to remain relatively intact, the EU déclassés' presence seriously questioned this narrative. While analyzing these interviews' combined narrative, I identified a widely held conception of Sweden having a "social contract" between citizens and the welfare state, in which the citizens outsourced their personal responsibility for strangers to the state, which takes care of those in need in exchange for labor and high taxes.[6] Historically, it was this "social contract" that would have eliminated the need to beg in Sweden. EU déclassés, meanwhile, constituted an obstacle to this fantasy, since they were not Swedish citizens or immigrant laborers. In light of this, several interviewees reported that their sense of responsibility for urban strangers had become activated for the first time in their lives. To them, begging was conceived of as belonging to other places, to those poor and unequal countries, something you maybe had stumbled upon as a tourist. It was also something *historical*, belonging to pre-welfare ages.

The way informants tackled this activation of moral considerations varied. These different mental strategies can be conceptualized as four ideal types of interpreting the problem and solution to EU déclassé begging.

First, there was the conviction that every EU déclassé was part of organized criminality—that is, they were simultaneously trafficking victims and perpetrators, deceiving the naive Swedes. The solution, then, was to ban begging, with the implication that both supposed victim groups—the trafficked panhandlers and Swedish pedestrians—would not have to be troubled by begging. This narrative, of course, was hardly separable from anti-Roma racist ideas, leading to the second ideal type of explanation: déclassés are victims of their culture, which has pacified them into work-shyness and exotic economic practices. Here the solution is a begging ban, to induce Roma into work and "society" (preferably back home).

Next is the third ideal type, which acknowledges the hardships of EU déclassés as genuine impoverishment, while also buying into the explanation of structural discrimination of Roma back home. However, these déclassés are other countries' citizens, and therefore their respective responsibilities, not Sweden's. It would be absurd to take responsibility for foreign citizens who do not qualify as refugees—the welfare state would collapse. What's more, begging is no solution to poverty. It only creates dependency and pacifies people into subordination. The solution is to induce the EU to exert pressure on the home countries to take accountability. Indeed, a begging ban might "send them a message" that Sweden does not accept this kind of social discrimination. Though this narrative does not necessarily call for official bans, the solution is to make sure the déclassés return to *their rightful place*. Notably, the causality between criminalizing begging in Sweden and conditions improving in the home countries is never thoroughly elaborated upon. Nevertheless, this gradually became the dominant interpretation of the begging question, embraced by politicians as well as many layers of the public. In the second part of this book, I trace and explain this process.

The fourth explanation, finally, is the "egalitarian" one, arguing that begging bans are ethically unacceptable. Because of natural human rights, it would not only be unfair to déclassés but also to potential ordinary residents like oneself if one would ever have to ask for assistance in public. It is also imagined that a begging ban would enforce racism while making Sweden callous and immoral. This is, of course, unacceptable, because Swedish moral exceptionalism must be defended. Against the third ideal type's commonsensical stand on citizenship, this explanation argues that EU déclassés are *economic* refugees, and that globalization makes national borders less relevant. The solution, therefore, is to accept begging and meet the déclassés with decency, knowing it will take time for them to emerge from poverty. However, this solution does not offer practical suggestions on how Swedish society might help EU déclassés out of said poverty.

The contradictions and internal antagonisms of these ideal types notwithstanding, I thought I had found an answer to the collective emotional aspect of the Swedish begging encounter: it had something to do with the relationship between the welfare state and the citizen and was a uniquely Swedish phenomenon due to Sweden's modern history as an omnipotent welfare state now in decline. As it turned out, however, this conclusion was all too ahistorical.

2   The Concrete's Historical Layers

As a quick perusal of the history of begging and poverty in the West reveals, there was hardly anything "exceptional" about Swedish emotional and moral reactions to begging in the 2010s. Consider, for example, the minor "moral panic" during the resurgence of begging in Stockholm in the late 1990s, in which the Stockholm police tried to frame begging as "disorderly conduct."[1] The discursive level also has deep roots in history. Let us cast our minds back to Victorian England. Reading Friedrich Engels's *The Condition of the Working Class in England in 1844*, one finds this letter to the editor of the *Manchester Guardian*:

> MR. EDITOR,—For some time past our main streets are haunted by swarms of beggars, who try to awaken the pity of the passers-by in a most shameless and annoying manner, by exposing their tattered clothing, sickly aspect, and disgusting wounds and deformities. I should think that when one not only pays the poor-rate, but also contributes largely to the charitable institutions, one had done enough to earn a right to be spared such disagreeable and impertinent molestations. And why else do we pay such high rates for the maintenance of the municipal police, if they do not even protect us so far as to make it possible to go to or out of town in peace? I hope the publication of these lines in your widely-circulated paper may induce the authorities to remove this nuisance; and I remain,
>
> —Your obedient servant, "*A Lady.*"[2]

Compare this "Lady's" words with this letter to the editor of a Swedish local newspaper from 2014:

Every time I walk through the town of Hudiksvall, several people are sitting scattered a bit everywhere. Either they sit and rustle with their little cans and tell people they want money, or they approach people and give them roses [squeezing] a note in your face forcing you to read it. It says all of their family is dead or that they are deaf, dumb, or have some other serious health issues and that they are homeless. [But] all this is just a big act! When the day is over and they've finished begging, their family members pick them up in new fine cars. If you live in Sweden, it is impossible for you to be impoverished and not have housing because the state is paying a lot of subsidies. There are housing allowance, child allowance, and a lot of other allowances they can get. Those allowances come from our taxes, and yet they have the guts to demand us on even more! This makes me really darned mad. My privacy is violated when they approach me and ask me to give them money. [As] a citizen of this town, I want to be able to feel safe when I walk around doing my errands. [Personally], I think begging should be outlawed. Let us citizens keep our right to move publicly without someone intruding upon our privacy.[3]

Although the latter is erroneous in believing "the beggars" have rights to Swedish state subsidies, the differences between the social policies of Victorian England and contemporary Sweden are striking. Nevertheless, what I identified as a social contract of outsourcing personal moral responsibility to the state seems to have been applicable even before the dawn of the social state. It's also worth noting that "the beggars" the Lady despises are neither racial Others nor foreigners; consequently, it would be too easy to disavow the discomfort at encountering racialized begging people as *only* a matter of racist sentiments. With all of this in mind, the remaining similarity between Engels's lived space-time and mine is the capitalist mode of production and its accompanying bourgeois ideology. Does this mean we can explain anxieties about begging as a historical result of capitalism as a system and ideology? The answer is yes and no. I'll start with explaining why the affirmative holds true.

Inside/Outside Capitalism—Inconvenience for the State

As capitalism has by now colonized practically the whole globe, the international and national production of wealth and poverty is mediated today through the capitalist system as a global, dominant mode of production. This system depends upon economic (and thus de facto political) inequality between two major social classes: capitalists and workers. Impoverishment is produced and perceived within this system. Looking upon history, we also see how begging has occurred as a social problem since the genesis of capitalist social relations. It also seems to be the case that the magnitude of both begging individuals and the moral panic connected to begging, within a given historical-geographical context, follows a cyclical conjuncture in tandem with the fluctuations of capital accumulation cycles. That is, within capitalism, begging is a latent constant yet something that is considered more of a social problem during certain temporal phases. These phases in turn intersect with phases of economic restructuring and/or crisis.

Following the Marxian tradition, I here make an analytical difference between "capital" and "capitalism." In the words of geographer Don Mitchell, following David Harvey, capital is "a political economic *process* with a central and necessary, if historically determined and evolving, *logic*," whereas capitalism is "a total social system rooted in and determined by that political economic process."[4] In this vein, "capital" can also designate the political logic of capitalist actors, whether as individuals, class, or institutions.

Given that begging is a practice of impoverished people who cannot support themselves through wage labor or property ownership, it is an expression of poverty. To capital, poverty and unemployment play a crucial role in its mode of production to generate accumulated value. As labor power is the only commodity that can produce value, capitalists need to exploit labor power by keeping the surplus value of production to themselves. The constant need to increase value accumulation (because that is the only way to keep value from evaporating) leads to a constant incitement to lower the cost of production to generate a larger share of surplus value. With the majority of the population left with no choice but to sell their labor power to attain a decent life, one inescapable cost reduction of production is forced competition among workers, as this keeps wages low. As workers do not own their own means of reproduction, unemployment equals poverty. Without poverty, or the risk of it, people would not sell their labor power nor compete with each other.[5] Of course, an employment contract by no means guarantees the absence of poverty—that is why unemployment, following the logic and interest of capital, always needs to entail more severe poverty than being employed.

Capitalist production undergoes fluctuations when there is a great need for workers, and when there is a great need to fire them. This leads to societal fluctuations of "overpopulation," expressed as unemployment and increased poverty. However, the cyclic production process creates a need to always have unoccupied workers ready to step in when demand increases, and a need to have these workers mobile to be allocated where demand increases. A relative proportion of the working class will always constitute an *industrial reserve army*: the unemployed whose labor is currently considered useless from a capitalist standpoint, but who are always available to either increase production or compete with other workers (through their willingness to lower the wage floor). This relative surplus population is stratified in a hierarchy of categories, correlating to their proximity to current labor market demands. As this system is hierarchical, someone needs, by necessity, to be at the bottom and thus the poorest. The lowest sediment is within the sphere of pauperism, and within this stratum exist those who are least expected to be considered employable. Marx argues the disabled, the ill, criminals, vagabonds, and outcasts belong to this layer.[6] Here we also find the "chronically" homeless and those who, for lack of other economic (or moral) options, turn to begging. Obviously, "unemployability" is something relative, due to capitalism's ever-changing demands and needs. As Marx explains: "It is already contained in the concept of the *free labourer*, that he is a *pauper*: virtual pauper."[7] He is "merely a *living labour capacity*," without "the objectivities necessary to realize himself as labour capacity." Stripped of their wage labor, every worker is a "beggar," a déclassé, from a political-economic perspective.

There is, however, an inherent contradiction to capital's relation to the unemployed poor. While capital needs reserve recruits on standby, it has no need for the individual who is not incorporable into current production schemes. Marx wrote, "the beggar, the unemployed, the starving" are "figures who do not exist *for political economy* but only for other eyes, those of the doctor, the judge, the gravedigger, and bum-bailiff, etc.; such figures are specters outside its domain."[8] Poverty is generated by capital and is inherent to capitalism, yet poverty's victims are useless to capital if they cannot be regarded as potential labor power. However, the other eyes for which "such figures" exist, such as the judge and the bum-bailiff, are, ultimately, the eyes of the state and its police. Capital is therefore in need of the state with its violence monopoly to discipline the working class into conforming to capital's needs. The state is also needed to protect private property. The "beggar's" practice of relying on others instead of engaging in wage labor is then overdetermined to be considered as socially disruptive—by not conforming to the work ethic, societal virtues of subjection, and the respect for others' property.

The capitalist state, in turn, needs capital to execute its power, while it also needs to regulate capital in different ways so as to save both the capitalist state and capital itself from the latter's socially devastating effects. This interdependence between the state and capital, and their relationship to "the beggar" as a disturbance of the social order, is neatly illustrated in Marx's account of "the so-called primitive accumulation": the nascence of capitalist accumulation in Europe. The absolutist state emerged in the social processes following the Black Death, and already in late fifteenth-century England and France, the owning estates began the expropriation of peasantry from their land by enclosures of commons. This dispossession, in tandem with the "primitive accumulation" of colonialism in the New and Old Worlds, would lay the groundwork for the capitalist system. The expropriated, now paupers and vagabonds, were to be disciplined into new workforces, which explains the anti-vagabondage and begging legislation's cruelty in punishment. In England the Vagabonds Act 1530 proclaimed nondisabled "beggars" were "to be tied to the cart-tail and whipped until the blood streams from their bodies, then to swear an oath to go back to their birthplace or to where they have lived the last three years and to 'put themselves to labour.'"[9] Subsequent legislation contained the possibility of forcing a caught "beggar" and his children to become slaves to those who denounced him. If caught several times, he was to be executed. Similar legislation was also found in France.

With the emerging establishment of capitalism, which replaced serfdom with wage labor, the anti-vagabond legislations in Europe became utilized as state-control instruments, disciplining the now "freed" proletariat into wage labor and fear of unemployment and idleness. In the following centuries, "beggars' detention centers" were established, along with correction establishments, prisons, and poorhouses.[10]

As was the case with former monasteries' almsgiving and infirmaries, the local poorhouses and their poor relief were entangled in a continuous struggle to distinguish between *deserving* and *undeserving* poor. Simultaneously, a distinction was made between those belonging to the community and those who were identified as strangers, informing the deserving–undeserving distinction. Those who belonged were prioritized, while outsiders were removed. Notably, the deserving were also those deemed unable to work (the elderly, sick, disabled, orphans, widows). The undeserving were not only "strangers" but also those considered able-bodied. In Bern, Switzerland, all non-belonging "beggars," such as French-speaking people, vagabonds, pilgrims, and Roma, were expelled already in 1481. Nevertheless, the problem of distinction remained, as the town in 1527 enforced all belonging "beggars" to wear tokens.[11] In the same year, in connection to the adoption of Protestantism and the expropriation of the Catholic Church, Sweden received its first (recorded) anti-panhandling legislation.[12] This occurred during the formation of the Swedish state, when Gustav Vasa made himself king of Sweden in 1523 following a "liberation war" with Denmark.

Swedish legislation regulating begging would continue, albeit in various forms, until 1982. Interconnected to different social upheavals—such as wars, land reforms and grabbing, pandemics, and bad harvests—legislation was modified to be either more liberal or less so. In longer periods, begging was accepted if one applied to the local authorities and received a license. With this, you could only beg within the domicile.[13] Different versions of local beggar tokens for each town existed until the end of the nineteenth century. Begging people were not to be mobile—instead, they ought to be kept "at home" to demarcate whose responsibility they were. Alongside the institutionalized local poorhouses, a wooden token called *fattigklubban* (the pauper club) circulated from household to household, marking whose turn it was to take care of vagrant strangers, temporarily visiting.[14]

It was not until the introduction of the welfare state in the early twentieth century that begging gradually ceased to be a social and police problem in Sweden. When begging was decriminalized in 1982 with the introduction of the new, more humanistic Social Service Act, begging was no longer considered a social issue. Indeed, several of my interviewees believed it had ceased to be an issue for good, thanks to my identified "social contract." In spite of the Swedish welfare state's success in radically increasing social wealth and diminishing inequality and impoverishment, poverty was never done away with. Neither was capitalism's inherent drive to compose an industrial reserve population.[15] What occurred with the social state paradigm was a shift of social policy from combating poverty's consequences to *preventing* poverty. As the social consequences of laissez-faire capitalism exploded at the end of the nineteenth century, a conjuncture of political interests overdetermined the successive *nationalization* of social policy: workers, social liberals, conservatives, nationalists, and capitalists (worried over the social unrest) saw the establishment of a social state as something desirable. The prevention tools were Keynesian economics, redistributive tax schemes, publicly funded social insurances, and collective bargaining.[16] Capitalist class society was maintained, but with a new governmentality of monetary redistribution and poor relief. With a countercyclical, demand-sided economic policy, supported by strong union organizations (likewise, industrial capitalists) and aiming for full employment, the unemployed were to be supported by social insurances (financed by their own previous or forthcoming labor), subsidies, and benefits—in order to be ready for reemployment as soon as possible. The municipalities' social offices were supposed to be the absolute last refuge. Those "unemployable" who could not take care of themselves were institutionalized and maintained there, hidden from public vision.

This Keynesian optimism, which purported to have found the strategy to abolish impoverishment, turned out to be utopianism. As the global capital accumulation regime of Fordism changed in the 1970s, the neoliberal movement would give rise to the reappearance of homeless and begging people in Western spaces in the 1990s.[17] Sweden was no exception to this development. The title of a report from the Social Services Department (Socialtjänstförvaltningen) on the *new* begging issue, from 1999, is revealing: *Begging: A New-Old Phenomenon*.[18] Begging reemerged on the heels of the property estate bubble financial crisis in Sweden (1990–94). In the "newest" return of begging in Sweden, EU déclassés showed up as a combined consequence of the neoliberalization of Romania (and other Eastern European countries), the enlargement of the EU, and the financial crises of the United States and Southern Europe, among other contributing forces. As shown throughout this book, the Swedish authorities' treatment of this begging population was in turn conditioned by Sweden's political-economic developments.

There is a discernible trend throughout capitalism's history of begging being a practice of those expropriated and excluded by the economy (and the state), turning said outcasts into "surplus populations" *for* the economy (and the state). However, this only explains the production of life conditions that encourage people to beg; it does not explain the overly emotional responses to the presence of begging. While the capitalist and ruling classes have a vested interest in keeping life in unemployment hellish and stigmatizing, this does not explain their parallel interest in chasing away begging people. If begging was to work as an advertisement of what happens if you do not labor, then it would be counterproductive to hide the ad from public view. Besides, it is not only the ruling classes that have throughout history condemned and panicked over begging—the aversion is probably almost as much a property of the working classes. And returning to the findings of my previous study, common perceptions of begging are not only aversive. They are, rather, ambivalent. This moral ambivalence is also discernible throughout the history of begging.[19] Could we find a clue to the causes of this emotional overreaction in the history of belief systems and their interconnection to capitalist reality?

Against Common Sense—Ticklish to Political Ideas

In a prototype of the most popular contemporary IQ test, the 1949 *Wechsler Intelligence Scale for Children*, one finds the following question: "Why is it generally better to give money to an organized charity than to a street beggar?"[20] If you do not agree it *is* better, then you're stupid. The fact that begging is not a good thing is here treated as common sense, with the decision-making process liberated from morality and emotions by the logic of reason alone. To Marxian theoretician Antonio Gramsci, "common sense" is a historical-geographical condensation of sediments of historical thoughts, sciences, beliefs, ideologies, and myths, together appearing as common truth to any given society: "Common sense is not a single unique conception, identical in time and space. It is the 'folklore' of philosophy, and, like folklore, it takes countless different forms. Its most fundamental characteristic is that it is a conception which, even in the brain of one individual, is fragmentary, incoherent and inconsequential, in conformity with the social and cultural position of those masses whose philosophy it is."[21]

The foremost utility with Gramsci's conceptualization of common sense is his emphasis on its *contradictory* character—how common sense can speak "against itself" on different social matters, by invoking opposing or incoherent statements about how reality and morality work. In the begging question, both in my researched space-time and in the longer history, the societal ambivalent stance on begging can be interpreted as one expression of common sense's contradictory character. Common values on panhandling catch the begging gestalt in what sociologists Angus Erskine and Ian McIntosh call the poor's double bind, articulated as a contradiction between "activity" versus "passivity."[22] Since the begging individual is "passive"—not wage laboring—they do not deserve help, because they ought to work "like the rest of us." Simultaneously, however, "the beggar" is too "active" to deserve help: by begging, a work-like exercise, "the beggar" is active enough to be "capable" of working "like the rest of us." Even though the speaker identifies "the beggar's" need as genuine, "the beggar" can still be caught in this double bind. One example is one interviewee, a well-off woman in her forties, who told me she could be annoyed with "beggars" because "it becomes a little bit like 'the sick role,' [always] being a victim, that you don't have any responsibility, at all; instead, you put it on everyone else. [I think this passivity] can be provocative because, in some way [it proclaims that] everyone else would be well-off and everyone else would have it so easy." This thought process seems to belong to the idea of workfare within neoliberal ideology, which holds that benefit receivers are "passivized" by "maintenance dependency" and ought to be "activated" by harsher welfare schemes. However, this belief is far older than neoliberalism.

In Sweden in the 1830s, parliament was debating "a new kind of poverty"—the pauperism of dependency upon municipal poor relief.[23] Different actors (politicians, intellectuals, clerics) argued both paupers and beggars were to be treated as reprobate abusers addicted to alms, who must be taught to become moral, self-sufficient individuals. The so-called social question of the nineteenth century circulated bourgeois interpretations of working-class poverty being a moral issue on behalf of the poor. This belief has persisted to this day, although fluctuating in political relevance and with changing language. Though it is obvious how this idea neatly dovetails with the interests of capital, I argue it is also an idea that is appealing to the working classes, as it speaks to commonsense morality: you ought to do your fair share, just like everyone else.

During the 2010s I stumbled upon the commonsensical statement that "beggars should work to earn a livelihood like everyone else" everywhere, such as when I overheard a heterosexual couple in their twenties at an open-air café in Stockholm, immediately after dismissing a begging man: "How can they afford iPhones when I can hardly pay my own phone bill?" Notably, I didn't see the déclassé's phone. They went on: "It's not giving money that I find hard, but 'this societal [thing],' that everyone has to feel guilty. [. . .] I have many expenses to pay bills and so on, like 9,000 kronor a month; should I then beg on the street? [They] have to work like everyone else." A hockey coach, in turn, tweeted, "I am in favor of labor immigration. But not begging. They don't help out!"[24] In a letter to the editor in a local newspaper, the pseudonymous SINGLE DAD wrote that he works more than forty hours a week to pay the rent, and when he gave some change to a "beggar," "she sat with DC shoes and talked on a smartphone, didn't even raise her eyes and say thank you. I cannot treat myself with DC [shoes]."[25] One Liberal local politician argued in favor of a begging ban, saying that panhandling "risks eroding the social contract, which has served our society so well. You work and contribute; society is there to support if you need help, but you do not depend on others unnecessarily. It was the implementation of this social contract that [made] begging bans unnecessary in Sweden."[26]

Not only do these quotations speak to the commonsense morality of deservingness and condemnation of free riding, but they also harbor the latent message that this perceived work-shyness is almost an insult to one's own efforts in a class society. This transference of capital's interests into societal commonsense morality is a key example of the classical Marxist notion of *ideology*—the beliefs (and interests) of the ruling classes universalized into common societal values and the perception of reality itself. In a dialectical twist, the social reality is (re)produced by practices following ideological perceptions of this reality, making these conceptions become more (or less) common sense.

What must be understood is that this moralization of the pauper finds its ideological appeal as a top-down dissemination of the elites' values, and also because of this morality's grounding in other ideologies, values, and experiences. Gramsci argues common sense might vary in content between different class positions (and likewise communities) because of divergent historical-social trajectories; nevertheless, there is some social common sense that is more common than others. What makes some social truths into cross-class universal values is these truths' capacity to be interpreted from different social positions as correlating to one's own reality. Such a social truth is, for example, the conviction that people who can work need to do so in order to deserve a good life, and that anything else would be *unfair* to oneself and also to the society to which one belongs. It is a curious fusion of bitterness and solidarity, which is what the politician above referred to. From a Marxist standpoint, this truth is partial: capitalists live off workers' labor, and it is, after all, possible to legally inherit wealth without having earned it oneself. But these kinds of exploitation do not appear as exploitation as explicitly as the begging individual's plea for alms.

But how can this work ethic be part of the dominant ideology of society? It is because hard work is the lived reality of the masses, uniting the well-off with the struggling. No matter that "work's" content and meaning differ tremendously between cleaners, artists, and managers—the *form* of wage slavery is something to which (almost) everyone can relate. The harsh reality of work appears as the means for one's living standard. This cross-class shared experience with work creates its own shared commonsensical values on the necessity of work and an imagined community of sharing the drudges of, and rewards for, laboring. It becomes a common sense of pride and respectability, as one perceives oneself *deserving* recognition, status, or a living by one's working.[27] In Sweden, where social democracy gained a dominant position during the twentieth century, the concept of "the diligent worker" has gained a stronghold in the public consciousness; one is supposed to be industrious, self-sufficient, and self-restrained.[28] Although the labor movement opposed bourgeois values and capitalist inequality, its critique of capitalism was based on the vantage point of the (male) worker demanding equality, safety, and a fair share of the surplus value. Labor itself was not questioned. Neither was the inherent morality arising from capitalist class society on the virtues of laboring and the sins of depending on others.[29] Consequently, the labor dogma remained intact (and still is so), as both representatives of labor and capital, both working and owning classes, supported this ideological understanding of labor's role in society.

The commonsensical proclamation that begging is not work (which it is not, from a capitalist standpoint, as it neither produces nor realizes value), and therefore is an inherently immoral economic practice, has cemented itself due to different class interests and experiences. This nonwork character touches something fundamentally social and at the same time personal, as it relates to one's own hardships. Here, the notion of fairness is inescapable. Therefore, it bears repeating that this morality is inherently contradictory and ambiguous. As commonsensical as it is that "all who can work shall work" (as I read on SAP's homepage), it is likewise commonsensical that those who *cannot* work and are *too poor* ought to get some help.[30] The continuation of begging regulations makes this evident; after all, if people did not give to "beggars," there would be no need to ban this practice. We must admit that there have always been "exceptions to the rule" of the labor imperative: those who are too young, too old, too sick, or not able-bodied enough. However, these exceptions are historically contingent and subject to disagreement on who qualifies as a "deserving" unemployed or poor person. After all, it was not long ago child labor was common sense in the West, and it continues to be so in too many places around the world.

Accordingly, the poor's double bind between activity and passivity is grounded in the social truth that some people actually deserve assistance, hence the perennial obstacle in defining who's deserving and who isn't, as human life trajectories are more complicated than rigid binarities, and the resources spared for the paupers are finite. This moral quarrel also arises in personal considerations of which destitute strangers to support, and how much, no matter if we talk about panhandlers, aid organizations, or fair-trade products.

This wicked problem of "deservingness," so readily elicited by the begging encounter, is mirrored in the three dominant political approaches to poverty in capitalist society: liberalism, socialism, and conservatism. In all three there are ambiguities on how to interpret "the beggar's" needs and moral character. These ambiguities have surfaced in political debates in Sweden on the parties' correct stance on begging ban's "either-or," especially among the liberal parties and SAP.

A 2017 newspaper debate between representatives of the Liberal Party reveals the symptoms of liberalism. Beneath the heading *Liberals Cannot Forbid Someone Asking for Help*, two parliamentarians claimed: "We proceed from a liberal perspective. Liberalism is about freedom. The freedom of one human being to ask for help does not harm another, nor does it diminish another person's freedom."[31] By way of reply, two other Liberal representatives countered with *Liberals Sure Can Prohibit Begging*: "Everyone understands that the foreign beggars' social rights are terribly met in their home-countries. However, this does not imply they have rights to the Swedish welfare system. [The] idea that our citizens should have a moral obligation to tolerate begging because of other countries' shortcomings is accepted by fewer and fewer. Poverty is tackled through education, work, and social reforms in the country where they are citizens."[32] This contradiction between liberal voices, and what might at first appear as an *illiberal* argumentation by the latter two, becomes intelligible if we understand the dispute as representing "the beggar's" formal human rights versus "the pedestrian's" commonsensical individual rights in the private sphere. While the latter Liberals argue from a commonsensical nationalist standpoint where each nation-state is supposed to protect its own citizens, they also refer to the problem being "the idea" that individuals "should have a moral obligation to *tolerate* begging." From this perspective, they agree with the letters to the editor in the beginning of the chapter.

As geographer Nicholas Blomley has pointed out, anti-panhandling legislation can rather effortlessly be interpreted as a protection of liberal rights; the twist is that the right in question is the approached citizen's right to be protected from the intrusion of "the beggar."[33] Tracing the liberal conception of freedom back to Thomas Hobbes, who argued liberty "signifeth (properly) the absence of Opposition [by which] I mean externall impediments to motion,"[34] Blomley argues this conceptualization of freedom is embodied in urban life nowadays. What he calls "the right to pass freely" is the commonsensical expectation that individuals' freedom of movement without hindrance by others is something to be protected in liberal public space. This commonsensical idea of personal freedom, enshrined in liberal thought, is countered, however, by another supposedly commonsensical liberal idea: the idea of natural (human) rights. Within the liberal worldview and the discourse of human rights, begging has been interpreted as an expression of the fundamental liberal rights of access to public space and freedom of speech.[35] In 2021 an ERRC (European Roma Rights Centre) third-party intervention in the European Court won a case against Geneva's criminalization of begging, which referred to the legislation as incompatible with the right to respect for private and family life and the right to expression.[36] However, as Blomley demonstrates, these rights do not undo, but rather *collide with*, the unquestioned rights of bodily autonomy and movement of the approached pedestrian. It is not about a real threat of physical harm—yet it is commonly understood as moral harm. As a consequence of liberal ideology's view of humanity as consisting of equal, atomized individuals, the begging interaction is, from a liberal standpoint, readily interpreted as a conflict between equal claims of rights between "the pedestrian" and "the beggar." And, as Marx said, "Between equal rights force decides."[37]

There is also another contradiction in liberalism's attitude to begging, which is rooted in the writings of Adam Smith. As a staunch believer in the public wonders of individual self-interest, Smith famously argued in his *Wealth of Nations* (1776): "It is not from the benevolence of the butcher, the brewer, or the baker, that we expect our dinner, but from their regard to their own interest. [Nobody] but a beggar chuses to depend chiefly upon the benevolence of his fellow-citizens."[38] However, he immediately follows: "Even a beggar does not depend upon it entirely. [The] greater part of his occasional wants are supplied in the same manner as those of other people, by treaty, by barter, and by purchase." This, theologian Kelly Johnson points out to us, reveals an ambiguousness regarding the function of begging in Smith's theoretical system. "The beggar" follows the doctrine of self-interest, yet does this by depending on benevolence. "The beggar" is "rational," yet "irrational." If self-interest accomplishes societal wealth through labor, "the beggar" is made useless by begging—but not by consuming alms in the marketplace. There is also a moral dimension to this. Notably, Smith was a moral philosopher by profession. If one reads his earlier writings alongside *Wealth of Nations*, one realizes that his whole social theory depends upon interpersonal honesty, trust, and self-control between alienated individuals for the magic of self-interest to generate economic growth for the entire society.[39] "The beggar," by relying upon others' benevolence, and with an incentive to stir up *negative* emotions in the economic interaction, thus becomes an obstacle to optimistic (if inherently stoic) Smith's view on humanity.[40]

This problem of behavior has its own history in liberalism, as liberal thought was also the origin of social Darwinism and its racialist ideologies of "development." Even John Stuart Mill thought the poor should be prohibited from voting, as they could not take responsibility for themselves due to their dependence upon others, and that "barbarians" needed despotism before they were to become mature enough for liberalism.[41] An updated variation of this theme is voiced in 2015 by a Swedish neoliberal think tank director who argues on his blog: "Remember that until 1965 we had a law called the Anti-Vagrancy Act, according to which beggars could be put into forced labor. It was this view on labor that turned Sweden into maybe the world's most eminent country. Our greatest gift to the Roma would be to teach them The Labor Imperative."[42]

HOLDING THE SOCIALIST LINE

Whereas liberalism is the ideology of the bourgeoisie, the ideas supposed to represent working-class interests, here generalized into the umbrella term "socialism," also include historical moral ambiguities regarding the begging practice. This is because begging is associated with philanthropy. Oscar Wilde explained socialist suspiciousness to philanthropy rather straightforwardly: charity was a medicine not curing the disease (poverty) but only maintaining it. By keeping the poor dependent upon the goodwill of the bourgeoisie, the structural oppression of the poor would not be extinguished. Only through political struggle would "poverty be impossible," which should be "the proper aim" of any struggle.[43] Workers' movements around the world have fought to restructure societies so that people can rely on social security during hard times instead of begging for survival. Probably the most popularly appealing idea of the welfare state itself was the eradication of the need for private philanthropy. By maintaining philanthropy's existence, "the beggar" becomes a potential (although not necessarily willing) "class traitor."

The idea that accepting begging would constitute an inherent threat to the maintenance of the Swedish welfare state is most prominently represented by social-democratic voices (but also old-fashioned Stalinists).[44] A case in point is this political editor's defense of begging bans as an option for the SAP government in 2015, arguing the labor movement historically would have "combated" begging: "People were to be relieved from having to stand with hat in hand before the master and the bourgeoisie asking for alms to make ends meet. Not only because it was humiliating [but] also that individual alms and gifts is an ineffective form of distribution policy. It only scratches the surface without changing the structure, creating inequality and leading to begging. [The] whole point with the solidary welfare politics [was] born out of this insight."[45] An opposite conclusion of SAP's history is given by a former SAP politician. He argues that the idea of regulating begging "is on a fundamental collision course with the Social Democrats' century-long work to eradicate [pauperism] and the striving towards an equal society." Where, he asks, is the "fighting spirit"?[46] Paradoxically enough, one could argue that both sides are true to the SAP's historical project and ideology of the *folkhem*. For context, the *folkhem* was a term appropriated by Per Albin Hansson, Social-Democratic prime minister and one of the founding fathers of Swedish welfare society, in a well-known speech in 1928. There, he envisioned Sweden's destiny to become "a good home": "In a good home, there are [no] favorites and no stepchildren. No one is looked down [upon]. No one tries to gain advantage at another's expense; the strong do not oppress the weak. [Applied] to society as a whole, this would require that we break down all the social and economic barriers that now divide citizens into the privileged and those left behind, the rulers and their dependents, the plunderers and those plundered."[47]

The debate on the "historically correct" stance on begging for SAP reveals a fundamental contradiction in the social-democratic ideological position on the matter. Begging itself constitutes the antithesis of the welfare society project, yet *prohibiting* begging is also a practice at odds with the labor movement's legacy of fighting poverty, not the poor. Notably, previous begging restrictions were never put in place by SAP governments—instead, they inherited the legislation from the era before universal suffrage. However, in spite of SAP's long tenure in power from 1932 to 1976, it was not until 1982 that begging was ultimately decriminalized by a new Social Service Act enacted under a right-wing government. Reasons for this delay might be found in the ideology of the diligent worker and the double-edged class ideal of respectability and temperance, which brings us to a second issue within the socialist idea tradition that begging actualizes: "the beggar's" *group affiliation.*

During a 2016 TV interview, former SAP prime minister Göran Persson argued in favor of a begging ban, reasoning: "We have always said in Sweden: thou shalt work, thou shalt stand up, thou shalt demand your rights. You are not to bend your knees to pray. [So,] I have a very simple suggestion [to the déclassés]. Go home and take up the fight."[48] This easy way out of dismissing the problem as a matter of national citizenship has a similar genealogy in labor movements' own identity-formation processes. Although "the beggar" is a victim of capitalism, it has, from a socialist standpoint, not been certain whether they belong to the *political subject* of "the proletariat." Is "the beggar" an ally, an enemy, or someone to ignore for the moment? Marx and Engels proved in different cases how the capitalist system of cyclical and structural unemployment forced members of the working class to beg for survival. However, they muddied the waters regarding potential worker solidarity with begging people (alongside homeless, prostitutes, drug addicts, outcasts, and minorities) by subsuming them within their opaque concept of the lumpenproletariat, or the "dangerous classes" at the very bottom of the social hierarchy. In *The Communist Manifesto* (1848), the lumpenproletariat is described as "the social scum, that passively rotting mass thrown off by the lowest layers of the old society."[49] They "may, here and there, be swept into the movement by a proletarian revolution; its conditions of life, however, prepare it far more for the part of a bribed tool of reactionary intrigue." Literature theorist Peter Stallybrass has noted the irony of Marx and Engels's accomplishment of turning the derogatory term "proletariat" into a positive identity, only to transfer its negative content onto a new identity within the proletariat.[50]

There are, however, anarchist and postcolonial theorists who celebrate the lumpenproletariat as the "real" radical subject of revolution.[51] While nineteenth-century anarchists were problematically idealist, Frantz Fanon dealt with the pragmatics of the colonial experience. In 1961 he argued that due to specific colonial class relations, the lumpenproletariat *could* actually be more revolutionary than the "formal" working class in the colonies. However, just like Marx and Engels, he cautioned that there was an equal risk of bribing the lumpenproletariat into becoming counterrevolutionaries. Meanwhile, Cabral, the inspirer of my analytical classification "déclassés," tried to grapple with this ambiguousness by dividing the lumpen into the "real" (bad) lumpen and the other potentially good lumpen, thus replicating the separation between proletariat and lumpenproletariat within the lumpenproletariat itself.

It could be argued that, rather than a theoretical conclusion, Marx and Engels's delineation was strategically tied to the specific political circumstances of the day. Nevertheless, the term "lumpenproletariat" and its derogatory content have been applied by socialists, and likewise fascist regimes, to justify degradation of dissidents or oppression of different minorities. In these discourses the socialist political subject "the proletariat" has been transformed into "the people" or "the nation." Symptomatically, in the twentieth century, "lumpen" often came to be used to label Roma minorities. Former Eastern-bloc regimes in Central and Eastern Europe, as well as Nazi Germany, used it to label Roma.[52] The term implied destructive "antisocial" behavior, work-shyness, criminality, and parasitic behavior.

Conservatism, a reaction to the optimism of liberalism, contains an unmistakable degree of pessimism on humanity and its capacity to change. This cynicism originates from a fear of "the rabble" threatening to drive civilization into a downfall.[53] Terrified of losing their privileges, the owning and ruling classes universalize this ideological fear to all classes through the reliable, affective, and uniting power of traditionalism.[54] As an allegory for this conservative anxiety about "the rabble" and the desire to maintain the current social order as a necessary (even if unjust) balance of terror, I here rely on the case Thomas Robert Malthus made against Adam Smith's economic optimism. Malthus's *Principle of Population* (1798) influenced the draconian poor relief laws of nineteenth-century Britain, Sweden, and elsewhere.[55] Accordingly, his ideas influenced the politics leading to the great famines in Ireland in the 1840s and Sweden in the 1860s. Malthus argued that the rate of food production did not match the increasing birth rates of the lower classes, which would, if unregulated, result in overpopulation and the end of society by starvation. It was therefore crucial to make sure the paupers were not to reproduce themselves too hastily nor, preferably, receive poor relief. Malthus argued this was not a matter of morality but a *natural necessity*.

In other words, the Malthusian solution to poverty is not self-interest but temperance—to respect the (Divine) order of private ownership, regulating (natural) class society. Here, the begging individual is someone relying on dangerous benevolence, threatening the social order by inducing bleeding hearts to upset the natural order of property relations.[56] This idea is primarily used by SD in the Swedish present context, although in a nationalist garb. "Paupers" have become "immigrants"; "overpopulation" is "mass immigration"; "civilization" is "welfare society" (or rather, "the nation"), and the solution is "expulsion" from the national territory. The homology with Malthusianism is primarily found in the urgency of the problem: it is not a matter of morality but of life or death. To wit, if we do not halt the growing numbers of needy (the non-Swedes), they will ultimately swallow us (the Swedes). In 2014 SD's legal policy spokesperson argued as much in a TV debate, urging for the "immediate" expulsion of all EU déclassés from Sweden: "It's not Sweden's responsibility to take care of other countries' [citizens]. The solution is not that these people come here. We already have a welfare system in Sweden that's on its way to crack for many, not least the Swedish health care system which has enormous problems with offering good and safe health care to our citizens. We cannot take on this responsibility. It's totally unreasonable."[57] To SD, begging, because of its explicitly racialized character in this time period ("the beggar" being both foreigner and an ethnic minority) is only one expression of their enemy, the territorial presence of racial Others. The quote could have as easily been pulled from a debate on undifferentiated (non-white) immigration. The problem here has nothing to do with morality, but the "natural necessity" of survival for the insiders.

Though the SD increasingly framed themselves as a "social conservative" party to disguise their fascist origins (and aims), there are other conservative parties: the Moderates—SAP's foremost rivals for the throne—with a liberal-conservative profile, and the Christian Democrats. As with liberalism and socialism, there is an ambiguity in conservative values on begging, especially if one introduces religious and virtue ethics within the conservative belief system. The "Christian" love message and the virtue of caring for the poor are also relevant to discourses on the begging encounter, and, notably, these discourses are far older than the capitalist mode of production! Accordingly, our genealogical inquiry of the historical roots of the current values and emotions on begging must extend beyond the capitalist era, as the existence of begging—and, likewise, perceptions of it—precede the current mode of production. It is true, after all, that while present production and interpretation of poverty are mediated through capitalism, this economic system is but one historical mode of production within the longer tenure of class society. But before I broach the role of religion and the Middle Ages, we must first explore the heretofore neglected *racialist* traces of these commonsensical statements on begging.

The Continued Insistence of Nation and Race

The rise of the nation-state as a political function (and organizer) of uneven capitalist development has helped to naturalize "the nation" as the imaginary equivalent of "society."[58] Political parties and movements translate their universal claims into local issues for the national territory and its population. "The working class" becomes "the people"; "the individual" becomes "the tax-paying citizen." This is relevant because this naturalization of national belonging allows the political ideas in Sweden the possibility to foreclose the ideological problems that EU déclassés' begging threatens to actualize: "the beggar" here in question is *a foreigner*! Through the power of a banal nationalism repackaged as common sense, the moral ambivalences on begging are rendered moot, sublimated into a social distinction between "us and them" and a policy discussion on geographical removal. As a large share of my interviewees stated commonsensically: the déclassés are another nation-state's responsibility, since they have formal citizenship somewhere else and do not qualify as political refugees. In an almost magical one-dimensional way, this "common sense" short-circuits moral considerations on whether déclassés are deserving or undeserving "beggars." By being nonlaboring noncitizens, and thus not contributing to the imagined national community, "these beggars" are by default undeserving. It does not seem to matter whether they are "morally" deserving care—the important thing is that they are *not Swedes' responsibility*. Two anonymous internet commentators on media articles about déclassés represent this common sense:

> It's NOT my responsibility to take care of them. It's a responsibility their homelands' authorities should take![59]

> The problem with Romanian beggars is chiefly Romania's responsibility and it's not solved by Swedes giving money to those poor wretches sitting on our streets. Put more pressure on Romania to not discriminate against their own citizens![60]

This common sense is available for purposes of both left-wing and right-wing interests. Socialist, liberal, conservative, and radical-nationalist politicians can therefore agree with each other that the only political issue the déclassés really represent is *people out of place*. This neutralizes the liberal agonies about what "freedom" and "individual responsibility" actually are (concerning both the begging and the approached individual)—likewise, the socialist dilemmas on how to handle emergencies within capitalist systems, and whose needs are to be prioritized in the ongoing class struggle. In a seemingly paradoxical way, all three political ideologies can agree with this argument by an SAP think tank director: "The solution [to the "beggars'" poverty] is to contribute to hope for the future in the home-countries—even if this in short-term means slightly worse opportunities for the individual, before s/he can receive a long-term, sustainable, and worthy livelihood."[61] This solution recalls my earlier presented third ideal type from the interviews. I have read statements with almost exactly the same phrasing as the quotation above from representatives of the Liberal Party, The Moderates, and the Christian Democrats, and by civil society actors, opinion makers, and the government. With this argument, the contradictions within the political ideologies are deftly shifted onto the begging individuals themselves. If only they return to where they came from, everything will be fine. For both them and us. Nevertheless, this intellectual consensus has, as shown in the book's second part, neither been dogmatically adhered to nor mobilized into practice immediately. In the adolescent years of the begging question, SD was the only parliamentary party stating clearly and consistently that déclassés' begging neither belongs in Sweden nor is the country's responsibility. But as I show here, this conclusion is not necessarily the result of sympathizing with SD. It is, rather, in light of our Gramscian perspective, commonsensical.

The doctrine of nations as separate and essential units of the world, and one's need to belong to a nation, normalizes a great many things that in turn naturalize the capitalist mode of production: the global alienation of the working class from each other; the trust and legitimacy of the state; the belief that one's own national economy's prosperity is the result of one's own population's industrious labor.[62] Within this ideology "the immigrant" takes the place of the racialized Other, although they are often interpreted as being the same. Indeed, European Roma's historical absence of a nation with a territory has facilitated the super-exclusion of them throughout Europe notwithstanding their actual place of birth or origin. The "denationalization" of Roma in Romania suffices as an example of this logic, as the EU membership has introduced the possibility of Romanian Roma being "European" but *not* Romanian—thus not really belonging (even though Roma have lived within contemporary Romania's borders since at least the fourteenth century). Along these lines a Romanian MEP (member of the European Parliament) stated in 2008: "The European Union enlargement was the last act of Roma liberation. Roma are today European citizens. Perhaps they are in absolute terms the truest European citizens because they are only Europeans."[63] In the déclassés' home countries, this is the dominant view of authorities on their supposed responsibility for "taking care of their own citizens," as is so often commonsensically stated in the Swedish debate.

So far, however, I have only spoken of nationalism as a universal, unconscious belief system. Nationalism requires a parallel belief in the specialness of one's own nation, making it distinct from others. Granted, the particular nationalist ideology of Sweden's national character posed somewhat of a moral and ideological obstacle to the commonsensical nationalist reason to ban begging. What I lay out above as a moral contradiction within the social-democratic ideology can also be said of the national self-image of Sweden: being an exceptional moral superpower guided by egalitarian values proclaiming equality, humanitarianism, antiracism, and solidarity. Per Albin Hansson's vision of "the good home" where "the strong do not oppress the weak" is echoed in my interviews with the idea that Sweden is a community where "we take care of each other." It is also echoed in the political discourse, as in 2017, when one minister explained that the government wanted to "stop begging" but *not* criminalize it, since "in Sweden, it should be possible to ask for and to receive help."[64] The other side of the coin of this national character is the idealization of Swedes as industrious and temperate, as begging is not commonly interpreted as having either of these virtues.

This contradiction is also *spatialized*. As nationalism requires a spatial-aesthetic regime supposed to express the national particular identity within the national territory, begging is "out of place" in Swedish space because of its aesthetic composition. As the Swedish self-image of its national character is explicitly ethical, this perception's spatial expressions are aesthetical-ethical—"aesthethical," one might say. In other words, the spatial visibility of begging in Swedish urban space disturbs the aesthethical landscape by displaying poverty and inhumanity (by the fact the destitute are not helped). In 2015 one columnist expressed concern in Sweden's major business magazine that Sweden's "trademark," which is intended to "be equated with various positive words such as empathic, caring, engaged and coequal," is threatened by the presence of "beggars," lamenting that "tourists' depiction of our welfare society is affected when a part of the streetscape in Swedish towns nowadays comprise destitute people begging for alms."[65] This sentiment was echoed by one of the interviewees, a man who implied that the practice of begging was fundamentally at odds with the national spatial-aesthetic of modernity, development, and Western values: "It feels like society is in some way becoming . . . like we're lowering the standards in our society. Because of these beggars. It feels like there are beggars everywhere! It's like we live somewhere in a third-world country."

This spatial interpretation of begging as intrinsically non-Swedish and externally sourced works as a political resource because of these "beggars'" status as foreigners. Had their profile been the same as the homeless begging Swedes of the 1990s, this solution would not be available. In that case one would have to instead deploy the social truth that proclaims begging to be a dysfunctional character trait. Regardless of nationality, they become undeserving through demoralization. Here, we encounter the attendant logic of *pathologizing* the poor's poverty as either moralization or racialization. As previously mentioned, poverty is, in bourgeois ideology, interpreted as a "social question" of deficient moral character. While problems like alcoholism and drug abuse, for example, were widespread among the Swedish begging population in the 1990s, that does not negate the curious similarities between historical approaches to the poor: first moralizing them in the nineteenth century, then medicalizing them in the 1990s, and then finally, in the 2010s, culturalizing them. Each of these discourses are variations on the same ideological project: turning the expression of structural inequality into the moral pathologies of deviant individuals— people who are not like "us."

THE DIALECTIC OF RACISM

In this book I treat racism as a dialectic between *structural racism* and *racist ideas*. As with the Marxist critique of ideology (where the material conditions of reality and the prevailing interpretations of this reality reproduce each other), racializing structures of society generate ideological perceptions of society along racialist ideas. These perceptions, narratives, and sentiments in turn replicate the racial order.

Anti-Roma Mythmaking

Starting with the sphere of ideas, the presence of anti-Roma racism in the discussions on begging is obvious. Closely related to the storied tradition of pathologizing the poor, we find historically resilient myths that Roma are inherently work-shy, lazy, immoral, and cunning, which are ready-made to be used in deliberations on why the déclassés are begging. This historical resource is made all the more expedient by the fact that all ideological positions in the debate came to articulate the begging subject as primarily "Roma," whether or not the problem is "discrimination" or "culture." Because of the obsessive use of the race signifier, its genealogical traces are always lurking within the debate. One constantly needs to take them into account, thus reproducing their relevance.

Along these lines one anonymous commentator on social media explains the ingenious cultural rationality of Roma begging:

> Working according to majority societal norms and, for example, going to school is no alternative for the majority of Roma. There are of course exceptions. Begging is no expression of "vulnerability" or sign of poverty

but rather a theatrical play to swindle the majority population to unconditionally give cash, food, and other utilities to the beggar.

It is no temporary solution for a healthy and strong Roma man or woman in their thirties to sit outside a [grocery store] with a mug in front of them. It is a life project, a carefully laid out career path. [Communicating] signs of "vulnerability" that give maximum exchange in the form of money in the mug etc. is an excellent skill for every beggar.[66]

Interestingly enough, the folklore of begging as a well-crafted scam has not only been the property of anti-Roma sentiments but has throughout history also targeted other begging strangers. In fifteenth-century France, for example, poems, plays, and stories displayed an enduring disdain and even hatred of begging people, since they were supposed to trick innocent spectators into becoming bleeding hearts.[67] Erskine and McIntosh identified a centuries-long discourse in Britain and Germany where "beggars," no matter whether they were deemed alcoholics or Romani/Travelers, belonged to an *alternative culture*, with a secret society of alternative norms and social codes. They find "almost" an element of "jealousy" on behalf of their detractors, as "the beggars" are depicted as (sometimes even rich!) charlatans and redeemed from societal constraints.[68] Romanticizing Roma "culture" as an "orientalist Other" has a long history within anti-Roma discourse, even among well-meaning advocates fighting for Roma rights.[69] However, one probable supporting factor in influencing these fantasies, when speaking of "beggars" in general, can be found in the continuous demarcation between welcome and unfamiliar paupers. Recall the interviewee who explained his sense of a lack of transparency in his encounters with EU déclassés (compared to homeless Swedes): he had "no idea" what the money went to, because he did not "know" them in the same way he believed he knew the Swedish homeless. While racial Otherness strengthens sensations of strangeness, there is also an economic dimension that makes "the beggar" a *spatial stranger*. Homelessness aside, someone begging for a living has an incentive to be mobile so as to not exhaust communities: one needs to find new benefactors. The resulting "nomadic lifestyle" is reflected in the historical experience of Roma communities in Europe.

While the idea that "the beggars" are simultaneously victims and perpetrators of human trafficking fits neatly into the anti-Roma myth of the Roma's fundamental wickedness, cultural racism is also used to identify déclassés as demoralized victims of their subordinating (underdeveloped) culture. Returning to the aforementioned neoliberal think tank director who argued that "Swedes" ought to teach "the Roma" to labor, we note that he defends his position against "all the alarmed counterarguments from those who still are obsessed with the shame of us being too well-off in our society, in Sweden: that Roma have been oppressed for centuries and that it therefore is up to the rest of the world to feel ashamed and prepare them a decent life. But this is not the case. We Swedes help the Roma more by encouraging them to become self-sufficient rather than supporting them with coins and bills in their paper mugs."[70]

Swedish Roma's History

Not only do the historical experiences of Swedish Roma prove the commonsensical nationalist maxim of "each citizen to each nation-state" to be anything but self-evident, they also demonstrate how entrenched current racist fantasies, persecution, and state oppression of Roma really are in Sweden. Indeed, as early as the sixteenth century, the presence of Roma in Swedish territory had been documented—that is, at the dawn of Swedish state power. The so-called father of the nation, King Gustav Vasa, for his part, aimed to expel all Roma to the province of Finland, and in 1560 the archbishop prohibited the baptism of Roma children.[71] The same year that saw the introduction of a royal placard that allowed local licensed begging, 1642, another placard was instituted too, urging every Roma and Traveler to leave the country—for if a Roma man was found, he was to be executed without trial.[72] In subsequent centuries Roma continued to live in Sweden, but they were relegated to an unpropertied nomadic lifestyle, occasionally taking "dirty jobs" the common people did not want.

In 1885 the Anti-Vagrancy Act was introduced, which remained in effect until 1965. Begging, alongside vagrancy and prostitution, was considered a "dishonest livelihood," and vagabonds were to be rehabilitated in workhouses. The curious thing about this legislation is that there was no crime to be punished. Instead, it targeted unsavory behaviors and character traits, which ought not to be criminalized; otherwise, the matter had to be taken to court. The intervention was thus implemented as a measure to prevent potential crimes.[73] Starting in 1923, Roma and Travelers were included within the legislation's "vagrant" category. The law was also incorporated into immigration legislation, resulting in an explicit prohibition on Roma to emigrate to Sweden. Significantly, this legislation was in practice until 1954, meaning it also affected Roma trying to escape the Holocaust. The law also made it almost impossible for Swedish Roma to emigrate from Sweden, since Swedish Roma and Travelers were commonly not registered as either residents or citizens.[74] In this sense Roma, even when they were natives, were still treated as noncitizens by authorities, similar to present-day déclassés. It was not until the 1950s that the state changed its attitude, and although Roma had lived in Sweden for five hundred years, it was not until 1999 that "Roma" was acknowledged as an official minority in Sweden—a self-proclaimed "multiculturalist" nation since 1975.

Per Albin Hansson's fabled utopia without "social and economic barriers" notwithstanding, anti-Roma racism did not disappear with the introduction of the *folkhem*. As late as 1948, a pogrom occurred in the town of Jönköping targeting so-called *tattare* (Travelers), although no one died. Between 1935 and 1975, 62,888 people were sterilized as a part of a governmental eugenics program, with the majority of sterilizations taking place in the first decades. Although the program's aim was not explicitly racialist, Roma and Travelers were overrepresented as victims of sterilization.[75] The biopolitical rationale of the eugenics program, it should be noted, did not follow the Nazi ideology's interpretation of race, as the overwhelming majority of those sterilized were white "Aryan" women. The motives for sterilization were several, albeit united in a eugenicist social Darwinist discourse of social engineering, with the primary aim of freeing society from social problems. It was against this background that not only Roma and Travelers were sterilized but also prostitutes, the "promiscuous," the mentally ill, the disabled, and pauper mothers. Of course, this is not to underplay the crucial influence of racist ideology upon the program. Of all the countries in Europe, only Nazi Germany surpassed Sweden in sterilizing more citizens for eugenicist aims. The reason *tattare* were targeted during this craze was because "their irregular lives were considered a severe social problem."[76] As a professor at the State Institute for Race Biology (founded in Uppsala in 1922) argued in 1944, "the social problems of the *tattare*"—who, he admitted, could not be genetically distinguished from Swedes—"cannot be isolated from the general problems occasioned in our community by the existence of persons leading vagabond and asocial lives."[77] The discursive genealogy between "asocial," "vagabond," and "Roma" needs to be taken into account when one considers that the Anti-Vagrancy Act was in 1965 abolished in favor of legislation on "subversive antisocial behavior," which carried with it several similarities to the former law. Because begging was interpreted as intrinsically antisocial, it was with the abolishment of this legislation in 1982 that begging was finally decriminalized.

The Racialization of Poverty

In the 2010s several opinion makers argued that although many different minorities are poor and discriminated against, no minority begged to the same extent as the Roma. Therefore, they recommended cultural assimilation—by outlawing begging, preferably.[78] This argument ignores the fact that because class society is hierarchical, some people must, by necessity, occupy the lowest stratum. Likewise, this claim is oblivious to the history of begging, wherein we see a tendency that different minorities, during different social formations' pauperization processes, have turned to panhandling. In Swedish, *fattiglapp* (pauper Lap) is a common invective meaning "pauper" or "bum," which originally referred to impoverished and begging Sami. As the crown's colonization of Sápmi took off in the 1600s, Sami populations were forced southward as they were increasingly isolated from their land and resources. Those who did not own reindeer and could not provide for themselves traveled from farm to farm, doing jobs considered "dirty" or begging. The *fattiglappar* or *tiggarlappar* (beggar Laps) were excluded from the historical equivalent of social citizenship, *laga försvar*, and they were not allowed (or forced) to join the army. To avoid becoming vagrants (and thus lawbreakers), those without *laga försvar* had to seek employment. The authorities in northern Sweden tried their best to drive the *tiggarlappar* "back home" to their presumed place of origin, passing different legislations to make sure they were not living within the county.[79] In Germany during the same time period, roughly 20 percent of the Jewish population were commonly known as *betteljuden* (beggar Jews). This lumpenproletariat lived impoverished nomadic lives as the combined consequence of rapid population growth, racist legislation on Jewish settlement, and disruptive political and economic processes.[80] Moving some miles further south, and to the present, it is not uncommon on northern Italian beaches to encounter African migrants trying to sell accessories that one could easily buy at a nearby shopping center—put simply, a more socially accepted performance of begging. All in all, these examples bear out the historical tendency that begging becomes a racialized practice when already vulnerable groups lose access to their previous livelihood and support systems.

This fact brings us to the materialism of racism, or as geographer Ruth Wilson Gilmore puts it, "the state-sanctioned or extralegal production and exploitation of group-differentiated vulnerability to premature death."[81] Within the capitalist system, racism as a signification process plays a crucial ideological role in reproducing inequality within the working class.[82] Specifically, the workforce becomes racialized, wherein people within a given social formation tend to occupy different positions within the production hierarchy, depending upon their complexion, religion, language, traditions, and so on. Within a racialized society, it must be underscored, *everyone* is racialized. Here, however, I use the adjective "racialized" in relation to the white norm—that is, in hierarchical steps beneath the highest position in the racialization hierarchy. Whiteness takes the highest position because of the global history of European colonialism and imperialism (different political modes of capitalism's historical development). Certainly, Sweden has been a part of this history as well. In the seventeenth and eighteenth centuries, the Swedish Empire included Finland, the Baltics, and parts of today's Norway, Germany, Poland, and Russia. Sweden also partook in the Atlantic slave trade, started its own East India Company, and had small colonies in the Americas and elsewhere. And, of course, there is the historical and ongoing settler colonization of the Sápmi. Meanwhile, in post-empire Sweden, whiteness has been fundamental to the nation-building process, as the dominant society has been white and with a relatively homogenous "ethnic" composition until the last decades.[83] This legacy looms large in the contemporary racial discourse of today's Sweden, where "Swede" in common speech equals "ethnic Swede," which in turn equals whiteness. A white Norwegian, for example, or a white Brit, could be mistaken for being a Swede. The common racial binary in daily speech is articulated as Swedes–Immigrants. This binary makes everyone who does not pass as "Swedish"—in other words, not pale skinned—into a (potential) "immigrant." Clearly, the commonsensical racialization in a Nordic context is thus dependent upon and sensitive to one's skin color, which means that even some Southern Europeans, for example, are thought to be "non-white."

The racialization of Swedish residents thus has a clear first racial division of two social positions, which with alarming frequency correlates to social class distinctions. Just like class is multileveled, racialization is a fundamentally hierarchical process of several relational social positions. These positions, lived as racial identities, impart different degrees and expressions of power, privilege, and oppression depending upon historical-geographical contextual circumstances. They are further intertwined with other subject positions due to gender, sexuality, body, age, health, and so on. This structuring of society into different class statuses, correlating to racial ideas, reproduces the labor hierarchy, the racist sentiments, and the racial pecking order. It is from this perspective that we understand racism in capitalism as a dialectic between material and imagined conditions. This means racist sentiments are a boon to capital when they do not turn into unproductive destruction or exclusion of demanded labor power. In this sense antiracist sentiments might also be an asset to capital, as they can help integrate more people into production and labor market competition. Capital's only moral, after all, is the self-valorization of capital. The best political strategy to accomplish this, in relation to racial questions, depends upon the historical-geographical context of political economy. Racial belief systems function nonetheless to displace capitalist inequality with racial difference, making people believe in the existence of a cross-class community called *the nation*, and making the racialized into the scapegoat for injustice. The intersectional non-white racialized positions, often with a family history of immigration, make them more likely to occupy the social stratum of the reserve army, which is more probable to be poor and more willing to accept wages below the level of "insiders." On the whole this makes racialized people in capitalist societies more likely to be ideologically interpreted as agents of inequality, burdensome government expenditures, and betrayal.

The racialization of Swedish poverty can be exemplified by the fact that while between 1991 and 2016 the cohort living in relative poverty in Sweden increased from 7 to 16 percent, this number, however, swelled from 11.6 to 27.4 percent for foreign-born adults—in comparison to the increase of 6.5 to 10.1 percent for natives. Significantly, Swedish poverty packs the biggest punch against single-parent households, the elderly, and immigrants born outside Europe. Sociologist Göran Therborn argues that being an immigrant in Sweden is to face three types of inequality simultaneously: in health, respect, and income.[84] This, however, ought to apply not only for (non-Western) immigrants, but for non-white Swedish residents *overall*, such as Swedish Roma—indeed, in 2010 a state report concluded that out of the fifty thousand Roma citizens of Sweden, "80 percent of adult Roma are estimated to be unemployed. A majority of Roma children do not complete primary school, very few continue to secondary school and even fewer reach university level. Functional illiteracy is not uncommon among adult Roma. Health problems start earlier, there are [lifestyle-] related health problems, health problems dating back from the times before

Roma were [residents], and life expectancy is judged to be clearly below average. Living standards are lower than average."[85]

Begging beyond Capitalism

Begging, as we know, is older than capitalism. Therefore, one avenue of inquiry into older trajectories of the begging question is to investigate the discourse of the Christian community in Sweden. Although one of the most secular countries in the world, Sweden has a long history of a powerful Lutheran state church. But what is most relevant to our case is the fact that, alongside humanitarian organizations and leftist-anarchist networks, the majority of NGOs and communities engaged in the relief of déclassés have been parishes. Indeed, Christian voices have been rather prominent in the debate, and, with minor exceptions, the majority have clearly positioned themselves *against* begging prohibitions. A case in point is a joint debate article signed in 2015 by representatives of Sweden's largest Christian denominations, proclaiming:

> Jesus gives us clear directives to give [these begging individuals] the same help as if it was him sitting on the street corner, wrapped up in a blanket, extending his paper mug. We cannot look the other way and lay the responsibility upon someone else, not if we are taking the injunction from the church and every Christian's Lord seriously. [Let] them instead become a living reminder of everyone's responsibility for the community and cohesion in-between humans, characterizing the good society which we together with many others want to be part of erecting.[86]

The only problem is that Jesus does not give "clear directives" on how the help is to be carried out. The only thing he does is urge people to care for the poor and love thy neighbor. Meanwhile, the implementation of Christian love for "the beggar" is left to profane interpretation, which has resulted in a history in which institutionalized religion has predominantly followed the interests of the state and capital. In 1869 a Swedish vicar objected to common "misunderstandings" that Christian love for the poor would take the form of giving alms and relief to paupers. According to him, Christian love entails galvanizing the pauper into industriousness and self-support, since the obligation to work was a divine punishment for the original sin; if there was a "common folk spirit" of not giving money to "stranger wanderers," "a given consequence" would be that these people "must stay at their right home."[87]

Here we must touch on a common oversimplification: the tendency to blame Protestantism for the capitalist work ethic and Western contempt for the poor. Granted, it is true that Martin Luther was hostile to begging, advocating anti-panhandling legislation and wanting municipal poor relief to be as restrictive as possible. However, Western European towns had already introduced regulations on begging and vagrancy in the fourteenth century, and as early as the tenth century there were ecclesiastical voices condemning begging in favor of forced work in order to counteract sinful living.[88] Although it's true that capitalism produces pauperization and migration patterns at an unprecedented rate, we must remember that impoverished outcasts and wandering strangers have existed in all agricultural societies. Though it was during the later centuries of the European Middle Ages that begging became a problem of "public" and "moral" order, as pauperism exploded in the wake of the Black Death and expropriations, begging before that was morally ambiguous at its best, sinful at worst. As a matter of fact, the theological question of whether begging is an expression of virtue or sin has existed ever since the debates of the Church Fathers.[89] During the medieval period, the church was a political institution maintaining the social relations of feudalism. On that basis the inherent ethical question begging raises—on what right the privileged have to their property, since the plea presupposes that it is in fact possible to share—needed to be neutralized. The ideological solution could be expressed in the symbolism of Jesus being both a beggar and king of humanity—both the destitute asking for God's love and God Himself giving His love to those in need. In this way Christ was to be found in the gift relation itself, in the social bond between the rich and poor, making humanity into one community.[90] Some contradictions were not so easily reconciled, however—like the paradoxical identity of the "beggar." Humility, patience, temperance, and diligence were all virtues, while gluttony, greed, sloth, and envy were all sins. "The beggar" could be associated with all of these characteristics—good and bad—making the Christian stance toward begging inherently ambivalent. With charity as a nonnegotiable imperative, a paradoxical moral was crystallized, reading something like this: blessed are those who give alms, but do not ask for them.[91] And since "work" was the penalty for original sin ever since the banishment from Eden, "free riding" was condemned.

Accordingly, there was a clear incentive even in the Middle Ages to distinguish between deserving and undeserving poor. As early as the thirteenth century, there were control systems during almsgiving at the monasteries, with tokens distributed to recipients of charity. This policy ensured that those who were not entitled to aid got none, and, likewise, no one received extra helpings.[92] Although it was a virtue to care for the poor, true deprivation—as opposed to religious renunciation—was not commendable, and the destitute were not persons to be admired. The rise of friars in the 1200s, following St. Francis and others, was an expression of a belief in the virtue of humility obtained by choosing poverty—to turn oneself to God instead of material possessions.[93] Of course, this practice is not limited to Christianity; mendicants and ascetics have also existed for thousands of years in Buddhism, Hinduism, Islam, and other religions. "The religious poor" is an "inversion" of "the beggar," since the latter does not beg out of contemplation. Moreover, mendicants are generally discouraged from accepting money as a gift, as their goal was to maintain their poverty, not overcome it. All of this made the friar virtuously humble—and "the beggar," in the eyes of religion and the public, anything but.

It would be erroneous, I believe, to blame the Christian ambivalence on the content of Christianity itself. To my knowledge, we have not seen any durable classless society in either feudal or ancient times, which means the dominant religions of these social formations faced, by necessity, a similar ambivalence. The fact that Buddha himself was a mendicant supports the existence of begging in antiquity. In ancient Greece, where Odysseus was said to disguise himself as a "beggar," there was also a distinction between deserving ("active") and undeserving ("passive") "beggars."[94] In fact, as far back as Middle Bronze Age Mesopotamia, old Babylonian letters between hungry applicants and state administrators indicate "the pejoritivization of the hungry, with hunger assimilated to moral ills." Hunger was further positioned "as the problem of *individuals*—occasionally of households— and not of communities." Notably, there were "no direct characterizations of the hungry as social parasites, but many responses to their pleas recast them as beggars, thieves, slackers, and whiners."[95] Thus, in my quest to find explanations as to *why* begging causes such overly invested, negative emotional responses, I have gone as far back in history as the earliest written records of humankind. In doing so, I have found that ambivalent or accusatory attitudes toward "beggars" are as old as penmanship, that there are class interests that benefit from these sentiments, and that the history and structures of racism and poverty have close interconnections. Even so, there's still no answer as to why these negative sensations arise, nor why there is such a frequent tendency of irrational victim blaming.

Psychoanalytic theory can provide some answers to these riddles. Before getting there, however, another question looms: Does the terminus at the Bronze Age mean that moral views on begging are fundamentally universal—a part of human nature itself? Here Engels once again becomes relevant, as he had an answer to the ideological conviction that some moral injunctions are eternal. Engels argued against Eugen Dühring's claim that some moral rules are essentially human because of their perpetual, universal presence, such as the moral injunction "Thou shalt not steal." Indeed, Engels argued that each developmental stage of class society—slave, feudal, and capitalist—has its own overarching moral theory reflecting its social (class) relations. Because said stages are part of the same historical development, these seemingly fixed injunctions can be found throughout all three stages, or so said Engels: "From the moment when private ownership of movable property developed, all societies in which this private ownership existed had to have this moral injunction in common: Thou shalt not steal. Does this injunction thereby become an eternal moral injunction? By no means."[96] In short, as long as private property exists, stealing will be a commonsensical crime. A slave can steal from a slave owner, a serf from a lord, a worker from an employer. In other words, theft is possible because property is enclosed from others. Meanwhile, in a society where resources are collectively gathered or produced and consumed—such as in hunter-gatherer societies or in utopianist visions of communism—robbery would not exist, since there would be no property to rob. With the advent of enclosures, it became an ideological fact that stealing is inherently wrong, because it violates the moral order of a class society—a society where people are divided into exploiters and exploited, owners and dispossessed. Within this framework the conceptualization of stealing as a sin becomes a commonsensical truth because both exploiters and exploited live in a social reality where the loss of one's own resources represents a threat to one's well-being. It becomes a violent act.

Nota bene: there is a marked difference between the category of "property" and the more socio-phenomenological concept of "possession." Since human life is simultaneously individuated and social, it is a cognitive impossibility to imagine a reality where individuals do not believe themselves and others to be respectively entitled to possessing things, whether it is food, clothes, bodies, children, animals, or care. Indeed, a dog, child, or enamored person can beg for food or love, but that is not the same thing as the social regulation of enclosed resources qua property. Nevertheless, the emotional tensions that are present in the negotiations of personal entitlements are readily repeated in negotiations of property relations, as is shown in the following chapters on psychoanalysis.

Begging, like stealing, has a long legacy in human societies; one is probably as old as the other. There is another important similarity, too: both practices stand in direct negative relationship to ownership. While "stealing" is seizing someone's property, "begging" is a plea for someone to relinquish their property to another. In that sense begging is inherently ethical and political—it expresses objective inequality, while recognizing the other's ownership and the option to give it away. Therefore, in a seemingly paradoxical way, begging simultaneously *recognizes* and *questions* property relations—likewise, the moral systems regulating them. While stealing is easily defined as a crime due to its violent character, begging blurs the distinction between interpersonal aggression and subjection. No matter the intention of the begging individual, begging is associated with collective anxieties, by virtue of its questioning of social interaction norms and property relations. Since both property relations and social interaction (both inseparable from societal morality) are often understood to constitute the very fabric of society, anxieties awakened by the begging gesture are readily displaced into anxiety over the fragmentation of the social itself. Although wage labor is a capitalist historical category, the drudgery of obeying authority, laws, and norms and the collective production processes are far older sensations. This is also true of the fantasies of free riders—a chronic source of victimization for "beggars." Racial Others, too, have been targeted by these fantasies—whether or not they were actually impoverished.

Marx, for his part, believed exploitation was a simulation of natural constraints, which in pre-class society was the cause of conflict. While the fear of alterity has its own psychic causes, the artificial production and maintenance of scarcity and insecurity in class societies, including capitalism, certainly fuel impulses of interpersonal and group domination. Political theorist Erica Benner argues:

> These impulses may appear as the expression of an incorrigibly conflict-prone human nature, while encouraging exploited groups to attach a high value to the characteristics which distinguish them from their exploiters.
> [Marx] did not expect the removal of exploitative class relations to bring an end to all interpersonal and social conflicts, but he did argue that those relations were an unnecessary source of intense and recurrent antagonism.[97]

Nevertheless, she continues: "It is certainly true that Marx failed, in his vision of communism, to spell out the ways in which the presence of others with distinct wills, desires, and group attachments must restrict the freedom of individuals in any imaginable society. [Additionally,] the prospect of domination, whereby one party asserts the power to define another's self-image, is never wholly absent from human relationships."[98]

Domination, aggression, interpersonal restriction on wills, desires, and group attachments—these phenomena cannot be wholly blamed upon either capitalism or class society. Since begging has, throughout history, been bound to these social qualities, we need to leave the conscious realm in favor of the unconscious realm of anxiety and desire to find a final answer for the emotionality and agonies of begging. Indeed, the road to this realm necessitates a confrontation with the widespread libidinal racist hatred and violence the EU déclassés encountered upon their arrival.

3 Abjection, or Hell Is Othered People

In Högdalen, a suburb of Stockholm, in September 2014, a tent camp housing déclassés was set ablaze. One man died of smoke inhalation, and another man had to have a couple of fingers amputated. The residents were convinced it was arson, although it could never be proven.[1] For years to come, local media stations would report on different variants of violence ranging from arsons and beatings in settlements to being kicked and spat on by passersby on the sidewalk. These attacks occurred throughout the country, and people of all backgrounds participated: teenagers, pensioners, civilians, guards, restaurant employees, native, immigrant, white and non-white Swedes, the healthy, and the sick. Indeed, terrorizing déclassés almost seemed to become a popular sport. As there never was any nationally coordinated survey or police operation that mapped, documented, and investigated these crimes as parts of a national pattern, it is impossible to identify the spread and development of the violence. Here, an enormous hidden statistic is to be expected—attributable, in part, to the victims' tendency to speak neither Swedish nor English, be illiterate, lack information on the Swedish legal apparatus, and be too disillusioned to believe reporting the crime would make any difference. Therefore, it is impossible to state the extent to which said crimes have been collectively coordinated. We do know there was an escalation of *reporting* on violence in 2015. This intersects with an escalation of arson attacks on refugee accommodations, which peaked in the autumn of 2015, during the height of the so-called refugee crisis.[2] The year 2015 also probably marked the greatest population of déclassés nationally present (or at least visible), and the issue of begging was still newsworthy to the media.

The terror attacks carried out against the déclassés can be understood as an expression of a micropolitics of ethnic cleansing. The overarching aim of such attacks, whether they include physical assault or verbal harassment, is to make déclassés vanish from one's territorial lifeworld by "voluntary" leave, pursuit, or extermination. By briefly touching upon examples of such politics, we return to my initial theoretical problem of this part of the book—that of the "irrational" emotions the begging practice seems to elicit. Here, this emotionality is articulated by, and discharged through, racist hostility. This violence symptomizes the relationships between poverty, deviance, and racism, yet it also forces us to try to analytically separate these phenomena, in order to better understand this particular kind of racist violence. Through an analysis of textually stated reasons for hostility toward the déclassés, we increasingly enter the "other scene" of the unconscious.

Regarding physical violence, déclassés were (and are) attacked at both their begging spots during the daytime and in their sleeping spots during the nighttime. The settlements were targeted for harassment, stoned, robbed, fired at, firebombed, set fire to, and otherwise menaced, as illustrated by the following exemplary events.

In 2014 in Perstorp, people sleeping in a car were attacked by ten individuals. The perpetrators smashed the windows and beat one of the occupants when he attempted to flee the car to seek help. The rationale for the attack was a false rumor of "beggars" trying to steal a dog.[3]

In a settlement in Gothenburg in 2015, a woman awoke to an unprovoked attack. Her assailant, a man carrying a "machete-like object and a hammer," stabbed her three times before demolishing three trailers and setting a tent on fire.[4]

In 2015 in Ängelholm, someone screwed a wooden board onto a trailer. The people inside could not get out while the aggressors pounded the walls. Another time, two perpetrators blocked the door of a trailer while someone used their car to try to roll over the vehicle with people inside it. Afterward the déclassés tried to move to another parking lot, where they were bombarded by rocks.[5]

In 2016 in a central park in Stockholm, it was common for déclassés to be awakened by drunk passersby urinating on them or kicking them in the stomachs, as there were several pubs on the other side of the street.[6]

On August 1, 2016, during nighttime, a police patrol stopped a forty-one-year-old man in a car in Eskilstuna. Inside the car they found Molotov cocktails and three cameras alongside a firecracker, axe, and smoke bomb. The man wore a balaclava around his neck. At his home the police found yet more weapons and receipts for bombs, as well as hard drives containing mappings, footage, and films of déclassé settlements in the area. What's more, his YouTube channel contained Nazi propaganda and various films on "beggar swine-filth in Eskilstuna," where déclassés' settlements were called "debris," "garbage," and so on.[7] This perpetrator's explicit Nazi sympathies make this case an example of a political lone wolf terrorist, who, together with thousands of likeminded others around the world, follow a white power political strategy named "leaderless resistance," which originated in the United States.[8] Applying a postmodern tactic, this strategy is based on nonhierarchical and decentralized networks, wherein individuals are to act as isolated warriors or martyrs. The lone wolves are instructed not to be official members of any organization or party, not to cooperate with others, and not to follow orders. This atomization of "the resistance" is thought to counter police investigations and the establishment's efforts to dismantle the movement: after all, if there are no organization and no leaders to catch—just anonymous individuals everywhere—the racialist "liberation war" will ultimately exhaust the enemy. As the arrest of the forty-one-year-old man indicates, déclassés in Sweden are familiar enemy targets, along with refugee accommodations, non-white Swedes, immigrants, mosques, synagogues, LGBTQ+ people, and left-wing organizations. Of course, we do not know how many of the attacks on déclassés and their settlements are carried out by politically motivated self-proclaimed lone wolves, who, it must be noted, are not alone in their hostility against déclassés.

The pattern of racist violence against déclassés is thus interesting to analyze as a leaderless racialist resistance war of a "collective unconscious," in the sense that so many of the assailants—especially if we take into account the more "innocent" violent acts of verbal abuse and humiliation—were probably not acting according to a political script or strategy. Nevertheless, from the perspective of consequences, they are on the same side in "the war." This serves as an uncanny correlation to the refugee accommodation arsons in 2015, where "ordinary" laboring family men with a local connection to the area were overrepresented as perpetrators.[9] Notably, these kinds of attacks were not novel in Sweden. In the early 1990s there was a similar flurry of arsons, with a similar profile of typical perpetrators. This rash of fires intersected with the largest refugee wave thus far and the entrance of a xenophobic party into parliament: the anti-immigration and anti-taxation populists Ny Demokrati, whose tenure in parliament only lasted one term.

But the "resistance" was not only targeting settlements—even more common were attacks on déclassés begging on the sidewalk by common pedestrians. Although the majority of penetrators were men, there were representatives of both sexes, all ages, and all backgrounds. Assailants spit at déclassés; cursed at them; threatened them; screamed at them; kicked them; beat them; poured liquids or ashes on them; threw food, cans, and stones at them; and so on. Here are a few telling examples:

In 2014 a grocery store owner in Gothenburg threw two buckets of water on a woman who was sat begging at the entrance. He then threw water "showily on the window, making her even wetter."[10]

Outside a shopping mall in Uppsala in 2015, an elderly woman attacked a begging woman, including intentionally kicking her framed photo of her children so the glass shattered and cut the photo.[11]

In Borås in 2015, a man named Ionut was run over by a moped rider in a crowded urban square. He sustained two bone fractures, a rupture in the lumbar region, scratches on the face, and bruises all over his body.[12] The crime, which was committed in broad daylight on a Sunday, was celebrated in a closed Facebook group, with comments such as:

This should be regarded as social work and rewarded with a medal.

I think all the world's misfortunes should strike upon those disgusting parasites; people are welcome to urinate on them, beat them [so] they take their things, clean up their feces piles and get lost.

Hahahahahhaa imagine his hospital bills hahahahaha.[13]

A few days later, in a central Stockholm park, Romanian couple George and Angelina rested in the grass after spending several hours collecting bottle deposits. A middle-aged man emptied a pint of battery acid on them.[14]

At a Stockholm subway entrance a few months later, on a Saturday evening, two drunk men in their fifties hit and kicked a begging person. Thankfully, two sixteen-year-olds intervened and asked them what they were doing. The men responded, "So? Don't you beat beggars?" and asked the teenagers if they were Swedes, adding, "You better be."[15]

In Stockholm in 2018, a man threw two big cobblestones at Maria, a thirty-seven-year-old begging woman. Hit twice in the back, she afterward described the pain: "It felt like the stone went straight through my body. I screamed for my life."[16]

Concurrently, there was another kind of violence spreading, although of a subtler nature: those trying to expel déclassés from public spaces by spreading false accusations. In two extraordinary examples, the perpetrators were actually caught. In Gothenburg in October 2013, a woman reported a man named Krasto to the police for theft, claiming he mugged her for 7,000 kronor and a tablet. After arresting Krasto, it turned out the woman's story did not match her cash withdrawals. She was convicted of false indication and was sentenced to probation and fines.[17] The other event went international. In August 2014 a man of about thirty stole a tablet from his son's kindergarten in Sjöbo and gifted it to a woman outside a store. Thereafter, he reported her to the police for theft. However, a security camera corroborated the handoff, and he was sentenced to four months in prison.[18]

The Enmity Politics' Language

Another typical strategy in this war was the dissemination of propaganda via notes outside grocery stores. Outside a store in Sävja (Uppsala municipality), an anonymous note claimed "the girl" begging there was "cunning; in addition to lying to the police, she shows her teeth and snarls when examined."[19] A photo of this note was shared on social media over four thousand times. The note also stated that the woman was part of an organized gang coordinated by a "highly educated" Romanian man making roughly 700,000–900,000 kronor per month through "this organized begging." Apart from hiding food, cash, and a cell phone beneath her blanket, the "cunning girl" was allegedly infected with tuberculosis, or so said the note: "If you get TB, maybe in a few years, you've probably been infected by a Romanian beggar." It is also common to misrepresent "the police" as the sender, such as in this note from 2015: "Call to the people of Gothenburg. The police urge the public not to donate money to beggars," because then "you as an individual support organized crime."[20]

In comparing these messages with social media discussions, they appear to echo conversations in closed Facebook groups and on Sweden's biggest internet forum, Flashback Forum—a free speech platform in a similar vein as Reddit and 4chan. Here, racist hate speech is flourishing and amplified against "beggars," often labeled as "Gypsies," who are frequently associated with disgust, disease, and trash. Consequently, they are often called "parasites," "rats," "filth," "animals," and worse. One user writes: "The local newspaper in Solna is despairing because of a suspected invasion of rats, close to the subway. Two-legged rats in the form of aggressive begging Gypsy dirt is, however, not written about! [I'm] convinced Gypsies are spreading more disease and misery than a whole colony of four-legged rats. Wow! How wonderful it would be if the municipality had an emergency number to call when two-legged Gypsy rats needed to be taken care of."[21]

In these spaces, users share stories of why they hate déclassés and what they (claim to) do to them as *revenge* and acts of *resistance*, thus replicating white supremacist fantasies of guerilla warfare:

> If one wants to fuck with them, you have to minimize their income. Why not scoff at those who give [money], destroy deposit bottles, [damage] their mugs, or complain to the shops facilitating their existence? Way more effective than to notify the police.[22]

ANXIETY

Excellent suggestions in your quote. It doesn't have to be big dramatic actions, like burning down their camps. No. Everyone can do something small. All resistance helps. [Why] not take the mug and keep the money? Or, if one doesn't want to touch the garbage: Pour a deciliter of ill-smelling liquid, like gas, vinegar, or butyric acid one keeps in a small bottle. [Another discreet] variant I've done sometimes is to "accidentally" kick away the beggar mug, or mash it with the cart. You just say "whoops" and continue. No one notices.

The harder we, the people, make begging, the better for society. As said, authorities, politicians, and media have abandoned us. The only ones who can do anything are us.[23]

[Unwelcome] new Gypsy neighbors are not always in their [filthy] trailer. Suggestion: when it's empty, you [bring] an opened can, with wonderful smelling [fermented Baltic herring]. [Go] to the [filthy trailer] when the place is empty; pour liquor around the door and window slots, and finish by pouring out those fine fish at the entrance to those ugly fish's trailer. If there's a Gypsy-car, it's a jackpot! Herring liquor on the windshield runs down in the intake, making the car acquire an odor even eclipsing the aroma of feces aroma, from Gypsies using the toilet without [toilet] paper.

Mean . . . ? Not at all! In love and war, everything is permitted. Herring makes the Gypsy plague move, to another spot. The good thing with herrings is nothing needs to get burned (I refuse to become a pyromaniac), and tires etc. are not damaged. Good luck, please return with extensive event reports! I felt like a bad boy when the beggar throne close to my office was soaked with herring. The happiness with the Gypsy [gone] triumphed over my guilt, however.[24]

On Flashback you also find maps uploaded so users can participate in locating settlements. While these excited conversations contain rather "extreme" language, mundane expressions of antipathy against déclassés are more common on more mundane social media platforms. In these posts the idea that déclassés are an enemy to the national "us" is foundational. A case in point of this discourse's potential "subtleness"—which pictures déclassés as a national threat rather than straightforward enemies—is the backlash against a private dentist in Halland who, in the autumn of 2014, fixed déclassés' teeth for free after her working day was done. Commenters expressed arguments along these lines: "If a dentist wants to volunteer to help these beggars then okay! But then they shall do the same for our own homeless, sick listed, the unemployed, pensioners, single parents, and others with shitty finances or barely make it day to day."[25] Here, the problem or "bad object" is identified as those who do not help "our" (Swedish) poor. However, it is rather obvious that the déclassés are also "bad objects" by acting as unjust beneficiaries of care—implicitly stealing sympathy and resources from those who have legitimate claims to the services they are accessing. Although the framing of the déclassés as changelings might present them as innocent, it is nevertheless evident that caring for them is treason. This comment thread embodies one of the problems about which journalists reached out to me for comment, and for which I didn't really have a good answer: Why this *passionate negativity* against déclassés? When treating killings, arsons, hate speech, and public complaints against solidarity with déclassés as different degrees of the same antipathy against impoverished, racialized, homeless, and begging individuals, neither a theory of Swedish welfare society nor a critical race theory of capitalism and class society can explain the passions within this fundamentally "irrational" hatred.

We then have to, again, turn to an understanding of racism as a dialectic between thought and materiality. We get nowhere, after all, by dismissing this hostility as "racism." Here racism cannot be the answer as to why this hatred and violence arise. Rather, it is the question. Namely, how does racism become such an affective force in these interpersonal reactions to begging and homelessness, and why is this racism fueled and expressed in a violent manner?

Manifest Motives for Hate

When we historize this collective hatred, we find that there are, of course, political factors that partly explain why the escalation of violence occurred during this time period (such as the fact that it took place within a great conjunctural crisis of the Swedish welfare state and its hegemony, as is explained in part 2). Returning to the previous chapter, we recall that scarcity and insecurity feed temptations of domination and hostility. Crucial here are the collective *perceptions* of scarcity and insecurity as a social possibility and thus reality, rather than the actual socioeconomic conditions of individuals. Swedish welfare society had for decades become increasingly unequal and segregated, while simultaneously more racialized along class lines. Notably, this increase in national inequalities is an international phenomenon—likewise the rise in electoral support for racist and radical-nationalist movements. Their main representatives in Sweden, SD, depicted "beggars" as a threat, or a nuisance, to the nation from the start. Then, as the normalization of SD and their ideology grew at record speed during the 2010s, their definition of the problem with begging and "beggars" gradually became commonsensical. Because this argument connected the problem to non-white immigration, and this problem in turn was urgent to the nation's survival, one might guess these assertions fueled a moral panic regarding immigration in general and déclassés in particular, triggering outbursts of violence. When we marry this political development to the democratization of internet communication, the lone wolf tactic is supplied with an effectiveness that local communities' place-bounded racist rumors and mobilization cannot match.[26] Crucially, lone wolf terrorism also increased in this time period due to radicalized Salafist supporters, as ISIS gradually lost ground in the Syrian war, encouraging Muslims in the West to wage jihad behind enemy lines.[27] Of course, in Sweden the white power faction has murdered many more people than the jihadist-Salafist camp, as the only successful attack of the latter was the attack on a pedestrian street in Stockholm in April 2017, killing five people.[28]

However, the political landscape does not by itself explain differences in values, emotions, and subject positions on begging Roma. Additionally, there also ought to be factors explaining the causes of the specificity of anti-Roma sentiments against begging homeless déclassés. While anti-Roma racism absolutely targets Swedish Roma, they are not subject to the same kind of treatment as the foreign déclassés because they do not face the same material circumstances as the visiting EU citizens. As discussed in the previous chapter, contempt for "beggars," outcasts, and the impoverished is a universal property of class society throughout history. Note that this ubiquitous "fear of beggars" has also affected white individuals. In the contemporary United States, homeless people are attacked regularly, including those who are white. In fact, hundreds of homeless Americans have been murdered by non-homeless people.[29] The point is, the aversion to the deviant "homeless beggar" represents a dangerous societal antipathy in its own right. Without underplaying the obvious racism at work in the aforementioned violence, there ought to be a material dimension to the hostility against déclassés, regarding their visual appearance in Swedish everyday spaces. And this appearance, the condensed effect of the spaces and practices of loitering, begging, failing to conform, and desperation, seems to work as a "trigger" for antipathy and hostility. However, it seems as if the race signifier, in identifying the visual traits of homelessness and impoverishment as the entities of a racial Other, together with the fact that this Other speaks an alien, non-white, language, pushes this trigger even harder. When interviewed in 2017 about their experiences of being victimized in Malmö public spaces, some begging déclassés deny they faced hatred and violence because of their Roma heritage, instead arguing the determining push was their begging. Three of the déclassés explain:

They don't like us because we are begging and they think that we don't want to have normal jobs. It's a pity because it's not true.

It is not because we are Gypsies that people think badly of us. It is because we are "beggars." They think we interfere when they go past us, we are in the way.

We beg, which many people do not like. They think we don't want to work. Furthermore, we are not Swedes, and many feel that we are exploiting Swedish society. They think that they don't have any responsibility for us because we are not Swedes.[30]

Here, the racial signifier that induces hostility is not "Roma," but "non-Swede." Again, this argument does not minimize anti-Roma racism. Rather, the racist identification process seems to draw three interconnected conclusions in the meaning-making process of the EU déclassés' appearance: (1) the Other is "deviant," (2) the Other is "non-Swede" (non-white), and (3) the Other is "Roma." This cognition process, if correct, yields a three-layer structure of contempt against the déclassé, which also explains this antipathy's ideological, discursive, and social genealogy in relation to other forms of racism and phobias regarding Otherness. In a study in the same town two years later, twenty-five déclassé respondents were presented with three options for the motives behind their perpetrators' attacks:

Ethnicity or race: seventeen votes
Skin color: three votes
Livelihood: eleven votes (nine votes = begging; two votes = collecting
   cans and bottles)[31]

The respondents could tick more than one option, and nine respondents ticked both the first and last choice. Eighty-four percent identified themselves as Roma. However, as both my media sources and this study indicate, the Roma déclassés are hated not only because of their Roma affiliation, but also for being deviant, homeless, begging, non-white, and non-Swedish. Nevertheless, in the Swedish media discourse, "beggar" and "Roma" became interchangeable metaphors. When the mainstream press and radio headlines mentioned the "Roma," the reader was supposed to understand this story was about Eastern European Roma EU citizens without right of residence being homeless and begging in Sweden, not about a member of the ten-times-bigger population of Roma Swedish citizens. A few examples include "The Police: Roma Are Forced to Pay to Beg"; "Roma on Gotland Collect Money for Refugees"; "Eviction of Roma More Expensive than Shelters."[32] In other words, the respondents' answers do not expose the potential that the perpetrator's perception of the victim's ethnicity/race and livelihood are ultimately the same, further blurring one-dimensional categorizations of hate crimes' intentions. The particular kind of racism delineated here might be aptly labeled xeno-racism, per Ambalavaner Sivanandan's description of the term:

> If it is xenophobia [i.e., the fear or hatred of strangers], it is—in the way it denigrates and reifies people before segregating and/or expelling them—a xenophobia that bears all the marks of the old racism, except that it is not colour-coded. It is a racism that is not just directed at those with darker skins, [but] at the newer categories of the displaced and dispossessed whites, who are beating at western Europe's [doors]. It is racism in substance but xeno in form—a racism that is meted out to impoverished strangers even if they are white. It is xeno-racism.[33]

The concept of xeno-racism works to not only uncover the racism obscured by deracialized language but also to point out the particular processes involved in how the encounter with something "xeno" becomes absorbed by and operationalized within a racialist logic. A childhood friend's grandfather told me, upon hearing the focus of my research: "Well, I guess I am a racist then, since I'm so fucking tired of these beggars." Given that I had neither mentioned "racism" nor "Roma," this conclusion reveals the inherent racialization of the Swedish begging question, as his feelings on begging had become inseparable from a discourse on racial difference, which has been fueled by both sympathetic and antipathetic voices. Giving the grandfather the benefit of a doubt, one might interpret his statement as an expression of actually being "so fucking tired" of the deviancy—that is, the "xeno"—of begging itself, but due to the dominant language he interprets this frustration as "racism." And then, being true to himself, he cannot curb his frustration; thus, he has to be a "racist." This brings us to the commonsensical appeal of SD, regarding the begging question. Because SD was, for several years, the only champion for the desire to make begging go away, the party was able to position itself as the only one that dared to address the "real" problems of society—a relatable prospect for those feeling they did not want to simply accept the continuous presence of begging. At that time the other parties presented no solution other than acceptance, while simultaneously blaming SD's sympathizers for being racists. As the anxieties of the refugee crisis became intersected with the begging question, I am not exaggerating when I say that, in 2015, begging individuals were to be found nationwide in everyday spaces—even in small localities with fewer than four hundred individuals. Refugees, meanwhile, were not people the average resident necessarily had encountered, yet fantasies about "the refugees" were stirred up. And "beggars" were almost daily encountered. Perhaps this is why my well-meaning dad, as an ideological Freudian slip, habitually misnames déclassés as "refugees."

The Sweden Democrat Ideology on Begging

If we look at how the discourse of racist antipathy forms the problem of déclassés, it seems unnecessary to invoke fantasies of the nation's doomsday. To motivate hatred and violence, the sole fact of the racialized "beggars'" territorial presence is sufficient. In SD's discourse on begging, the Malthusian urgency of "rescuing welfare" and the attendant claims that all organized begging is criminal are supplemented by an argument that is probably even more appealing, due to its commonsensicality: deviancy itself. In August 2015 SD paid for an enormous ad in a subway station in Stockholm, addressing tourists in English:

SORRY ABOUT THE MESS HERE IN SWEDEN. = (
WE HAVE A SERIOUS PROBLEM WITH FORCED BEGGING!
INTERNATIONAL GANGS PROFIT FROM PEOPLE'S DESPERATION.
OUR GOVERMENT [sic] WON'T DO WHAT'S NEEDED.
BUT WE WILL! AND WE'RE GROWING AT RECORD SPEED.
WE ARE THE OPPOSITION AND WE PROMISE REAL CHANGE!
WE ARE THE SWEDEN DEMOCRATS!
WELCOME BACK TO A BETTER SWEDEN IN 2018!

Accompanying the ad was a mural of a homeless Roma woman sleeping on the sidewalk with her back turned to passersby, surrounded by the text: "Sweden should do better than this!" Here an explicit mention of the welfare state collapsing is absent. It is not needed. What's more, the issue of criminality is simply a contemptuously racist "bonus." Within this framework "the beggar" becomes an ideological condensation of the roles of victim, perpetrator, and, above all, "mess." A couple of months earlier, when SD had demanded a ban on foreign begging, forced visa identification for Romanians and Bulgarians, the presence of more police, and an end to all possibilities of social support for déclassés, the notion of spatial deviancy was the prime motif: "People are disturbed, worried, and negatively affected by the beggars and the slum communities being more prevalent in our communities. Migrant beggars occupy private land and disturb business owners, and our parks, where children are playing, are not infrequently used as toilets. This is not acceptable."[34] One of the authors, the infamous politician Kent Ekeroth, also announced SD's demand for a begging ban in 2011. In a radio documentary on Ekeroth's political journey, he discloses his desire for an extralegal expulsion of "immigrants" (even if they fled death sentences) who dare to side-eye someone: "If they are threatening, cocky, behaving badly—expulsion. Immediately, no questions. [If] they side-eye someone, it will be expulsion on principle. [It] should be enough with stealing a bike—expulsion. Pooping on someone's plot—expulsion. Sitting on their porch, being cocky, saying this is mine—expulsion."[35] The similarity between this diatribe on the problem with "immigrants" and the problem he presents with "beggars" is obvious: both concern "the racial Other insulting me on my territory." In a 2015 post on his blog, Jan Sjunnesson, chief editor of SD's bulletin, urged citizens to "reclaim the streets" from "beggars":

Put yourself in front of the beggar who's bugging you, and you want to go. Stay next to or in front of their paper cup or sign, not on their stuff. They can otherwise use that against you. They know exactly what rights they have. [If] they touch you, you have won and can accuse them of molestation, which is a fussy method they [use]. You are simply blocking their activity with your body until they move. Then you follow them. If they pack their things, you have won.

[You] have the right to stand wherever you want, and apparently, beggars have the right to sit wherever they want as long as it is a public space. [The]

ANXIETY

streets, squares, shop entries, and places today sieged by beggars are *yours*. You have the right to be there and stand wherever you want. Show this by taking back public space, kindly but firmly.[36]

The racial Other is sieging *your* space. This is crucial, since the racial signifier "non-Swede" marks the déclassés as intruders: an enemy. This perceived enmity, however, seems to be primarily rooted in (as absurd as it sounds) bad behavior. Earlier the same year, a twenty-five-year-old man continuously persecuted and abused people begging in Kista (a Stockholm suburb), once pouring lighter fluid on tents and throwing belongings from a footbridge. He was also probably the one who punched Maricica Cojocaru in her stomach and kicked her to the ground. By August 2015 he had been reported twelve times for assaults over a two-month period. When questioned why he hates "Roma" so much, he first explained it is because they do not have the same right to be "here" as himself, since they are "*not Swedish*." Then he goes on to say that they have destroyed Kista by cluttering it and sleeping outdoors. Finally, however, what seems to be worst of all is that they "behave badly": "They are not behaving normally. Once I sat next to a woman on the subway who loudly guffawed while speaking on the phone. I think they should take a course in etiquette or something."[37] This reason for racial hatred echoes Ekeroth hating "immigrants" for side-eyeing others. It also resonates uncannily with the argument the racist Swedish serial killer Peter Mangs presented for the reason he shot non-white Swedes in 2009 and 2010: "I was bothered by their presence. They insulted me. Drove around in their cars as if they had a right to do so."[38] The twenty-five-year-old's words also recall Sjunnesson's "reclaim the streets" campaign. When confronted, Sjunnesson explained to a journalist: "Many people are irritated, not being able to move effortlessly on the streets. They are molested and feel bothered. [Therefore,] one must harden oneself and become impolite, rude, and bothersome oneself. We Swedes are not used to this, because we are generous and good-hearted, not aggressive people."[39] Notably, this argument resembles the problem with begging described by "A Lady" in a letter to the editor and reprinted by Engels, and likewise the more recent letter to the editor from someone whose "privacy is violated" by the begging encounter. It is as if the déclassés, as racial Others, not only behave deviantly by begging and being homeless but also act like this out of aggressive intentions toward the observer (i.e., "the Swedes")! What is this if not an example of psychoanalytic projection? Take Sjunnesson, who believes his aggressiveness is not his own—rather, it is the Other's aggressiveness that he must defend himself against!

The aforestated irrationalities, overreactions, fantasies, and projections that undergird racist violence tell us there is something else going on in the begging encounter that cannot be sufficiently explained by history, capitalism, or ideology. There is an unconscious dimension to this. Accordingly, I commence my psychoanalytic interpretations below.

Enter Psychoanalysis via Abjection

Contrary to what one may expect, properly applied, psychoanalysis is a materialist theory, not an idealist one. Theorist Fredric Jameson explains, "To say that both psychoanalysis and Marxism are materialisms is simply to assert that each reveals an area in which human consciousness is not 'master in its own house,'" though the decentered areas differ.[40] In Marxism it is the class dynamics of social history, while in psychoanalysis it is the unconscious mental processes reacting to stimuli. Although unconscious processes might be experienced as "timeless," they have historical origins and trajectories, just like the human organism itself is an unfinished historical development of evolution. As human transformation is always caused by its social-environmental context, psychoanalysis investigates the borderlands between biology and culture, the physical and the mental.[41] As such, it invariably becomes a philosophy, which is also the way I apply it here.[42] If treated consequentially, it works as a philosophy of the existential, the ethical, and the political. What's more, it is erroneous to argue psychoanalysis's focus is exclusively individualist. Its ontology implies an intrinsic *social* reality that is also changing, as unconscious suffering and desires are sublimated through—and simultaneously generated by—historical-geographical language, practices, and rituals.[43] Regarding the dialectic of racism, psychoanalysis mediates the mutual influence of structural racialization and racial ideas, as psychoanalysis relates to the liminal spaces between sensation and thought.

Having offered this brief defense of psychoanalysis, I begin with the theory of abjection, as it gives some initial answers to the problems presented earlier in this chapter. In the next chapter I proceed to more complicated theoretical implications.

The racist violence in question is of a fundamentally spatial character, with the aim of exterminating the territorial presence of déclassés in one's lifeworld. Its stated problem is the spatial presence of déclassés and their supposed rude behaviors, deviant practices, and evil intentions. The language constructing this problem and solution depicts Roma déclassés using metaphors that connote mess, filth, and vermin. Of course, this linguistic trend, which equates the racialized Other with objects of disgust, is well established in the history of racism. It happened in Nazi Germany, and so too does it happen in contemporary Sweden. This first step of "dehumanization" (or, rather, the transformation of the Other into an evil and dangerous human), a process that lowers the social thresholds for racist physical violence, is called *abjection*—the conversion of the Other into an "abject": a disgusting object. Abjection implies a sense of disintegration on the part of the subject, its spaces and communities included, by an intruding transgressing object. This process also targets other marginalized groups, such as the homeless and sexual minorities. But how does this strategy come to work, and why is it so effective? And what is the spatial implication of abjection's logic?

Anthropologist Mary Douglas once famously argued that "dirt" is "matter out of place."[44] Groups orient their community around certain rules of conduct, which define the group's norms, morality, and boundaries. This particular order reveals what the particular group, in the final analysis, actually is. Spatially, this ordering implies, by necessity, that some things belong to some spaces, whereas some things do not: things in order are "pure"; things out of order are "dirt." Philosopher Julia Kristeva applied this insight to the unconscious dimension, noting that some phenomena are more prone to cause phobic reactions than others.[45] What phenomena such as feces, insects, pests, and putrefaction share, as an existential quality, are their common capacity of being experienced as transgressing the body's demarcation against the external world. Symbolizations of diseases, sickness, and death, and associations to these, activate sensations of bodily fragmentation. Abjection, however, has the nasty habit of being anthropomorphic, turning nonnormative Othered bodies into unconscious representations of these dangers. When Jewish people were called "rats" in Nazi propaganda, they were made into a disease of the social body, an evil matter, out of place in the pure racial nation, that needed to disappear. When Gica's teenage attackers called him "the rat," this language probably facilitated their ultimately fatal abuse of him. The scandalous insight psychoanalysis provides is that racial abjection is not only a collective discursive strategy; it implies collectively embodied and affecting sensation—that some people really sense disgust and fear of the racial Other's perceived Otherness. Nevertheless, discursive strategy mobilizes these bodily sensations, as language is affective through its symbolic power of triggering associations, fantasies, and emotions.

Geographer David Sibley spatialized Kristeva's abjection theory by applying it to practices of spatial exclusion of "deviant Others" (racial Others, Roma, teenagers, etc.) from purified spaces. Ultimately, abjection refers to a process of demarcating selfhood, aiming to uphold a clear border between purity and filth and, through this method, locating oneself within a social (contingent) order of things. As racial abjection implies, this demarcation of selfhood also takes place on a collective level, as human beings are fundamentally social creatures who define themselves as members of a larger group of unifying similarities. Sibley's point, however, is that the world of inanimate objects "also provides a context for selfhood."[46] Life always takes place. Lived spaces become, through their material, aesthetical, and social orders, tacit and unconscious supports of selfhood. When these spatial orders are (registered as) disturbed, this disruption can be sensed as taking place within one's self. Crucial once again is that this is not merely a "language game"; we are talking about real bodily-mental sensations.

Relying on psychoanalyst Melanie Klein's object relations theory, Sibley highlights the individual psyche's foundational intersubjectivity. To apply continental philosophy jargon, every "subject" needs an "object" toward which it is directed. Though the individual identifies itself as a subject, separated from others and with its own will and wants, it nevertheless depends upon other persons in order to exist. The human being is nothing (both cognitively and materially speaking) without its social existence. This is demonstrated by the human child's exceptionally long dependence upon others to survive. As Klein explains, an infant is fundamentally dependent upon an external object for its own survival: "the (m)other." As an infant develops self-consciousness, it recognizes its own separation from its original object (its caretaker/s) yet also comprehends its continued dependence upon this object to receive nutrition, safety, and pleasure. This contradiction prompts the desire to possess "the object," as the child feels abandonment and pain when separated from its (perceived) source of fulfillment. However, with the establishment of subjectivity, the child unconsciously fears being swallowed by the object—it wants to maintain its subjectivity, which it only can pursue by keeping a distance, a demarcation, against the object. This is a basic overview of object relation theory.

Subsequent phases of socialization make the subject inscribe this original object relationship to constitute the unconscious basis of other relationships. Problems arise as the child's mind continues to maintain a *transitivist* subjectivity—its demarcation between inside/outside, between subject/object and me/others, is never definitely set. The demarcation needs to be continuously explored, negotiated, and defended, as the subject always depends upon its social surroundings to map out this demarcation. Because the child originally equated sensations of pleasure and suffering with different external impressions, these impressions become symbolized as different objects with (unconsciously perceived) inherent characteristics of being good or bad to the subject. "Good objects" elicit pleasure; "bad objects" cause suffering. "Abjects," meanwhile, are objects that transgress the object order—in other words, a kind of bad object. But these objects are then easily, thanks to symbolization and fantasy, turned into human beings with different expected characteristics.

This transitivist worldview causes the subject to be constantly engaged in simultaneous processes of *projection* and *introjection* (externalizing and internalizing). Locked inside one's own body-mind, all sensations are sensed from within one's body-mind. Nevertheless, the causes of some of these sensations ought to come from the outside—from the material surroundings and from other people's actions. Freud argued: "We are threatened with suffering from three directions: from our own body, which is doomed to decay and dissolution and which cannot even do without pain and anxiety as warning signals; from the external world, which may rage against us with overwhelming and merciless forces of destruction; and finally from our relations to other men."[47] The same goes with pleasure. But with suffering threatening the subject from three directions—although all suffering is initially sensed from within—cognition risks confusing the causes of suffering and their original locations. External forces are introjected to become part of one's own self, and vice versa; internal beliefs and sensations are projected into others' properties and intentions. Bad traits readily become others' (individual or group) characteristics; good traits readily become one's own (again, individually or as a group). This results from a wish to distance oneself from sources of suffering. Recall Marx, Engels, and Cabral's efforts to split the working class into good objects (the proletariat) and bad objects (the lumpenproletariat), or the perennial distinction between deserving and undeserving poor. While these attempts at subdivision have their manifest historical reasons, they simultaneously contain unconscious dimensions of projection/introjection.

In this way this transitivist lived reality helps explain those beliefs that implicate the déclassés as the cause of their own assailants' aggressiveness. Having interpreted the origin of this aggressiveness as external, rather than from within, the antagonist's aggressiveness turns into a defense against this projection.

The spatial aspect of this unconscious logic should not be underestimated, as it also helps address the dignity of identity regarding these matters. Namely, Sibley's geographical point is that the material properties of space themselves become part of one's identify formation. If déclassés' begging and homelessness result in disturbances of previously naturalized social-spatial aesthetic orders, and these structures are unconsciously lived as parts of one's very own self, these transgressions should affect some people as if they are personal intrusions beneath one's own skin. In research concerning, for example, the social tragedies of gentrification and forced migration, researchers appear to take this transitivism for granted when they discuss "senses of displacement"—as though an alienation from one's familiar surroundings causes psychic and existential suffering.[48] But if these assumptions are to be true, they ought to work for everyone facing involuntary spatial alteration—not only the dispossessed, but also the privileged. This argument is crucial in order to better grip the causality between geographical aesthethical change and nationalist-racist rage. Living in a social reality of commonsensical, banal nationalism, where the nation's territory is treated as a collective "home," and racial/foreign Others are identified as causes of spatial disturbance, this unconscious sensation of selfhood (being extrabodily expanded out in space), activates the national identification between oneself, "the people," and "the territory." In this way the abject intrusion of a racialized "bad object" not only becomes an intrusion into one's personal sphere, or one's local community, but also one's nation. Although unconscious, this process nevertheless depends upon history, geography, discourse, ideology, and the lived reality of class society. Here language is crucial, as it provides the subject with the mental symbols, associations, and narratives in order to make sense of its own sensations. If "the nation" is commonsensically believed to be one's "good object" (among other goods), without which one cannot exist as a separated individual, the sensation of fragmentation via racial abjection becomes transferred into the fragmentation of the nation.

Let me illustrate this dramaturgy with a blog post with the apocalyptic title "Everything falls apart" ("Allt går sönder") from June 2015, written by a former Social Democrat who turned into an "immigration-skeptical" blog author: "For the third morning in a row on my way to work, I see feces and toilet paper in the playground close to the subway. [Some] hundred meters away piles of trash bags, IKEA bags, strollers, and carts along with the beggars' mobile homes and clutter. [If] you are sleeping for free under the open sky in Sweden, you shall not leave excrement or other things as gifts to those living here and paying for this."[49] He continues to describe an urban landscape where law and order seems to have retreated, and where the loitering of "beggars" is described interchangeably with their bad manners and rudeness. He blames the prime minister who is supposed to sit in his ivory tower separated from, and ignoring, this growing sense of social disintegration. He mentions his immigrant friend "Ali"—a "deserving" immigrant who functions as the story's antithesis to the déclassés. Ali is a political refugee, an industrious wage laborer, and a victim of his unworthy counterparts: "The beggars and jihadists are ruining it for people like him who don't want anything other than to work hard and earn his livelihood in a lawful manner. [Ali] is drawn into the hate and contempt [growing] each day." The magic of the racial signifier is obvious here: all of a sudden, "beggars" are part of the same problem as the Salafist terrorists—they are both racial Others and represent something morally bad (evil). What started as a complaint on spatial loitering has in the end become a prophecy of the downfall of civilization and the nation itself, through the presence of immoral racial Others. And this is also a personal, existential threat, as he concludes: "I fall apart. Ali falls apart. Sweden falls apart. Everything falls apart."

This straightforward description of fragmentation illuminates the relationship between abjection, spatial purification, and morality. Mary Douglas argued that social orders of purity and pollution have less to do with hygiene and more to do with maintaining social and moral boundaries within a given group, in order to preserve group identity against its constitutive (however contingent and changing) out-groups. This implies that social notions of purity and filth are a matter of morality; "dirt" equals "wrong." From this perspective socio-spatial orders of purity imply moral landscapes where these orders are performed and transgressed. Ergo, if something doesn't belong, it's also morally wrong. Recall representations of Swedish urban landscapes as places where impoverishment and begging are something out of place and time. Here, something nationally out of place becomes anti-national and anti-moral. Remember too the aforementioned voices who argued that déclassés and other racial Others need punishment because of their "bad behavior" and lack of manners. Begging, which is moralized by its spectators, has throughout history been designated by determining structures and interests a moral misdeed. Through this lens we're able to grasp how these perceptions imply a moral violation in a moral landscape (begging being a socio-spatial disorder), and how this offense is, in turn, readily interpreted and perceived as sensuously *revolting*: dirt. The same logic is applicable to the abjection of homelessness itself.

These associations between different binaries of linguistic signifiers (moral/immoral, good/evil, purity/dirt, in-place/out-of-place, nation/Other) also help us understand the perpetual obsession with claiming all déclassés are criminals. As previously mentioned, this conviction tends not to discriminate between victims and perpetrators, treating "them" as all being the same. Moreover, the actual criminality of trafficking does not appear to be the real issue here, since those shouting the loudest do not seem to care at all about the victims of said trafficking. The real crime is spatial deviance, with the victims cast as pedestrians. Within this racist discourse, "criminal" is simply a metaphor for "evil human." A criminal is a person whom society deems to be doing something exceptionally morally wrong. The flipside is that this insufficient argument creates its own social reality. The sensation of evil creates an evil object, an evil person, and then racist discourses and ideologies with their symbols provide these sensations with an intellectual interpretation, building this sensation into a moral conviction. In this way, the conviction of the Other being "evil" finds its narrative ("criminality"), which provides an intellectual foundation for the newfound conviction that the Other is criminal. Consequently, one can go out in the world and identify the déclassé's cell phone as a proof of the criminality (they are lying about their poverty and thus are criminal), since the narrative has already been established. No matter the evidence—the déclassés' "luxury" items or "bad manners"—the conviction of the Other's evilness arises from the original sensation of spatial "dirt" being "evil." As is developed in the next chapter, when one considers the relationship of psychoanalysis to ethics, moral sensations are inherently sensuous and affective, no matter how hard rationalists try to make them into analytical units in the abstract.

This triad of purification, morality, and spatial transitivism, when inter-related with historical-geographical racialization hierarchies, makes racist sentiments regarding the spatial appearance and practices of racial Others violent and dangerous. These sentiments receive affective support from unconscious agonies on self-demarcation, fear of dirt, and evil. Obviously, however, not everyone reacts to déclassés' presence with racist abjection. This Kleinian conceptual apparatus is rather undynamic if it is going to explain the contradictory general common sense of the Swedish begging question, the interconnection of abjection processes with political insti-tutional logics, and, most importantly, my originally identified emotional kernel that sympathetic and antipathetic minds share. Thankfully, Jacques Lacan's "post-object relation theory" allows me to grasp this reality's con-tradictions and seeming heterogeneity.

4 Anxiety and Ethics

Mary Douglas once claimed, "Where there is dirt there is system."[1] She continued, "Dirt is the by-product of a systematic ordering and classification of matter, in so far as ordering involves rejecting inappropriate elements. This idea of dirt takes us straight into the field of symbolism [. . .]. [Dirt] is a relative idea. Shoes are not dirty in themselves, but it is dirty to place them on the dining table." This explanation provides an ideal introduction to Lacan's triad of the psyche's orders: the Imaginary, the Symbolic, and the Real.[2] Translating these orders into Douglas's formula "Where there is dirt there is system," the Real is "dirt," the Symbolic is "system," and the Imaginary is "there is"—in both cases.

More specifically, the Symbolic is the social ordering of a system where different phenomena become different relational signifiers—that is, symbols referring to other signifiers/symbols. Here Lacan puts a twist on Freudian psychoanalysis, understanding the unconscious as a function of the Symbolic order, per his famous statement, "The unconscious is structured like a language."[3] This implies that the Lacanian unconscious is fundamentally *social*, and thus, from a social-scientific analytical perspective, more similar to Foucauldian discourse than Freudian repression. As such, the unconscious is found within language and cultural systems of signs and symbols. Due to language's inherent intersubjectivity and the human cognition's intersubjective constitution, it is "transindividual."[4] People, therefore, are unconsciously and libidinally invested in the Symbolic order of their imagined communities.[5]

Next in our triad is the Real, which, as theorized in this book, designates reality as it exists outside and within the human mind's imagined and symbolic lifeworlds. While the Real is itself without agency, the social world with its contingent systems of morality, language, and ideology is, in philosopher Marc De Kesel's words, "a major 'reaction formation' against the overwhelming field of stimuli that is reality, the field of the 'real' that keeps beating against our symbolic system."[6] Recall Freud's quote regarding the three directions of suffering. Here, the encounter with the Real is an involuntary confrontation with suffering—"the overwhelming field of stimuli" issuing from the internal, external, and relational spheres. However, as the subject is a symbolizing and fantasizing being, it can generate pangs of suffering with its imagination alone. The sight of Douglas's shoes on the dinner table might, for example, generate disgust due to their inappropriate location in the social-spatial system. The Real dirty shoes are Real because they reveal the arbitrariness of reality outside the moral order, a chaos inducing displeasure. Whereas one might "very well know" Douglas's shoes are not dirty per se, and, indeed, that dirt is a social construction, this conscious knowledge probably wouldn't negate one's unconscious vexation at their "dirtiness," nor the anxiety brought on by disarray in one's socio-spatial system. Jameson explains, "It would be a mistake to think that anyone can ever really learn to live with [the Real] any more than the most lucid subjects of psychoanalysis ever really achieve the habit of lucidity and self-knowledge; the approach to the Real is at best fitful, the retreat from it into this or that form of intellectual comfort perpetual."[7] Consequently, an involuntary brush with the Real often amounts to abjection.

The strength of the Lacanian triad, with its emphasis on the inherent interconnection between language and the unconscious, is that the triad can also be applied on the level of ideology, discourse, and institutional logic. Here, the Real resembles the concept of "anomaly." If we examine the déclassés' territorial presence in the Swedish nation-state, they are, structurally, a symptom of the Real of Sweden's welfare legal systems (rephrased, the welfare state's Symbolic order). They don't qualify as any group category entitled to social or citizenship rights, leading them to become regarded as "out of place"—both legally and emotionally. Nevertheless, here they are!—their spatial presence is "for Real." However, just as dirt is a necessary "by-product of a systematic ordering," symptoms of the Real are unavoidable consequences of the Symbolic and Imaginary's classification systems. This unites psychoanalysis with historical materialism, as the latter's Hegelian conceptualization of "contradiction" can be interpreted in two ways: capitalism's unintended outcomes and the Real of historical development as such. Jameson argues that, in short, the Real is simply "history" itself.[8] The Real entails historical *change*, revealing that capitalism and bourgeois society are not, in fact, natural orders (as imagined) but historical systems in constant struggle.

Before turning to a psychoanalytic critique of ideology, however, we must understand the role of human agency within ideology. While Marx was correct in arguing that humans don't make history under circumstances of their own choosing, he was equally right in claiming that humans nevertheless make their own history.[9]

Pleasure and Suffering

Universal to the human condition is the *perceived* pursuit of pleasure and avoidance of suffering. As Freud discovered, human beings are polymorphous pleasure-seeking animals, which implies that they can derive pleasure from any object.[10] Notably, this pleasure principle doesn't mean that humans are inherently "hedonistic." Rather, humans attain gratification by negating overstimulation or escaping suffering. Due to various contradictory factors in the psychic apparatus, however, the subject tends to repeatedly cause itself to suffer, even though it convinces itself that it doesn't do so intentionally. Paradoxically enough, some suffering can register as pleasure, hence my italicizing "perceived" in "perceived pursuit of pleasure," as this pursuit readily yields the opposite of its intended outcome.

Clearly, "suffering" and "pleasure" are complex phenomena. To make sense of them, we must first understand that biological life is a reaction to stimuli. When tensions, such as tiredness or hunger, are registered by the body, the organism seeks to alleviate them. By satisfying one's needs—by sleeping or eating, for example—bodily strains desist. Neurological life can perceive friction or tension as suffering, and the upheaval of this as satisfaction and pleasure—but this is not the only way. Because pleasure is the discharge of tension, it can build up its own excitement, making the excitation pleasurable. Examples include the exhilaration derived from play, sex, sports, the arts, humor, and violence. Nevertheless, suffering is inescapable. Humans develop different kinds of defense mechanisms to neutralize, negate, or expel this distress. While humans may find these defense mechanisms pleasurable, they can also cause suffering.

Thinking back to object relations theory, we can better elucidate the Kleinian distinction between "good" and "bad" objects by establishing "pleasure" and "suffering" as the initial phenomenological binary of sensations. Through the infant's socialization into the Imaginary and Symbolic order, this binary is sublimated into symbols representing pleasure and suffering to the subject, socialized into representations of good and evil. These biological judgments are not based upon a Darwinist survival instinct—throughout humankind's history, people have, after all, chosen death over the prospect of unrelieved suffering. Instead, these judgments follow, as other ethical considerations tend to do, a "pleasure principle," in which humans use pleasure as their guiding principle for determining what's good. In this sense, ethics is constitutional to being, as this biological precondition is socialized. Freud said, "One thing only do I know for certain and that is that man's judgements of value follow directly his wishes for happiness—that, accordingly, they are an attempt to support his illusions with arguments."[11] Here, the "wish for happiness" is the search for pleasure. Social morality equips the subject with both arguments and illusions in its quest for happiness, imparting a system of good and evil signifiers—that is, a Symbolic order including morals, laws, norms, and aesthetics. Significantly, the subject conforms to the Symbolic Law even when it suffers from obeying social authorities, from one's superiors to laws to norms of conduct. It can of course also derive pleasure from transgressing this law, just like it can suffer (and maybe also feel pleasure?) from the potential punishment. While the fear of reprisal is one source of conformity, another is the desire for recognition from, and community with, others—the subject, after all, is an inherently social being. This renders the philosophical question of whether humans are inherently altruistic or egoistic meaningless, as this binarity relates to two sides of the same coin. There is an unconscious dimension to this statement, however, which probes the very constitution of cognition itself.

Subjectivity and Extimacy

Lacanian theory understands subjectivity itself to be an imagined structural relationship between a perceived ego and its Other. "The subject" is this unconscious imagined relation.[12] If we return to Klein's theory on the genesis of subjectivity, initial dependency on an external object is marked at the core of the child's evolving cognition. Note that here we talk of "the Other," not "the object." Lacan's famous mirror stage is a metaphor for the birth of this intersubjective subjectivity, as the infant recognizes its own mirror image. When the child identifies the reflection as itself, it misrecognizes (or miscognizes) this image as being itself.[13] This inaugurates the child's entrance into the Imaginary order, whereas the Symbolic order assimilates the child into language and culture mediated by the caretaking Other.

The Imaginary order is the order of the visual: as the child realizes its separation and demarcation as a separate body (and mind) from its external surroundings, it identifies the phenomenological world composed of different identities and units—or, as Klein contends, objects. As the child initially identifies its ego as being outside its body, in the mirror, the child conceptualizes its own unconscious subjectivity as a relationship between this imagined ego and the Other entity (its gaze) perceiving it. Subjectivity, therefore, becomes a dialectic between these two gazes. The subject can judge its own ego from the perspective of the Other, and the Other from the perspective of the ego. What it cannot do is to overcome this split, this gap between its thought and its thinking. That is why Lacan refers to a *split subject*, changing Descartes's idiom to "I think where I am not, therefore I am where I do not think."[14] This Real lack of coherence between (self-) image and spectator is foreclosed and displaced by the subject's fantasy, a capacity of the Imaginary order. The Real of the subject—that it does not actually exist as a clear, demarcated individual unit—is obscured by the Imaginary and Symbolic. However, the Real (of this lack of coherence) lingers, as the subject's abbreviation of reality's "overwhelming field of stimuli" into different Imaginary identities always risks breaking down. Through the Imaginary, the subject believes itself to have a coherent identity—or identities—with certain characteristics and traits.

The Symbolic order signifies the subject as an identity with relations to other Symbolic identities ("man," "white," "heterosexual," "Swede," "non-Swede," "beggar," "Roma," etc.). But these orders are contingent, as the Real (of history) reveals. This creates a tragic tendency of conservatism on the part of the subject—it tends to want to keep to the order of things. That is how it believes itself capable of navigating a fundamentally unstable reality, where a part of subjectivity's support is to be found *outside* the individual—in the external Other.

The Lacanian "Other" is varied in its content depending on the psychic context. It might, for example, designate one's caretakers, beloved, social relations, society, space, and Otherness. The Symbolic order itself is unconsciously treated as an Other to the subject, replacing the original caretaker relationship with the authority of society itself. Consequently, painstaking conformity to social rules evokes the pleasurable sensation of obeying one's authority qua parent, toward which one might have a contradictory relationship of love and hate. This, in turn, actualizes the notion of transitivism, as subjectivity becomes (through the mirror stage) inherently *empathetic*. Notably, empathy is not sympathy, but the capacity to imagine the feelings of Others, which means that the identification of Others' suffering readily becomes registered as one's own suffering. A typical empathetic reaction is when a child hits another and then cries in imagined pain, or how one starts to laugh and have fun because someone else is laughing. Another—perhaps surprisingly—is the sadist's pleasure in torturing their victim by placing suffering within the Other's body.

This transitivist subjectivity has geographical implications. Geographer Paul Kingsbury has highlighted the Lacanian concept *extimacy* as a description of the structure of subjectivity.[15] A neologism of "exterior" and "intimacy," extimacy describes this Möbius-like cognition, wherein there is not only a part of the subject located *outside* the individual, but also a part of the Other—people, nonhuman life, physical and nonphysical phenomenon—is located *inside*. We might then talk about extimate space constituting the "smallest" scale level of human perception: a scale that takes place in between bodies and their socio-material environments, where the classical demarcation of "outside" and "inside" one's body (and mind) is blurred. Here, a sentimental place, individual, or thing is experienced as a constitutive part of what I am. Extimate space may also take place in between one's body and mind: as surely one's own body can be experienced as Other to oneself. The concept of extimacy demonstrates that the Other is a more dynamic conceptualization of the split subject's "object" than the Kleinian scheme. The subject's object is an Other, and this Other can be found both inside one's own thoughts and outside, in the existence of others' thoughts.

Anxiety and Desire

What does all this have to do with the hatred and racist violence on begging? How does it relate to the begging encounter? Ultimately, it deals with my original problem: the shared emotional kernel. It also informs my statement, following geographer Jesse Proudfoot's groundbreaking lead, that the unconscious dimension of the ideal typical begging encounter is a forced encounter with the Real of the Other, in the shape of *anxiety*.[16] This assertion requires further elaboration.

Lacan identifies "anxiety" as "the instant when the subject is suspended between a moment at which he no longer knows where he is, and a shift towards a moment when he will become something in which he will never be able to find himself again."[17] Anxiety occurs when the subject loses its coordinates within the Imaginary and Symbolic networks and temporarily forfeits its unconscious ego-Other relationship. It also briefly loses itself-as-subject, which is registered as a Real threat of extermination—the dissolution of subjectivity itself. Anxiety is, then, among the worst imaginable kinds of suffering to the unconscious subject. Because anxiety does not have a specific phenomenological object, it differs from other emotions. Fear, hate, and love all have a relationship to an object. Anxiety's object, meanwhile, is the Real itself—the radical negativity within the Imaginary and Symbolic. For the unconscious subject, anxiety is worse than death. In order to relocate its ego-Other relationship, the subject must transfer, project, internalize, or displace anxiety onto a feeling qua object. Phobia is the expression of a displaced anxiety that is made unconsciously manageable, by projecting anxiety onto an object you can fear or dread. With fear, as with love and hate, you (think you) know what you are in relation to the Other. But just as phobia is something "irrational," endowed with the displaced psychic energy of excited anxiety, this "neutralized" anxiety still lurks and feeds in the shadows. Accordingly, the displacement of anxiety readily reinforces anxious sentiments, since its *actual* source is not addressed.

The encounter with the Real of the Other is an anxious affair since it implies an encounter with the Other's desire. If "anxiety" is a sublimation of suffering, "desire" is the socialization of "pleasure"—or, rather, the pursuit of pleasure. As suffering and pleasure are different degrees of excitation, anxiety and desire are in a relationship with each other. If anxiety is the loss of the unconscious subject's coordinates in the Symbolic and Imaginary orders, desire is the subject's direction within them. Because the subject yearns to overcome its inherent split between ego and Other, the subject desires the Other. But the Other, as a Real Other human being, has its own subjectivity—its own desires. Because the subject empathetically identifies the Other as both itself and another entity, it then desires what the Other desires. Put simply, this means humans' hopes and dreams are inescapably socially affected and constructed: their origin is always external. The Big Other of society (with the Symbolic as Other) teaches us what, whom, and how we desire.

With that said, the Other's desire also implies a philosophical issue of foundational existential alienation. To return to the dawn of subjectivity, the original separation from the (m)Other, the infant is alienated from the Other, as it does not yet speak the same language. The language it goes on to learn is Other to it; it is an alien practice to which it needs to assimilate. Nevertheless, language (a symbolic system) is the only way to reach the

Other. At first, communication with the (m)Other will be both a struggle and source of disappointment, due to the (m)Other "not getting it." Every caretaker has experienced the child's frustrated crying of not receiving what it "really" wanted. Perhaps even the child doesn't know what it wants. Upon reaching adulthood, this confusion lingers. The Other continues to constitute *alterity*—other beings' wants and needs are always to be interpreted, and one can never be sure if one has done so correctly. There is a dialectical twist, too: the subject can itself never know what the Other really wants, because (and through that) it can never know what it "really" wants itself. Because we cannot really "know" the Other, we can never truly "know" ourselves. Because we are socialized into an originally alien language and can only grasp our own thoughts and feelings in communication with others, our perceived thoughts, aspirations, desires, and dreams are never solely our own constructions—there is an aspect of our thinking which is not "our own," and therefore Other to oneself.

This problem of a lack of transcendence resembles the Kantian problem of the Thing-in-itself: a piece of reality believed to be out of reach to the senses and cognition. As Hegel argues, however, there is no hidden Thing-in-itself of secret knowledge within either the Other or the subject.[18] Following Hegel, Žižek argues that it is the very *idea* of this "real" knowledge that is the Thing-in-itself: the miscognition there appears to be a Truth, an essence within the phenomena. For Žižek, then, the Thing-in-itself is nothing but a radical negativity.[19] It is the Real, appearing as what Lacan called a *lack*. The point, therefore, is that there is no way to "really" know either the Other or oneself because there is nothing, after all, to "really" know. Notably, this conclusion doesn't render the subject's ignorance of itself or the Other moot—rather, it indicates that this void cannot be filled, and this lack within subjectivity and intersubjectivity is a source of anxiety, as well as desire, regarding the Other.

This lack is inscribed into language as language's Real dimension—its lack of successful meaning making of the Other and its desire. Lack is then a precondition for interpretation, meaning, and ethics. It constitutes *difference* and, through that, the need for communication. This need leads to a ceaseless underlying question of what the Other actually wants from one, and what one wants from the Other. The subject-child desires pleasure to never abate and imagines this wish of ultimate satisfaction to be within the Other's sphere—if only the child finds a way to reach the Other. Henceforth, the subject is thus caught in an impossible double bind between a desire for fusion with and separation from the Other. Contradictory enough, the subject still desires distance from its Other, as a merge with the Other would mean the end of subjectivity. Consequently, the prospect of an involuntarily merge with the Other is a cause of anxiety, representing loss of subjectivity.

Anxiety in the Begging Encounter

This rather convoluted explanation of complicated concepts eventually leads us to an ideal-typical begging encounter on behalf of the pedestrian. Here we find the encounter with the Real of impoverishment under capitalism is not only the encounter with radical alterity but also with an Other subject *desiring* your help. When the Other urges you to decide whether you will help them, it is an inescapable interpellation. The pedestrian can choose to ignore the call, but this is also a decision made in response to the Other's desire. Setting aside the moral ruminations on who deserves money and how much (which are anxious considerations themselves), it is clear that the human who begs is in such need that they desire as much as you're ready to give of yourself. Here the common expression regarding charitable considerations, "Where does one draw the line?" is not only a parable but the unconscious existential question: "Where *is* the line between the Other and myself? How much can I give of myself without giving myself away? If I surrender, the voracious desire of the Other will swallow my whole subjectivity!" This is, of course, not really what's on the table—it's a question of whether you can spare some change, please? Nevertheless, I argue, this is what is staged in the unconscious subject's mind, which explains the historically recurrent, excessive expressions of anxiety, suspiciousness, fear, and hostility against begging individuals.

We might liken the begging interaction, on the registered unconscious level, to an interaction with "energy vampires"—those who one feels are unbearably demanding of one's attention and sympathy to a threshold where one desires to break free from them, so one does not fall apart. The difference, in material reality, is obvious. Because begging is about *poverty*, it doesn't need to be practiced as a "guilt trip" for these sensations to be the "irrational" response. Seemingly, it's enough for a begging person to simply be there, registered within one's field of vision, in order for anxiety to take place.

Begging is per se a prayer for help. While this appeal can then be cultivated into an economic profession, this in no way erases the gesture's ethical kernel. Even if the gesture is presented under false pretenses—whether the stated need for the money is an exaggeration or a lie—the gesture remains the same. Someone is reaching out to you and asks, "Will you help me?" As a rule, you cannot be 100 percent sure the Other in front of you is deceiving you or not. Moreover, if the Other now is fooling you to get some cash, this act of deception still expresses a need on behalf of the deceiver—after all, they went as far as trying to mislead you to obtain your gift. Remember you are not tricked here into buying anything—only to give. If physical force, or the threat of it, was involved, the interaction would cease to be begging and instead would become robbery. Nevertheless, this desire is often unconsciously registered as an *aggressive* threat, since the unconscious subject experiences the Other's desire to be so overwhelming that it threatens to dissolve the subject. This actualizes processes of projection and introjection, because the prayer's implicit expression of need forcefully activates the subject's empathetic capacity, and the subject imagines the Other's hardship or suffers from the ethical gesture's insisting force. This mirroring of negativity potentially causes a confusion of whose suffering the subject actually experiences: Is it my own suffering, or is it the Other's? And whose will is it that informs my decision on whether or not to give? The demarcation ego—Other trembles, causing anxiety to signal to the subject that the Other is on its way with its forceful desire to obliterate you.

Recall my encounter with the crying begging woman in the subway car and her desire's *power* to affect all the rest of us, now being forced to contend with her presence and desire. This power issued from her capacity as a fellow human being to bring attention to herself with her actions, but also from her plea to the public. The question demands a response, even if the answer is a nonanswer in the shape of silence. There is undeniable power in this, even if this power is expressed as a simple request for some change. What this reveals, then, is a possibility of agency that is available to every human, even if they are materially powerless. This power of asking calls to mind Žižek's claim that "questioning is the basic procedure of the totalitarian intersubjective relationship."[20] Here he relies upon a compelling thought formulated by psychiatrist Aron Bodenheimer: there is something obscene in the very gesture of asking a question—something obscene in the question form itself.[21] This is because "the question lays open, exposes, denudes its addressee, it invades his sphere of intimacy."[22] Notably, this indecency lies both within the police interrogation and the child's innocent inquiry into why the sky is blue. Although the request of "the beggar" is not a question regarding a "what?" or a "why?" in its manifest content, by asking, "Will you?" it impels the addressee to respond, to become responsible for the Other. When the child repeatedly asks the parent, "Why this?" and, "Why that?," the real stake, Žižek and Bodenheimer argue, is to expose the impotence of the parent (here an authority)—their incapacity, yet also their responsibility for this incapacity.

This sublimated aggression against the subject—in the sense of the subject's registering of the received interpellation, since it ultimately doesn't matter what the Other's intention really was—is perfectly exemplified by the begging encounter. This is because the interaction's very material conditions determine the interaction in a certain way. There is a curious homology between the child's repeated questioning of "why?" and the begging gesture: not only is the subject induced to decide whether to give but also how to behave, and if to give—how much. It is not uncommon for begging individuals to press for even more than they received and not taking "no" for an answer. This is a rational behavior for an economic agent whose need for money triumphs their fear of coming off as rude. Yet this pressuring of the subject might easily appear as a provocation, a provocation probably also causing shame, because of the revealed impotence of the subject. Žižek says:

> A question, even if it refers only to a given state of things, always makes the subject formally responsible for it, although only in a negative way—responsible, that is, for his impotence in the face of this fact.
>
> What, then, is this point in the other at which the word fails, this point of impotence at which the question as such is aiming? The question as such creates shame because it aims at my innermost, intimate kernel [. . .]: at that strange body in my interior which is 'in me more than me', which is radically interior and at the same time already exterior and for which Lacan coined a new word, *extime*.[23]

This is also a source of provocation, of feeling cornered, because the repetition of the question, by its very form, appears to aim, as Žižek says, at "something else"—this "intimate kernel" of the Real within the subject, "at what is in the subject more than subject, at the *object in subject* which is constitutive for the subject." And this is why the overwhelming presence of the Other makes the subject's demarcation of an ego—Other relationship tremble, signaling anxiety: the Other desires me, that is, my "me" (the subject's object, which in the end doesn't exist). Anxiety is, after all, when the subject is "suspended between a moment" where "he no longer knows where he is" and a future where "he will never be able to find himself again."

I, for my part, certainly felt anxiety in the subway car, as I had so many times before and afterward upon encountering the begging gesture. My anxiety, in strategic contemplation of how best to maintain my relationship to the Other, was projected in multiple directions. Would I give money to the begging Other? What if She desired more than I was willing to give? What if She didn't accept a refusal, as She had done with others? What do the Other passengers think and feel? How would They react if I gave, or refused to give? How would I react if an Other were unkind to this fellow human who begs? What do I desire myself? Don't I desire Her to be happy? Don't I desire to stop Her suffering? Do I desire Her to stop crying because I want Her to be happy or because it makes me suffer? Do I actually desire

Her to go away? Do I (the ego) really want that? Is that really my own desire? I thought my ego was sympathetic and solidaric. Don't I desire my ego to be better than this? And so on. Notice how I depict my thoughts as if there is an Other *within* myself, thinking, reacting, and desiring in opposition to what I thought was myself—"I think where I am not." At last, recall how an Other exclaimed, "She's faking it!" prompting an aggressive reaction to this Other, an aggression I am convinced was channeled due to my own anxiety.

Granted, this post-construction of my own agony is coming from someone whose job was to analyze this agony. It is, therefore, an intellectualization of a process that was actually simpler and more straightforward, which I assume I shared with my fellow commuter: I (or we) felt bad about the situation. That's what matters. Reflections aside, the Real sensation was that it felt bad, because of my unconscious empathy.

At last, we here discover the common ground between the middle-aged passenger and me: our sensation of anxiety in the midst of the begging encounter. Scandalously enough, I believe this general apprehension to be universal—that it is a shared experience between me and the hateful, murderous people abusing and torturing begging individuals. I further contend it is a somewhat shared experience between me and the begging Other. Based on the acknowledged stories of violence, hatred, and contempt affecting begging people, we can guess the latter are probably pretty anxious while begging. Add this dimension of anxiousness to the material deprivation and desperation of having migrated halfway across Europe to beg, often initially to find labor, but in vain; having to sit in the same place for hours in snow and rain, with the fear of harassment and violence from passersby or competing street fractions (as well as from security guards and the police), and with extremely low access to sanitary conditions and with the risk of acquiring different diseases as a consequence of the constant exposure to the dangers outdoors (such as bladder infection or frostbite); and, for good measure, the psychic stress of financial anxieties, fear of harassment, worries about sick relatives back home, the danger of the police tearing down one's settlement and the resultant possibility of needing to find a new place to sleep at short notice.[24] This anxiousness I cannot claim to share at all. But I can *imagine* it, with the power of my empathy and its meaning-making resources of the Imaginary and Symbolic orders, and their complementary social belief-systems.

The differing uses of the empathetic interpretation of the begging encounter and its anxiety is where the similarity between me and the racist hatemongers end (I hope, anyway). Because anxiety needs to be neutralized, it can be transformed into sympathy, antipathy, or apathy toward the Other. I argue all three are different *defense mechanisms* in handling sensations of suffering—of turning anxiety into a grounded sensation. These strategies are ideal types, and in reality they might be fused. "Antipathy" is the trajectory I have touched upon most so far, which is why I start there, beginning with the bold assertion that "apathy" is ultimately a subdued version of "antipathy," though it can be generated from both antipathetic and sympathetic trajectories.

Antipathetic Interpretations of the Begging Other

THE CAPACITY OF AGGRESSIVENESS

Here "antipathy" means the cultivation of anxiety into aggression. It implies the displacement of one's internal sense of suffering onto an entity outside the ego-demarcation. In this way, a topology is established, where suffering condenses into an evil object (the cause of suffering). At this point, anxiety is displaced upon the Other, who is the supposed cause of one's anxiety. Now, not only is my own anxiety the Other's hostility ("The Other *wanted* me to feel uneasy. Why did they do this to me? It has to be an aggressive intention!"), but also the "lack" of the Other is gone, per Proudfoot's observation: "The other does not lack, instead it deceives: the lack is not real, *the other is whole but hostile*."[25] The subject also legitimates this fantasy from the aforementioned obscenity and provocation of the Other's question, implicit to the question form itself. As Žižek points out, this is also the form of "totalitarian" intersubjective relationships, and as we cannot deny there is a certain power exercised even by powerless subjects interpellating others, might we not think there is potential here on behalf of the antipathetic subject to project this sense of power as a "totalitarian," authoritative kind of power? If this would be the case, it would help explain the warlike rhetoric on déclassés outline previously: they are an *oppressive* enemy.

This fantasy also illustrates the pleasure that the projecting subject achieves with this unconscious maneuver. Since the subject here cannot accept the existence of the Real, and cannot accept the Other's (material) lack to be genuine, a narrative takes shape: not only is the Other hostile but also deceitful. This, in turn, induces exciting fantasies of the evil Other deceiving me or us, so they can take something from me/us. Add to this paranoia the social construction of this Other as foreign and racialized. Now, the hostile dishonest begging Other is also the *evil racial* Other, who oughtn't be here in the first place! In this way, the emotion formation becomes aggression or fear, to make the Other disappear—fight or flight.

Here racist ideas enter the anxiety aroused by the begging encounter as an *interpretation tool*, which neutralizes anxiety into a bearable emotion in which the subject maintains its distance and relationship to the Other. Aggression and fear, however, have the nasty habit of becoming amplified, due to the excitement they generate: a "perverted" kind of pleasure. Still, aggressiveness needs to stem from at least some real experiences—it cannot only be attributed to fantasies where people (mis)interpret others as aggressive. There are aggressive people out there, all around us, as our media diet constantly reminds us of. Because empathy makes subjects capable of identifying themselves in others, and vice versa, the Other's simple human capacity for aggressiveness is always lurking in subjects' interpretation of the estranged Other's action. People are then, as Freud concluded, not merely "gentle creatures who want to be loved," but "on the contrary, creatures among whose instinctual endowments is to be reckoned a powerful share of aggressiveness."[26] To justly assume aggression's potential in others, however, tends to be amplified through the combined influences of the Imaginary's simplification of the world into good and bad objects and a given society's ideological reflection of racialization orders. To rephrase, some Others, through their social signification, become *representations* of aggression. As phenomena are classified, some subject positions, and through that, some bodies, are, through the lens of the dominant normative gaze, interpreted as more aggressive than others. Through the unstable subject's likelihood to embrace the familiar and avoid the unfamiliar, the "strange" Other is then overdetermined to become such a fetishized representation of human destructiveness. The begging individual is then in turn, and as the historical record demonstrates, overdetermined to be a "stranger."

Crucially, these senses of paranoia and abject hate are not exclusively dependent upon racist sentiments. The antipathy described here has also targeted begging and homeless people who are not racialized Others. There are two reasons for this similarity between antipathy toward begging and homeless people and racial difference. First, the begging individuals relevant here are racialized. Second, human cognition is finite and consists of a limited repertoire of reactions. Although the social reality is complex, humans' psychic and emotional reactions to this complexity are, by necessity, not as heterogeneous. What enables us to discuss empathy and the human condition in the first place, after all, is a certain kernel of shared bodily prerequisites. Due to cognitive finitude, there are similarities between racism, homophobia, fear of the poor, and other anxieties about alterity. From this perspective, "alterity" is something contingent, historical, and ideological.

We can also situate antipathetic sentiments on begging people within common sense folklore, as widespread ideas of "beggars" and Roma being criminals function as fantasies regarding the Other's aggression. This interpretation helps us better understand the semantics of "aggressive begging" as something that demands police intervention in the United States, or Swedish residents' sensation of *otrygghet* (a tricky Swedish word combining "lack of social safety" and "insecurity") as a reason to ban begging. When, for example, the Moderate Municipal Council of Ekerö defended the municipality's outlawing of begging in 2019, he wrote: "[Maybe] what is most important is not to risk vulnerable people being exploited [. . .]. We have become aware of perceived *otrygghet* from municipal residents in conjunction with this money collection. One shies away from recycling [at recycling stations]. One sees loitering and misuse of public space, consolidating a feeling of lawlessness."[27] With a passing reference to human trafficking, the mayor foregrounds the "feelings" of the taxpayers as the real political issue. The aggressiveness doesn't (necessarily) belong to "the beggars"—rather, people want to be protected from their own sensations of aggressiveness by removing the poor from public view.

The Deceiving Other

Intertwined with fantasies of aggression is the conceptualization of decep-tion. As with aggression, it is not erroneous to expect the existence of deception in the world, but this possibility is here exaggerated by projection. Upon reviewing the history of begging, we discover a recurrent portrayal of the Other as deceptive. Since this depiction is so common, one doesn't have to be a lone wolf terrorist to believe "the beggar is faking it"—just ask my fellow subway passenger. Still, the conviction that all déclassés are criminals, or the idea they are cunning free riders rather than poor, is, upon consideration, strikingly irrational. Proudfoot argues the benefit to applying psychoanalysis to the begging encounter is to make sense of people's seemingly unreasonable willingness to buy the myths of "beggars" being wealthy charlatans. With a theory of the unconscious, there is a rational foundation for the role of these fantasies in anxiety management. What's more, people can very well know that these convictions are likely fantasies, but they nevertheless find such a pleasure in believing in them that they continue to treat them as truth. What matters to this rationale is not the intellectual content of deception, but the form: "the strange Other" = "deception." These fantasies of deception seem to be an unconscious response to the inherent alienation at the heart of the subject itself. As the subject is alienated from its Other (never really able to know the Other's thoughts), they use fantasy and symbolization to cover this gap within the Imaginary, filling the voids with meaning or displacing them. The Real, however, is always within. Meanwhile, the Imaginary can turn a lack of knowledge about the Other into an exciting fantasy: "The Other is whole but hides something from me." In this way, one's ignorance becomes the Other's intentional obfuscation.

Regarding "beggars'" perceived deception, there is the recurrent anxiety of *not knowing where the money goes*. Consequently, fantasies of criminal or sinful consumption become sufficient explanations. Because the recipient lives somewhere else and returns there, the financial chain of custody is unclear. One only has the Other's word—but how can one be certain they are trustworthy? In 2012 an editor shared their suspicions that déclassés are trafficking victims: "They all say they are here by choice and will return home in a couple of weeks or months. The problem is, however, that a trafficking victim would provide the same answer."[28] When one makes this supposition, the Other's response is moot; the fantasy is confirmed regardless of the answer. However, this lack of transparency applies to almost all other economic transactions as well! After all, one doesn't really know where one's tax money goes, nor what sellers do with their payment. The decisions of charity organizations, too, are beyond one's control. The difference is that other transactions are ideologically cloaked by a commodity-fetishist fantasy of *reciprocity*. Normally one doesn't care how vendors spend their profits or how charities allocate donations, since one's money, phenomenologically speaking, went to the commodity—the transaction is finished. One believes the charity organization is run professionally, since one purchases the reassurance of doing something good.

Note that this comfortable variant of alienation is also the norm of social interaction while navigating urban spaces. In a city one passes by hundreds of individuals every day whom one treats like "things." By alienating those Others, one enables urban coexistence. This is neither a good nor a bad thing. Human cognition, after all, could not handle "taking in" every urban individual one meets. That people leave each other alone makes urban life bearable. This is also why begging individuals in Sweden, only a couple of thousands, were sometimes experienced as an "invasion." Begging individuals, through their mere presence, interpellate you, making you into a subject with a relationship with them. You are activated into an ethical subject, forced to make a decision in the situation at hand. This inescapability creates a question of *who the Other is*, because you now have a relationship with the interpellating Other. One local letter to the editor lays out these uncertainties in 2014: "One needs to consider that we do not know anything about [the beggars'] background. [And] where are they when they are not sitting next to the shops? Where do they live? What do they do? How much does it cost to travel from Romania and Bulgaria to Sweden to beg? Can there be any truth to the rumors claiming this is organized begging?"[29]

Problematically, there is some truth to rumors of criminality and deception, since there of course are cases of déclassés deceiving, lying, stealing, and kidnapping. Considering the life conditions these people face, however, one might expect it to be more common than it seems to be. Besides, déclassés are human too; like everyone else, some are "immoral." For example, there are those who fake handicaps to garner sympathy, a begging strategy dating back to the Middle Ages, at least.[30] One clip shared over 185,000 times shows two individuals in Umeå, who feigned a handicap while begging, walking into a grocery store no longer limping.[31] People use such examples of "deception"—which could also be interpreted as a work performance to deserve help—as proof that déclassés aren't in need.

There are also cases when good-natured individuals have been tricked. In 2015 I interviewed one senior citizen in Borås who, together with his wife, furnished a Romanian couple with fundraisers, temporary housing, and other things, only to realize a year later that the couple had not been honest about their living conditions back home. The pensioner couple was disappointed, but they did not stop being involved. Instead, they started an after-school program in a Romanian village. To them, the couple was obviously in need, no matter their distortion of the truth.

Finally, there are the trafficking cases. Although there seem to be few relative to those begging voluntarily, they should not be ignored. One man, for example, was sentenced to twelve years in Romanian prison for forcing eight men to beg in Uppsala for months. The victims had been tricked into traveling to Sweden with the promise of construction jobs. Instead, they were forced to beg up to thirteen hours per day. The perpetrator, who threatened them with a gun, sword, and axe, profited at least one million kronor from the scheme.[32] In another instance a Bulgarian family forced their thirteen-year-old daughter to beg for two years in Dalarna. While several civilians reported this to the police and social services, they both did nothing to help except attempt to pass off the responsibility to each other.[33] With that said, trafficking is already criminalized, and these cases do not nullify the déclassés' economic needs, which would not be satisfied by outlawing begging alone. Additionally, the existence of poverty-induced criminal exploitation does not undo the pathology of the racist fantasies of criminal "Gypsies." Žižek explains: "Remember the Lacanian proposition concerning the pathologically jealous husband: even if all the facts he quotes in support of his jealousy are true, even if his wife really is sleeping around with other men, this does not change one bit the fact that his jealousy is a pathological, paranoid construction."[34] He then exemplifies this with the racist "pathological, paranoid construction" of anti-Semitism, which would not cease to be racism even if it turned out there really were Jewish people who were immoral, swindling, or criminal.

The other source of fantasies of deception is the aforementioned appearance of the material conditions of déclassés. Let's start with begging itself. Déclassés' stated reason to come to Sweden is to make an income, which means begging individuals prefer cash donations above food. For some civilian observers, this precondition is interpreted as a proof that déclassés aren't poor. One civilian in Hudiksvall, for instance, told a reporter: "Giving them food has not always been appreciated. This is a sign that they are not begging for survival, but cash."[35] Another such "proof" is that déclassés can afford cell phones (to keep in contact with each other, both in Sweden and back home), as pointed out by the café guests I mentioned in a previous chapter.

There are also "deceptive" dimensions inherent to being unhoused and unemployed. Homeless déclassés do not, as a rule, have any Goffmannian backstage to which to withdraw—neither when taking a break nor calling it a day, and for many, not even when one goes to sleep. At all times they are forced to use public spaces as private places. Not only is this abnormal behavior and a source of abjection, but it also publicly exposes all personal behavior. Sleeping, eating, socializing, washing, cleaning, crying, fighting, laughing—everything takes place in public. This context forces déclassés to be perpetually evaluated by the public and creates impressions they are uncivilized, loud, and impolite. Further, this lack of a "backstage" makes every déclassé's practice of behaving differently in different contexts very explicit. Because begging is an economic practice, one needs to treat it as such. By "taking off the mask," the impression is that begging déclassés are *acting as* "beggars," as Flashback users and others believe. Granted, this is, to a certain extent, correct. No one, after all, is a beggar—like all other social roles, it is temporarily performed.

The last stand in defending the fantasy of the nonexistence of lack is conceding its existence, but short-circuiting one's own moral subjectivation in the face of it. One has three options: first, to blame the victim, like the middle-aged man who passed a begging woman in Gothenburg with a sign claiming she had six children at home: "Six children! I don't believe that! And one shouldn't bring children into the world one can't support anyway."[36] Alternately, one concludes that the Other's suffering is not one's legal responsibility to undertake. It is a matter for social services, the state, Romania, or the EU. This option is close to an "apathetic" stance. Here, the evil object is the thought of anxiety itself, which one then uses "mental aggression" to disavow. One learns to ignore the desirous Other and the ethics surrounding them, preferably with the aid of ideologies that insist that caring about the begging Other is pointless.

Encountering "the Human"

All these different strategies of escaping the anxiety of the Real—of empathy and the Other's alterity—are the consequences of the begging interaction being an objective interaction of inequality. For this reason I argue that the anxiety of not knowing the Other is the encounter with the human condition itself: the intersubjective alienation between ego and Other. This, in turn, makes the ideal-typical encounter with the begging individual an encounter with the human itself. "The human" is, to me, the realization that the Other is Other. One does then not only realize one's Self's *finitude* in the confrontation with the Other's phenomenon.[37] Dialectically, one also encounters oneself as an Other, when recognizing one's Self as Other to both the Other and to oneself. In other words, the human is the core of radical negativity, the Thing-in-itself of a lack of meaning. Why the human is ideal-typically encountered in the begging encounter is because of the fundamental nonrelationship of equality, revealing the lack between and within, appearing as the Other's overbearing desire for my possessions, readily confused as the desire for one's ego. When it comes to the EU déclassé's position, the Other is not only poor but also a national and racial Other. These three layers of alterity lead Swedish discourses on begging to readily misinterpret poverty as culture, which is also in capital's interest. What's more, the encounter with "cultural" alterity is a rupture in the Symbolic interaction between subject and Other. It manifests itself most obviously in the linguistic confusion between déclassés and Swedish residents: as a rule, they do not know each other's language, which by itself is a tremendous source of tension. This frustrated communication intersects with the lack of the Other's desire in the begging interaction—the begging gesture is a concrete manifest desire expressed as a concrete straightforward request: *money, please.* Paradoxically enough, just like Hegel's resolution of Kant's Thing-in-itself, there is no inherent Other desire beneath this conspicuous desire. The lack is expressed in the very gesture of begging and the absence of a satisfaction of this lack, as this lack is the absence of the subject's capacity to end the Other's suffering—not only your fellow neighbor's suffering, mind you, but also the Other of poverty itself.

This intersection between the fellow Other and the Other of the social itself helps us recognize the political aspect of this encounter with anxiety. The EU déclassé's double exclusion from the political Imaginary and Symbolic order in the Swedish context, both lumpenproletariat and national/racial Other, makes this social position an overdetermined symptom of the Real on both the intersubjective and the social scales. The EU déclassé's positionality reveals the Real of the ideological and political structure, in the sense that this position's non-place within the specified network of right-bearer categories makes the EU déclassé a symptom of the reality beyond these categories—the categories' fundamental contingency and incompetence in addressing the real condition of humans. This, in turn, corroborates historical accounts of begging individuals being perennial extimate outcasts across social formations—they are simultaneously outside and inside society, with no assigned place but nevertheless taking up space there. It is also in this sense that the begging subject is the human condition, which it also shares with the national/racial Othered subject—the universal of humanity, as the only thing we can call "humanity" is the negation of the social order. This is so because every order is contingent and particular, whereas the negation of every order is constant. In Žižek's words, following philosopher Jacques Rancière: "[The] point of inherent exception/exclusion, the 'abject,' of the concrete positive order, [is] the only point of true universality."[38] Unfortunately, the emotion that best correlates to this point of rupture in the Imaginary and the Symbolic is anxiety.

As morality is fundamentally the same thing as language—an incomplete structured order of signifiers of equivalence guiding good and bad acts—the rupture of the human is an entry to ethics. Simply put, the negation of the moral order is where ethics has to step in to bridge the gap. Therefore, we now turn to ethics, to address what the individual sympathetic to the begging individual now must confront.

Sympathy and Ethics

SENSE OF GUILT

In this chapter we have examined the begging encounter from an anti-pathetic perspective. We now enter a sympathetic perspective, where the subject has tamed anxiety by transforming the Other into a "good object"—the begging déclassé, in other words, is interpreted as an impoverished individual in genuine need, a "deserving" poor person. Even here, however, the Real of anxiety is displaced, not neutralized. In this case the most common sensation of the sublimated anxiety is perhaps *guilt*: guilt for not doing enough for the Other; guilt for finding the Other's begging disturbing; guilt for desiring the Other to be gone; guilt for averting one's eyes and ignoring the Other; and so on. These feelings of guilt have tortured me, at least, during my years of conducting research. Psychoanalytically speaking, sensations of guilt and shame are aggression turned inside—against one's own "ego." Whereas the antipathetic directs aggression at the external Other, the guilt-tripped diverts it toward the internal Other of the ego. Guilt, like shame, is a horrible sensation, and one needs to find strategies to cope with it. One strategy that appears spectacular, though probably common, is presented by the neoliberal think tank director who concluded the solution to begging is to "teach the Roma" to work. He started his piece by confessing:

> There has been an imagination that blocked logic and decelerated my thinking. This blocking imagination is the [. . .] feeling, 'I am ashamed for doing well.' As long as that feeling dominated me, it was impossible to reach any other conclusion than the beggars deserved free board and lodging and dental paid by the municipality.
>
> My philosophical breakthrough came when I exchanged this imagination with a version of the implication, "I deserve to do well." I actually think I do. Sure, life has given me a lot of luck and help from others, but I have also worked hard. With this vantage point, all of a sudden it was possible to think. Human cohesion depends basically on people uniting in the realization of common projects. One works and pulls in the same direction. Imagine a soccer team [in a soccer game]. All of a sudden, two players leave the field, pull up paper mugs, and start to beg among the audience, whereupon the team loses. To abandon the joint efforts to look after oneself is disloyal.[39]

He then goes on to defend himself against those "obsessed with the shame of us being too well-off in our society" and who feel sorry for Roma due to their historical oppression, as he has now realized he has nothing to be ashamed of. Here, the unconscious short circuit occurs when this disavowal of shame is transferred into the Other's flaws. Rationally, he did not have to take that extra step. Nevertheless, he did, transforming his suffering into the pleasure of loving himself, with the bonus of racist guilt-tripping: it is the Roma who ought to be ashamed, as they are "disloyal"!

I, for my part, have tackled my sensations of guilt by sometimes avoiding the grocery stores where begging individuals with whom I'm acquainted are known to be operating. I am not alone, as the writer of one letter to the editor tells about her middle-aged female friend who "nowadays doesn't visit shops where beggars sit outside. She becomes so downhearted by this, she said, so she chooses shops with no beggars. She said she earlier [gave] 20- and 50-kronor bills, but nothing helps. They are nevertheless sitting there the next day."[40] Even when people sympathize with begging individuals, therefore, many of them turn away, performing the same pattern as if they were antipathetic or apathetic to the latter. There are similar mechanisms at work when handling suffering through the Other's desire.

GOOD DEEDS AND PATRONIZATION AS RESCUE

Nevertheless, thousands of people all over Sweden have gotten involved in efforts to help déclassés—as individuals, volunteers, NGO workers, neighbors, community members, business owners, politicians, municipal employees, and so on. Some have gone above and beyond in this effort, like my acquaintances at the volunteer network HEM (Föreningen HEM—hemlösa EU-migranter) who, each day, devote several hours of their time and energy to helping déclassés. In addition to this, there are those who have opened their homes to déclassés they met on the streets; activists who have protested evictions; and individuals who have organized fundraisers for begging people, found jobs for them, and invited them over for dinner. These concerned citizens, who come from all walks of life, include men, women, nonbinary people, students, workers, pensioners, the unemployed, those on sick leave, the disabled, wealthy people, the poor, those with families, and single people. Déclassés, meanwhile, are themselves known to do good deeds. They find and return the dropped wallets of passersby, save people from falling off their wheelchairs, give coins to young pedestrians so they can buy ice cream, and more. Some have befriended Swedish residents. Others have become their lovers. Some have even been considered for adoption. The list goes on. To be sure, déclassés have made a big impact on residents, who in turn have been motivated to assist their begging neighbors. Review of all these good deeds shows it is obvious that they cannot only be done out of guilt, self-fulfillment, or kindness. There have to be senses of righteousness out there—moral, ethical, and political convictions of what is right and wrong.

Note, however, that even the most rational or sacrificial good deed cannot escape the dialectics of pleasure and suffering. In several accounts of Good Samaritanism found in my empirical material, the bond of friendship or acquaintanceship seems to generate its own pleasure, enhancing the relationship of help and hospitality. Of course, this doesn't always have to be so. One can help others without becoming their friend, and establishing a social bond does not necessarily end interpersonal suffering. What if the Other doesn't want to be my friend? What if the Other is unlikeable or finds me unlikeable? How do I really know that what we have is friendship, and not manipulation, since the Other's desire might (righteously) prioritize my money?

One solution to such agonies is to objectify the Other as a one-dimensional representation of victimhood or goodness, potentially facilitating one's own perception of oneself as a good-hearted and moral individual. The danger of such a strategy is the possibility of patronizing the Other when they do not agree with your definition of the correct solution to their problems. In the capitalist era, the bourgeois social question, religious social work, philanthropy, and radicals disappointed in the working class have been haunted by the desire to turn the Other into a demoralized, immature, or ignorant victim who doesn't know what's best for them. As with social fantasies of deception and aggression, there might be some truth to claims that people don't know their own self-interest and need guidance from others. It is only when this partial truth becomes "pathological"—distorted to serve the interests of the powerful—that it escalates to an ideological problem. One such example is the Christian NGO worker who in a debate article claimed that "these people's real poverty is primarily not about money" but rather "*utanförskap*" (social exclusion).[41] The solution, then, is to offer the Other "authentic friendship not based upon giving" and to teach them "stewardship"—in short, a more romantic version of the old workhouses.

One Roma rights activist, a Swedish Romani herself, responded: "The Roma issue in Europe is not an issue of love or being a parent to them. It is an issue of human rights. [One] does not have to love people to show solidarity. I work actively to help the beggars in my hometown to obtain a better future. I do not love them all. Some of them I don't even like. That's the case with humans. Some are roses, and some are asses. It is a human right to behave like an ass too."[42]

While I don't think she's correct that it's a human right to be an ass, the point still stands.

SELF-INDULGENCE?

However, other voices swing to the other extreme by arguing that those who place money in begging hands are doing nothing but buying their own sense of self-indulgence. In December 2016 renowned ethicist Ann Heberlein claimed that giving to "beggars" was nothing but complacency: since people seem to find pleasure in giving away money, they are only doing so for their own good.[43] Others have gone so far as to liken giving money to déclassés with purchasing sex from trafficking victims.[44] Here the evil Other is not primarily "the beggar," but the immoral benefactor who secretly enjoys others' suffering (probably also one's own pain in having to face "beggars"). Note, however, that abstaining from giving doesn't undo the consequentialist aspect, and one can hardly do "good" without feeling any kind of pleasurable sensation. Within Heberlein's logical framework, one must suffer to accomplish a good deed. This, however, only inverses the signifiers.

Heberlein's intervention does, however, actualize the extimacy of care—of how egoism and altruism are different aspects of the same property. Because part of the ego can be found in the Other, and vice versa, the desire to do right by another person is also the desire to do right by oneself. This correlates with the original dialectics of pleasure/suffering. Let's exemplify this psychoanalytic argument by allegories:

If my back itches and I scratch it, I have relieved suffering and feel satisfaction. I have done good to myself.

If my friend is grieving, my friend's sense of grief makes me suffer too. I
comfort my friend; she feels better, and then I experience the pleasure
of the shared suffering having been relieved. I have done right by my
friend if she ceases suffering.

If I meet a begging individual and give her some change, I feel pleasure
by relieving the shared suffering in our interaction. It feels good that
she was grateful, or because I did the right thing.

Let's flip the allegories:

I cannot reach the itchy spot on my back. My exertion to make my
suffering cease fails, causing more suffering through the exertion of a
tension-laden effort.

My friend is inconsolable. In spite of my ministrations, she won't stop
complaining. My grueling efforts take energy, to no avail it seems.

Meanwhile, the middle-aged female friend feels "nothing helps." Even
though she gave "beggars" money yesterday, "They are nevertheless
sitting there the next day."

Regarding the begging encounter, the non-begging person is facing an
ethical circumstance where they must navigate an individual situation that
is the outcome of global structures of injustice. To acknowledge the individualization of a structural problem, however, does not undo the ethics of
the individuated lived situation at hand. I, for one, know several leftists who
believe themselves to have "cracked the code" by interpreting the begging
issue as the consequence of capitalism, a system in which "ethical consumption" is an impossibility. Of course, this strategy of apathy is as unfruitful
for the Other as the belief the Other is demoralized. Even if they're right,
after all, that doesn't undo their disavowal of individual responsibility for
answering the Other's interpellation. If I give a bill to a begging neighbor,
they will not stop being poor immediately, but they will be less so than
before. Abstract politicizing cannot change this fact. With that said, the risk
remains that I unwittingly support human trafficking. Then again, I involuntarily support a lot of immoral things through my consumption and taxes.

The point is, though one is paradoxically doomed during the begging encounter to become a sinner by never doing enough good, this fact does not undo the responsibility to make an ethical decision. From an ethical perspective, there is no system guaranteeing a fail-safe manual of doing right in every case. We face, therefore, the Real of ethics.

THE SUPEREGO AND ETHICAL SYSTEMS

In my research some interviewees describe a nagging voice inside their head that, as a forty-year-old man confessed, says something like: "Now's the time to show whether you are someone who gives or not." Notably, it's not the begging person asserting this, but rather the internal Other by way of the *superego*—the Other's desire within. According to Lacan, the superego is a sadistic agency that appears in the cracks of the Symbolic. This is because it is the personification of the categorical imperative, which is fundamentally oppressive in its demands.[45] This conceptualization of the superego is derived from Freud's *Civilization and Its Discontents.* There he argued the moral injunction to "love thy neighbor" is, if taken literally, an impossibility, making the subject guiltier the more they try to adhere to this precept. Significantly, this guilt is masochistic in character, as it derives from the internal superego's aggression against the ego.

To escape the superego's torture and make coexistence bearable, the subject is guided by laws, norms, morality, and ethics. When one encounters begging and, upon recognizing the Other is in need, wants to be a righteous person, ethics are supposed to help one decide what is the right thing to do. But the problem is that ethics cannot, by itself, provide an *objective* answer to this question, with regard to the lived reality of the interpersonal and particular begging encounter. Nevertheless, ethics is the last resort in trying to ground morality in universal objectivity, and the desire for ethics is the desire to escape the agony of risking wrongdoing.

Ever since postmodernity became trendy, there has been a common academic praise of, and attempts to introduce, "anti-deterministic" ethical systems, intended to derive ethics from the fluidity, contingency, and ungraspability of every identity and situation. Unfortunately, this celebration of undecidability confuses the ethical "ought" with the ontological "is"—the very *purpose* of ethical systems, after all, is to counter and tame reality's painstaking undecidability. To ground ethics in reality's contingency is only to describe how reality already works—not to designate what ought to be right and wrong. That is, what people want from ethics. Accordingly, the ethical philosophies of relevance here are the systems that people turn to in order to revel in the calming guarantee of what is the right thing to do. In order to demonstrate the field's overall problem with ethical consistency in the begging encounter—namely, its impossibility—it should be sufficient to investigate said confrontation through the lens of the three classical "Western" ethical systems: *virtue ethics, utilitarianism/consequentialism*, and *deontology*. Following a historical-materialist analysis, much like the abstraction of historical modes of production into the developmental stages of slavery, feudalism, and capitalism (or, in sociologist Immanuel Wallerstein's updated terminology: mini-system, world empire, and world economy), I here argue that the three ideal-typical ethical systems can be found in different contextual variations throughout the world in history and time—a development attributable to ethics and morality's dialectical relationship with the socioeconomic order it represents.[46] Virtue ethics, for example, has its origins in premodern history, including ancient Greek philosophy, monotheistic religions, and Confucianism. The sub-Saharan ethical philosophy of Ubuntu is also, arguably, a type of virtue ethics, as it teaches virtues over precise rules and causality models. Meanwhile, deontology, or duty ethics, is classically associated with Immanuel Kant and Western rationality, but its form of a categorical imperative could be found in the Ten Commandments and in communitarian importunities to share.

Virtues are about a precise balance of characteristics. It's a virtue, for example, to be generous and caring toward those in need. If one is too generous, however, one becomes ostentatious. Conversely, if one is too economical, one becomes miserly. "The beggar" risks transgressing virtues constantly—turning humility into greed, laziness, or jealousy.[47] With virtue ethics, it becomes impossible to apply an objective guide to navigating the begging encounter, with definitive guidelines for accessing each party's virtue at any given moment.

With consequentialism, the problem of "the beggar" becomes a matter of deciding what would be the best and most useful consequence of one's actions. But then one must ask, Consequences for whom? If for "the beggar," "the giver" has problems tracking the money's chain of custody. From "the giver's" perspective, giving may encourage "the beggar" to ask for more in the future. By not giving, however, "the beggar" would probably continue begging, too. With utilitarianism, Lacan argued, following Jeremy Bentham's lead, the good becomes *fictitious*.[48] In the wake of God's death, the subject itself decides what the good is. This enables the subject to treat ethics as a fiction, where the good can readily become the subject's own good.

With Kantian deontology, God's death cannot be an excuse to use one's own definition of "good" to determine what is ethical. The good then takes on a new incarnation as an entity outside the subject, in the universal of reason. This exogenous entity has an authoritative force, and compared with the previous systems, we find *duty* as the form guiding right and wrong here—thus closer to a commanding imperative that concretely tells the subject what to do in the situation. Notably, the difference between the divine injunction to love and the categorical imperative is minimal. In Kant's prescription, one has to depathologize the good and thereby cannot escape superego's demand. In the begging interaction, therefore, "the giver's" responsibility becomes to unconditionally give to "the beggar." The problem is that even this good would become pathologized, as it would be impossible for the majority of people to achieve in every empirical case.

Moral philosopher Colin Radford used the hypothetical begging encounter to prove that the longing for foolproof moral principles guiding private actions is done in vain. The only principle that guarantees consistency is to never give to anyone. Those advocating for this moral position

> neither wrongly nor irrelevantly, invite bleeding hearts to consider the
> question of whether one should give in to kidnappers.

The motives for doing so are parallel to those for giving to beggars. By doing so one can save a life, help someone in the most terrible need by paying the ransom. Nevertheless we should resist that all too human, immediate, concerned response which can save the life of an innocent victim. One should not do so because, by so doing, one encourages kidnappers. If no one ever gave in to kidnappers, kidnapping would cease.

[However,] if no one begged because they knew that it was pointless, that would not mean that no one who might have survived by begging would not die because no one would help them.[49]

Significantly, Radford concedes that it is "clear that we may properly, and sometimes we should, give to beggars, although I cannot specify the occasions on which we should do so."[50] The psychoanalytic lesson of this conclusion is *not* a celebration of this undecidability. Rather, this lack of certainty is a source of anxiety—it leaves the subject with the (often painstaking) decision on which occasions qualify as appropriate ones to give.

If we think back to Freud, his objection against the biblical command to unconditionally love one's neighbor is also a retroactive rejection of what we might call Levinasian ethics. Emmanuel Levinas, a central figure in postmodern philosophies, searched for an ethics transcending rationalism and grounded in experience. He likened the ethical with a face-to-face encounter with the Other, whose very presence constitutes a perpetual, unconditional, and nonreciprocal responsibility for the Other: "It is precisely insofar as the relationship between the Other and me is not reciprocal that I am subjected to the Other [. . .]. My responsibility is untransferable, no one could replace me. In fact, it is a matter of expressing the very identity of the human I, starting from responsibility [which] is what is incumbent on me exclusively, and what, humanly, I cannot refuse."[51]

Levinas's "responsibility" is of a Kantian kind, since it is not refutable. The supposed difference, however, is that the imperative does not come from reason, or from the superego, but from the Other's existence itself. Consequently, it is meant to escape the pathologization of a dictum, which Kant's own imperative, however it aimed at the opposite, leads to if taken literally.

Further, the Levinasian depiction of ethics as an undecidable encounter with the face of an Other, which constitutes a nonreciprocal responsibility for them, appears to be particularly applicable to the begging encounter's ethical problem. With that said, Levinas's abstract reasoning doesn't help us with the concrete of the situation—it only states that you're responsible for the Other and cannot demand any reciprocity. Responsibility, of course, can mean many things, and is all too readily used as an excuse for exercises of power. If it is to mean anything in the hypothetical begging encounter, it must imply the responsibility to help the Other—to give them money—without requiring reciprocation. Let's then hypothetically apply the Levinasian position to the begging encounter, as a Kantian axiom for ethical action.

First, you cannot discriminate between whom to give to or not; you should give to everyone. A common truism in the Swedish discourse is that since Sweden has to such an extent transformed into a cashless society, one never carries change. I hear this all the time, as an instinctive defense, bodily expressed like this: ¯_(ツ)_/¯. Still, ATMs exist. If one is to follow the injunction, one can always go to a machine and withdraw cash. How much? You alone decide, perhaps using factors such as your economic situation, familial responsibilities, and so forth. All these objections are morally applicable, but they do not undo the injunction: only you can decide that your loved ones' best interests, or your own, trump the Other's. As long as you have money, you can never deny it is your own freely made decision to withhold money. In the end one cannot escape the responsibility to the Other's desire.

You could try, however—by, for example, transferring one's responsibility for the Other to the Other themself. If it's ultimately my own choice to accept or refuse my responsibility for my neighbor, then couldn't one argue that "the beggar" has the same free will to decide whether they are going to beg or not? Surely, this is true. They could instead have chosen to live an even poorer life or pursue other activities such as stealing, drug dealing, or prostitution (which several no doubt do on the side in order to make ends meet). Failing that, they could have sought foreign work opportunities, offered by strangers who could very well be either benefactors or slavedrivers. However, both Levinas and Kant would argue the Other's potential immorality—of not fulfilling the categorical imperative—in no way affects your own responsibility to follow the imperative. The raison d'être of deontology, after all, is to "save" ethics from such relativizations by making the rule universal—beyond profane personal considerations.

As a final objection against the demand to unconditionally help the Other, one must set *a limit* to where "helpfulness" becomes "self-extinction." Once again, this limit is yours alone to determine, a decision complicated by existentialist concerns. The fundamental free choice of suicide, of sacrificing oneself for the Other, might be a solution. The Levinasian injunction, however, should not allow that: by terminating your own existence, you escape your ongoing responsibility for others. Ultimately, not even death salvages you from the Other's desire.

The impossibility of accommodating the Other's desire, this never-ending responsibility, is a highway to anxiety and suffering. We learn this in Bertolt Brecht's *The Good Person of Szechwan*, a play about a woman who always tries to adhere to the gods' prescriptions for goodness. This strategy culminates in her having to invent a selfish and exploitative alter ego in order for her to be able to proceed with her social life. When the gods appear before her at the end, she laments:

Your original order
To be good while yet surviving
Split me like lightning into two people. I
Cannot tell what occurred: goodness to others
And to myself could not both be achieved.
To serve both self and others I found too hard.
Oh, your world is arduous! Such need, such desperation!
The hand which is held out to the starving
Is quickly wrenched off! He who gives help to the lost
Is lost for his own part! For who could
Hold himself back from anger when the hungry are dying?
Where could I find so much that was needed, if not
In myself? But that was my downfall![52]

The Real of being encountered with the Other's desire, the Real of no reassuring ethical solution on which to rely, leads to the desire for the presence of a Third—a Big Other of society, mediating between the subject and its Other.[53] The moral canon on good and evil masks the abyss of free will in order to enable subjects to reduce their suffering in social interaction. The presence of the poor has prompted various (incomplete) moral laws aiming to regulate the good through a Symbolic order. In Medieval Europe, for example, there was the distribution of alms; then, in premodern Sweden, the circulation of the pauper club regulating whose household's turn it was to look after the pauper. In the United States, meanwhile, there is the celebration of philanthropy and charity. In Nordic welfare states, the taxes are supposed to accomplish the societal good in one's place. With the introduction of homeless magazine vendors, the civilian is furnished with the neat routine of ritually performing the good by buying a paper once a month for a determined price. To compare with "the beggar," the street vendor undoes several anxious considerations found in the Levinasian extreme—you can now act as if you do not have to decide yourself how much you should give and when. The same goes for supporting aid work with direct debit, fair trade and ecological consumption, and climate compensation. To paraphrase Erich Fromm, you escape freedom.

I am not moralizing here—I simply repeat Žižek's argument that there is no deeper meaning to suffering.[54] The common desire to neutralize the ethical sphere into a moral order does not undo the desire to do right by my neighbor; instead, it sublimates it into a more comfortable—and hence more doable—routine. Žižek argues that the ideological use of Other surrogates who believe in the good (or doing what is good) in the place of oneself does not make the belief in the good less sincere. Similarly, one might enjoy watching a sitcom in spite of not laughing along with the laugh track.[55] As Žižek argues, every ethics must rely on a *fetishist disavowal*:

> Is even the most universal ethics not obliged to draw a line and ignore some sort of suffering? [. . .] Imagine the effect of having to watch a

snuff movie portraying what goes on thousands of times a day around the world [...]. Would the watcher be able to continue going on as usual? Yes, but only if he or she were able somehow to forget—in an act which suspended symbolic efficiency—what had been witnessed. This forgetting entails a gesture of what is called fetishist disavowal: "I know, but I don't want to know that I know, so I don't know." [What] if that which appears as an inconsistency, as the failure to draw all the consequences from one's ethical attitude, is, on the contrary, its positive condition of possibility? What if such an exclusion of some form of otherness from the scope of our ethical concerns is consubstantial with the very founding gesture of ethical universality, so that the more universal our explicit ethics is, the more brutal the underlying exclusion is?[56]

In Sweden the snuff movie analogy became a Reality in everyday spaces, as exemplified by this fifty-year-old interviewee, who said:

People don't want to be bothered ... in their everyday life, I think. I don't mean "bothered" by a person begging for money but bothered by the phenomena, I guess [...]. The phenomena that there are people in need of money. That there are poor people in the world, and that there are drug users, alcoholics, and ... I want to walk from my apartment to work ... and think everything is okay. And later, I want to open the hatch to the TV news sometimes and see there are other things.

With the advent of begging déclassés in Swedish urban environments in the mid-2010s, I argue, this ethical problem became, for conscience-ridden subjects (including me), a *conscience-phenomenological catastrophe*.

In order to save ethics from cynicism, Žižek stresses the necessity of deciding what kind of suffering one is allowed to be "the exception to the rule." The encounter with this "limit" of ethics, which holds true for both individual and societal morality, is homologous to confronting the radical alterity of the Other. If it were not for the "failure" of ethics—its limited capacity to furnish every ethical situation with a correct answer—there would be no need for ethics in the first place. After all, ethics work as a substitute for the lack in the Symbolic, the Real beyond ideology. If it was not human to error, human would not in fact be human, and the desire to do good wouldn't exist.

Of course, the fact that exceptions must be made doesn't automatically justify exempting déclassés from norms of ethical treatment, as has become common in Sweden. What one must take into account is the injunction that, so says Lacan, is the ethical maxim of psychoanalysis: "Have you acted in conformity with the desire that is in you?"[57] Here I interpret this precept to be an examination of one's ethical position on one's own desire. Have you conflated your desire for your own good (qua pleasure) with the desire for the societal good? The good, it must be noted, cannot be reduced to an absolute static ideal, as it depends upon one's historical-geographical context rather than being relativistic. Regarding the personal issue of the begging encounter, therefore, you can ask yourself, "Do I support a begging ban because I desire what's good for 'the beggar' or what's good for me?" For Sweden, the problem was the successively spread belief that banning begging and expulsing the poor was for the poor's own good. This mindset also motivates the desire to outlaw begging to save one's neighbor from trafficking, without considering that a begging ban that makes no *real* efforts to fight poverty does nothing good for those begging except sparing oneself anxiety.

In 2015 one journalist reflected upon his own development in contending with the suffering of the begging encounter. To that end he described the process of the encounter becoming normalized and slowly growing numb to it. "This time you did not stop. Even though she waved at you [. . .]. And you felt ashamed, but somewhere one needs to draw the line. And it was hard, but it becomes easier. [. . .] You think such weird thoughts in this new *annoying* world. This world which leans in and tests you. You hate to be tested."[58] Nevertheless, he is anxious because his four-year-old, who has never experienced a time without begging, does not seem to care. Ironically, he exclaims in italics, "*Maybe it's just as good to forbid them, so our children grow up into good people. Who can help them if we fail!*" He concludes, "You have not even thought your weirdest thoughts yet." While this columnist presents this conclusion as ethically absurd, several opinion makers have seriously argued for banning begging for the express purpose of avoiding dampening Swedes' concern for strangers in need. Though the argument has been prominent in social-democratic defenses of the welfare state's solvency, right-wingers have deployed the same rationale. The editor of Sweden's leading business magazine, closely associated with the Confederation of Swedish Enterprise, has argued, "One should not be allowed to beg. It is destructive for the one begging and the surroundings slowly getting used to facing utmost distress. Social security nets are fundamentally based upon the public's sensitivities and ability to react to poverty, and one should look after that capacity for empathy."[59] These thoughts were echoing the former chief editor of *Dagens Nyheter*, a self-proclaimed liberal: "The habit of seeing bottomless poverty with no cure makes us hard also toward people maltreated in health care, children with abusing parents, women in need of sanctuary from their tormentors. The basis of welfare politics in the citizens' empathy and sensibility is weakened."[60] Notably, these authors misunderstand "the basis" of welfare state solidarity, which is a sense of shared interests, and not sympathy with the vulnerable. How, one wonders, can one preserve Swedish compassion for others, if said compassion cannot withstand the presence of strangers in need? Here we see how the unconscious works as a social network joining together individual desires with ideological interests, and, likewise, how individuals are libidinally invested in commonsensical nationalism. However, the argument is not only racist—turning the racial Other into a threat to national cohesion—it also has the convenient quality of being available to both the left and right as an argument.

Because of my interpretation of the functions of the unconscious, I'm prepared to concede that this desire for banning begging may be genuine in its proclaimed aim on a conscious level. However, it is *perverted* by the unconscious desire to not only escape the suffering caused by encountering begging but also the losing of one's righteous self-image. Ultimately, the subject can only encounter itself in its confrontation with the Other.

Having traced the roots of the anxiety of begging, we can now conclude that this anxiety is overdetermined not only by the history and logics of class society exploitation, capitalism, and racialization, but also by the fundamental alienation at the heart of subjectivity itself. However, now another question arises, which regards the interconnection between politics and the unconscious. If it in the end doesn't matter whether individuals are morally sympathizing with or despising "the beggar," since the result tends to be likely the same in the end, nothing is theoretically standing in the way of presenting the upheaval of the begging gesture by societal means, with the aim of ensuring that no one turns to begging for survival. This solution would lie in everyone's "interest," in the sense that no one (especially not "the beggar") wants to experience begging. It also intersects with the "spirit level" argument, that more societal equality is in everyone's interest since it reduces social distrust, anxiety, illness, and overall unhealth on behalf of the whole of state populations.[61] Nevertheless, the common solution throughout history, with few exceptions, has been to expel the poor—to make begging go away from one's sight without fighting their poverty. We already know this inclination in capitalism is due to the omnipotent logic of capital, but how is this tendency mobilized into popular support? How does ideology make use of the unconscious for political objectives?

5 Ideology, or Enjoying the National Thing

How are personal anxieties about the Other's desire translated into politics? The answer is ideology, which mediates between the personal and the social. Here, in this book, "ideology" is not merely a set of political ideas, but the three Lacanian realms mobilized into a persuasive fantasy of a commonsensical social reality. Specifically, the Imaginary and Symbolic are consolidated into a taken-for-granted order, into *senso comune*, with political implications and consequences. Critically, it is ideology that gives reality meaning, and as Fredric Jameson contended, "'meaning' is always ideological." After all, ideology "is how you designate the situation specificity of all thought and all positions (no matter how universally articulated). Ideology is what comes naturally to a species made up of individuals as we are: namely, that we can never reach 'the universal,' that everything we think is slanted and conditioned by the situation in which we are formed, from the existential and psychoanalytic all the way to class, nation, race, gender, and so forth. This is the deeper sense of 'metaphysics' and indeed of 'meaning' [itself]."[1]

Implied here is a difference between reality and perception. In Marxian dialectical thought (drawing on Hegel's corpus), reality consists of a totality that, due to contradictory processes and relations, is in constant movement.[2] This whole, ungraspable to human cognition, equates to the Lacanian Real. Through the Imaginary and Symbolic, human cognition abstracts this overwhelming totality into a cognitive map, with the Imaginary turning reality's processes and relations into abstracted units, and the Symbolic forming a relational network of these abstractions. Notably, abstraction of reality is inescapable, but *how* this process occurs varies. Although every person abstracts the world from their own perspective within a historical-geographical context, their abstractions are influenced by socially dominant interpretations—caretakers and institutions, in other words, teach them what to believe about how the world works. Consequently, dominant abstractions of reality constitute ideology. With that said, ideologies exist in the plural, and in contradictory relations to each other. Together, they comprise, and are subjected to, the *dominant ideology* of a given society.

Gramsci's "common sense" is a perfect illustration of ideology in action. Although common sense upholds various truisms (some fundamentally contradictory), some common sense is more common than others. Accordingly, a dominant ideology consists of the most prevalent "common senses" and contains fragments of both myth and reality, similar to how ideology universalizes partial truths rather than disseminating outright lies. Here the interconnection between ideology and the Imaginary order becomes evident; in the last chapter, we observed how reasonable considerations regarding the existence of interpersonal aggressiveness and deception were displaced, fetishized, and projected onto imagined hostile Others qua "beggars." This is how ideology works, by amplifying some facts and diminishing others. Naturally, this affects how humans abstract information, with some abstractions—namely, ones that benefit ideology's overarching Imaginary and Symbolic orders—likelier to crystallize than others. Likewise, certain ideological abstractions take shape out of their power to appeal to individual psyches' Imaginaries within specific socio-spatial surroundings. For ideology to be treated as reality, people must be *libidinally attached* to it. Consequently, ideology equips subjects with productive displacements of the Real. If, for example, the Real of a social order—its incoherencies, injustices, horrors, and sufferings—is successfully commonly abstracted into an Imaginary Other that embodies these Real properties as its essential characteristics, this Imaginary Other becomes part of ideology.

By simplifying the world into demarcated identities/units through the Imaginary, these reifications become imagined as harboring essential characteristics—"essential" in the sense that that these characteristics originate "from within" and are eternal. However, all that is solid melts into air. As time passes, a leaf changes color and decomposes, revealing that it

ANXIETY

was only ever the temporary appearance of a leaf. However, interrelated circumstances, processes, and relations caused the leaf to momentarily appear as such. This does not mean the leaf's appearance was false; rather, every phenomenological identity is the sum of its temporal-spatial appearances and its obscure processes and relations. In the Imaginary, however, time and space are "frozen," causing these appearances to be perceived as essences. In this way "poverty" becomes "poor people" becomes the destitute's "inherently poor character"—then is individualized, pathologized, and culturalized. "The beggar" is a Roma, homeless abuser, cunning idler, or something else inherently evil in a manner befitting the ideological scene and cast. Troublingly, this conflation of appearance and essence implies an inversion of *cause* and *effect*: poverty, the cause of begging, becomes the effect of begging. Recall the neoliberal think tank director who, in a perceived "philosophical breakthrough," decided that because his hard work yielded great wealth, "the Roma beggars" deserve their poverty since they choose to beg instead of working hard. Alternatively, consider the widespread social belief in Sweden (and elsewhere) that "begging does not end poverty," as if that would be a sound argument for outlawing it—that if only they stop begging, "the beggars" would end that very poverty that initially led them to beg.[3] For Marx, this confusion between cause and effect (likewise, appearance and essence) was characteristic of bourgeois ideology, which he likened to a "fetishism" that "transforms the social, economic character that things are stamped with in the process of social production into a natural character arising from the material nature of these things."[4] Given my Lacanian ontology, where Imaginary miscognition is constitutional for subjectivity, we must understand bourgeois ideology as a certain kind of fetishizing—benefiting certain interests.

Unconscious Ideology

Critique of ideology, like Foucauldian discourse theory, is often accused of determinism, with detractors raising the question of whether it's possible to step outside discourse/ideology, an omnipotent force that constructs subjectivity itself. Thankfully, psychoanalysis provides clarity, because while ideology certainly conditions and determines subjectivities, it cannot erase the Real. This matrix enables us to distinguish between reality and appearance—the very reason I can discuss abstractions of reality in the first place, since their incoherencies are now discernible. Consequently, I can "step outside" ideology on a reflective level, but my *unconscious attachments* to ideology aren't so easily undone.

As Žižek argues, ideology is an unconscious social fantasy structuring our social reality itself.[5] Following philosopher Louis Althusser's appropriation of Lacan, Žižek argues the power of ideology is not found primarily in the content of thoughts themselves, but in the *performative* aspect of behaving as if ideology was truth. The last chapter's elaboration on the need for an ethical fetishist disavowal illustrates this point: "I know, but I don't want to know that I know, so I don't know." People can be well aware that what they believe is not the truth, but the pleasure they receive from ideological thought processes, conclusions, and actions reinforces said beliefs. The common suspiciousness of "beggars" being deceptive, fraudulent, or even rich is such a symptom of ideology. People ought to know, if they were to give it serious thought, that the prospect of the begging Other's hidden riches must be a fantasy. Nevertheless, they believe it, because it facilitates their unconscious strategies of negotiating their feelings of anxiety and desire for the Other. This social fantasy becomes Ideological with a capital *I* since it serves the interests of the ruling classes—specifically the interest to short-circuit moral and political considerations on economic distribution and equality.

Strikingly, the distinction between conscious knowledge and unconscious belief makes the classical liberal idea of education as the solution to social "ignorance" and conflict fall short: people can be well educated, intellectual, and critical, while simultaneously embracing "ignorant" beliefs and practices. To see how the liberal market of facts and opinions does not magically generate greater insights, one need only peruse social media's passionate and hostile discourses. Clearly, the problem is not "lack of knowledge"—it's that humans, in order to believe a truth claim, require the involvement of their anxieties and desires. People can hold a moral belief that all humans deserve a decent standard of living, consider themselves duty bound to help their neighbor in need, and well know that begging individuals are in genuine need. Nevertheless, they might *behave* as though they are mildly antipathetic, ignoring the Other on the sidewalk. On those grounds this behavior is an ideological performance, as it reproduces a social reality where decent living standards are not a human right and racialized impoverished outcasts continue begging.

The emphasis on ideology as practice highlights ideology's dialectical relationship to the socio-material reality it represents. Because ideological beliefs inform action, the social world is molded to appear as ideology prescribes it to be. To revisit the dialectics of racism, racial ideology reflects a world that appears hierarchically divided into different races, which guides subjects and institutions to reproduce this appearance. As we know, however, where there is system, there is dirt. The incapacity of ideology to swallow reality in its totality causes contradictions to emerge all the time in our ever-changing world, as ideology continually tries to adapt to changes it is partially guilty of enhancing. In this way the Real of ideology both threatens and facilitates ideology.

The Dominant Ideology on Begging

A "dominant ideology" in the singular implies the condensation of fragments of "minor" ideologies, discourses, and historical layers of different ages' values and moralities. As such, ideology is not logically coherent, as the social reality it represents is itself filled with struggles. There is also scale to ideology, as there is a globally shared dominant ideology that upholds capitalism as the natural order, and there are dominant ideologies undergirding each nation-state—each with its own perceived national exceptionalism.

Regarding the dominant ideology on begging, there are two scale levels to consider here: the "universal" ideology upholding capitalism, which itself contains traces and fragments of previous ideologies inherited from older modes of production, and the "particular" ideology maintaining the Swedish nation-state. Before we investigate contemporary Swedish ideology's relationship to begging in part 2, we must abstract the dominant capitalist ideology on begging, as the universal ideology dominates, and thereby informs, nations' particularist ideologies.

To conclude previous excursions into the historical and unconscious layers of current public attitudes, begging is *overdetermined* to be interpreted as a moral wrong. Abstracting the perspectives of different class positions, institutions, and ideas, begging is a potential moral offense for the following:

class society: begging questions the naturalness of enclosed property and existing property relations.

capitalism: begging questions the naturalness and social productiveness of wage labor and reciprocal economic exchange.

capital: alongside aforementioned concerns, begging encourages "unproductive" expenditure and likewise disturbs the gentrification and commercialization of public space.

the state: begging constitutes disorder through its dubious legal and moral character and the uncontrollable mobility of subjects.

the bourgeois class: for all aforementioned reasons.

the working class: begging disrupts taken-for-granted norms on deserv-ingness and respectability. If begging is racialized, the dominant race's working class might project it as a "lifestyle" that exploits members of their demographic, whereas the dominated races fear its resultant guilt by association.

institutional religion: begging complicates the idealist conception of humanity as loving, caring, and humble.

nationalism: begging disturbs the imagined community of fraternity and solidarity.

liberalism: begging perverts the idea of self-interest.

conservatism: for the same reasons as class society, religion, and nationalism.

socialism: begging complicates visions of the proletariat's struggle.

urbanity: begging challenges norms of social interaction, mobility, and private integrity.

aesthetics: begging transgresses ordered spaces of purity and dirt.

patriarchy and racialism: begging, through its submissiveness, exposes
human weakness and dependency.

the unconscious: the begging interaction has a remarkable capacity to
stir up anxieties regarding the Other's desire, forcing the subject to
confront its Other (in potentially every sense).

Nevertheless, people continue begging, since people continue to give. That's why begging is overdetermined to be, but is not deterministically, wrong. Parallel to this overdetermination, after all, runs the counterbalance of human sympathy and desire for the Other:

In class society, the injunction to love thy neighbor has an ideological
function, as it enhances the social fantasy of a community between
rich and poor.

Among the bourgeoisie, it is virtuous to care for the poor.

Among the working class, giving can be an act of solidarity.

In institutionalized religion, caring for the poor is both virtuous and
demanded.

In liberalism, each individual bears fundamental rights to express themselves and pursue happiness.

In socialism, the destitute is a fellow victim of capital.

In the extimate unconscious, there is the desire to overcome suffering
and establish communion within the (internal and external) ego-Other
relationship.

On the whole, it is fascinating to observe the consolidation of different class positions and ideas into a prevailing ideological truth that claims begging is *socially disruptive*. As we know, this structural moral determination is materially attributable to the regulating role of property in class society, where scarcity is artificially produced and maintained. But I also argue this consolidation is due to the emotional kernel of anxiety for encountering the human Real in its desirous lack—in its radical negativity, where no Imaginary or Symbolic symbiosis appears to be possible for the anxious subject trying to rediscover itself.

This human Real is within and between every human being as a reality and potentiality to be encountered, but it is also, through class society's structuring of property and power, ideologically located at the subject positions that rupture this social and moral order through their excluded positionality. Due to the universal character of this anxiety—identifiable as a shared sensation among one's fellow neighbors thanks to one's empathetic capacity—this fetishization of anxiety via Othering becomes inverted into a positive condition for a community of all those believed to share this sensation. As desire is the dialectical counterpoint to anxiety, this perceived shared anxiety can become a mutual desire for a common aim—namely, to eliminate the cause of this anxiety. This is where ideology becomes relevant, as this emotional investment in a perceived shared community of similar subjects helps displace the human Real that exists between these subjects onto the shared object of the "community's" Other. That is, through the conversion of anxiety into hate or love, a community is discernible and imaginable. To illustrate this logic, consider "the beggar" and ideology's "commonsensical" construction of labor: "the beggar," who causes anxiety, doesn't work, in perceived contrast to "the worker" and "the capitalist," which means the latter two have both work and anxiety about "the beggar" in common! Add the racial signifier, and we see this ideology qua nationalism come into play. The Real of labor—that work is certainly not a shared experience across classes in terms of its material content—is concealed by the projection of the hardships of labor upon the perceived cause of personal anxiety: "the beggar," the poor, the racial Other. This leads us to subjects' unconscious attachment to ideology—the belief in a shared Thing that enables people to believe in ideology.

Enjoying the National Thing

In order to function as a "force" fueling and guiding practices in certain directions, ideology requires a collective emotional attachment to unconscious objects of desire: common ideas or symbols believed to give pleasure and community, as the subject is fundamentally alienated from yet desires its Other. One such sublime ideological object is a fetish in which a group's members (un)consciously view themselves as a community. The fetish of work has already been mentioned as an example of this—the content of labor is secondary to (or even in the way of) the belief structure, as what matters is the form of the shared "Thing" upon which it is possible to project different desires and experiences. Žižek calls this kind of fetish the *National Thing*, "the way subjects of a given ethnic community organize their enjoyment through national myths."[6] Douglas's point that a community's existence is due to its ordering of things implies the continuation of ordering—a "way" to "organize their enjoyment." A given community cannot be conceptualized as real based solely on social identification. Žižek explains, "The bond linking together its members always implies a shared relationship toward a Thing, toward Enjoyment incarnated."[7] Discourse is not enough. People need to invest themselves emotionally in a believed shared Thing to feel a sense of community, especially in mass societies.

This National Thing is the object of both nationalist politics and banal nationalism, as it signifies the idea of the particular nation itself. Because "the nation" is not a metaphysical object, but a historical category and unconscious point of reference for organizing the territorial politics of states and movements, this sublime Thing cannot be grasped. Here the capital *T* is a clue: the National Thing is a nonappearance of the Thing-in-itself, which, as we already know, cannot metaphysically exist as anything other than a negation preceding its own idea. Nevertheless, it functions as an Imaginary "good object," which is the perceived hidden mediator between the subject and those who share this association. What's more, it's the precondition for the idea of the existence of "the good home" or *folkhemmet* envisioned by Per Albin, further expressed by the assertion of the former chief editor of *Dagens Nyheter* that "the basis of welfare politics" is "the citizens' empathy and sensibility" for each other.[8] In sum, it is the Thing that "the beggar" reveals doesn't exist!

Regarding the performative character of ideology, the National Thing is socially treated as the hidden cause of social similarity between people in habits, rituals, traditions, and behavior. This similarity is commonly labeled "culture," and Žižek calls it "our way of life." As the subject is finite and needs to demarcate a degree of distance from Others, the National Thing necessarily excludes some appearances and practices as Other to it. To understand the National Thing's resultant sensitivity to abjection, we must consult Žižek's theorization of *racism as fantasy*. According to him, racism (on the side of ideology in the dialectic) is the fantasy of theft of Enjoyment. Though "Enjoyment" means "complete pleasure," in this book it designates the pleasure of community—of the subject believing itself non-alienated from the world and fused with its (good) Other.[9] This definition implies a latent fear that Others, as in "the nation's Others," will steal or destroy the National Thing. It also feeds suspicions and jealousy that the (bad) Other Enjoys its own Thing at the subject's expense. In times of social upheaval and insecurity, this latent fear becomes ideologically productive. Žižek explains:

> We always impute to the 'other' an excessive enjoyment: he wants to steal our enjoyment (by ruining our way of life) and/or he has access to some secret, perverse enjoyment. In short, what really bothers us about the "other" is the peculiar way he organizes his enjoyment, precisely the surplus, the "excess" that pertains to this way: the smell of "their" food, "their" noisy songs and dances, "their" strange manners, "their" attitude to work. To the racist, the "other" is either a workaholic stealing our jobs or an idler living on our [labor]. The basic paradox is that our Thing is conceived as something inaccessible to the other and at the same time threatened by him.[10]

These fantasies' similarity to the abjection of déclassés is obvious. Here again, the "irrational logic" of hating the racial Other simply for being Other reemerges. We also see the paranoid confusion of the Other's enigma with their deception, and how this fantasy of deception creates incoherent paradoxical fantasies of the Other being simultaneously passive and active, rich and poor, dumb and cunning. The Other's Otherness—termed "the human" in the last chapter—is readily determined by ideology to be the perceived essential characteristics of society's minorities. "When it comes too close," this gestaltization of Otherness "disturbs us, throws the balance of our way of life off the rails."[11] It is not the Other human per se but their perceived alterity that "can also give rise to an aggressive reaction aimed at getting rid of this disturbing intruder." Notably, this hostility has a function within ideology, since "what we conceal by imputing to the Other the theft of enjoyment is the traumatic fact that *we never possessed what was allegedly stolen from us* [because] enjoyment constitutes itself as 'stolen.'"[12]

Through the fantasy of it being stolen, ruined, or lost, the National Thing of Enjoyment might continue to exist as a belief. If out of sight, the subject preserves the fantasy of its existence by blaming its invisibility on intentional efforts to hide it. This way the Thing might paradoxically come to appear to exist *within* the figure of the Other—where, after all, is it to be located on the cognitive map, if not at the actor believed to possess it? This accusation helps explain the need for all the national narratives of a bygone "golden age" that is now lost, or on its way to be lost if the nation does not reorient itself around the National Thing. Such a narrative finds nutrition in the belief in "bad guys": those who are believed to be either intruders from the outside or the enemy within. Amid a period of social turmoil, people become more anxious and nostalgic about the times prior to crisis. Consequently, this narrative of "theft of Enjoyment" becomes desirable.

Nonetheless, the gap between ideology's promises and reality's disappointments is constant, which always latently feeds fantasies of scapegoats. One such delusion, prevailing since antiquity, is that of "beggars" secretly enjoying themselves on the back of others' hard work. This suspicion, which treats work as a "National" Thing, fits within an ideology that proclaims society's wealth is attributable to everyone's *equal* participation and *solidary* hardship; consequently, paupers can become the cause of one's personal drudgery and conformity. Because of its association with economic as well as socio-existential reality, labor in capitalist class society makes a perfect ideological condensation of the location of the collective Thing. Labor's ideology also legitimizes the protection and distribution of property, which begging inherently challenges. Although people can well know this distribution is unfair and feel discontent regarding their positionality within capitalism, they may still unconsciously believe this is the way things ought to be in order for reality to be coherent—their own existence as specific subjects included.

This thesis appeals to the idea of an inherent conservatism within the subject and, likewise, the idea of phobia being preferable to anxiety. After all, with the current order, or with the phobic object, you at least (believe you) know who you are in the Symbolic order. Still, the subject's character is progressive, too, since the world is constantly changing, whether the subject likes it or not, and the discrepancy between ideology and reality feeds desires for what's beyond what already is. The Thing is always there as a touchpoint for the subject's desire, which, collectivized, easily becomes the desire to overcome the gap between the subjects and their Others and the end of suffering altogether—toward Enjoyment.

Žižek's parade example of the function of ideology as a fantasy of stolen Enjoyment is Nazi Germany's anti-Semitism. At that time Nazi ideology depicted society as an autonomous harmonious social body, where all classes were in cohesion due to the Thing of racial purity. This ideology's Real was the class struggle and the Depression. By turning "the Jew" into the desired object (the cause of desire for the Thing), Nazi ideology took "its own failure into account in advance."[13] If only the Jew was exterminated, it contended, racial cohesion would be realized. Following this logic, the category of Jew was expanded to encompass all ideological enemies, from capitalist to Bolshevik, primitive to civilized. This consolidation served to maintain ideological desire and Enjoyment of racial hatred and mobilize these feelings into a political force.

Reflecting on chapter 2, we can see how the ideologies of liberalism, socialism, and conservatism work along similar lines: in liberalism, the Thing is within "individual freedom"; for socialism, "termination of economic exploitation"; for conservatism, "harmony between classes." "The beggar" qua object constitutes obstacles for all three, whereas its function as driving ideology fits best within conservatism's fear of "the rabble." This is because the conservative ideology explicitly locates the human Real as the *deviant* position—the position threatening to make the terror balance between classes contingent and unnatural. As we have seen, liberalism and

socialism can adopt this structure too, but the deviant's position in these ideologies is more ambivalent due to the way they condense the Thing. In conservatism the deviant instead becomes almost a pure negativity of the Thing.

THE NATIONAL THING = THE BELIEF IN COMMUNION
IN DISTRIBUTION OF PLEASURE AND SUFFERING

If this theory is to inform a critique of ideology, which also takes the
material dimension into account, the collective Thing ought to have a
political-economic foundation that enables it to be productive (even though
it only exists as a mental shroud that disguises its material and metaphysical nonexistence). To place the Thing in an analysis of a given political-
economic context, one must nonetheless begin with the universal lack
of symmetry between the subject and its Other. What makes the subject
able to continue as a subject is a miscognition of the Real of the Other
(and thereby themself) that occurs when one projects a fantasy that the
Other and subject share, or do not share, the Thing—the social itself. If
the Thing is a positive phenomenon, believed to end suffering and elicit
pleasure by neutralizing the Real, the political implication is that the Thing
designates the social relations where the subject and its (good) Other share
and distribute pleasure, desire, and suffering. The Thing, then, becomes the
projection of *social concern* and *solidarity* between neighbors, as suffering
and pleasure in a material world with artificial scarcity and ownership often
are expressed as poverty, redemption, and wealth. Therefore, the binary of
pleasure-suffering can here be sublimated into welfare-poverty. For each
social formation there is a "moral economy" of expected rights and duties
between subjects, classes, and the state—informed by, and informing, ideology as common sense.[14] This contextual moral economy gives "content"
to the perceived National Thing of each nation-state's population. In other
words, the "National Thing" relates to a moral economy that is believed to
be shared and honored. Those who claim to represent a certain "people"
must legitimize their power by maintaining and delivering this Thing of
a common moral economy of goods, rights, duties, suffering, pleasure,
and desire. Notably, proponents of counter-ideologies that challenge the

dominant ideology must also appeal to a moral economy that is recognized, albeit allegedly hindered or suppressed by the powerful. As none of these moral economies can ever be complete (not in class society, anyway), ideology perpetuates itself by never actually realizing the "ideal society" it proposes. Instead, it gives people a common direction in a changing world, persisting so long as it continues to mobilize subjects' anxiety and desire along those lines.

In the historical-geographical context of the Nordic countries, we might interpret "welfare society" as a metaphor for this National Thing: "welfare society" signifies the foundation making "society" into an entity of Nordic subjects in communion with each other, which also implies the societal distribution of economic and moral pleasures and sufferings. Classically, the Nordic welfare state is believed to guarantee social security (*trygghet*) to its members, which assures everyone's equality, as the dominant ideology holds that the state ought to distribute trygghet and resources in a way that is equal among classes, ages, and genders. The reciprocal relationship that "equality" implies, however, eludes the begging interaction. In contrast to Per Albin's vision of the folkhem, where everyone has trygghet and equality, "the beggar" and the EU déclassé are neither socially secured nor equal to the rest of the Swedish population (except in the humanist respect of intrinsic human dignity, maybe). In this way the EU déclassé's mere territorial presence disturbs the Symbolic aesthethical-spatial organization of the National Thing, which, in turn, causes chain reactions along the signifiers that articulate the Thing, activating fantasies of the Other's theft of the subject's Enjoyment—namely, the latter's community and ontological security. Recall the liberal former editor who argued that begging constitutes a threat to the preservation of "welfare society" on the grounds that it would make people empathically numb to the sufferings of neighbors. Given my argument that the National Thing ought to imply a belief in solidarity between subjects (bridging the alienation gap and "neutralizing" the Other's Otherness), this editor appears to believe that the "object-cause" of "welfare society" is the social bond between individuals, an Enjoyment of *solidarity* that "the beggar" threatens to steal. Here ideology not only tries to displace "the human" Real, but also the Real of itself. We discover that the material effects of welfare society do not exist due to individuals' or collectives' capacity for concern or altruistic actions. Of course, care, solidarity, and altruism obviously exist, but not in the sense of an essential substance "within" certain individuals or a *folk*. Humans do not simply make history under circumstances chosen by them—their desires are caught in the dialectical totality of class struggle, ideology, and uneven geographical development.

Another pathway for mobilizing anxieties regarding the Other's desire is, as discussed in chapter 3, in service of racialist ideologies. In this case the racial Other destroys the Thing of the racial social order. This ideology demands its own Thing of solidarity, in which the Malthusian view of the world's finite resources turns the poor's plea for sharing into a hidden attack against "the people's" Thing. This Imagined order is also applicable to the dominant ideology of welfare society, if "welfare" itself is understood to be finite and scarce. Think back to the accusations of sympathy stolen from poor and homeless Swedes when a dentist helped foreigners—a theft of Enjoyment of trygghet and equality. The political movement that convinces Swedes to attribute these anxieties to the theft of the National Thing will garner not only passionate support but also powerful political allies. An ideology that cloaks the uneven distribution *within* the national economy as "scarcity," and disavows scarcity's artificiality under capitalism, fits the interest of capital.

This observation does not only mark the end of this book's first part, where I set out to answer why begging constitutes a social problem by searching for the universal in the particular case of Sweden's mid-2010s and reflected on reactions to the presence of begging EU déclassés. In fact, this observation also hints the beginning of an answer to the following question, which set the stage for the problem central to the next part: *What happened in the Swedish begging question?*

PART 2   Hegemony

The Particular in the Universal

6   The Swedish Ideology, or Missing Exceptional Equality

In late spring of 2014, back when I interviewed the Stockholmers, Moderate prime minister Fredrik Reinfeldt fell out with SD in a debate on the latter's demand to criminalize begging: "Do not turn humans into the problem. It would be a hunt on individuals already very vulnerable, and I don't think we should argue that way."[1] Some months later he added, "One should be aware that these are poor and vulnerable people who need totally different types of efforts to get a better life than to face a prohibition on the possibility to ask others for money."[2] The same day the new leader of SAP, Stefan Löfven, stated, "Poverty is impossible to prohibit; that's something one needs to do something about," and "to prohibit begging is no solution."[3]

At Christmas time, two years later, Löfven, now prime minister, explained his party was looking for different strategies to "stop" begging, whether by prohibition or a permit system, because "it is never acceptable to have to see people get on their knees begging. It is so degrading and far away from social-democratic ideology, so somehow this must stop. [We] must show a difference, that we actually gradually make sure to remove it, because it is an inhuman situation."[4] The following year Reinfeldt's successor, Ulf Kristersson, demanded a nationwide ban on begging, arguing that nothing else works and that "we must stop begging; it is not dignified in Sweden."[5]

Before the national election of 2014, SD was the only party that supported begging legislation. Before the subsequent election in 2018, both SD and the Moderates clamored for national prohibition, whereas the Christian Democrats' and SAP's leaderships wanted to enable local legislations to draft their own laws on begging. What happened in between these years that made the leaders of both the largest left-wing and the largest right-wing party change their minds? What had previously made them agree on the moral offence of prohibition? In short, what made the dominant ideological stance on the Swedish begging question change? The short intelligible answer to what happened between the interviews of 2014 and 2016 is the so-called refugee crisis, peaking in the autumn of 2015. But how did begging relate to asylum reception, except for the superficial level of migrants being in need?

In this second section of the book I argue that the *actual* crisis that led to this political shift was one of hegemony of the Swedish state and its ruling fraction's (the national dominant) ideology. This juncture concerns the governing of the welfare-capitalist state and therefore is, ultimately, a symptom of ongoing class struggle. The political-economic contradictions that the begging question helped reveal were between capital and labor, expressed in different parts of the state complex and regarding different components of the reproduction of the social order. The threat to the hegemon was not the immigrants themselves, but the growing popular support for the radical-nationalist, ultimately fascist, counter-ideology of SD. What partially neutralized this imminence was a concession to this counter-ideology by the dominant bloc controlling the state, capital, and media, which constituted a shift in the dominant ideology's stance on Swedish "moral exceptionalism" and antiracism. Following this pivot, the ideology's moral contradiction on begging—where neither begging nor its prohibition belonged in Sweden—was successively dissolved. What I argue made the counter-ideology gain such unexpected popular support was the widespread belief that the National Thing of Swedish welfare society, or what I term *exceptional equality*, was threatened to be ruined by the racial Others crossing the border. This support, in turn, was enabled by backlash against several decades of neoliberal politics. Those steering the political field and the state initially underestimated the counter-ideology, but when a conjuncture of political and racial processes occurred in the autumn of 2015—the exceptional degree of asylum reception numbers, the growth of the visual presence of EU déclassés and their provisional settlements in public space, and the rise of terrorism against non-whites accompanied by the tremendous rise of preference for SD in opinion polls—the ruling fraction turned to coercive measures to punish migrants in order to secure their hegemonic power. However, the reversal was intended to be executed such that Sweden's ideology of moral exceptionalism and exceptional equality was spared this crushing blow. A year after arguing for the borders to be closed to refugees, as Sweden needed "breathing room" to deal with those who had already managed to enter the country, the prime minister insisted begging was "an inhuman situation" that must be "stopped."[6] Note, however, that though the dominant attitude against EU déclassés grew harsher from 2015 onward, it nevertheless took three more years of realpolitikal tactics to finally "resolve" the lingering moral contradiction on begging prohibition in Sweden.

Due to the begging question's inescapable interconnections between race and class, state and capital, ideology and reality, rights and responsibilities, space and place, and anxiety and desire, its historical evolution during the 2010s lays bare this burgeoning crisis of hegemony more clearly than many other contemporaneous social issues. Within this perfect storm, the EU déclassés' territorial presence—coupled with their external or liminal social positionality in the citizenship realm, labor market, housing market, legal field, and ideological sphere—signified the Real of Swedish ideological constructions of moral exceptionalism and the welfare-capitalist state apparatus.

In this chapter I present the Swedish ideology's configurations before and within the crisis. After explaining this ideology's political-economic history, racial structure, and place within a global context, I probe the begging question's political-historical development. Within this narrative I then investigate the begging question's political setting in order to explain how this issue intersected with a polyphony of political contradictions within the state apparatus. I have chosen to name this cluster of contradictions, which concerns short-circuits within the fields of citizenship, labor, and housing, *the Borromean welfare knot*. This knot helps explain why it grew so complicated, even for benevolent political actors, to solve the begging question in an egalitarian way. Crucially, the regulating anxieties of theft of Enjoyment safeguarded the extrication of this knot.

A Definition of Hegemony

Understanding the politics of the EU déclassés as revolving around a larger political struggle—namely, hegemony—enables us to understand the historical changes that, at first, rendered begging in Sweden "uncriminalizable" and then later made the practice in commonsensical need of policing. According to historian Jan Selling, a discursive momentum regarding Roma rights took hold in Sweden in the early 2010s, with a peak in 2013–15.[7] This momentum, which pertained to the rights of both the Swedish Roma and EU déclassés, marked the moment when the latter's situation was closest to becoming a *social* issue, which meant that there was a possibility of taking a different political path. However, this impetus was foreclosed when the begging question combined with the refugee crisis, signaling the *global* momentum and rise to prominence of racist-populism. For those in power hoping to secure their hegemony—that is, popular legitimacy—it became more important to confirm the xeno-racist wave than advocate for rights of the Roma.

Here *hegemony* is applied in a Gramscian sense, as the method by which the ruling bloc of the state maintains the dominant ideology of a given social formation. As Stuart Hall and his colleagues explain: "When a ruling class alliance has achieved an undisputed [authority,] when it masters the political struggle, protects and extends the needs of capital, leads authoritatively in the civil and ideological spheres, and commands the restraining forces of the coercive apparatuses of the state in its defense—when it achieves all this on the basis of [consent,] we can speak of the establishment of a period of hegemony or hegemonic domination."[8] Crucially, hegemony is achieved when the rulers manage to ground their governing in a combination of coercion and consent, but with an emphasis on the latter. When popular consent falters, a crisis of hegemony occurs, with counter-ideologies growing in political power, affecting common sense, electoral results, and, in turn, the state rulers' governing. Although there are always counter-ideas and oppositional interests, "the 'exceptions' to the general [rule] do not often spawn counter-ideologies capable of challenging the over-all hegemony of 'ruling ideas', thus leading on to alternative strategies of struggle which take the transformation of society as a whole as their object."[9]

The most apparent symptom of a hegemonic crisis is a change in rulers' approach to governing, going from a preponderance of strategies on extracting consent from the masses to coercion and repression. The rulers employ the latter strategy either to repress the opposition or to appease the oppositional movement questioning their legitimacy, as their governance appears to be failing in the eyes of the masses. In this story the rulers adopted the latter approach, with the objects of coercion primarily being EU déclassés, refugees, and non-white immigrants. The main oppositional force and counter-ideology is represented by SD and their growing popular support, increasingly backed by powerful fractions of capital and the Right. Whereas SD never entered governmental power or exceeded electoral/statistical support above 20 percent during the 2010s, from 2014 and onward they functioned as the parliamentary balance of power. Consequently, the dominant bloc of agonistic parties and interests made a fifth of the population into kingmakers and primary definers of societal problems, to maintain, increase, or conquer governmental power as they saw fit.

Theories on hegemony have differing answers on which actors can achieve hegemony and at what scale. According to theorist Nicos Poulantzas, "hegemony," under a capitalist mode of production, fundamentally pertains to the dominance of the political-economic system—the reign of capital. *State hegemony*, however, requires a coalition of different class fractions who together constitute a dominant bloc. Note that, within this bloc, there are two distinct fractions: the hegemonic fraction—"the one which guarantees the general interest of the alliance and whose specific interests are particularly guaranteed by the state"—and the reigning fraction—"from which the upper personnel of the state apparatuses is recruited, i.e. its political personnel in the broad sense."[10] This distinction between the two demonstrates that hegemony is not found "within" the state alone. Rather, it relies on cooperation between class fractions and actors from both the state apparatus and civil society. Additionally, it indicates hegemony can be achieved by a reigning fraction even at the expense of some of the interests of the constituent parts of this collective.

Guided by Poulantzas's observations, I understand "hegemony" as consisting of two levels, with the hegemony of capital relying on the hegemonic function of the state to fulfill the role of legitimate political ruler and monopolist of violence, a replication of the difference between the global dominant ideology and a national one. The state must be governed; therefore, its hegemony must be constantly upheld by the state's reigning fraction, which secures consent via a dominant ideology. With that said, this ideology must at times neutralize—or adapt to—harmful counter-ideologies; otherwise, it becomes replaced by them—its representatives included. It's worth noting, however, that though the hegemony of the reigning fraction of the state faces crisis on occasion, this might not—and generally does not—lead to a crisis of *capital's* hegemony. If, on the other hand, the political order collapses, which might happen if a crisis of the reigning fraction isn't curbed, this breakdown can affect the legal, social, and political structures upon which capital accumulation is based. From this perspective, all hegemons and their crises under capitalism and class society are symptoms of class struggle—the Real of capitalist class society's imagined community. This implies an unconscious dimension, as the state is governed by individuals who are also subject to the dialectics of anxiety and desire. Just as the potentiality of aggressiveness and suffering can be registered as an Imagined real threat due to the revelation of said potentiality, hegemonic gatekeepers are also susceptible to "irrational" fears. Even if it is not realistic to expect civil war or a dramatic, Mad Max–style "breakdown" of the social order at hand, the dissonances signaling the very potential of havoc can incite moral panic in the corridors of power.

The hegemony relevant in our story is the hegemony of the reigning fraction of the Swedish nation-state and the dominant ideology of this constellation. Here the reigning fraction consists of the government, the parliamentary parties' leaderships, and state bureaucrats qua officials, investigators, lawyers, social workers, and police officers. From the large-scale abstracted perspective of the reproduction of capitalist state hegemony, it doesn't much matter if the government is controlled by social-democratic or right-wing parties, since they are ultimately part of the same reigning fraction. With the institutionalization of popular-democratic politics, the established parties' representatives became increasingly merged with the governing logic of the state apparatus. Of course, struggles are played out within the fraction between parties and actors, which to a certain extent affects the content of the dominant ideology and the implemented politics of the state. When there is a crisis of state hegemony, however, and the reigning fraction registers instability in the whole of the social formation, they share an interest in maintaining order. In this way the different political antagonists in the corridors of power bear a contradictory relationship of both cooperation and competition with one another, like capitalist actors. This contradiction of interest is crucial to understanding how the right-wing and left-wing governments of the studied era can simultaneously be regarded as "enemies" and "allies," and how an initial hegemonic enemy (in this case, SD) might successfully be made an ally.

In figure 1 I map out how I believe this theory of hegemony plays out in relation to the psychoanalytic critique of ideology and the dialectic of racism as elaborated up to this point. For pedagogical reasons some faculties appear in boldface, while the topological relationships with arrows indicate the relations of influence. The purpose of this chart is primarily to facilitate this book's argument, although I believe it may prove useful to further studies engaged in the relationship between racism, capitalism, and national politics.

The dominant ideology of a nation-state territory is also the ideology of the nation. To understand how the begging question could become a symptom of the Real in Swedish ideology, we first need to concretize this ideology and its relation to the National Thing. Having married Žižekian ideology critique with a classical Marxist interpretation, I present the political-economic foundations and history of this ideology. After that we reach the ideology's racial structure, bringing us closer to the National Thing that was so greatly threatened by the presence of the begging EU déclassés.

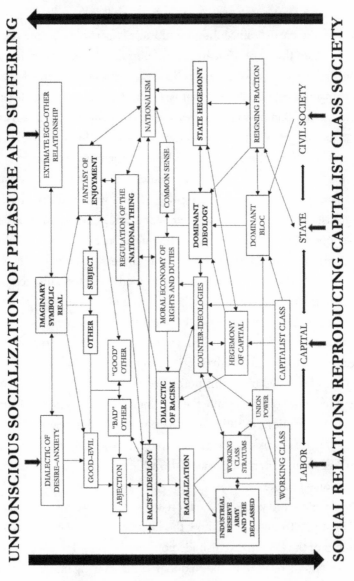

PRODUCTION OF ARTIFICIAL SCARCITY

UNCONSCIOUS SOCIALIZATION OF PLEASURE AND SUFFERING

SOCIAL RELATIONS REPRODUCING CAPITALIST CLASS SOCIETY

IDEOLOGY AS UNCONSCIOUS SOCIAL FANTASY

1. Topological map of the book's theory of hegemony. Created by author.

The Swedish Ideology's Political-Economic History

As revealed in the interviews, the relative absence of visual poverty has commonly been explained through the narrative of the successful folkhem welfare state project. Significantly, the Swedish state has a history of being perhaps one of the most omnipotent presences in the lives of anyone who resides in a liberal democracy, with a remarkably high degree of popular trust.[11] The welfare model, or *the Swedish Model*, which constitutes both the state and the associations of labor and capital, was however not the natural result of a harmonious consensus between "the Swedes" and "the state," but the outcome of struggles and compromises between different political interests throughout the twentieth century.[12] Like Gramscian common sense—and ideology in general—the Swedish Model's "morality" is a contradictory patchwork of values and interests. This has in turn made the folkhem available as a National-Thing-signifier of ideological struggle, as Left, Right, and fascism all claim to represent folkhem values and continuity.

Though the folkhem implies a nation where the weak and poor are taken care of, and where everyone treats their neighbor as an equal, Sweden has always been a class society. Indeed, historians Urban Lundberg and Klas Åmark explain that while the Scandinavian welfare states contain a broad social insurance system, they constitute "at the same time a system with strictly controlled and needs-tested poor relief/social assistance."[13] Whereas the "general principle" of Swedish welfare systems became "security against poverty and need," this general principle has been accompanied by economic and moral stipulations that determine one's eligibility, which means "the system is not treating all citizens alike, but creates and upholds differences between them, according to gender, age, place [in] the labour market, income, and so on."[14] These distinctions indicate the existence of an overarching *dual* system with two dominant categories of social safety nets in Sweden: one is "universal," tied to citizenship/residency and guarantees basic securities, and the other is based on labor performance following an income compensation principle.[15] All of this reveals a difference between ideological equality and equal treatment.

Nevertheless, this ideology proclaims equal security against suffering, guaranteed by the state and its representatives. In a nutshell, people should not have to beg in Sweden, and the state ought to take care of this. Upon inspecting this ideology's aesthethics, we observe a state responsibility to deal with both the poverty of "beggars" and the sight of them. While ideological trust in the state is constitutive to the belief in the folkhem, geographer David Jansson argues that the folkhem ultimately was a state project that aimed to create "a new, modern nation."[16] This celebration of "newness" and "modernity" is inseparable from the supposed *exceptionalism* of Swedish identity. While a given nation's belief in its own exceptionalism is embedded in the very fabric of nationalism, Sweden is among a few other "lucky" nations whose exceptionalism is corroborated by international recognition as such. Jansson explains, while distinguishing between the idea of U.S. and Swedish exceptionalism:

> "Swedish exceptionalism" is grounded primarily in the idea that the country is a "moral superpower," and this reputation has its seeds in the establishment of the welfare state (sometimes referred to as the "Swedish model") from the 1930s onward. [For] a world on the cusp of a second devastating world war in a generation, [in 1936, U.S. reporter Marquis Childs portrayed] the Swedish welfare state as an effective compromise between communism [and] capitalism, a "middle way." Thus from a political economy perspective, the Swedish model [represented] the ultimate compromise between social democracy and global capitalism.

Jansson goes on to argue that one of the folkhem subprojects aimed to create a modern nationality from above "as imagined by experts and technocrats [whereby] 'social engineers' and planners would scientifically discover and devise the most efficient and best ways to do [things]. The *folkhem* is in part a project involving the creation (we might say *engineering*) of a new, modern, Swedish subjectivity."[17] If we set aside how exceptional the social engineering of Sweden was (or is), it is not farfetched to argue this "post-political" view of planning and social policy—as a matter of expertise—is a massive aspect of Sweden's self-image. Consider, for example, how two researchers interpreted Sweden's latest exceptionalism, namely, its COVID-19 strategy (guiding recommendations rather than lockdowns or restrictions): "Sweden's democratic system of government has a more pronounced epistocratic element than other comparable countries."[18]

It's worth considering whether this belief in technocratic rationalism as a substitute for politics is an ideological reflection of the material base, as the Swedish model of labor market politics has, since the 1930s, been based on negotiation and compromise between representatives of labor unions and capital, with as little intervention from the state as possible. Potentially, the common thread between this economic arrangement and the technocratic element is a belief in *rationality*: there is a pragmatic way to do things, which idealism and passions hinder. Since Swedish class struggle was robust in the early twentieth century, with recurrent strikes and a close shave with revolution in 1917, capital benefited from a peaceful, collaborative labor movement—the most well-organized working class of the world, according to historian Erik Bengtsson.[19]

THE SOCIAL-DEMOCRATIC APPEAL

This brings us to Swedish social democracy and its dominant role in shaping the social formation, state, and ideology. SAP has been the largest party since the official introduction of "universal" suffrage in 1921 and has for the following hundred years held governmental power for seventy-six years combined. By disavowing revolution in favor of reforming capitalism, SAP's leadership has continuously presented themselves as a voice of reason and fairness, representing not only workers but also the *folk* of Sweden.[20] In the late 1880s the workers' movement founded both the SAP and the Swedish Trade Union Confederation (Landsorganisationen i Sverige, or LO), initiating an ongoing alliance between the two that has allowed the former to rely upon labor's support in the class struggle while they attend to the responsibilities of being the nation's fathers. With its reformist brand of state capitalism, SAP conceptualized the folkhem as the harmonious home of the Swedish people, where labor and capital cooperate with one another, and individual freedom and collective responsibility can coexist frictionlessly. As mentioned, when Swedish ideology encountered the begging question, this ideology was very much that of the SAP, as they have been the dominating political force to which ideology's other interests must refer. That SAP managed to hegemonize its ideology can be credited to their and LO's mid-twentieth-century economic policy (including the Rehn-Meidner model), which established income security as the dominating principle in Swedish welfare systems. This means socioeconomic trygghet is guaranteed in cases of sick leave or unemployment, with payouts that correlate to one's income. Because this generous system benefited "all" wage laborers, not just the lower working-class fractions, it helped to win the support of its middle strata.[21]

It was also this shared *class-conscious* interest between the lower- and middle-class fractions of workers that helped to explain the historical ideological cohesion and consent for the folkhem project in the first two-thirds of the twentieth century in Sweden. As Bengtsson explains, in the nineteenth and early twentieth centuries, the Swedish monarchy was an exceptionally unequal and undemocratic country in comparison to the rest of the West.[22] Although a cultural Sonderweg from the precapitalist ages is commonly understood to have laid the groundwork for modern Swedish "equality," the fact is that Swedish politics from that time period were controlled by a plutocracy of the landed aristocracy, bourgeoisie, and wealthy farmers, who opposed democratic reforms. In this way the socioeconomic and political inequality of the Swedish oligarchic state paved the way for a broad and strong socialist-liberal alliance between the manual, agricultural, and intellectual working classes, struggling for both economic and political equality. To compare, Germany's class struggle turned into a united front of the middle and upper classes against the lower strata, facilitating the road to fascist hegemony.[23] Whereas Germanic interwar fantasies of the theft of Enjoyment became effectively exploited in favor of a hegemonic anti-Semitism that legitimized corporatism, the Swedish political landscape enabled the lack of Enjoyment to become progressive, where Enjoyment of the National Thing was envisioned as a part of the future-to-come, not lost in the past. In the Swedish imagination, therefore, this "futuristic" Thing wasn't stolen or destroyed, but withheld—and not by a racial Other, but a "plutocratic" Other. Gradually, this Thing became incorporated into the folkhem state with the aim of creating (what Jansson termed) "a new, modern, Swedish subjectivity."

But what about the ancien régime of the Right? Following Norway's 1905 disaffiliation from its forced union with Sweden, and in the zeitgeist of the fin de siècle, conservatives sought political inspiration in corporatism and "national socialism"—a pivot facilitated by the historical bonds between Prussia's and Sweden's intellectuals. In fact, conservative political scientist Rudolf Kjellén, famous for coining the term "geopolitics," invoked the folkhem concept even before SAP did. In his usage, folkhem was similar to the German Volksgemeinschaft, which would become a sort of signifier for the Nazi ideology's Thing. If we compare the socialist and reactionary interpretations of the folkhem, the common thread was a harmonization between territory and nationalist fraternity. Without claiming the folk-hem concept itself, but appealing to the reactionary Thing, the Moderates (then Allmänna valmansförbundet) initially embraced Hitler's seizure of power. In 1933 they formed vigilance committees and held a great mass meeting "against bolshevism and class struggle," where speakers celebrated Germany's "national revolution."[24] This occurred within a political crisis in which SAP had not yet achieved state hegemony: while SAP had won the previous year's election (after the military killed five unarmed workers during a demonstration), SAP struggled to secure their parliamentary majority, and a new election was on the horizon. When Hitler dismantled the bourgeois parties that had helped him ascend to power that same autumn, and SAP began to cooperate with the Farmers' League (today's Center Party), the Moderate's leadership did a volte-face and condemned authoritarianism, prompting their youth movement to break with the party to become full-blown supporters of Nazism. Though the political fortunes of this radical-right movement, Sweden's National Association, withered away following the Second World War, they appear to be SD's closest pre-decessors.[25] Amid all this tumult, the Left-reformist signification of the folkhem Thing became dominant, while the Moderates lost the leadership of the Right to the Liberals and the Center Party.

The late 1960s marked an ideological shift, with growing leftist criticism of SAP and its welfare state for being alienating and conformist. Post–oil crisis, this critique came to be monopolized by the Right.[26] As neoliberalism spread in the early 1980s throughout the world, SAP came to be controlled by politicians representing a neoliberal "Third Way" economic policy (this time in between neoliberalism and Keynesianism), and the deregulations and privatizations of the welfare state took off—and continued ever since. Consequently, the Swedish ideology became saturated with libertarian values on freedom of choice and "entrepreneurship," as well as a greater emphasis on *deservingness* in social care. In my interviews I noted a marked presence of the notion of individual freedom, as a majority were against begging bans on principle—it was a restriction of an individual's right to freedom of expression. Ever since the dawn of the welfare state, humanist individualism has been part of the Swedish ideology, thanks in large part to the working-class alliance with liberal reformist intelligentsia, the tee-totalers, and the Free Churches.[27] As a matter of fact, what usually strikes international observers of Swedes as exceptional is the degree of individualism and anti-traditionalist values. Post-1968, however, individualism was successfully appropriated by the Right following a conjuncture of critiques of SAP's "state authoritarianism" from both the Left and neoliberals. Indeed, the abolition of begging legislation in 1982, following the introduction of a new more humanistic Social Service Act, might have been a symptom of this convergence.

As in other countries, the "individualization" of the dominant ideology went hand in hand with changes to the political economy. The Swedish welfare state, after all, was founded on the social relation between industrial capital and industrial labor.[28] However, due to Sweden's economy being heavily based on industrial exports—thanks to Sweden's ability to stay out of WWII, subsequent availability to supply both war-ridden Europe and the liberated colonial world with the goods they required, and an ideal geopolitical location—the stagflation crisis of the early 1970s called for structural reforms. To enhance finance capital circulation among both businesses and households, SAP deregulated all financial markets in 1985. Increasingly, the dominating capitalist actors shifted from hired business leaders to pure capital owners. At the same time, a real estate bubble frothed until its crash in the early 1990s, which sparked the country's greatest financial crisis since the Depression. This crisis, in turn, was ideologically interpreted as a failure of "the too big public sector," with both right-wing and SAP governments passing harsh reforms, including public sector cutbacks, the decentralization of social care, and the termination of a national housing policy. It was in this aftermath that the first recurrence of begging occurred.

The Moderates, for their part, regained their role as leaders of the Right opposition in the late 1970s. By changing their ideology to liberal conservatism, a better fit for the neoliberal strategy, they appeared to be closer to the folkhem ideology's proclamation of *political* equality than old-fashioned reactionism. In the first decade of the 2000s, the Moderate's leader Fredrik Reinfeldt successfully rebranded his party as the New Moderates, an appropriation of the UK's New Labour and Germany's centrified Christian Democratic Union. They framed themselves as the "new labor party," embracing a doctrine of neoliberal workfare with a (somewhat) "welfare-friendly" discourse. With the party thus revamped, Reinfeldt then forged a coalition with the remaining three right-wing parties (the Liberals, the Center Party, and the Christian Democrats) called the Alliance, which seized power for two mandate periods: reigning 2006–14. Crucial to their electoral victory was their targeted criticism of public health insurance, presented as too generous and exploited by cheaters. Put differently, their victory was due to their successful mobilization of the fantasy of theft of Enjoyment of the welfare society, as they promised to restore the nation's lost industriousness and comradeship through the signifier of "work."[29] This counter-ideology succeeded because it convinced enough people there really were "Others out there" stealing Enjoyment at the expense of hardworking people, which further implied a moral economy in which some people are undeserving of welfare. While benefits have always been conditional, this way the dominant ideology became suffused with a considerable degree of jaundice against the poor—against the Other. It implied and facilitated a shift in class alliances, with a shared interest between the upper and middle classes against the lower layers of the working class and against the declassed—who, due to the changing racial composition of the population, became increasingly non-white.

Of course, this revanchist ideology would not have won people's hearts and become fused within the dominant ideology if it was not for Sweden's growing socioeconomic inequalities, which had already begun to swell in the 1980s but later became anchored to the ramifications of the 1990s crisis. In 2015 an OECD (Organization for Economic Co-operation and Development) report stated that in Sweden, "the growth in inequality between 1985 and the early 2010s was the largest among all OECD countries, increasing by one third."[30] While the report grants that "Sweden still belongs to the group of most equal OECD countries," this membership, as political economist Sandro Scocco argues, is only attributable to the increasing inequality in all other countries. To put the numbers in perspective, contemporary Swedish inequality rates are similar to the United States in the 1980s, and back then the United States was already considered an unequal country.[31] Before the 1990s, Swedish unemployment was roughly 2 percent, but since then 7 percent has become the average figure.[32]

As it was SAP that governed during the aftermath of the financial crisis (1994–2006), a number of voters ultimately concluded that the party had failed to deliver the dominant ideology's promised National Thing. As a result parliament has been dominated by right-wing parties since 2006, which has made SAP dependent, on the one hand, on the internal splits of the Right and, on the other, the neither-left-nor-right Environmental Party and the Left Party to secure a majority. The latter, which until 1991 was named the Left Communist Party, has been continuously stigmatized by both the Right and SAP, as their historical fidelity to Moscow made them a threat to SAP's and LO's cooperation with capital. With that said, they have always championed SAP governing before the Right, which made them, on the whole, a safe ally. Although their current ideology and program is similar to that of SAP in its heyday, they, with some exceptions, never exceed 6 percent of the votes. Therefore, in the wake of the public's loss of trust, SAP's shrinkage has diminished the potential to pass progressive reforms in parliament. Even if SAP was to go to the left, their prospects remain the same, as too many workers turned to the Moderates in the beginning of the 2000s and then to SD in the 2010s.

The Moderates, naturally, must have known their political power depended upon their ability to refrain from explicitly attacking the ideology of folk-hem equality. It was from this perspective that their politics followed with maneuvers that did not bury the ideology but slowly excavated its material base. Although the Alliance's policies were neoliberal, and welfare was extensively privatized during their tenure, they never attacked social security systems benefiting the middle and upper stratums—such as child allowance and paternal leave. Their deregulation of the health-care and education sectors into free choice markets with public and private alternatives kept the services tax funded but enabled private companies to receive the same public funding as public competitors without hindering profit outtakes. To put this in perspective, the only school system similar to contemporary Sweden was that of Chile until 2015.[33] In 2015 the revenue on welfare services was 32 percent, compared to 20 percent for the whole service sector.[34] While health care and education were still formally free of charge, hospitals and schools turned into "winners" and "losers." That way the upper-class strata maintained the privileges of the "universal" folkhem model, while the lower classes became increasingly disadvantaged. In this vein, the National Thing of the folkhem was gradually transformed into a contradictory *split object* of neoliberalist infiltration and social-democratic values. Increasingly hollowed from within and more and more excluding the poorest, the welfare state is incrementally becoming a folkhem for the well-off. While the number of billionaires has increased from 35 in 1997 to 206 in 2019, and the country's richest 1 percent's share of the total wealth was estimated at 41.9 percent in 2017, the state ideology of "equality" prevailed, with representatives of both labor and capital making respective ideological use of it.[35] Even so, the contradictions of this paradoxical ideology continued to grow, and hegemony's treatment of the EU déclassés became symptomatic of this.

The Swedish Ideology's Racial Structure

In 2010, the same year that I understand the begging question arose, SD entered parliament with 5.6 percent of votes.[36] Remarkably, Jimmie Åkesson, their leader since 2005, has claimed his political role model is Per Albin Hansson (the Social Democrat who popularized the folkhem concept); in fact, he wrote a book called *The Modern Folkhem*.[37] Just as the Moderates labeled themselves as "the new labor party," SD has presented themselves as the last defenders of the Swedish welfare society. When they call themselves "social conservatives" to obfuscate their racialist and fascist values, the aspect of this "conservatism" most appealing to supporters is, in all likelihood, nostalgia for "the golden years" of the folkhem. In this mythical folkhem, not only did no one have to beg, but there also weren't any *nonwhite* people stealing Swedes' Enjoyment of welfare, trygghet, and solidarity. This appropriation of the folkhem myth, in which the National Thing qua equality is redefined as "racial similarity," is a dialectical reemergence of the signifier of the proto-fascists, wherein the folkhem's enemies are the national traitors of socialism, liberalism, and racial Others. Because historical traces of notions of racial homogeneity are embedded in the Swedish ideology's fabled harmonious national home of the *folk*, we must revisit the Swedish historical dialectics of racism to better understand how the racial dimension of Swedish ideology became mobilized during the begging question's timespan.

It's worth repeating the notion that the racialization of the begging question isn't merely attributable to the commonsensical aspect of relevant "beggars" as foreign language–speaking noncitizens. As state and popular anti-Roma racism has spanned five hundred years alongside other racisms, it naturally affects Swedish common sense and perceptions of what the problem with EU déclassés' begging is. With that said, Sweden also has a modern history and international reputation as an *antiracist* nation, in light of its protest of imperialist wars, opposition to apartheid, and standing as the greatest international aid donor. In 1975 parliament voted for Sweden to become Europe's first official multicultural nation, and the country has taken great pride in proclaiming its anti-nationalistic sentiments. From this perspective, excessive patriotism has been commonly regarded with suspicion, and it was not until 2005 that the National Day became a public holiday. According to researchers Tobias Hübinette and Catrin Lundström, this seeming contradiction is a century-long development of the Swedish *whiteness regime*, encompassing three phases: White purity/Old Sweden, White solidarity/Good Sweden, and White melancholy. This trifecta helps us to historicize Swedish racial capitalism.

THE POLITICAL ECONOMY OF WHITE SOLIDARITY

Prior to WWII, the nationalist project mobilized the myth of Swedes as the whitest of the white—the embodiment of Eurocentric beauty standards involving blondness and blue eyes. Although Swedish *territory* has always accommodated different ethnicities, the Swedish *nation* has been remarkably homogenous. While Finns, Jewish people, the Roma, the Sami, and others have lived in the realm for centuries, the dominant ethnos has been (population-wise and culturally) domineering to such an extent that the minorities have been continuously subalternized.

With its aggrandizement as one of the world's wealthiest and most equal countries, Sweden has been branded as a solidary, "colorblind" nation. As the race concept is commonly thought to be inseparable from racism qua Nazis, Swedish discourse has widely treated theories of critical race studies and racialization as an awkward import from U.S. discourse. However, Hübinette and Lundström argue that the whiteness regime of Good Sweden constituted a white supremacy of antiracist whiteness, explaining: "Proclaiming 'good whiteness' was in fact the ultimate white position in this era of decolonisation and civil rights movements, and Sweden without doubt played this part *the best*."[38] What's more, Swedes became so white that they became, in a way, noncolored—elevated beyond race. Notably, in the late 1960s, Sweden was a pioneer in non-European adoption, which was sanctioned by several influential voices as a necessity to diversify the racial landscape and teach Swedes to shed lingering xenophobic sentiments.[39] For decades Swedish nationalism has been an inversion of explicit patriotic celebration, with Swedes too "enlightened" to indulge in such charades. One might link this "anti-nationalist nationalism" to the folkhem celebration of modernity, as well as the narcissist mirroring of the "big Other" of U.S. cultural imperialism. Equally worth pointing out is that these values benefited the Swedish political economy, which had strong economic ties to the "Third World," and, following the postwar economic boom in the 1950s–60s, required significant labor immigration to maintain and expand the accumulation of capital, as well as welfare schemes. To this end, immigrants during 1950–2014 generated 85 percent of employment growth and expanded the economy by a fifth.[40]

With an ageing population, Sweden will require large immigration flows to *maintain* a contemporary degree of welfare produced. This implies, alongside practical considerations, an ideological interest on behalf of the welfare state itself of maintaining a dominant antiracist ideology—that is, if we understand the "welfare state" as a coagulation of interests of both labor and capital. The former benefits from the maintenance of a united front against the destructive fantasy of theft of Enjoyment. If racism qua ideology is dominantly articulated, bitterness toward the Other's Enjoyment becomes a powerful threat to working-class solidarity. In terms of capital, labor immigration fills the opposite ideological function: the layering and splitting of the working class into interclass competition. At the same time, capital demands social order and cooperation among classes in order to avoid upsetting production and circulation; domestic "race wars," after all, tend not to be good for business.[41] In this way fractions of capital benefit from siding either with racist or antiracist ideologies, depending on what is forecast to secure *the order* of production. In the Swedish context, both capital and the welfare state have encouraged labor migration due to foreign labor power's lower costs. From this perspective Swedish capital's ideological actors have also traditionally embraced an "antiracist" stance—inviting white and non-white workers to get along with one another. Accordingly, the modern Swedish Right has since WWII generally proclaimed anti-nationalism—Reinfeldt, for example, was a stubborn opponent of SD.[42] Therefore, as it has managed to secure contradicting interests of labor and capital, Swedish colorblindness has been hegemonic.

With that said, capital only desires immigration that is exploitable within the existing national labor market's demands. Simultaneously, the cooperating unions only desire the level of *labor* migration that does not threaten to circumvent (and then hollow out) the collective bargaining agreements and social security systems. In light of these parameters, let us consider how EU déclassés fit into the picture: the ideal-typical EU déclassé is (formally) nonskilled, as they often do not have, or cannot prove, previous labor experience. Further, they lack the relevant language (Swedish or English) or literacy. To be under serious consideration for employment in the contemporary *formal* Swedish labor market, one is expected to have graduated from upper secondary school (which is free of charge for Swedish residents). As such, "low-skilled" formal job opportunities that do not demand these qualifications are objects of *global* competition—most berry pickers, for example, are migrant workers from countries such as Thailand, Bulgaria, and Ukraine.[43] As neither labor nor capital desires the immigration of the declassed street worker, they become a symptom of the Real of both standpoints' Imaginary and Symbolic. Because of their contextual "unemployability," this position of combined political and economic exclusion does not structurally constitute a threat to either side in the class struggle. They might, however, become a resource in the class struggle, if anxious fantasies entangled in the lived reality of racism and racialization target them as an abject or an intruder, stealing Enjoyment.

Notably, the specific positionality of the EU déclassé did not exist during the age of Good Sweden, as the country never held its borders unconditionally open. Before Sweden's, Romania's, and Bulgaria's membership in the EU and its legislation of free movement, the unemployed could not immigrate to Sweden legally if they had not managed to get refugee status. In 1969, for example, world-famous antiracist SAP prime minister Olof

Palme explained why forty-seven French Roma who had survived the Holocaust and fled from continuous persecution did not deserve asylum in Sweden: "We can't cope with receiving so many Gypsies in Sweden."[44]

In lieu of free movement, the regime maintained the "original" Swedish Model, which aimed to help "deserving" immigrants become equal social and economic members of society—though not immediately. Because they are new to the country, immigrants tend to populate the lower ranks of the workforce. In other words, this position is not only a product of discrimination; there are objective knowledge barriers that one encounters in a new land. According to Scocco, this (racialized) layering was supposed to be compensated with the technologies of social mobility: those on the bottom rung with lower incomes are meant to gradually elevate.[45] In this way Good Sweden intersected with the folkhem-Keynesian policy, which redistributed incomes according, first and foremost, to a life-cycle perspective through the social insurances—funded by the individual's own labor participation. While this model always accepted income inequalities, the existence of ladder steps within an "exceptional-equal" society was legitimized by the idea that *everyone* was supposed to advance socioeconomically. It was along these lines that the American dream was collectivized, but with an "intervening state" regulating institutionalized "trickle-down effects." This socioeconomic elevation only works by minimizing the low-income sector—if the latter is kept tight, while growth continues, workers advance upward; otherwise, the low-income sector expands. That way, the immigrated workforce fulfills the reformist political economy's purpose of maintaining a foundational low-income sector—performing the labor that natives no longer want to do themselves yet cannot do without—while not broadening this sector. Fundamental to the success of upward mobility in this model—even for those entering at the bottom—is the implementation of social equality in interactions with social institutions. Namely, class inequality is supposed to be offset by *equal access* to a relatively high standard of social security in terms of access to education, social and cultural capital, housing standard, and income.[46] All these levels of equality have gradually decreased in Sweden alongside an expansion of the low-income sector—a result of political reforms favoring capital's interests. Capital, after all, prefers the expansion of the low-income sector and immigrant labor competing within this sector. Even if capital tends to side with anti-immigration and populist Right politics, it will, for this reason, never abide a total closing of the border. Instead, the ultimate fantasy would be immigrant workers without rights, desperate enough to accept any wage and conditions, however inadequate, and a breaking of worker solidarity with the unions so that these circumstances become the reality of every worker.[47]

In sum, while the political economy of the Swedish welfare state depends upon internal class inequalities (not to mention its need for an uneven world economy as to exploit labor power abroad) and desires racialization of the national labor force, it nevertheless disseminated a dominant ideology of social and racial equality—contradictorily (but not paradoxically) benefiting the interest of capital and labor. To uphold such a multilayered ideological meaning of "equality" as a moral good—with "equality" implying social, political, economic, gender, and racial parity—a dominant commonsensical construction of *fairness* is required, which is expected to be upheld by the state. Such an idea of fairness is at once a source of solidarity and envy. A perception of fairness, where, in Per Albin's words, *no one is favored*, is the condensed outcome of the class relations' buttressing a National Thing of "exceptional equality." Of course, though giving EU déclassés real resources of poverty alleviation—housing, livelihood, education, health care—would in no way be favorizing in a material sense, it would, in the lived ideological reality (in individuals' Imaginary relationship to their Real conditions), be perceived as favoring.[48] This is because the "ordinary" working (white) people don't attain Enjoyment for free but have to earn it like everyone else. Hence, social policies that explicitly aim to accommodate certain minority groups always risk incurring xeno-racist backlashes. This, by the way, is why the Swedish welfare model of the twentieth century became commonly supported—egalitarian redistribution must appeal to the universal and appear to be universal, in order to secure electoral consent.

When SAP governments reduced labor immigration as the economic boom slowed down, greater emphasis was placed on refugee immigration. Since then Sweden became (in)famous for its relatively liberal refugee policy (with a fluctuating degree of "humanitarianism"). Increasingly, immigrants arrived from farther away from the Nordic realm, while simultaneously the neoliberal paradigm gained new ground. In this way the latter's restructuring of the welfare state intersected with the increasing presence of non-white Swedes. Significantly, these two correlating (not causal) trends continued until the appearance of the EU déclassés.

At the transition to the 1990s, a conjuncture of events seriously destabilized Good Sweden's self-image. In 1989, a year after SD's founding, the SAP government radically albeit temporarily harshened the refugee policy to counter the record number of refugees, many of whom were Bulgarian Turks. Simultaneously, white power movements gained popularity among youth, while riots, murders, and arsons (against refugee accommodations) spread in concurrence with the eleven shootings of non-whites by a lone-wolf terrorist called "The Laser Man." Right before the financial crisis escalated, a xenophobic-populist party, Ny Demokrati, entered parliament. Although this party imploded after the following election, the asylum policy went back to "normal," and reports of racist violence decreased, it nevertheless became more difficult to deny the existence of a "race question" in Sweden.[49] Furthermore, Sweden's racial composition has, in tandem with the radical increase in the inequality rate, heterogenized in a relatively short period of time: in 2000, 11.3 percent of the population was foreign-born, with the majority originating from Finland. Meanwhile, in 2020 the figure rose to 19.7 percent, with the majority now from Syria and Iraq.[50] Notably, this fifth of the population is overrepresented in the roughly fifth of Swedish labor power who has become precariatized (facing insecure employment or unemployment) in the wake of the 1990s crisis responses and then the Alliance's structural reforms.[51] Due to their lower rate of long-term employment, this demographic has lower possibilities to fund their welfare than the rest of the population. With a growing racial feature of the industrial reserve army, and the accompanied racialization of residential segregation, there should be an escalation of racist fantasies that the Other desires one's job, money, and welfare—especially since the rising inequality rate has deprived people of goods that they feel morally entitled to. When the Alliance scapegoated the benefit receivers, it was unconsciously understood among many, I dare to say, that the sector of the unemployed in need of being "activated" and forced to work was, most likely, "immigrants."

To articulate a collective perception of a simultaneous loss of both previous whiteness regimes, Hübinette and Lundström christen their third regime "White melancholy." This white melancholia, I argue, is then reproduced in the reactions to the spatial presence of racialized begging individuals in what is supposed to be one of the world's most modern, prosperous, and equal countries. Within this framework, support for sd and begging bans signifies the mourning of Swedish white purity, whereas its counterpoint laments Swedish white solidarity and opposes bans. With that said, it's not that simple: the "white solidary" Sweden image did not contain begging, and, what's more, defending the presence of begging would risk engendering a social acceptance of racial discrimination and impoverishment.

Post-Exceptional-Equality Melancholia

"White melancholy" is inspired by cultural theorist Paul Gilroy's concept of "postimperial melancholia," which designates white England's disavowal of the loss of senses of omnipotence: the loss of (Colonial) Empire, or to rephrase, their National Thing.[52] Broadening the national melancholia relevant to this story—and, indeed, the rest of the book—I argue that the analytical signifier for the National Thing of the folkhem might be conceptualized as *exceptional equality*. This means institutional and popular responses to the begging question express a Swedish *post-exceptional-equality melancholia*. In other words, the folkhem proclaims not only equality, but exceptional equality, as the national ego-ideal has depicted Sweden as an exceptionally modern, solidary, equal nation—a moral superpower. Speaking of a melancholic feeling toward equality instead of whiteness helps us bridge the themes of racism and capitalism, if "equality" is, in this context, understood to imply a racial dimension.

Freud distinguished between mourning and melancholia, writing, "In mourning it is the world which has become poor and empty; in melancholia it is the ego itself."[53] This recalls Lacan's topology of anxiety, where the subject loses itself (that is, the believed ego–Other relationship). In mourning, the subject grieves a lost external object. With the subject's ego lost, the mourning process is wrenched, as the subject, on an unconscious level, cannot come to terms with whether the object is truly missing. Consequently, the sense of loss is internalized but not actually confronted: the subject submits to repeated acts of suffering while repudiating the loss.

It is useful to marry this purport of melancholia with the fantasy of theft of Enjoyment, as the latter disavows "the traumatic fact that we never possessed what was allegedly stolen from us."[54] The melancholic fantasy of loss or theft of the National Thing also helps us understand the curious *repetitive* character of this perception of social disintegration and national loss. While some commentators would argue that Sweden's exceptionalism was lost in 2022 once and for all due to SD's successful election and the abandonment of the country's centuries-long neutrality policy with its NATO application, already in 2000 geographer Allan Pred argued Swedish exceptionalism was forfeit in the 1990s due to the financial crisis, racist violence, and a racialized labor and housing market.[55] However, some would argue this exceptional equality had already vanished in 1986, when Olof Palme was murdered. Then again, the year 1976 might also suffice as heralding "the end" of the folkhem: SAP lost governmental power for the first time since 1936; there was an inflation crisis; and entertainers sang "Var blev ni av ljuva drömmar?" (Where did our dreams go?), referring to SAP's abandonment of their old aspirations. Or take the origin of Nordic noir, the social realist crime novels about police detective Martin Beck, written in 1965–75 by Maj Sjöwall and Per Wahlöö, which were collectively titled *The Story of a Crime*.[56] Notably, the stories' overarching crime was the slow deterioration of Swedish welfare society, as SAP betrayed the working class. Although writing from a communist perspective, Sjöwall and Wahlöö's depiction of social deprivation and poverty in the folkhem was but one addition to a more general critique in the late 1960s of the "unfinished welfare" and class society disguised behind the facade of equality.

Throughout modern Swedish history, there appears to be a cyclic repetition of the sense of loss of Swedish exceptional equality and a cyclic repetition of melancholic denial as a defense mechanism. Here, the psychoanalytic lesson is that this object never existed in the first place. Nevertheless, we observe an unconscious experience of this phantasmatic object *being lost* and an inability to accept it. The concept of the National Thing, as a structural property of ideology, allows us to realize there is nothing exceptional about Sweden feeling this sense of *lack*, as it is both constitutional for subjectivity and for the imagined community itself. However, while it's possible to argue that there was "always" a golden age and it was "always" better before, this sense of loss becomes more urgent in times of crisis, whether perceived or actual: in short, when social anxieties regarding the possibility of scarcity and violence are accumulating. As we have seen, the 1990s were such a period in Sweden, as were the 2010s. The main difference between those phases is that during the 1990s, SAP's parliamentary dominance was not broken, and SD was a marginal party—still considered racist and neo-Nazi, which explains their ban on Nazi uniforms during meetings in 1996.[57] This time around, to an unprecedented extent, Swedish post-exceptional-equality melancholia became a crisis of hegemony on behalf of the state and its rulers.

A FIFTY-YEAR MELANCHOLIA OF DEMOCRATIC CAPITALISM?

When SD entered parliament in 2010, this constituted a national shock, as it was commonly believed exceptional Sweden was spared the parliamentary presence of far-right parties.[58] Be that as it may, the political, economic, and social developments of Sweden are not spared from global processes. It would be naive to expect the growing support for racist counter-ideologies in Sweden to be only the causal outcome of national politics; the rise of authoritarian, racist populism was global, and the pathway of Swedish political economy and unconscious symptomizes the universal of global capitalism's development. After all, the cyclical activation of collective melancholia is not limited to Sweden: anxieties on the loss of white England were prominent during the 1960s–70s, early years of the 2000s, and Brexit.[59] What's more, it's academic common sense nowadays that "neoliberalism" has been politically relevant since at least the 1980s—perhaps earlier, since its initial infiltration into economic policy emerged in the late 1960s. Additionally, in the Global North, widespread popular perceptions hold that everything was better in the shimmering postwar decades until the 1970s crisis, the "neoliberal shift," and "globalization." In other words, whereas the golden age lasted for roughly twenty-five years (1945–70), the neoliberal global regime of capital accumulation will have soon reigned for double that time span. Just like the recurrent anxiety on the folkhem Thing's evanescence, there appears to be a temporal correlation on a global scale in (at minimum) the Global North regarding the loss of the "harmonious" Keynesian, and white, era. Might we understand this global melancholia regarding the slow putrefaction of societal Enjoyment (of the desirable, pleasurable fantasy of non-alienated communion between strangers) to be *one single* fluctuating political "crisis" ranging for over half a decade?

Economic sociologist Wolfgang Streeck argues the international economic crisis of the early 1970s might be understood as not yet over, if we understand the subsequent political-economic development as a delayed crisis of democratic capitalism. Since the Great Depression, states worldwide have deployed three successive strategies of maintaining the expenditures needed to keep a political-social equilibrium, where capitalism and popular democracy can coexist. Without fail, all three phases culminated in a great crisis, with the subsequent paradigm setting out to avoid the pitfalls of the preceding one. When postwar economic growth stagnated in the 1970s, the ideal-typical "tax state" was replaced by the "debt state," where state indebtedness would compensate for the lack of growth without increasing taxation on the capitalist class. Next, in the 1990s, the new norm became the "consolidation state." To facilitate the cutting of public expenditures, public debt was transferred into private debt through financialization:

"a large-scale experiment of taking away from the state the investment necessary for the future of a capitalist political economy" and its citizens.[60] This
development represents a cyclical repetition of crises, for each one further
"de-democratizing" the state as inequality steadily rises, unemployment
rates grow, central banks escape public accountability, and governments
do what's necessary to fulfill capital's dictates to attract investments. As
Streeck argues, these "monetary methods of generating illusions of growth
and prosperity" have progressively diverted the national-political conflict's
scene away from average citizens' daily lives and their capacity to partake.[61]
The scene successively shifted from the union's wage struggle to parliamentary elections, then to private loan and insurance markets, and then, finally,
"to a realm of international financial diplomacy completely remote from
everyday life, whose issues and strategies were a closed book for everyone
except those directly involved, and perhaps even for them too."[62]

While this thesis is compatible with our understanding of the politics of
hegemony, the question remains: Is there a causality between these cyclical
capitalist crises and the cyclical loss of the National Thing? I believe so.
Compare the rather absurd continuous ritual of lamenting the folkhem since
the 1970s to this day with the attempts to postpone democratic capitalism's
ragnarök (end of the world)—each phase moving the Thing of democratic
power and social equality further from the public realm. In its own way,
the Swedish government's and the class fractions' controlling of the state
has followed the same script, which has postponed the acceptance of the
loss of the folkhem by hollowing it out from within, at a pace slow enough
to maintain the ideology with its increasing contradictions. The growing
support for authoritarian populism—in Sweden as elsewhere—becomes
even more intelligible if we understand this development as a "return of
the repressed" desire for the Thing qua the cessation of suffering (artificial
scarcity), ideologically transferred into the eradication of the Other stealing
the Thing (causing suffering). It then becomes historically specific if we
interpret the mobilized racist passions as a displaced melancholy regarding
the loss of expected democratic influence over one's own life.

This analysis is not intended to downplay the political force of racist fantasies themselves; cognitively, the anxiety of the Other's desire precedes the class struggle. Thinking back to Stuart Hall, however, and his question regarding the circumstances that give racism "its effectivity, as a concrete material force," the general answer to this query is conditions that facilitate fears of losing access to the Thing. For racial hostility to become politically relevant, racial Others' territorial presence must be successfully ideologized as a threat to one's relationship to Enjoyment. In the 2010s a conjuncture of political, economic, and social changes, which was global in scope, produced just such an Imaginary, which was shared by enough people that it became a powerful counter-ideology against the dominant ideology of political liberalism generally and, in Sweden, the neoliberalized social-democratic national ideology of exceptional equality.

Since the stagnation of productivity in the 1970s, we have witnessed a "return" to the capitalist geopolitical core of Marx's "primitive accumulation," in the shape of what geographer David Harvey terms "accumulation by dispossession."[63] In short, capital has found a way to extract value through enclosures of previous common goods, such as public welfare institutions. This geographical "inversion" through the exploitation of the capitalist core by dismantling previous historical victories of organized labor (when labor power is imported from the world economy's peripheries, and there isn't any serious geopolitical counterforce of "socialist nationalism," nor any continents left to steal in order to absorb European "surplus populations") prepares the reemergence of popular nationalism.[64] Significantly, this reversing wave of colonial dispossession is reflected in the change of the previous dominant configuration of the social Thing of Enjoyment from a lack to a loss: from being potentially feasible in an optimistic vision of the future to utterly impossible due to the perceived inevitability of widespread sociopolitical regression (brought on by global warming, or the return of feudalism by the superrich or Eurabia).

It is clear that the EU déclassés' presence in Sweden is a *symptom* of these global processes, as they unfolded after the latest global financial crisis of 2007–8, which originated as a U.S. housing bubble. This starting point of the crisis of the "consolidation state" spread across the Atlantic, where the Euro crisis not only affected Portugal, Ireland, Italy, Greece, and Spain, but also Romania and Bulgaria, which had recently joined the EU and adopted its free movement principle. While economic recession in the East encouraged labor migration westward, Southern Europe's crises swept jobs away from Romanian Roma (and others), prompting many of them to travel to France and then be expelled to beg in Sweden and elsewhere. Moreover, the financial crisis functioned as one of the triggers of the Egyptian uprisings in 2011, culminating in the Arab Spring and the subsequent destabilization of the Middle East and North Africa.[65] The Libyan war broke down the previous agreement between EU and Qaddafi to block immigration from Africa, while Syrian and Afghani war refugees were used by Turkey and Russia to put pressure on the EU. The latter's Dublin Regulation stated refugees were to seek asylum in the first EU country in which they arrived, but the closest member states, Greece and Italy, were heavily affected by the Euro crisis and, as a result, "encouraged" people to proceed northward.[66] It is against this backdrop that the Swedish refugee and begging questions intersected, in the political-economic sense—not because both indigent migrant groups are racial Others or foreigners, but because they were fleeing from, and their arrival actualized, the multifaceted consequences of finance capitalism and capital's revanchism. This includes Sweden's politics of dispossession: while Sweden was relatively spared the financial crisis, this reprieve was to a fair extent offset by the Alliance's reforms during 2006–14. As an example, the Alliance implemented tax breaks (including the abolition of wealth tax) that reduced the state's revenue by $27.7 billion per year while they, at the same time, increased VAT and excises—regressive taxes instead of progressive.[67] By drastically lowering payouts of the health and unemployment insurances, setting an upper limit for days of sick leave, and changing legislation to enable more temporary hiring, they weakened union power and social protection on the labor market. Consequently, it became possible for Swedish residents to be rejected by both health and unemployment insurances, causing more people to depend on municipal financial aid.[68] This has shifted an unprecedented level of responsibility onto the shoulders of the municipal social service offices, which now have, in some cases, the final word on whether people are to receive *any* financial support. In this way, the declassed position of Romanian Roma in Sweden reflects a level of foreclosure that is possible even for Swedish residents.

It is rather revealing that the Alliance years intersected with the tremendous rise in SD votes: from 2.9 percent in the 2006 election to 12.86 in 2014.[69] Instead of returning to SAP, disappointed voters found themselves taken in by the reactionary appeal of racist protectionism. When popular consent for the rule of the reigning fraction of the state diminishes, voters, noting a marked discrepancy between the dominant ideology's promises and their lived reality, have come to believe their rulers do not share the fundamental values of "the people." After all, the hegemony of the rulers' ideology has transformed class interests into "national values." Reflecting on the political development of Sweden and elsewhere during the Alliance's years, Scocco argues that a change occurred among voters. Previously, economic-political values dominated voters' preferences; however, "when economic development defaulted, and they felt politically abandoned, parts of the electorate were instead guided in their flaw-finding by their constitutional moral values. [Contrarily to common belief,] traditional gender and national values have [actually] decreased in importance [for people], but their political power is growing."[70] This is extremely important, considering Hall's caution against generalizing the power of racism. According to this thesis, racist ideology in Sweden, as in other countries, became a more potent political force, but it did not necessarily become more widespread in terms of the public's common (that is, expressed and conscious) values. The trend of the last decades shows an increase in "liberal"—as opposed to "authoritarian"—values among all Swedish class positions, while class consciousness remained intact (the lower the position, the more left-wing). Although the more authoritarian tendency is found in the poles of the strata and among the petit bourgeoisie, it is probably not personal class consciousness that has weakened, but the relationship between class and politics.[71] In other words, it is the political convergence of the traditional parties, the decrease in politicians who share the same background as their voters, and the increased focus on sociocultural issues that explain why workers abandoned their former representatives. These three factors were embedded in the begging question itself. Before the refugee crisis, there was a consensus from left to right in parliament to neither prohibit nor present any other solution to begging. Further, while opinion polls showed that the majority supported banning begging, this was not reflected in parliament. Third, "the beggars" were effectively hegemonized to be labeled as *a cultural Other*—Roma, before any other social positionality. The only party that explicitly went against the hegemonic stance on begging was SD, which was also the only party presenting a "solution" to the problem, while the reigning fraction's continued inaction increasingly appeared as an unwillingness to listen to the will of the people.

Fascist ideologies prefer a social fantasy where the class struggle is substituted with a conflict between "the people" and "the elite," wherein the latter, because of their moral decadence, ushered in a Trojan horse of racial enemies. Unable to face the political contradictions within the welfare state apparatus, the Swedish hegemony's initial shared front against SD facilitated this ideological fantasy. As one SAP-aligned political scientist said in 2016, it was not unreasonable to imagine "a strong connection between SD's successes and that the beggars showed up before the food shops. People believe, namely, what they see with their own eyes, not what the politicians are babbling about in the media."[72]

7   The Tolerant Stance of Inaction, 2010–2015

Amid SD's entry into parliament in 2010 the world's collective anxieties regarding terrorism and insecurity, including the emerging topic of global warming, lingered on from the previous decade. In Sweden these anxieties were reflected and enhanced by the loss of a parliamentary majority for both the Left and Right blocs. For the duration of the decade, the coalitions found themselves caught in a political paralysis brought on by both their traditional opponents and the steadily growing SD. In this way public anxieties and political insecurities reinforced each other. According to one political commentator, "it became hard to govern Sweden" in the 2010s: "The perpetual proximity of governmental crisis, in combination with the existing political blocs no longer able to govern, made politics into a perpetual election movement."[1] Thinking back to the previous chapter, one wonders if there could be a more apt description of a crisis of hegemony.

A watershed moment in history, 2010 marks not only the parliamentary origin of this hegemonic crisis but also the genesis of the begging question as a national affair. Though a few begging "Eastern Europeans" had appeared on the streets before this time, the national discussion only really began in earnest following the French government's deportation of thousands of Roma back to Romania and Bulgaria, a decision unanimously denounced by Swedish editorials as "a shame for Europe." On the heels of this condemnation came the revelation that the Stockholm police had deported twenty-six Romanian Roma for "devoting themselves to loafing/begging," a practice that turned out to be routine, with the police referring to outdated provisions in immigration legislation from when begging was unlawful. Notably, these clauses had their initial origins in the anti-Roma immigration legislation of the early twentieth century, wherein "Gypsies" were to be denied entrance alongside vagrants, prostitutes, and all others who conduct "dishonest livelihoods." Following this revealed crackdown, a debate on anti-Roma racism ensued, with the European Council's commissioner for human rights condemning the action as ethnic discrimination. The Moderate minister of migration, however, defended the police, arguing that not only is begging "dishonest," but also that "Roma" are "more inclined than other groups to come here and support themselves this way," and that the EU's principle of free movement was not intended to facilitate begging in Sweden.[2]

The next year the justice ombudsman ruled that, since begging was not prohibited in Sweden, the deportations were unlawful, stating, "Nowadays, it must be considered nonnegotiable to ground interventions in liberties and rights on juridical interpretations assuming authorities and courts are to make arbitrary judgements of moral character."[3] Against the backdrop of this ruling, which signaled juridical acceptance of begging, local politicians resolved to make every effort to oust "the beggars." Already a few months before the ombudsman's decision, Sala's municipality attempted to outlaw begging via the Public Order Act, pledging to "get rid of illegal activity based upon trafficking and criminal activity."[4] This maneuver was rejected by the county government as an insufficient reason to invoke the statute. Another appeal to the Public Order Act came in 2014, when the Södertälje police tried to fine three people for begging, but this was struck down by the Crown Court. On the whole the begging's social dimension appeared, from a "conventional" legal standpoint, to make it near impossible to label begging as solely an economic activity in need of local permission according to this law. This meant that the only feasible way to outlaw begging on the local level was to juridically frame it as not a moral disturbance, but a *practical* one. By making a distinction between active and passive money collection, in which "active" money collection entailed walking around asking people for support, the Crown Court opened the door for this logic to be legally implemented.[5] After all, this practical issue of "disorder" could be restricted, leading to successive attempts to limit déclassés' begging to a seated activity. Not only did this echo the historical double bind between activity and passivity of the pauper, as laid out in chapter 2, but presumably this injunction intensified the begging strategy of congregating outside entrances to grocery stores, shopping malls, and other crowded passages. Shop owners and clerks each handled this development differently, as the déclassé could be alternately interpreted as an economic competitor transgressing private property, a public nuisance for customers, or a harmless person in need of somewhere to be. One grocery store owner complained to a reporter: "We want to be as humane as possible, and this is a kind of catch-22 for us. [Some] customers are disturbed by the beggars, other customers by the fact that we shoo away those who beg. And if we turn away beggars, they often come back after ten minutes."[6]

Among these options, confusion reigned on how one ought to proceed. In the news, for example, myths and hearsay abounded regarding the potential connection of "the beggars" to "mafia" networks. By 2011 SD's Kent Ekeroth had already demanded a nationwide ban: "The reason is actually very simple: beggars destroy the street scene and also constitute a direct disturbing issue for many honest citizens visiting streets and squares. [Begging is mainly] an immigrant phenomenon we import by being too lazy or unwilling to do anything about it."[7] During this mandate period (2010–14), SD had only received 5 percent of votes, and other party representatives hoped their presence was only temporary. The Alliance had secured their second mandate but no longer had a majority. Neither they nor the other bloc—"the Red-Greens," consisting of SAP, the Environmental Party (EP), and the Left Party—wanted to cooperate nor converse with SD. Consequently, Prime Minister Reinfeldt's only option was to try to split the Red-Greens by working with EP, the mandate period's third largest party, whose political-economical ignorance, yet strong "value profile" of multiculturalist humanism, enabled a compromise on a new migration policy. This policy secured the Alliance's *labor* migration policy (which one OECD report deemed one of the most liberal labor migration regimes of the association), while giving undocumented children the right to health care and education, and undocumented adults the right to acute health care.[8]

For the Right this realpolitikal chess board made the tactical stance on the emerging begging question problematic. While certain fractions within the four parties favored criminalization, it was strategically more important to nurture the relationship with EP and their own (social liberal and former-SAP) voters than to risk being blamed for doing SD's errands. Additionally, sentiments of international solidarity and antiracism pervaded the traditional social liberalism of the Liberal Party; in fact, prominent Liberal politicians had set out to champion Roma civil rights in Sweden and found the begging question to be relevant to this cause. It was all of these factors, therefore, that determined the New Moderates' further emphasis on humanitarianism and neoliberal multiculturalism. There were, however, some complementary overtures on behalf of the Right on the begging matter. In 2012, for example, the Moderate minister of justice called for a prohibition against "organized" begging—alleged to counteract human trafficking—while the Center Party presented a similar suggestion, with their legal spokesperson explaining: "Many believe they are doing a good thing when they give to someone begging. However, actually, the money ends in the pockets of a profiteer. [This] is slavery."[9] Nevertheless, the spokesperson did not want to criminalize begging itself, since "we don't want to chase the beggars, they are victims themselves. We want to get those organizing begging to profit." He likened his suggestion with the legal approach to prostitution, where purchasing sex is illegal, but selling it is not. The same year, the minister on migration joined five other European ministers pushing for the reintroduction of visa requirements for Balkan asylum-seekers—a measure intended to counteract Roma immigration.[10] On the whole the stance of the Right government was notably ambivalent in its balancing of considerations in order to secure hegemonic consent on national values.

The New Antiracist Counter-Ideology's Momentum

The reigning segment faced other challenges too, including what the (imagined) silent majority thought about matters that appeared to be more about race, tolerance, and morality than about economic redistribution.

Social media platforms such as Facebook and Twitter had just become new public spheres for debate—what trended there appeared to represent the vox populi. Further, 2012 saw various debates on cultural appropriation, racialization, stereotyping, media representation, white privilege, blackface, the n-word, discrimination, and cancel culture.[11] Just as the events that occurred on the cusp of the 1990s had prompted a national awareness of racism, the parliamentary entrance of SD seems to have energized movements and actors pushing for an "updated" color-conscious antiracist ideology—primarily inspired by Anglo-American discourses on structural racism, postcolonialism, and third-wave feminism. In this way, a new generation of non-white Swedes, with greater cultural capital than their (non-white) immigrant parents' generation, called out Swedish hypocrisy and hegemonic whiteness. While it is possible to analytically term their struggle a "counter-ideology" following Hall et al.'s categories, the general movement's ideology was too vague, too in line with the current social order, and too weak in actual political power to be "capable of challenging the over-all hegemony of 'ruling ideas.'"[12] Additionally, most debates referred to representation (in literature, art, theater, television, media, advertising, and entertainment) without seriously attacking the economic structures. Nevertheless, for a couple of years Alan Pred's critique of Swedish self-denial of cultural racism was now at the center of public debate. This ideology probably also won acceptance due to several exceptional, intersecting racialist events. In 2011–12 two racist lone-wolf shooters made headlines: first, the Norwegian mass murderer (and SD sympathizer) Anders Behring Breivik, who massacred seventy-seven people (the majority of them underage), and then Peter Mangs in Malmö, convicted for two murders and seven attempted murders. In another 2012 scandal, Ekeroth, along with two other high-ranking SD politicians who had armed themselves with stolen iron pipes, drunkenly called a Kurdish-Swedish comedian a "wog monkey," jeering, "This is my country, not yours." Finally, in 2013 Nazis attacked an antiracist demonstration, signaling a return of the presence of white power movements.[13]

That same year, two additional events that involved the police put the anti-racist counter-ideology on the radar of the reigning faction of the state. On the heels of aforementioned new rights for undocumented migrants in 2013, the media exposed a police campaign to crack down on "illegal immigrants" by stopping people in public spaces and forcing them to identify themselves. With so many non-white Swedes being stopped, accusations of racial profiling were difficult to dismiss. Then, to solidify the begging question as part of the counter-ideology's questioning of the state, news broke that the Scania police kept a secret illegal register of 4,741 Swedish Roma citizens. Of this list, 1,320 were children.[14] According to Selling, this revelation constituted a "game changer," prompting a discursive momentum on Roma rights in Sweden: "Mass media in general started to side with Roma, both in historical material and in the contemporary situation for vulnerable EU migrants." Consequently, "the topic of 'Roma' was suddenly trendy in the editorial offices."[15] This momentum was sustained thanks to decades of work by the Swedish Roma civil rights movement up to this point. Ever since Sweden's official recognition of Roma as a national minority in 2000 (together with other minorities, as Sweden ritually integrated itself into the EU's political-legal frameworks), the movement had increasingly identified with the discourse on historical responsibility for the Holocaust. With these two signifiers of "national minority" and "historical responsibility," Roma activists issued demands for the state to become involved in highlighting Roma history and addressing both anti-Roma racism and substandard Roma living conditions—a struggle that made a significant advance when in 2010 the Alliance granted the request of the Delegation on Roma Issues for a white paper. While the Alliance made it clear that they only wished the paper to focus on the horrors of the twentieth century, rather than contemporary discrimination, following the leak of the police register, however, the government announced the appointment of a two-year Commission on Antiziganism.[16] Shortly after its creation, this commission declared that the begging question was a matter of anti-Roma racism and structural discrimination, where the solution was to grant the Roma their unconditional human rights of protection, accommodation, access to health care, and clean water.

The final defining event of 2013 was an acclaimed story in *Dagens Nyheter*, in which reporters had followed several begging individuals back to their home villages in Romania. This investigative report related a convincing picture of genuine poverty and hardships among Romania Roma that was difficult to dismiss as inauthentic.[17] Rather quickly, the dominant media discourse adopted the narrative that begging was a survival strategy for mistreated Roma, with attempts to frame begging as a vehicle for criminality now dismissed by opinion makers as expressions of prejudicial sentiments. In this way the culturalization and moralization of the begging question cemented the "Roma" signifier as interchangeable with "the beggar." What's more, thanks to the integration of discourses on historical responsibility and racism into an ideology of human rights, a Symbolic order took shape, wherein the EU déclassés' hardships became articulated as a "lack of human rights." Naturally, the solution was to grant them these rights. Alongside the commission, several representatives for this human rights ideology emerged—Amnesty International, Civil Right Defenders, Save the Children, Médecins Sans Frontières, the Swedish Church, the City Mission, and prominent lawyers—who from then on became dominant spokespersons of behalf of the subalterns.

Notably, all these actors were, as evidenced by their very legitimization, nonpolitical in the commonsensical sense—with one exception. Within this political landscape, a feminist party with parliamentary aspirations, Feministiskt initiativ (F!), received much media coverage. For their alleged lack of interest in feminism and intersectional issues, their charismatic leader had previously broken with the Left Party, for which she had been a successful leader in the 1990s. Thus lauded for their "wokeness," F! seemed to be a force to be reckoned with: a political channel for the antiracist counter-ideology and, in turn, growing popular solidarity for the EU déclassés. Clearly left-wing, the party situated its politics within an ideological framework of human rights: these rights were the antidote to oppression and purported to have an immense power over states. Significantly, their EU parliamentary candidate, Soraya Post, a Swedish Roma, put Roma human rights at the very center of her campaign proposals. On this basis a vote for her would be a vote for taking action at the European level for the sake of déclassés. It was against this backdrop, therefore, that she, in 2014, managed to secure her party's first (and only) seat.

HANDLING POLITICAL CORRECTNESS

In the end this convergence of a widespread ideology of humanitarianism on the begging question—drawing on Swedish ideology and carried out by the media, philanthropic civil society, institutions of human rights, and some politicians—came together to discourage the reigning fraction of the state, including the government, parties, and police, from cracking down on the growing presence of EU déclassés. With the leadership of all parties—except sd, that is—now clearly stating their unwillingness to ban begging, the police had, in their caution, refrained from intervening in events in a way that could be interpreted as racist. Further, since begging was determined not to be a public order problem, police did not intervene when agitated citizens urged them to "remove" déclassés out of sight.[18] Likewise, there was a marked lack of intervention into the presence of begging people in pseudo-public spaces such as subways and train stations—so when it happened, it became news.[19]

At this time, the temporary ascendance of the intersectional and antiracist position in Swedish media—spanning from roughly 2012 to 2016—fueled widespread fears of doing, saying, or thinking the "wrong" thing on issues related to racism. This anxiety was amplified by a national self-image that was still reeling from the emergence of sd, the novelty of social media platforms filled with antagonism, and, among businesses and media companies, an obsessive fear of trademark damage via the risk of backlashes and boycotts. As an anecdotal example, one private individual, interviewed on her thoughts on the growing presence of "beggars," told a reporter, "You're not allowed to speak about this, to think anything, except feeling sorry for them."[20] This expression of a fear of a "thought police" accusing one of racism was a recurring theme in discussions about my research with relatives, friends, and strangers during these years. (Remember, too, my subway car and Christmas dinner incidents.) Another effect of this discursive climate was anxiousness among politicians, officials, business keepers, and managers to make an effort to curb begging and informal settlements that could potentially draw public ire. At the same time, however, the state did not seem to take any steps to help déclassés out of poverty, relegating the problem to a status quo that was easily interpreted as cowardice on behalf of public actors. Notably, this accusation came from both sides of the begging question: those antipathetic toward the déclassés were angry with the state not taking a hard line, while those sympathetic were angry with the state for not extending social support.

Amid this ambivalence, in late 2013, well-known political scientist Bo Rothstein suggested a Swedish Third Way of legislating begging: criminalizing giving as a means of punishing the perceived perpetrator rather than the victim, who no longer was the "Roma trafficker," but a "naive pedestrian." This phrasing suggests a turn toward a narrative of social engineering compatible with the Swedish ideology—wherein begging is "destructive":

> To punish these extremely vulnerable, socially excluded, and obviously suffering human beings contradicts our humanity and sense of what's right. Simultaneously, it must be obvious that more alms and continued street begging cannot be the solution to these people's social misery. [So far,] no one has been able to put forward a reasonable solution to this new and particularly depressing feature in the Swedish cityscape.
>
> [Instead of alms,] totally different, more encompassing, and more structural efforts, in the form of education, access to health care, and different forms of social and medical rehabilitation need to be applied. There are strong reasons to believe that as long as street begging [gives] a livelihood, sufficient structural actions from society will [default].
>
> I am convinced that [my suggested prohibition] would send important signals about the serious underlying problems this occupation is based upon and therefore enforce more encompassing structural [efforts].[21]

This sympathetic albeit deeply ideological self-deception (of believing in a causality where state prohibitions against helping the poor will *cause* structural social efforts on behalf of the same actor) was met with ridicule and accusations of Rothstein wanting to criminalize "compassion."[22] Nevertheless, his suggestion became a point of reference in the debate's subsequent years, presumably due to its ideological reasonableness, which upholds Swedish righteousness while counteracting "the beggars'" presence.

The Parliamentary Anticlimax of 2014

In 2014, as the national election approached, begging became a political national issue. It was also this spring that local newspapers reported on the sudden and unprecedented presence of "beggars" in small towns and villages all over the country, and I conducted my interviews.

Due to the emotional moral symbolism of begging itself, and the reluctance within the reigning fraction to publicly delve into the complex nitty-gritty of what could actually be done to help the EU déclassés, all political issues surrounding the increased presence of déclassés became subsumed within the abstract symbol of "the begging ban." Due to politicians' personal morals and pangs of conscience, it was easy to take a stand on this simple either-or question—yes or no to banning begging; plus it made for good publicity and helped further mystify the relationship between poverty and racism. SD, of course, embraced this moralization of the begging question, as they were the only ones taking a stand against "the elite," with advertisements in the Stockholm subway that read, "IT IS TIME TO STOP THE ORGANIZED BEGGING ON OUR STREETS." EP's leader, meanwhile, reacted by appealing to the Swedish ideology: "To attack someone who cannot defend themselves, is that something you think should be Swedish?"[23]

Despite this seemingly united moral front, the political establishment was not internally cohesive in their stance on the issue. After all, the classical political ideas were, as we know, ambiguous on the virtues and sins of begging, symptomized by local politicians from the SAP, the Moderates, and others in support of begging prohibition. Granted, these voices usually articulated their desire in a manner that was in keeping with the Swedish ideology. One Moderate, for example, argued that prohibition would free "the genuine poor," "mistreated Roma" from the forces that "cemented" their poverty and encourage them to find work.[24] These assertions were immediately dismissed by Reinfeldt, who countered that the ultimate solution was to put pressure on the home countries through the EU.[25] Likewise, his SAP opponent, Stefan Löfven, had to go through the same motions—dismissing a ban-friendly colleague and then arguing for a vague solution in "the home countries."[26] Consequently, the political reigning fraction, before the national election, stated the following as one: banning begging is morally wrong and does not do anything to combat poverty, referring to criminality is xenophobic, and the solution is to "put pressure" on the home countries and enact some unspecified "structural reforms" in order to make the Roma employable. Notably, there was no tangible counteroffer to the public's desire to find a way to end begging without—and instead of—criminalizing the practice. Overall, the question of what practical steps the Swedish state could take to help the déclassés was seldom brought up. In a notable example of this reticence, the Alliance's coordinator on homelessness explained that while he opposed prohibition and denounced rumors of organized criminality, "EU citizens who come here to beg do not have [a] right to the Swedish welfare system." If they would, "then the system would crack," which is why "the solution is to be found on the beggars' home ground."[27]

There was, however, another destitute racial Other approaching the borders in greater and greater numbers: the refugees fleeing from the escalating Middle East and North Africa (MENA) wars. The refugee crisis towered on the horizon. Looking back on it, Reinfeldt appeared to have misread the public sentiments, when he, in a now infamous speech prior to the election, urged the Swedes to "open their hearts" to the refugees. With estimates predicting a refugee reception on par with the 1990s' Balkan wars, Reinfeldt admitted this influx would drastically diminish the budgetary space for social reforms. In this way, it was possible to interpret Reinfeldt "admitting" receiving refugees was a costly affair—conceding that they would Enjoy something at Swedish citizens' collective expense, when he pleaded: "I want to remind you we are a nation that has stood up and been open back in times when people have faced hard rigors. [Now,] I appeal to the Swedish people to have patience, to open your hearts to see people under strong pressure with threats against one's very life who [are] fleeing to freedom, fleeing to better conditions."[28]

The national election went on to be a catastrophe for the reigning fraction—the only winner was SD, who enjoyed tremendous success when they increased their support from 5.7 percent to 12.86 percent, thereby becoming the third largest party and securing both blocs' powerlessness. While SAP lost most votes to SD numerically, the Moderates did so proportionally, prompting Reinfeldt to immediately step down as party leader.[29] F!, for their part, failed to enter parliament and would never build upon their momentum. Forced to adopt a new strategy, SAP, for the first time, formed a government with EP, while excluding the Left Party; Löfven's plan was to try to attain a centrist hegemony, into which the "communists" could never be accepted. This was a risky strategy, as this government could only come into being via the Alliance's benevolence or breakdown. Naturally, this ignited fractions within the right parties—especially among the Moderates and the Christian Democrats—who urged cooperation with SD. Meanwhile, to save "the nation" from "mass immigration," SD defied praxis and voted for the Alliance's shadow budget in a bid to undermine the government.

In Sweden, governmental crises were unusual, and when Löfven threatened to call for a new election, this option was dramatic. (It had not occurred since 1958.) To avoid this the Alliance and the government reached an agreement, the December Agreement, in order to exclude SD from influence and make the country governable: the minority government was allowed to implement their budget, the Alliance was to abstain their votes, and this agreement, it was decided, would last for two electoral periods. Like SD, the Left Party was kept out of this pact. This solution led to a rather bizarre political short-circuit, as the Löfven government still had a right-wing budget for 2015, and the Alliance was now supposed to let their antagonists implement unwanted reforms. To rephrase, the agreement passivized both sides, as the government would not dare to put forward controversial social reforms—such as giving déclassés social rights—due to their practical minority. Simultaneously, the Alliance was also pacified, a development that proved particularly provocative among liberal-conservatives, as the Alliance had had several bills outvoted when they were in minority government. Finally, and maybe worst of all for hegemony, this agreement made SD's counter-ideology—which framed their party as the only opposition against "the establishment"—appear accurate. However, fractions of the capitalist class saw their chance to capitalize upon the situation, as some of the most powerful business leaders, representing financial capital, private schools, trade and service businesses, and public relations, started courting SD to win their support. By the end of the following year, SD agreed to most of capital's dictates, a pivot that would secure a dominant right-wing parliament if only the idealist Right would come to its senses.[30]

In this "Bonapartist" situation, the foremost problem was faced by the leaderships of the two largest parties. While there was political leverage within both SAP's and the Moderates' legacies to clamp down on immigration, the realpolitikal and ideological landscape was such that they were subject to something of a double blackmail: first from SD, and second from the smaller parties upon which they were dependent (who could afford to make more principled stands in accordance with the Swedish ideology). By rejecting SD, SAP had to rely on EP and (unofficially) the Left Party, while the Moderates had to lean on the Liberal and Center Parties; all those necessary minor partners had clear "humanistic" profiles. In this way the two major parties faced a catch-22. Not cracking down on immigration risked inducing SD's continuous growth, while the latter's genuine Völkisch nationalism would proclaim any austerity measures to be too weak. However, if the Moderates and Christian Democrats joined forces with SD, they would risk losing the majority as well. Amid this "ungovernable" situation, EU déclassés and refugees continued to arrive on Sweden soil. Whereas the EU déclassés were relatively few in numbers—roughly five thousand individuals—their visibility, due to their homelessness and begging, made them more tangible in everyday life. As early as 2014 there were reports of hate crimes against them, while the problem of non-allowed settlements started to garner more media attention instead of begging prohibition. Ultimately, something had to be done to resolve the begging question, which simultaneously managed to secure the state rulers' hegemony by upholding the Swedish ideology.

In early 2015 the government initiated a one-year, one-man investigation, appointing state lawyer Martin Valfridsson as national coordinator for "vulnerable EU citizens temporarily residing in Sweden." His assignment was to devise a framework of cooperation and exchange of experience between authorities, civil society, and NGOs and to disseminate knowledge about the rights of déclassés in Sweden.[31] To rephrase, Valfridsson, alleged to be an "unpolitical" authority (representing Swedish law), was tasked with giving the state apparatus and society a common direction on how to handle the social questions of the déclassés. The choice of a lawyer for such a social issue was overdetermined: due to the parliamentary situation of a Red-Green government cornered by both the neoliberal Right and SD, referring to the law instead of values would neutralize the political antagonisms hidden beneath the begging question. After all, with a hegemony in crisis, values of the rulers are combated by popular forces and therefore need to be framed through the coercion of law. Additionally, Valfridsson, through the lens of the Swedish folkhem ideology, represented the rational technocrat, steering the folkhem in the prudent, yet inherently good, direction. Finally, the troubling human rights ideology needed to be neutralized by the state's own interpretation of law. In this way the government signaled to the electorate they were poised to carry out the maintenance of the current moral economy of rights and duties—that is, to protect the National Thing, its exceptional equality included.

8 The Borromean Welfare Knot

One may wonder, Why did neither the Alliance nor the Red-Green government initially "do anything" about the increasing presence of begging, homeless, EU déclassés? The answer is that the realpolitikal and ideological playfield aside, a complex machinery of legal, social, and political relations of the state apparatus and the Swedish Model presented obstacles to locating this sociopolitical subject within the state's Symbolic network and Imaginary categories.

With the justice ombudsman's denunciation of the Stockholm police's deportation of EU citizens, it was legally impossible to simply chase them out of the country—that is, if one wanted to comply with the EU's freedom of movement policy. The closest one could get to enacting such a solution would be to ban begging and homelessness altogether, as was the case in sd's role model country, Hungary.[1] To do the opposite, and follow what the ideology of exceptional equality actually appeared to prescribe, would involve giving the EU déclassés access to reasonable accommodation, health care, education, and some sort of social benefits. As we already know, however, the fantasy of the theft of Enjoyment within a racialized capitalist class society would only permit that if it were perceived as a preexisting, unconditional right for all Swedish citizens. Unfortunately, for all of the exceptional equalities of Swedish welfare society, this was not the case.

The regulation of wealth and artificial scarcity in a capitalist society—that is, the management of the National Thing—follows signifier chains leading through different social fields, where certain legal categories (of people) have certain rights and other categories have other rights. To explain why it proved so hard for the personnel of the state to comply with the dominant ideology with regard to the EU déclassés, we need to abstract those Symbolic structures and fields in order to map the "impossible" Real position in which the EU déclassés happened to find themselves within the Swedish welfare systems. Notably, this mapping procedure will reveal how the EU déclassé position symptomized not only the duality between national citizens and noncitizens, but also the dualities within the social apparatuses and the population itself. Further, it will demonstrate that the fate of EU déclassés was not merely a side issue of immigration regulation: indeed, it concerned fundamental political-economic contradictions at the very heart of the exceptional-equal Swedish Model.

The liminal existence of the EU déclassé in Swedish bureaucracy can be located within the Real's position within a Borromean knot of the three crucial legal-political fields that comprise the Swedish Model: *citizenship*, *labor*, and *housing*. In order for right-bearing subjects to enter any of these fields, they must enter the others as well. If only the EU déclassés had the right of residence—a practical social citizenship—they would have the right to education, health care, and social benefits. Granted, that would not guarantee them a job, without which they resort to begging. In any case they can only receive residency if they have a formal job, or a realistic chance at getting one. To apply for a formal job (with a sufficient salary), they need the requisite education and somewhere to stay—after all, it is difficult to seek and perform labor if you don't know where you're going to sleep that night. Housing, then, is needed, but to secure such an accommodation, you need to have an income, housing allowance, or help from social services—which you can apply for if you have the residence. To add to this elaborate catch-22, there are Swedish citizens and residents who are unemployed, homeless, or both, an increasing number of whom do not even qualify for the right to basic social assistance from local social services.

With all this in mind, let us review each of these legal-political fields, one at the time, to see how they became successfully actualized over the duration of the begging question and the hegemonic crisis.

Citizenship: A Real Position within the Rights

Due to the déclassés' political-judicial status as unemployed EEA (European Economic Area) citizens without right of residence, they are outside the social categories of Swedish citizens, those with UN refugee status, asylum-seekers and the undocumented, immigrants with residence permits, and EU citizens with a right of residence. This ambiguous legal status of being neither "citizen," "resident," nor "refugee"—because of their official home country citizenship—places the EU déclassé beyond both the legal sphere of citizenship and human rights; after all, the raison d'être of human rights is to compensate for a lack of national citizenship.[2]

Notably, EU citizens' right of residence in another country is obtained only if one is officially employed, studying, in possession of enough financial assets, or related to someone who meets these requirements. Other than that, the only rights afforded by institutionalized social care schemes are potential short-term social efforts on behalf of municipalities according to the Swedish Social Service Act, which states their responsibility to aid *everyone* within its territory in case of an "emergency" (due to risk of serious harm and death)—which, as a rule, translated into municipal-funded bus tickets back home. Additionally, the dominant interpretation of the law excluded the déclassés from asylum-seekers' and the undocumented's right to subsidized medical care; because of their EU citizenship, in other words, they are formally not "undocumented."[3] To understand what this looks like in practice, one need only consult the case of the Luleå-based begging woman Alina-Elena Dima, who, in 2015, was originally billed 55,000 kronor for postnatal care—while for residents, childbirth costs nothing (except a couple hundred kronor for using the facility).[4] Meanwhile, many Romanian (and especially Roma) citizens lack Romanian health insurance and are not covered by the relevant EU legislation. Further, the absence of a practice of registering EU citizens crossing national borders within the union has enabled déclassés to stay uninterruptedly in Sweden for years, perpetually caught in an official legal temporariness—as they are expected to stay for only three months, authorities can use this temporariness to foreclose the activation of social rights.[5]

There are, however, conflicting legislations that question this restrictive interpretation of authorities' responsibility. Children's rights, for example, are more protected in Sweden than adults', wherein no distinction is (supposed) to be made regarding nationality or background. In 2016 it was estimated that about a hundred children of "vulnerable EU citizens" resided in Sweden.[6] According to Swedish law, every child is to be protected from the risk of harm, which could be interpreted as a legal responsibility to provide families access to shelter, health care, and the like. While some municipalities concurred with this, it has been more common, when children are involved, that the authorities immediately encourage their families to go back home. Due to the risks of losing custody rights, déclassés are incentivized to leave children in the care of relatives back home when they travel to Sweden, reinforcing widespread myths that déclassés are "bad parents."[7] To further complicate matters, the UN Child Convention stipulates every child's right to education, sparking debate on whether Sweden ought to allow déclassé children to go to school there or else hinder children, somehow, from coming to Sweden in the first place. Notably, the same problem did not concern undocumented children, who always could be deported.[8]

There was also uncertainty about how to interpret the reach of municipal responsibility according to the Social Service Act, which could be understood as a duty to provide shelter and sanitation. From this perspective, some municipalities erected provisional subsidized shelters (often in trailers on municipal land) or funded NGO shelters explicitly targeting déclassés, while others did nothing. Likewise, the legislation protecting squatters was robust, which led to confusion on what to do with informal settlements if they became "permanent."

Probably the trickiest legal challenge, however, was how to deal with the embeddedness of international human rights conventions within Swedish law. These laws stipulate the responsibility to guarantee fundamental human rights for every individual, no matter their origin, on behalf of Sweden within its territory, including the right to shelter and housing, sanitary conditions, health care, education, and nondiscrimination. According to

Amnesty International (which for the last few years became perhaps *the* definitive voice fighting for déclassés' rights in Sweden), these rights are nonnegotiable from a juridical standpoint, and it is inaccurate to refer only to Swedish or EU law in order to escape responsibility—since, after all, these conventions are binding for Sweden and must be considered when interpreting national law.[9]

All of these aspects under consideration render the EU déclassés' relationship to asylum-seekers curiously contradictory—both were the political subjects with least practical rights in Sweden, albeit in different ways. The EU déclassés, for example, have, through their EU citizenship, the right to enter and reside in Sweden for ninety days per visit. Meanwhile, the asylum-seekers could be deported but have the right to accommodation, protection, and social assistance while their asylum application is pending, and they could be "hidden" from public view to a completely different extent than the homeless EU déclassés.

Labor: Contradictions within the Swedish Model

WHO DESERVES TO BECOME DESERVING?

As we continue to explore the differences between the statuses of the refugees and the déclassés, we discover that there are various publicly funded programs put in place to integrate legally recognized refugees and immigrants into the labor market—namely, complimentary adult education and validating programs. This "benevolence" on behalf of the Swedish state and associations actualizes the aforementioned dominant function of *labor* to maintain the welfare society. While the continued public funding of education is inherited from the "universal" aspect of the Swedish dual welfare model (tied to citizenship/residence, just like the social insurances for unemployment, health care, sick leave, and pensions), this funding is expected to be *repaid* by one's labor. Setting aside values on social rights, the Swedish Model's political-economic rationale is a public investment in productivity, where workers finance and consume welfare in accordance with individuals' fluctuating productivity capacity. In light of the theft of

Enjoyment, this is crucial: hegemonic consent for the welfare model is not rooted in individuals' "altruistic" funding of other people's education and health care, but rather in the collective "egoistic" interest in supporting a social consumption fund. In this way the welfare state's continuation is legitimated by the cross-class dominant moral economy, since it equalizes incomes and expenses for individuals over their life cycle—not because it redistributes money between individuals.[10] Nevertheless, the welfare state's insurance function and need-oriented construction does, in practice, serve to balance out incomes. Poorer people, for example, tend to have poorer health and therefore receive more subsidized health care. This inherent tendency of the system to "give more" to the poor provides pabulum to the ideological belief that Swedes "care for each other." What's more, it incites political debates on whether the "only" function of taxes is to finance welfare services, or if they should also flatten income differences.

While this counterbalancing effect has (due to the politics of previous decades) become increasingly less efficient, the dual model's predominant reliance on the principle of income security establishes a wageworker solidarity before a citizen solidarity. Ultimately, the national Enjoyment of "social citizenship" is not based upon national citizenship, but labor participation—indeed, a privileged, high-educated, and employed immigrant enjoys more welfare than noneducated, unemployed refugees and poor natives outside the security nets. We can also observe the dialectic of racism playing out in the multileveled causalities of neoliberalized schooling and the harsher grading system implemented in 2011: in 2021, 13 percent of the pupils finishing primary school were not qualified for upper secondary school, which is practically mandatory in order to secure a formal employment in contemporary Sweden.[11] Those who are failing school and entering the formal labor market are disproportionately non-white (foreign-born or second-generation) living in the poor suburbs. What's more, if they're male, they're likelier than others to join the emerging criminal network of "gangs" gunning down or blowing up each other and feeding common perceptions of "cultural incompatibility" in Sweden.[12]

In view of the system's privileging of a wage-earner solidarity, the attraction to SD must be interpreted, in part, as the desire for a caring national community of exceptional equality, where your right to security is not based upon your labor value, but rather your intrinsic human value—which is fetishized as your national belonging. Here, we must return to the historical binary of deserving and undeserving poor. Within nationalist fantasies of racial homogeneity, it is believed that this distinction could be placed along racial and territorial lines; that way, only one's racial comrades are able to unconditionally enjoy the Thing of trygghet. The folkhem project, for its part, aimed to turn the whole state population into deserving subjects through political-economic (and eugenic) means. Since the economic policy aimed for full employment, "everyone" was supposed to become a contributing worker and thus be entitled to support in hard times. In the wake of the crisis in the 1990s, when this aim was officially abandoned, the Swedish Model now amounts to a model for full employment without *policies* for full employment—a deficiency that further complicates the hypothetical integration of EU déclassés into the formal labor market.

During the 2010s there were neither state efforts nor debates on whether to establish specialized educational or training programs to help EU déclassés become "activated" workers—with the exception of partially publicly funded local initiatives by NGOs.[13] By way of explanation for this inaction, it could be claimed that it would simply be too expensive, as their degree of dispossession demanded public inputs on par with illiterate refugees—indeed, they would need not only paid adult education (often even spelling classes) and vocational training, but also accommodation, health care, and other social efforts. In other words, turning them into deserving poor by institutional measures would, undoubtedly, be costly. However, to fund the integration of immigrants is less expensive than the support of native-born residents, since the latter are given free education up to the age of nineteen, among other expenses. Then again, the native is born into a territorial citizenship, which commonsensically confers deservingness on the racial and national in-group. With that said, the accepted asylum-seeker has earned national investment by becoming a fellow laborer, even if they need the same degree of effort as the ideal-typical EU déclassé (same goes for those with a permanent residence permit through family ties). Once again the déclassé is caught in-between the right-bearer categories of citizenship and human rights, since the only remaining way for the unemployed Other to secure a moral-economic guarantee of deservingness (that is, to become "contributing" labor power) is to be accepted as a "deserving refugee": attainable only through the officially recognized refuge from *political*—not economic—oppression. Without this guarantee, the refugee also becomes a déclassé.

However, contrary to public authorities' commonsensical nonresponsibility for helping déclassés obtain jobs, legislation states that the Public Employment Office (PEO) must grant any EU citizen a personal meeting with an officer if requested—even if the applicant does not have a Swedish civic number or right of residence. Strikingly, two reports on déclassés' conditions in Sweden from the City Mission and Amnesty International noted an absence of adherence to this rule in practice. The City Mission, for example, recounts how PEO officials in two different towns rendered opposite judgments on two former bakers' eligibility to obtain work: in the first town, the baker was identified as a case to support, since there was a shortage of bakers in Sweden, while the second baker, in another town, was dismissed as a "hopeless" case.[14] Amnesty International, for its part, writes:

> Eleven of the 58 interviewees had been to [PEO]; most others had not even heard of it. Of those who had been there, only a handful had managed to register as job seekers. Several individuals told Amnesty International they had wanted to register but had been treated with suspicion and faced discriminatory remarks. Sometimes officials at [PEO] had refused to help them, even though they have a duty to do so under Swedish and EU law. Nobody Amnesty International interviewed had been helped by [PEO] to find work.
>
> When Amnesty International accompanied Alex, a 30-year-old Roma man living in Malmö, to [PEO], the official first refused to receive him, arguing that he could not help him because Alex did not have a Swedish

identification or coordination number. It was only when Amnesty International insisted that [PEO] had a duty to obtain a number for him that the official agreed to let Alex in.

Such attitudes suggest that "vulnerable EU citizens" are confronted with structural barriers, which further entrench the poverty and marginalization they experience and, in turn, feed discriminatory perceptions about their unwillingness or inability to work.[15]

The case of PEO reveals not only the problem of discrimination but also the déclassés' legal status as *temporary* residents. Normally, no efforts are made by the PEO before six months' uninterrupted residence, illuminating yet another catch-22 of undeservingness: the déclassés cannot qualify for employment efforts until after 180 days, but as unemployed persons, they cannot stay for more than 90 days. As Amnesty International observes, this exclusion of déclassés reinforces public perceptions of déclassés' aversion to contributing to the community.

"UNEMPLOYABILITY"

When déclassés were asked by the media, they almost always said they would prefer to work instead of begging. Given the commonsensical celebration of "work" as the antidote to poverty, we might say that it lied in "everyone's" interest to secure the déclassés some jobs. As early as January 2015, however, well-renowned neoclassical economist Lars Calmfors (notably against begging bans) cautioned the public that giving "the beggars" jobs would probably not end begging in Sweden:

> If we secure some jobs for them, then the expected benefits of traveling to Sweden increases. Then it becomes rational for so many to come that most of them will nevertheless fail to obtain employment. The latecomers then continue to beg, waiting for job opportunities to come along. Thus, street begging remains. [. . .]
>
> If we instead are primarily interested in ending street begging in Sweden, we will not accomplish this by creating jobs for beggars (if we do not give occupations to everyone, which, of course, is impossible).[16]

Of course, we should not expect a mainstream economist to contemplate a third option other than "jobs" and "begging." Equally unsurprisingly, he ignores the fact that "jobs," on their own, do not necessarily undo the continued need to beg. After all, many begging déclassés labored part-time: in low-skilled jobs in temporary positions, mediated by people they met on the street; in the "informal economy" as super-exploited unreported labor; in both formal and informal sectors back home or abroad for temporary periods of demand (such as in agriculture). Even if one manages to land temporary formal employment, it is only a time-limited occupation, affording one an insecure temporary stay in a foreign country, with a great deal of spare time and significant economic incentives to continue begging "on the side." As an NGO chairman based in Lund explained to me, "many work on an hourly basis," but "not to the degree one can leave the street permanently, unfortunately." To complicate matters, there are the moral distinctions of what counts as "work": busking was considered by several of my interviewees "almost" like a job, and some EU déclassés were involved in prostitution, thievery, and human trafficking—both as victims and perpetrators.

Notably, the "beggars'" degree of employability is not homogenous: some had former official employment; some had day-labored with payment on the spot; others had never labored. Granted, those old enough to remember the fall of Nicolae Ceaușescu generally had been employed at some point (at least according to the official legislation on compulsory labor). With that said, the Romanian educational system's systematic discrimination against the Roma has been longstanding: many have never finished school, and many lack any formal education whatsoever. To put things in perspective, I was once told by an NGO member who volunteered teaching Swedish to déclassés in Stockholm that, in each lesson, new pupils in their twenties showed up, not even able to spell their forenames. On the opposite end of the spectrum, in my media material there are myriads of examples of life trajectories in which "beggars" worked for wages outside Sweden before the financial crisis. Relevant exemplars worked as pavers, farmworkers, construction workers, basket weavers, factory workers, cashiers, plate artisans, stablemen, bakers, bricklayers, painters, bartenders, receptionists, guardians, and even international (female) martial arts masters before they found themselves begging abroad and sleeping in cars.[17] All these former laborers explain in interviews that they either were fired or found their wages so severely diminished that they could no longer support themselves. What's more, the social systems in Romania made begging abroad economically rational: in 2018 the Romanian unemployment benefits for minimum wage earners was $83 for six months—*if* one paid the Unemployment Insurance Fund fee, that is, which people working minimum wage seldom do. Further, the monthly allowance of social benefits was $31, while the price level was about half of the Swedish Consumer Price Index.[18] Consequently, if one made $10 by begging for one day in Sweden ($1.25 per hour, if working eight hours), one had, in six days, almost doubled the monthly benefit rate in Romania.

Another factor that served to deplete formerly workable livelihoods was the vanishing demand for traditional crafts associated with Roma culture—such as baskets, brooms, and ladles—as multinational discount companies (such as the Swedish chain IKEA) remove the need for handcrafted everyday objects, and Romanian forests are enclosed (in favor of companies such as IKEA).[19] Nevertheless, in Swedish towns it's not unusual to encounter people trying to sell various crafts at usual "begging spots."

During 2014–15, parallel to the explosion of efforts to help refugees in civil society, and in accordance with the Swedish ideology, there were local and personal initiatives all over Sweden to help déclassés find "work." My media sample tells of individuals, small companies, franchise units, churches, networks, and families who helped, or tried to help, déclassés obtain jobs. Sought occupations included shop employees, cleaners, gardeners, carpet weavers, scarf weavers, flea market sellers, vegetable vendors, construction workers, snow shovelers, berry pickers, farm laborers, fast-food employees, stablemen, musicians, and even actors and extras for theatrical plays or movies (playing "themselves").[20] Sometimes these jobs led to success. Sometimes they did not—as is so often the case with humans. A few times déclassés refused job offers, doing so for various reasons, such as the uncertainty of the job leading anywhere, separation from one's children, and their state of homelessness—all factors that make it difficult to plan for one's future. Meanwhile, the jobs that did materialize were temporary, low-skilled, and (almost) undeclared. It bears noting that to obtain the right of residence—thus, the right to welfare—the job needs to be legal and sufficiently well paid. This is where the *political* contradictions on labor in the Swedish Model enter the picture.

THE NATURALIZATION OF THE INSIDER-OUTSIDER HYPOTHESIS

In 2015 an association in Mariefred (a locality of two thousand residents) was celebrated in the media for their "success" in "removing the beggars from the street," a feat achieved by civilians who created a staffing agency for the sake of "the six Roma" present in town.[21] As the spokesperson explained, "beggars" in "quaint little Mariefred" became "an astonishing contrast to the idyll here. It is horrible if the children are to grow up seeing people so debased." Now, the Roma performed "simpler" jobs for the inhabitants, "like gardening, window polishing, or cleaning," salaried at 70 kronor per hour. In this regard the agency thought they had found a legal loophole: the tax authorities didn't have to be contacted if salaries were less than 999 kronor per employer and year. However, it turned out they overlooked the fact that employees did not receive their expected EU insurance cards. This oversight made them into uninsured workers, since no one paid their social fees or taxes—which is normally the responsibility of the employer. When confronted with this, the spokesperson explained, "This is very difficult and hard to know how to help and follow these rules. We are talking about very simple services [here]. There are no social fees or taxes, or anything like that paid for this. If they are to work according to the collective bargaining agreements, how do we then make Swedes hire them for these salaries?"[22] After this revelation the agency became a legal company, which both secured slightly higher salaries for the Roma and enabled clients to make tax reductions. This procedure had been made possible by the Alliance as Sweden's own incarnation of "union busting," achieved through tax reductions instead of institutional changes. Consequently, labor power that could have been invested in the public sector was instead transferred to the cleaning of private households. What's more, the maneuver lowered the lowest wages in Sweden by 50 percent.[23]

This anecdote symptomatizes the prevailing ideological depiction of the source of the EU déclassés' "unemployability," if one was not to blame their "culture." After all, Swedes would not demand déclassés' very simple services if they weren't sufficiently cheap, so here the evil object must be bureaucracy. From a right-wing perspective, this object signifies the Left, which has, through collective bargaining agreements, made the Swedish Model "overprotective" of Swedish workers. We see this reflected in a conservative editorial written the same year:

> When the Moderates [discussed] begging bans, the Left was quick to condemn [them]. Correctly, they stated that poverty and begging do not disappear only because we don't see it on our streets.
>
> [However,] it is harder to see how the same Left can dismiss lower entry wages in Sweden, even if that would provide jobs for more people and create new entries to the labor market. The labor movement knows, of course, low-income jobs exist in other countries [and that those] are a first step out of poverty for many.
>
> It appears, simply, as if the Left is most interested in not having to see lower wages and simpler jobs here, on our streets. Thus, not even lower entry wages would give those who beg a chance to enter the labor market. That's the Left![24]

Notably, this narrative of implicating the Left as thieves of Enjoyment has been invoked by the Swedish Right since at least the 1980s. It follows the insider-outsider hypothesis, which depicts a horizontal society where innocent unemployed "outsiders" are not able to compete with the privileged "insiders" on the accurate market price of labor power due to the latter's unions, labor law protection, and insurances.[25] The perceived "outsiders" have varied in subjectivation—spanning immigrants, refugees, youth, and the chronically ill—but ultimately concern the industrial reserve army itself. In the first decade of the 2000s, the Alliance successfully mobilized this theory, wherein their ideological scapegoat of Enjoyment was simultaneously the egoistic "Left" and the "social beneficiary."

Interestingly enough, however, the editorial that linked the "beggar" to this ideology was but one of a few exceptions to the rule: with regard to the begging question, this narrative was hardly mobilized at all. Equally curious is that no counternarrative was brought forward by the Left (SAP) either. It was not until after the refugee crisis, when SAP started to advertise themselves as the saviors of "the Swedish Model" (as a melancholic defense of the National Thing of Enjoyment) that a description of the relationship between the EU déclassé and the Swedish Model was presented by them. Three SAP politicians, in favor of banning begging, wrote in 2017:

> The Social Democrats' response to poverty has never been alms. Begging is not a job and should not be cemented as a phenomenon in our society. [Sweden] should counteract begging and its causes [which] in reality, ultimately concerns our relationship with other countries and their citizens.
>
> [The] question of begging needs to be solved urgently. The perspective of the work of the government is to defend and develop the Swedish Model. In that model, begging is not an answer to poverty.[26]

What, then, is the answer to the déclassés' poverty within that model? Apparently, it's the vague model itself, since that signifier symbolizes "jobs" and trygghet. In this way, regarding "beggars," these Social Democrats seem to prove the insider-outsider hypothesis correct, but with the opposite moral implication: we must defend the border against "the outsiders," who are the problem of other countries and their citizens anyway. This inversion of the horizontal ideology, where the subject's Enjoyment is threatened by the outsiders instead of the insiders, was, of course, the radical nationalists' idea as well. What's more, after the refugee crisis, this would *also* become the dominant interpretation of the Right in general, though its original aim—to crush the unions and expand the low-income sector—remained intact.[27] Here we can see some precursors to the transformation of the dominant ideology of hegemony, in which the xeno-racist counter-ideology has managed to make both capital and labor follow its lead.

While we don't want to get ahead of ourselves, it must be noted that this coming shift (after hegemony's crisis in late 2015) would not have been able to occur if the insider-outsider theory did not correspond to widespread perceptions of one's Imagined, lived reality. The insider-outsider hypothesis, in its original incarnation, appeared to be plausible because it helped to make sense of the inherent and increasingly discernible duality of the welfare systems. After all, there really was a qualitative stratum of "insiders" and "outsiders," increasingly racialized, within the working class, but the distinction was hierarchical before horizontal. However, in a dialectical irony, this correlation between ideology and reality was actually facilitated by the implementation of the hypothesis in the immediate wake of the 1990s crisis, when the economist who coined the theory, Assar Lindbeck, architected neoliberal reforms that were intended to save the economy—including the relinquishment of full employment as a policy goal. When the reforms' outcomes only broadened the gap, the ideology's failure was interpreted as proof that not enough had been done, as the outsiders were now even more "outside." Amid the remarkable silence of representatives of both capital and labor on the begging question (and disinterest in incorporating the issue into their competing ideologies), this ideology was further naturalized—after all, what was the EU déclassé if not the perfect outsider to the labor market and society?

Within the ideology of Swedish moral exceptionalism, fueled by genuine desires for solidarity, the initial response (after "beggars" were sanctioned as good objects) naturally became efforts to help them find work. As benevolent civilians tried to shepherd their begging neighbors into the labor market, they encountered webs of rules regarding registration and payment—including obstacles to déclassés' ability to be paid, such as their lack of bank accounts and civic numbers. When the reigning fraction of the state did nothing to facilitate this procedure (whether following a right-wing or left-wing logic), the depiction of the EU déclassés as outsiders to the institutional labor market gained further ground. What's more, when representatives of labor joined the Right in framing them as outsiders who did not belong to the Swedish Model, the hegemonic force of this ideology increased all the more. The initial sympathy among civilians, I contend, turned into apathy, as their engagement in efforts to help did not end the presence of begging; on top of that, the barriers they encountered helped reproduce notions of the EU déclassés as not only outsiders but also, ultimately, "unemployable." Seemingly, there was no foreseeable solution other than to either make them return home or else accept begging—an acceptance that is difficult, given the anxiety brought on by the Other.

Why did "the beggars" not become objects of desire for either labor or capital, but only a Real of their battleground? One answer is historical, and the other is structural. The first concerns the begging question's temporary intersection with the growing refugee issue, which appeared to constitute a greater obstacle to the ability of the state apparatus to govern. As we know, there is a moral-political priority to accept the "deserving refugee" as someone who is going to stay in the territory, whereas the EU déclassé position entails a temporary visit. While the staying refugee must, by necessity, become a tool of the class struggle within the nation-state, this did not have to become the case with the EU déclassé. Nevertheless, the symptom of the latter's "unemployability" reveals that those in command of Swedish hegemony lacked answers regarding what to do with those so impoverished that they were not considered integratable. Since we know there are also Swedish people struggling with long-term unemployment, this revelation constitutes a *structural* problem built in to the contemporary welfare state apparatus itself and its foundational dual character. With neither the legal status of deservingness nor housing, the déclassé is *declassed* from being a consideration of both labor's and capital's dominant associations: a "specter" to capitalists and a "passively rotting mass" to unions, to paraphrase Marx. Without the education needed to acquire the relevant level of competence demanded by the regulated labor market, the déclassé is neither capital's nor labor's business—after all, it's not up to the unions to "create jobs," and there's no compulsion on capitalists to create jobs out of kindness. Further, there's no demand for shoe shiners and the like in the Swedish labor market; to expect such demands could be generated purely for the sake of solidarity would be nothing but naive. Ultimately, the only institution that could have invested in the EU déclassés as a labor power to formally exploit in accordance with the contemporary labor market's actual demands was *the state*—but while the state could have taken actions to train, retrain, or support the unemployed, it is not expected under post-Soviet capitalism that any state introduce universal mandatory employment.

Housing: A Monstrous Hybrid

THE HUMAN RIGHTS STANDPOINT

For the reigning fraction, the EU déclassés' housing question was not as easy to ignore as the labor question. After all, their homelessness was a tangible, visible, and spatial problem that affected the electorate in their daily lives. (Remember the terror acts carried out against the settlements and their inhabitants.) This issue also appeared more mobilizable to proponents of the human rights ideology, who in this case could effectively combine the force of law with the idea of historical responsibility for Roma's contemporary marginalization and, at the same time, appeal to the Swedish ideology's moralism. Due to the legally binding UN and EU human rights conventions on the right to housing, shelter, and sanitary conditions, it was considered wrongful to evict déclassés without offering them alternative accommodation. For example, three representatives from a legal association on social rights argued in one article:

> In several cases, the European Court of Justice has ruled that [such] evictions constitute a violation of the European Convention [. . .].
>
> The European Social Charter, which Sweden has committed itself to abide by, also applies to other groups, including Roma and Travelers, regarding the rights that are linked to life and dignity.
>
> This includes that no one can be evicted, not even from an illegally occupied place, without the dignity of the persons concerned being respected and without alternative housing being made available.[28]

Additionally, the scene of police officers chasing away poor homeless Roma from settlements served as an uncanny echo of the dark history of Swedish Roma. For the lion's share of the twentieth century, Swedish Roma and Travelers were systematically denied, or conditionally granted, access to housing. Occasionally, the racist sentiments behind this discrimination were blatantly expressed: in 1923 the national committee for a new Poor Relief Act recommended the national expulsion of all Swedish Roma by restricting their mobility so severely that they would leave voluntarily.[29] There was also a common municipal practice of fining Roma in order to hinder them from settling, a procedure guided by combined racist and economic incitements to keep poor-relief expenses low.[30] Another strategy, lasting into the 1960s, was to maintain arbitrary deadlines for Roma settlements: they were (maybe) left alone for a couple of weeks and then torn down by the police, who escorted the settlement's residents out of the municipality. Notably, this policing practice had no legal support and, consequently, was hardly documented by officials.[31] These procedures involving the constant, forced displacement of Roma not only normalized the cultural expectation of them to be "nomads," but also effectively excluded them from becoming official citizens; their lack of registration (because they were never any municipality's formal responsibility) rendered them, in several regards, practically stateless. In her autobiography, Roma civil rights activist Katarina Taikon (1932–95) sheds light on this experience, explaining that, in her childhood, while being denied access to housing, her family's lack of sanitation options and resultant uncleanliness were used as a justification for not giving them access to reasonable accommodation.[32]

This history influenced various critics of the authorities' contemporary treatment of the déclassés' homelessness. In 2014, for example, a déclassé settlement in a Stockholm suburb was set ablaze, causing one man's death. Immediately thereafter, an enforcement officer, assisted by one hundred police officers, executed an eviction against the sixty settlers, who agreed to peacefully leave but were not allowed to bring their personal assets, and each was charged 600 kronor. These actions were condemned by the chairman of the newly appointed Commission against Antiziganism—also the former Council of Europe commissioner for human rights—who saw this procedure as a continuation of the Swedish state's historical treatment of the Roma:

[This] police action was brutal and unjustified. [Such] actions must be implemented regarding the human rights of those affected. They ought to be prepared by conversation—[with] a translator—and offered an alternative. [. . .]

Unfortunately, Sweden's antiziganist history has a topical reflection. [The] eviction [put] the affected Roma under further strain in an already vulnerable situation and confirmed their experiences and senses of living in a hostile environment.

With what credibility can we criticize other countries' treatment of Roma when the police force [enforces] political decisions that violate their rights?[33]

THE COMMONSENSICAL STANDPOINT

It must be stressed that while the idealism of natural rights became a powerful force in negotiating the housing question, so too did the commonsensicality of the capitalist moral economy. To paraphrase the moral genealogy on the relationship between begging and stealing: while the issue of begging was morally ambiguous, the issue of *squatting* was considered a definitive moral wrong. In other words, the act of settling on others' (private or public) land was a commonsensical *crime*—the "deservingness" of the poor perpetrator in question notwithstanding. And, as we know, "criminals" ought not to be rewarded but punished. Further, while the side of those in solidarity with the déclassés argued that they were homeless in Sweden, it could also be argued that they were *not* homeless—since they (ought to) have housing in their home countries. When, for example, Amnesty International in 2019 urged Swedish authorities to guarantee déclassés' human right to accommodation, the development leader for the national coordination of "vulnerable EU citizens" denied that this was a human rights issue, since "no one" is "forced to sleep rough" and that "you are not homeless just because you have your home in another country."[34] Disputing the fact that déclassés are in fact homeless in Sweden inevitably leads to the conclusion that their settlements, sleeping arrangements, and loitering are expressions of uncivilized and immoral behavior—that the déclassés use public spaces as private places *deliberately*. A case in point is a local politician's reaction to some déclassés' settling in an inner-city schoolyard in Stockholm in 2016, where the employed found feces (abjection per excellence). Ignoring the practical impossibility to find free public toilets in Swedish cityscapes, he stated:

> It is utterly unreasonable that in Stockholm schools, one must start the day by cleaning the schoolyard of clothes, debris, leftovers, and feces. These people have also been repeatedly asked to leave kindergartens and schools, so they know the deal very well, yet this behavior continues. [The] present situation is disastrous from the perspective of children. [In] Sweden, Swedish law applies, it applies to everyone staying here, and it says it is forbidden to sleep in public spaces. Nevertheless, the police choose to look the other way and not hand out fines. That is unacceptable. We can never accept illegal settlements, much less our children's playgrounds being used as [toilets].[35]

Of course, he is not asking himself *why* "these people," who "know the deal very well," continue with their immoral behavior. That they are houseless and have no access to toilets is not compatible with the ideological statement that no one in Sweden needs to sleep rough. Through the prism of Swedish ideology, then, such an abnormal practice cannot be understood in any other way than as an expression of a character trait: "they" "know the deal very well," yet continue to do this to "*our* children." Such perceptions made the human rights proponents' claim regarding lawbreakers' right to housing even more absurd from the perspective of the dominant ideology. In one telling example, a bourgeois editor, responding to an anarchist network that defended déclassés' settlements by claiming "the right to housing should be unconditional," countered: "It is not without wondering if this is irony? Maybe [a statement] to exaggerate the unreasonableness of socialism? One who has paid a million or two for one's home can, in any case, not avoid feeling fooled."[36]

While the Swedish *grundlag* (constitution) stipulates that housing is a social right guaranteed to the public, such an unconditional right was not the de facto reality of the Swedish housing regime. Here the theft of Enjoyment came into play, prompting an indignant reaction: "How could the squatting, uncivilized, Roma pauper foreigner receive an unconditional right to housing, when this right has not been afforded to hard-working, tax-paying, Swedish citizens?!" What this actualized contradiction on the Swedish right to housing reveals is an ongoing sense of national melancholia regarding the loss of the folkhem housing model—the built environment of exceptional equality.

THE TRAJECTORY TO THE CONTRADICTION OF
EXCEPTIONAL-EQUAL HOUSING

Folkhem Housing

While the local discrimination of Swedish Roma would prevail in subsequent decades, *The Gypsy Investigation* in 1956 marked a historical break with the continuity of Swedish state-sanctioned anti-Roma racism with its recommendation that the state take the initiative to make Swedish Roma and Travelers into citizens with social rights.[37] Its proposal, which held the state, rather than the municipalities, responsible for funding and organizing special programs to assist the Roma in education, housing integration, and the labor market, was prompted by the tendency of municipalities to only show concern for their own budgets and to neglect Roma residents. The timing of this shift was no coincidence—it occurred in the heyday of the folkhem project, when a new housing system was established in order to address the outstanding housing deprivation of the 1930s. Here the interests of the state, labor, and capital intersected to produce high-quality housing on behalf of all classes. (Capital, for its part, desired cheap working-class rentals as a means of avoiding paying higher wages.) Against this backdrop a housing policy was established in which tax-financed subventions and regulations encouraged private and state-owned constructors to build cheap high-standard rental units; at the same time, municipally owned public housing companies were introduced. During 1965–74, one million housing units were built, signaling an end to the housing shortage in Sweden in the 1970s. With that said, many of these constructions would lay the groundwork for the continued segregation and racialization of the Swedish housing market.[38]

What was remarkable about the Swedish housing model was its *universal* ambition—its aim of building exceptional equality. Sociologist Ingrid Sahlin summarizes, "It did not contain any separate solutions for poor or other— according to landlords—less desirable or profitable households. Everyone should have good housing conditions, and housing should be a social right, not a commodity."[39] Nonetheless, the capitalist market remained the distribution mechanism. What the universal model did was adjust the power dynamic and transaction between tenants and landlords; construction and rent were subsidized, and poor renters could obtain housing allowances. Consequently, the establishment of the social right to housing effectively amounted to the state's responsibility to enhance all citizens' *opportunity* to participate as customers.[40]

One result of this paradigm shift was the absence of *social housing* as a housing alternative, likewise a tacit banishment of it in the dominant ideology.[41] After all, public housing companies and rent subsidies made "social housing" an unnecessary category; plus, the whole project's rationale was a dismissal of separate solutions and standards that divided people into classes. With regard to the political situation under discussion in this book, the crucial legacy of this era was the discursive dismissal of separate class standards of housing. When the neoliberalization of housing followed, therefore, this dismissal prevailed, making "no housing" preferable to the acceptance of "slum communities." When, for example, both neoliberal and anarchist actors in 2015 suggested the possibility of arranging settlements for EU déclassés on municipal land with electricity, water, and sanitation (ironically labeled "well-planned slum communities"), investigator Valfridsson dismissed this option. Without offering an alternative, he explained, "I do not think any municipal politician wants that. Then, the municipality takes on the responsibility for slum communities that we have worked so hard to erase [from Sweden]."[42]

Financialization, Hybridization, Contradiction

Following the productivity crisis of the 1970s, the subsequent global capital accumulation regime became increasingly dependent upon finance capital and built city-environment investment. Notably, the safest capital assets are the entities that people cannot do without—such as housing. Here we see the continued relevance of Streeck's thesis regarding the outsourcing of the funding of democratic capitalism: by deregulating financial markets and transferring funding costs from the state and companies to the housing applicant, capital could invest in housing while keeping wages low and decreasing taxation. In this way housing turned into a unique commodity form: both a financial asset and site of risk, promising returns to buyer, seller, and the bank. Consequently, it lies in all parties' "interest" (except those renting and the homeless) that housing prices rise, and the construction of ownership units are prioritized over rentals.

One might argue that from the perspective of Swedish hegemony, this ultimately global housing regime of financialization belongs to the ideological Real (as an absent cause) of the crisis of hegemony. Looking only at the financialization of the economy, Swedish capital's financial character has spurred the hollowing out of the welfare systems, rise of inequalities, and vanishing of "exceptional equality." As mentioned in chapter 6, the U.S. housing crisis caused chain reactions that led to the increased presence of both EU déclassés and refugees in Sweden. When interpreted this way, the financialization of the built environment constitutes a global ideological Real of democratic capitalism. As geographer Don Mitchell argues, "urban space's deepening commodification as city space" has led the built environment itself to become the "central locus of capital accumulation in the contemporary economy."[43] Further, because the commodification of urban space involves making it "attractive" to customers, the inevitable uptick in homelessness caused by deregulations of public housing regimes makes the presence of homeless people in this space "unattractive." Here, abjection receives a political and ideological cause and function.

Though the changes of the folkhem housing system had already begun in the late 1960s, a clear shift occurred when the SAP government deregulated the financial markets in 1985, leading to the 1990s' financial crash. In 1991 the newly elected right-wing government closed the Housing Department, never to be reintroduced. Additionally, they allowed municipalities to begin selling their public housing cohorts, terminated the legislation enabling municipalities to distribute apartments according to social considerations, and canceled state loans and investment grants for construction.[44] In 2011 the Alliance legally mandated that public housing companies operate "in business-like forms." That same year *The Economist* estimated the Swedish housing market to be one of the world's most unaffordable and overvalued.[45] Although an investigation in 2016 revealed a housing shortage in 250 out of Sweden's 290 municipalities, this shortage was not attributable to an over-all lack of housing, but rather *affordable* housing.[46] Simultaneously, since the 1970s, housing has become the largest personal asset class in Sweden, accounting for roughly 45 percent of total wealth.[47] This acquisition of a wealth inheritance within families has been crucial in cementing Swedish class inequality. Because home ownership is considered a financial invest-ment for the future, buyers believe themselves to secure their own trygghet and grow less interested in "supporting others" through taxes. Ultimately, these housing investments normalize a capitalist mindset among the priv-ileged, encouraging a cross-class alliance with an imagined shared interest of not upsetting this moral economy of homeownership.

Strikingly, it is possible to argue that the housing system of the 2010s shares more similarities to the system before the 1930s than the one that came after that. After all, contemporary housing is mainly guided by market principles, there is a shortage of affordable rentals, and private profit-seeking actors dominate construction.[48] In 2015, for example, fewer than 20,000 housing units were constructed in Sweden, roughly the same amount as in the 1930s (and an astonishing contrast to 1974's peak of 110,000 units).[49] Another parallel to the laissez-faire era is the growing rate of homeless-ness and the increasing responsibility taken by civil society to care for the homeless. For our purposes, another significant similarity is the return of Roma provisional settlements—and the policing of them. This "repetition of history" highlights the need to understand racism as a dialectic: the "socialization" of the Swedish Roma's homelessness in the mid-twentieth century followed the nationalization of social responsibility and counter-cyclical economic policy, aiming to prevent poverty rather than addressing it. Next, the racialization of the EU Roma's homelessness accompanies the devolution of social responsibility and racialization of the housing market, following the neoliberal revanche of capital. In the debate, however, this semblance of similar historical conditions was rather superficially treated as an object of desire (to counteract), with both the people fighting for déclassés and those fighting for "order" accusing each other of wanting to reintroduce the pre-folkhem Swedish landscape.

Just as the labor question represents a political deadlock in the class struggle, with ambivalence regarding whether immigrants are to be used as a battering ram against the Swedish Model of laborer protection, the housing question of the déclassés implies a similar short circuit. This struggle between Left and Right concerns the zombie-like survival of the "exceptional," "universal" housing model. As geographer Brett Christophers argues, the contemporary Swedish housing system is not one of total neo-liberalization, but a complex, "monstrous" "hybrid of legacy regulated elements on the one hand and neoliberalised elements on the other," which plays a pivotal role "in the creation, reproduction and intensification of socio-economic inequality."[50] This hybridity is made evident in the fact that market rents are still not the norm; instead, the rent levels are collectively bargained among tenants' unions and landlords, and there is a use-value approach in setting rents. Another expression of this amalgamation is the hegemonic rejection of social housing as an option to housing the growing number of homeless people. The Left, for its part, wants to shield what remains of the old system against market forces, while the Right has been too anxious to conform to the dominant folkhem ideology of equality and avoid initiating a debate on actual housing for the poor. In this way the déclassés' homelessness symptomized an unholy alliance of an unwillingness to address the contradictions of this monstrous hybrid on behalf of society's poorest. So too did the housing of the refugees, albeit in a different way: during and after the refugee crisis, there were several incidents where moral rage was spurred by the revelation that municipalities rented or bought ownership shares for temporarily accommodating refugees.[51] Contradictorily, the absence of citizenship rights gave refugees *human* rights of accommodation while they awaited asylum evaluation or relocation. This "unconditional" right to housing was not enjoyed by the Swedish homeless, since housing isn't actually unconditionally guaranteed in Sweden. This perceived preference for the refugee Other at the expense of homeless natives was registered by some as a severe disturbance of the moral economy of fairness. Moreover, it reinforced racist fantasies of "the elite" being in collusion with refugees to steal public resources.

With all of this in mind, it is clear why it seemed so difficult to find a "fair" solution on behalf of the "temporarily visiting" EU déclassés. If they were acknowledged to have an unconditional right to housing in whatever form, on behalf of the state, then another choice would emerge: Should this housing form be of radically lower standard than the rest of the housing stock (thus ruining the ideology of equality) or of an equal standard (thus destabilizing the moral economy of rights)? Plus, the latter option implied an "unfair" competition against private landlords, camping owners, and builders—exaggerating "the unreasonableness of socialism."

A MORAL-BUREAUCRATIC GRAY ZONE

In a 2015 editorial, *Dagens Nyheter* described the municipalities' treatment of the déclassés' homelessness as playing out in "a moral-bureaucratic gray zone."[52] As aforementioned, municipalities handled the housing question differently. While municipalities' attempts to solve the déclassés' homelessness involved unique problems, such as having to strike a balance between national and international laws (and counteracting opposition against "cementing" "slum communities"), it's worth mentioning that the editorial's description applies the broader national landscape of homelessness as well. In a national estimation from 2017, more than 33,250 people were identified as homeless in Sweden—5,900 were in "acute homelessness," while the rest were homeless people accessing different forms of temporary solutions. Notably, this number included neither EU déclassés nor all those tens of thousands of people who had eluded the authorities. Out of the official number, in any case, one in five did not have any social problems other than their lack of housing.[53] There has been no national housing policy for decades, so there has been no homelessness policy either. Instead, the issue has been neutralized by efforts to shift the homeless out of public sight and contain them in various schemes that offer temporary solutions.[54] Indeed, homelessness has become a *local* political problem: a responsibility for the municipalities' social services, brought about by the cutbacks and reorganizations in the wake of the 1990s crisis. In 2019 it was revealed that municipal officers in Stockholm bought rental contracts in small rural towns for their "own" homeless populations, dumping their responsibilities on these much poorer municipalities—a repetition of the historical trends presented in chapter 2.[55]

Deprived of their former right to relocate people to vacant rental apartments, municipalities have turned to partnerships with local NGOs and private companies, in which the partners run different accommodation operations. As public goods turned into markets, and these tax-funded markets were regulated New Public Management style, 2008 saw the implementation of complicated legislation related to public procurements of private services. The Law on Public Procurement declares that public buyers must choose the cheapest alternative among those promising to fulfill the assignment, forcing municipalities and counties to scrutinize what services they could fund without thwarting these new markets (as in "positive discrimination"). This, of course, created a legal maze for public actors, with confusion regarding which NGO operations they could fund, how much they could give, and what they could demand from them. Some of the larger towns, in their efforts to assist the déclassés, tried to circumvent this legal labyrinth by cooperating with the City Mission's initiated advice-and-support centers called Crossroads—targeting EU citizens and third-country nationals "living in vulnerability or homelessness," partly publicly funded and connected to other NGOs.[56]

To make matters worse, the very policing of the déclassés' homelessness turned out to constitute a moral-bureaucratic problem of its own. According to Swedish law, eviction procedures were the responsibility of the enforcement officers—not the police—who were required to identify every trespassing individual and listen to their reasons for trespassing.

Since the trespassers in question often lacked documents and spoke neither Swedish nor English, proper identification was a complicated matter. Enforcement officers also had to take into consideration the "exceptional" notion of Allemansrätten, a constitutional yet vaguely defined freedom to roam on others' land. This ancient right, integral to Sweden's saga of exceptional equality, affords a couple of hours' or days' stay in green areas if nothing is destroyed. In several cases it could not be proven whether déclassés violated the Allemansrätt. Further, on account of the cornered position of the state's representatives following the "antiracist momentum," the police, by invoking the eviction legislation, appeared rather passive in many cases of trespassing—at least, according to the commonsensical view of private property. Besides, Valfridsson claimed to "have heard officers say that there's no point in imposing fines on this group because they have no money to pay."[57] Such a lenient attitude regarding the executives of the state's responsibility to maintain law and order was, of course, not considered to be "fair" toward other lawbreakers: "My concern as a lawyer is that this type of consideration is not taken by the police if it is a Swedish homeless person who fulfills his needs or camps in a park. [By that,] I mean that we cannot treat any group in society differently, but apply the legislation as it is set." This logic, in accordance with the dominant ideology of equal treatment and fairness, was to become one of Valfridsson's main strategies as he set out to solve the begging question alongside the looming "refugee crisis."

9   The Conjuncture, 2015–2019

In the spring of 2015, a small, temporary window was opened for the initiation of a discussion on social policies on behalf of EU déclassés— exemplified by a magazine reportage in which all parties declared their official standings on the begging question.[1] While it was unanimously considered self-evident that "the home countries" were primarily responsible for solving this problem, several parties suggested supplementary efforts on Swedish soil: the Left Party advocated for municipal parade grounds with clean water and sanitation; EP wanted to make it easier to obtain a coordination number in order to seek work; the Center Party planned to present suggestions on integration in the autumn; and SAP encouraged municipalities to make greater use of EU funding for Roma inclusion. Still, it must be acknowledged that, in view of the structural situation at hand, these suggestions were rather modest. In any case the temporary window was already closing, and the (re)turn of the begging question into an issue of law and order loomed on the horizon.

Accumulating Anxieties of the Others

One crucial event in this process, I submit, was an initiative to turn the déclassés into street paper vendors. In early 2015 the Stockholm-based volunteer network HEM had begun working with a Norwegian association that published a magazine made exclusively for Roma to sell. For context, street newspapers had existed in Sweden since 1998, as the public considered street magazine vending not to be begging but "deserving" work. While the Gothenburg-based magazine *Faktum* took on déclassés as salespeople, their Stockholm-based sibling, *Situation Sthlm*, did not—their mission served registered homeless people only. HEM, for its part, had no money, no business knowledge, and no facilities, so they sold copies of the magazine to presumptive sellers on the streets for a reduced price, who were then allowed to keep all the profits.[2] Immediately, the media celebrated this project as *the* solution to begging in Sweden, and the magazine was distributed nationwide. According to an author whose story was included in the first issue, her goal was to promote dignity: "I think I, like most people, feel grief when I see people sit and beg in the streets. And that is the point of this; one is not to beg, but they will be allowed to stand up and look us in the eyes when one sells this book."[3]

Rather quickly, this success story turned into a disaster. First of all, bank rules against accepting large amounts of cash (or any cash at all) prevented HEM from turning déclassés' cash revenues into bank accounts.[4] What's more, the magazine became a competitor with established street papers, creating an *actual* market for a commodity that was not supposed to have one. As the public looked on, rivalries between native and foreign vendors intensified, feeding perceptions of déclassés stealing income opportunities from "our own" homeless.[5] While regular vendors received job training and followed a code of conduct, the EU déclassés were not registered as vendors and had no binding standards of conduct—indeed, the majority had never vended before and were given no formal training. Besides, they were not only competing with "Swedes," but *with each other*. Many simultaneously begged while trying to sell too. In all likelihood, they did not want to be "rehabilitated"; they needed money. This brought about a rather surreal sight in larger public and commercial spaces in the bigger towns: in March 2015 I remember walking a distance of two blocks in Stockholm Central Station and met no less than eight people competing to sell the same issue. Conditions were not improved by "shady" networks infiltrating the business, as native street vendors were threatened with knives to leave their selling spots in Gothenburg.[6] Worse yet, copycats popped up, tricking déclassés into buying and then trying to sell "magazines" with incomprehensible Google-translated texts, further diminishing the reputations of street magazines and the déclassés. Vendors of *Situation Sthlm* reported that many customers expressed "shame and malaise regarding their own irritation and anger" toward "beggars": "'Am I a racist because I think this way?' an elderly woman asked me when she bought the paper from me. [. . .] she was tired of being asked for money by six, seven people every ten meters on her way to the store. And that they asked her to withdraw cash if she said she didn't have any money."[7] Another vendor reflected, "It has become too much of everything for people; they cannot stand it, don't want to. The last straw became the EU migrants and the begging. Everyone is shutting down. In the end, there's only hate left. That's hard."

With this said, HEM's ill-fated attempt at creating jobs cannot be interpreted as proving the "unemployability" of déclassés, as *Faktum*, by contrast, salaried roughly five hundred "Romanian and Bulgarian Roma" at the end of 2015.[8] Besides, HEM's implosion was attributable to an absence of resources, facilities, and institutions' (state or private) support. Most notable of all was the media's (and public's) naivety in believing that any "low-skilled job" would, by itself, be an antidote to extreme poverty and exclusion. This naivety, of course, further strengthens our thesis that the anxiety of begging itself made people instinctively desire any solution but begging's continuation. Symptomatically, the desire for déclassés to "stand up and look us in the eye" turned out to be even more disturbing and fear-inducing than their "passivized" begging.

Amid the failure of this "quick fix," the budding realization that "the beggars'" visit was not likely to be temporary began to take hold; likewise, it became obvious that their needs were more severe than previously expected. A local support group in Småland, for example, had collected 100,000 kronor for "long-term" projects in the déclassés' home countries in the previous autumn, believing "the beggars" could now return home for good. They were surprised, therefore, when the déclassés returned a couple of months later, demanding their share of the money, as their problems were immediate and personal, not "long-term."[9] Simultaneously, the settlements expanded in numbers, alongside the accumulation of received refugees, the reports on the horrors of ISIS, and European terrorist attacks by radicalized Salafists. As it started to become "too much of everything for people," all these issues (together composing an "everything") ideologically signaled, alongside "anxiousness," "racial difference" as their common denominator. Sensing the turn in sentiments, the Moderates, in April, amid a growing crisis both within and without the party (because of their losses to SD, backlash against the December Agreement, and growing dissatisfaction with their leadership), once again suggested the criminalization of "organized" begging—reissuing the proposition from 2012.[10] At the same time, fractions of capital discovered that the issue made for an excellent resource for the normalization of SD. Some weeks later an editorial in the financial magazine *Dagens Industri* demanded prohibition, citing a local scope of supposedly criminal begging.[11] Finally, in June the neoliberal think tank director memorably discussed in part 1 wrote his piece—hereafter, he would mobilize support for SD in various ways.[12]

Here it is crucial to repeat that these attitudes were not universally shared among "the people"—as mentioned, during the same period, significant engagement for the benefit of both déclassés and refugees took off nationwide. In this way the foreign-Other-in-need became a dominant object of desire, but this object's relation to desire varied between the ideal types of "desiring to help the Other" and "desiring the Other's disappearance." As Valfridsson would phrase it in his report, there became a "dynamic of extremes" between those burning down déclassés' settlements and others blocking evictions and finding new settlement spots.[13]

However, as the focus of the begging question's media content increasingly shifted to the settlements, "the beggar" went on to become a "perpetrator" in a legalistic sense. Initially constituting a moral problem, "the beggar" now became an *order problem proper*—a problem in need of policing. Through an ideological conflation of cause and effect, the problems of déclassés' homelessness became interpreted as a consequence of begging itself: columnists and politicians identified urban encounters with loitering as part of "the problems that follow begging," prompting some to demand a national begging ban because of this.[14] Meanwhile, a liberal columnist complained of finding excrement in a Stockholm suburb and "the politicians snoozing" away the problem: "I certainly do not want a begging ban. But the widespread laxity toward the problems following begging risks incurring serious consequences. When municipalities and the state fail, we can get a situation where people start to want to 'take matters into their own hands.' We have already seen disgusting examples of physical attacks [on] poor and vulnerable beggars."[15] It was also in this suburb, during this period, that a twenty-five-year-old man continuously persecuted déclassés, hating them for not behaving "normally" (see chapter 3). It was in this context that the columnist continued: "It is the resignation itself that constitutes the biggest issue. In the name of poverty, people can take the liberty of occupying land, erecting slums, building rubbish heaps, and littering the streets and squares without anyone lifting a finger. The Sweden Democrats just thank and receive." Here we witness a growing crisis of hegemony of the state's legitimacy and emerging calls for law and order. When law is not followed, the "state fails." Correspondingly, the columnist's proposed solution is to recruit more security guards—this way ironically paraphrasing sd's own stance. So did the Moderates in Stockholm, who wanted to create *municipal* security guards to hinder déclassés from sleeping outdoors, since the government "does not take people's anxieties seriously."[16]

In September this accusation regarding the settlements' threat to the legitimacy of the state and police was amplified by a public service televised reportage on a large settlement in a private vacant lot in Sorgenfri, central Malmö, that housed up to two hundred residents. With no access to water and sewers, it constituted an "environmental hazard" according to the authorities, who had tried in vain to secure the correct juridical grounds for eviction. To add to the drama, this case was presented alongside an incident in the countryside in which an elderly couple living abroad had their holiday cabin occupied by déclassés, with no attempts from the police to try to evict them.

Unsurprisingly, this story garnered great attention in the press. A liberal editorial complained about the police's excuse that these evictions were the responsibility of the enforcement officer: "This logic is incomprehensible. [Back] in the day, suspects could be prosecuted for trespassing. Is it really totally impossible to intervene in all these cases acknowledged this year? It [appears] as if the police choose to look the other way. In those

HEGEMONY

communities affected, frustration is growing."[17] In seeming agreement, the general counsel of the Swedish Property Federation wrote, "Concerning the living conditions of EU migrants, in many cases, the situation is undignified partly from a humanitarian perspective; no one should have to live like that in Sweden, but also from a legal state perspective. [We see] a remarkable passivity from the authorities. We have constitutional protection of ownership in Sweden, and the incapacity of authorities to help does not belong in a legal state."[18] A former judge concurred, too: "There are no excuses for the police not identifying them. It seems to me as if the authorities do everything they can to avoid troublesome decisions. [An] eviction must be carried out by force, and the police do not want that kind of attention. [Shortsightedly,] one avoids being in the loophole of negative attention. Instead, it results in long-term consequences; it leads to distrust toward the state's ability to maintain law and order."[19]

Notably, the primary "bad guys" here are the police—and, ultimately, the state itself, which is not protecting private property. Symptomatically, the déclassés are presented in this screed as innocuous lawbreakers, victims who "should not have to live like that in Sweden"— thereby securing the continuation of the Swedish ideology. One telling example of attempts to maintain this ideology within this aggravating contradiction was the Red-Green government of Malmö's response to an open letter from residents of the settlement themselves. Alexandro, Ana, Constantin, Ionela, Larisa, Nelu, Nicoleta, Nicusor, Maria, and Paul had argued against tearing down their makeshift home, writing:

If we who are living [here] get evicted, dispossessed of our possessions, and hence are forced to sleep on streets and in parks, if our settlement disappears and we are subjected to violence in the city—is that better than us staying on [this vacant lot]? We are poor, in all ways possible, but we do not hurt the city in any way. We are not coming here to cause troubles, but to make money for our families.

[Our] lives here in the settlement work well. We feel safe, we can sleep, we are not subjected to as much violence as other EU migrants living more scattered lives. It is, in all ways, an advantage to the town that we have this settlement.

[If] the City of Malmö does not want us staying here, on this poisonous ground, we wish another form of accommodation. Give us work and housing, then Malmö will not have any problems with begging.

We could live like common people like you, like the municipal [politicians].

Our lives are hard. We pray that you never have to be in our situation. We wish you all the best in the world. [. . .]

Thank you for reading.[20]

The City of Malmö's sober reply read:

We are deeply sorry for the situation making you feel forced to travel all the way to Sweden and that many of you do not find any other livelihood than begging.

It is upsetting that EU countries are treating some of their citizens this [way.]

We are welcoming you to Malmö to try and find work and accommodation. You have the same right as other EU citizens to try for three months to find a sustainable income.[21]

For context, the anxious management of the settlement issue took place within an intensified media frenzy of interconnected social issues, including "immigration," "violence," and "the state lacking control." One notable event involved an Eritrean refugee, who, when his asylum application was rejected, went to IKEA in Västerås and murdered two strangers, thereafter stabbing himself.[22] Parallel to this, popular support for SD, according to the polls, steadily increased for the duration of the year. To further elucidate the conjuncture of social anxieties in Sweden that crystallized that year, I (once again) permit myself to quote an article at length—this time, a speculative chronicle from late August written by a retired journalist. The headline is telling: "The SD Monster Is on Its Way to Swallow Us All."[23] I've placed it within its broader context to show that while "beggars" are only mentioned in passing (emphasized), the begging question's racialization had become integrated into a much larger crisis of hegemony itself:

> Each new table sends shivers of terror [up the spines of] the Social Democratic leadership, which seems completely frozen with fear. [However,] the Left's leadership pretends that nothing has happened and hopes everything will be fine [tomorrow].
>
> [People tell me,] "This country is falling apart. [I] fear the future." [What] they are talking about is the sharp increase in immigration of [refugees].
>
> Sometimes I see signs that Sweden is not what it used to be. Every day the trains stand still somewhere in the country because a line has fallen. Every day [there is] news on absurd waiting times in the emergency room. Streets and squares are often as dirty as in Istanbul and Cairo. *Now there are beggars sometimes only a few tens of meters apart, not only in Stockholm, but in almost every town and major municipality in the country.* Hand grenades are thrown at the police in Malmö. Gangs shoot sharply in Gothenburg.
>
> But in the center of Stockholm, well-dressed, beautiful, and well-trained men and women move [among] increasingly expensive apartments on the market. [Here,] everything shines prosperity.
>
> [Hatred] is growing online. The tone is sharpened in the debate. The fear of the stranger, the deviant, the different, spreads.
>
> [Sweden] is not on the brink of collapse, but the changes are so great, rapid, and forced that the fear that is spreading makes the SD monster bigger and bigger every day.

Here "beggars" are situated alongside Swedish youth shootings in suburbs—"gangs" composed primarily of disillusioned second-generation "immigrants" who are floundering in the education system.[24] Here, we see how the begging question represents but *one* symptom of widespread perceptions of "societal disintegration," and that this approaching catastrophe is interpreted as *mainly* caused by the increasing spatial appearance of non-white individuals, intertwined with emerging inequalities. Interestingly, the journalist's analysis intersects these sensations with the gradual breakdown of infrastructure due to neoliberalizations (of the railway, the health care system, and the housing market) and the polarization between rural and urban areas. In this way we discover a conjuncture of processes, constituting a state of moral panic, and a crisis of hegemony ("the leadership," we're told, are "completely frozen"), with the dumbfounded ruling bloc lacking answers on how to maintain consent. To once again quote the political scientist who noted a correlation between the sight of "beggars" and public support for SD: people believe "what they see with their own eyes, not what the politicians are babbling about in the media."[25]

Caring Rationality

But was "the leadership" really paralyzed? Regarding the problem of déclassé settlements, there did indeed appear to be confusion on how to proceed. In terms of the refugee numbers, meanwhile, this was not initially the case—the reigning fraction of the government and the state believed that they could ride out the wave of racial anxieties. Indeed, after the death of Alan Kurdi, Löfven, speaking at a *Refugees Welcome* demonstration in Stockholm, continued to defend a solidary refugee policy: "My Europe does not build walls, we help each other. [Those of you gathered here] show that people really depend upon each other. It's all of you who make Sweden into a country to be so proud of. [Now] we are going to speak about solidarity again."[26]

However, when it came to the EU déclassés, the government had begun to signal quite another attitude, though they still tried to comply with the Swedish ideology and the force of the still influential antiracist momentum. Since springtime, their appointed coordinator on the begging question, Valfridsson, had given interviews and written debate articles where he had informed the public of his juridical conclusions regarding Sweden's responsibility for the déclassés. In hindsight, his unspoken assignment must have been to somehow find ways to decrease the territorial presence of EU déclassés while simultaneously neutralizing the claims of the human rights ideology's appeals to law and morality.

After decades of intensifying capitalist contradictions, the Borromean knot, alongside the influx of refugees, had overdetermined the political solution to "the beggars": their discrete removal. With the EU déclassés' position mired in deadlocks and complications, they became—in contrast with the Symbolically more integrated (and therefore deserving) refugees—structurally "undeserving" poor. Nevertheless, this removal of the "undeserving" (who could not be deported) needed to comply with the dominant ideology and its proclaimed solidarity with those racial Others *as if* they were "deserving," since the previous momentum had made it difficult to discursively construct "the Roma" as "undeserving." Hence, what was needed was a discourse and an ideological fantasy where the National Thing of Swedish solidarity could be celebrated, while simultaneously making the situation so very hopeless for the déclassés that they would voluntarily leave. What was needed was a Swedish ideology on *caring rationality*: a rationality of technocratic expertise on behalf of the state, which could then explain why it was in everyone's best interest to facilitate the déclassés' "return home." Valfridsson, therefore, needed to be both rational and caring in his recommendations to thwart their continued stay. Put differently, he had to convince the public that the Thing of solidarity between rich and poor, soon to be ruined by the EU déclassés, could only be saved if the latter were to visually disappear.

In his first attempt, Valfridsson warned in an interview that the allocation of municipal land for legal settlements would reintroduce the "slum communities" that "we have worked so hard to erase." Next, alongside a charismatic NGO representative who had worked in Romania for a Sweden-based Christian charity called Heart to Heart since the 1990s, he advised the municipalities against letting déclassé children attend Swedish schools. Bucking the human rights ideology's demands to adhere to the UN Child Convention, they cautioned that "the good risks becoming the enemy of the best."[27] What's more, they argued that the convention's requirement that Sweden provide children with education did not explicitly stipulate *where* this had to happen; plus, by hindering déclassés from coming to Sweden, their children would have a better chance at receiving uninterrupted schooling back home (ignoring those countries' insufficient and discriminatory educational systems).

As contributions exploded following *Refugees Welcome*, Valfridsson and the minister of social affairs wrote a piece "recommending" that the public not give alms to déclassés, but instead to charity organizations working on "long-term, sustainable change" back in the home countries:

> Swedes [are] generally open and generous. This is something we should defend and nurture. This generosity also leads us to give to fellowmen asking for money.
>
> [However, this money] has the best utility in the hands of [organizations working in the relevant countries and with long experience of practical work in place]. By supporting long-term, sustainable work for improved education, livelihood, health, and structural reforms, more will see a meaningful future before them and following generations in the home countries.
>
> Let us continue to give money and tell our children that it is important to help the vulnerable human being. But let us do it in a way that leads to real, sustainable change.[28]

In a following article, where she noted that the government had donated 50 million kronor to an EU fund and initiated a bilateral dialogue with Romania and Bulgaria, the minister elaborated: "Sweden has a long tradition of contributing to changing structures for diminished economic vulnerability and the implementation of rights. If one prefers to instead, or to also, give to the person begging on the street, one should do so. We believe [however,] the money has much utility [among the organizations,] so people can, sustainably and in the long term, build their own lives with school, jobs, and housing."[29] Certainly, this line of reasoning would pass muster in the previously mentioned proto-IQ test ("Why is it generally better to give money to an organized charity than to a street beggar?"). Nevertheless, it remains an ideologically charged conclusion, since there is no immediately obvious reason *why* this would be the case. Let's say, for example, that 5,000 individuals beg in Sweden for 365 days (although not the same individuals, uninterruptedly—people migrate back and forth), and everyone makes 100 kronor per day by begging. In the end, this generates more than 180 million kronor per year without intermediaries and bureaucracy. Granted, this sum also goes to work expenses (traveling, food, and supplies in Sweden), but it's still more than three times the government's donation.

Even so, this benevolent reason was state sanctioned by Valfridsson in his role as an *expert*. But what expertise, exactly, did the lawyer acquire during his months as a coordinator? It may dismay the reader to find out that, in his state report, released in February 2016, there was *no research* whatsoever backing up these types of claims. Save a few quotations from actors attending a conference, who asserted that begging is no "long-term" solution to poverty—which no serious debater had ever claimed—Valfridsson did not have to rely on any facts when he stated: "To donate money to the one begging *risks* cementing the beggar role and not leading to any *long-term* change for the group. The children's schooling *risks* suffering, and the beggar role *risks* becoming inherited by the next generation."[30]

As emphasized, he uses the signifier "risk" to appeal to the ideological dimension of belief, desire, and anxiety. If you articulate the issue as a "risk," you apparently don't need to concretize the likelihood of these presumptions actually happening. Instead, it's enough to state the very possibility of future suffering (from the Other's desire)—to present it as commonsensical that begging is destructive. Here we once again encounter the power of the unconscious displacement of anxious fantasies concerning human capacities for evildoing into fantasies about the Other, and then concluding these qualities are inherent to the Other. The lack of hope and change, and the potential of "cementing the beggar role" (whatever that means), is here reified as the anxious object of "the beggar" itself. Further, the use of the empty signifier of "long-term change" facilitates an ideological inversion of space and time. By not specifying the time of the anticipated change, we do not know whether it is forecasted to occur next year, in the next generation, or after Judgement Day. By situating "change" in "the home countries" (or rather, *not here*), spatial and temporal uncertainty fuse to create a desire-laden ideological *belief*: if only they return home, everything will be fine (for them and for us). To make "the beggars" spatially disappear, in other words, is to assure ourselves of a happy ending that is staged elsewhere.

In this way the ideology of solidarity remains intact. Wishes for happiness create illusions with supporting arguments, to paraphrase Freud. It was in this manner that this belief became endorsed by hegemony's representatives as a basic political truth: we need to get rid of the Other, in a Swedish way. Upon inspecting the work of these representatives of "expertise" (playing the role of what Lacan and Žižek term "subjects supposed to know," or analysts called upon to "somehow guarantee" the reliability of the information we choose to believe), we cannot help but conclude: What is this work, if not ideology production?[31] In essence, these subjects were tasked with obscuring the Real—that there was no actual "long-term" solution on the horizon—and disavowing the Thing of the social bond's nonexistence by turning toward the believed cause of this fantasy's ruination.

To strengthen this argument further, and connect it to an analysis of the attempt of a dominant cross-fractions alliance (bridging the state and civil society) to secure hegemony in unruly times, I present the following statements for the reader's consideration.

When the state representatives recommended Swedes cease almsgiving, several members of the commentariat were outraged. Other opinion makers, however, found their recommendation—to scrutinize the "deep emotional question that begging is" by asking oneself rationally, "Where does my money make the most impact?"—"totally reasonable."[32] Simultaneously, Valfridsson's writing partner, the NGO representative who had joined him in opposing children's rights, claimed in various articles that begging was not a "long-term solution" and that "the migrants do not want to be here. They want more than anything to be at home," but they do not "see any other options for income and survival in the *short-term*" than panhandling abroad.[33] This supposed knowledge was reiterated in Valfridsson's report: "The majority of those coming here to beg do not see their future here. They want to go back to their home-countries. Considering their lack of language skills and education, it is not realistic to think most within the group would get jobs in Sweden. By being here, they also risk losing out on possible opportunities for livelihoods in their home-countries."[34] Of course, those "possible livelihoods" were not specified. However, the NGO representative had worked on establishing such "opportunities" in some villages, which was both used as an argument for the existence of long-term solutions in the report and an excuse for Löfven to state that he, personally, did not give to "beggars," but donated regularly to Heart to Heart—a rather unknown local organization.[35] Further, the promise that someone was attending to the needs of the déclassés back home enabled the minister of social affairs to claim later on (in 2017), when there was a *temporary* absence of déclassés in the cityscapes, that "the EU migrants have it better and better in their home countries," because "the long-term work to improve conditions in the home countries makes a difference." (Notably, her colleague had to disavow this statement only one year later, acknowledging that "obviously" not enough had happened "since we [still] have beggars left on the streets.")[36]

In late 2015 fractions of capital in Stockholm joined forces with the NGO representative, as a coalition of real estate and commerce owners of the inner-city shopping areas, and NGOs launched a campaign called Help People Begging—*support our fundraising for change in Romania*. Having placed big pink pots in the shopping quarters, these actors, in a joint article, argued,

> Right now, the help is most useful among aid organizations on the ground in Romania, not in individuals' paper mugs. Especially if the *long-term* goal is that people should not have to beg at all.
>
> We are not saying one should not give to beggars; we say that there are developments in place in Romania that in the *long-term* will hinder vulnerable EU citizens from being forced to travel to other countries to beg.
>
> [Our] core belief is that immigration is good and enriching, EU membership and labor immigration has been good for Sweden, and that we have a moral duty to receive refugees. Bearing that in mind, we are deeply worried about the begging, partly because it is not dignified for the people begging but also because it is no *long-term* solution to the problems of vulnerable people in, for example, Romania. Partly because it *risks* affecting public opinion in a way that threatens openness.
>
> [It] is not about getting rid of beggars. It is about creating opportunities for vulnerable people in their own home country.[37]

In addition to the anxious desire to comply with the dominant ideology ("It's not about getting rid of beggars"), attempts to make begging into a question of "immigration" were symptomatic of how the problem was generally constructed: namely, as having nothing to do with the Swedish political economy, nor poverty really. In the quotation above, for example, the "openness" under alleged "threat" refers to SD. In short, Swedes need to get rid of racialized begging, so that Swedes don't become racists, which would threaten capital interests.

Looking at these texts in combination, we can see how actors from the state, civil society, the media, and capital united to sanction this benevolent narrative of "getting rid of beggars" without explicitly endorsing repression. Indeed, *every one* of these voices was against begging. This was also Valfridsson's conclusion as a lawyer: "Criminal law should not be used to fight poverty. Nor is it relevant to make it a criminal offense to donate money to beggars. Criminalizing humanity only creates a tougher society without solving any problems."[38] If only the municipalities and civilians refused to extend money to the déclassés on Swedish soil, so that they would voluntarily return home to seek "long-term" "opportunities," "criminalizing humanity" would not be necessary.

This begs the question, however, What did these "opportunities" back home look like in practice? Heart to Heart, for its part, initiated a basket-weaving project for Roma in a Romanian village, selling the baskets in Sweden for 350 kronor each. In the national press, the NGO representative heralded this as the first step in implementing long-term change, as the project was to be carried out by a social enterprise with fair employment conditions.[39] Unfortunately, a public service investigation program discovered in the spring of 2016 that this was not the case: in reality, there was no registered company, no pensions, and no social fees; the twenty-five workers received only 30 kronor per basket and had not signed any contracts; and many had given up and returned to beg abroad.[40] All this was revealed, however, *after* the publishing of Valfridsson's report and the climax of the refugee crisis. It was within this conjuncture of crises that Valfridsson's legal expertise was deployed in order to do its part to save hegemony.

The Crisis of Hegemony

In October 2015 the refugee numbers peaked, with 10,000 arrivals per week. That year, 163,000 total immigrants arrived (whereas 50,000 emigrated), and approximately 80,000 were estimated to receive asylum. To put things in perspective, there had been a net immigration of approximately 55,000 people per year since 2000.[41] On top of this, European leaders had not listened to Löfven's call for a shared responsibility, with the notable exception of Germany, which welcomed the largest total cohort. Sweden, however, received the greatest *proportional* number of immigrants. While this number was low vis-á-vis the sum of asylum-seekers in the EU in 2015 (1.3 million)—and nothing compared to the global total number of refugees (60 million)—Swedish openness was *exceptional* in the European sense. From 2008 to 2017, Sweden received half a million asylum-seekers, comprising 5 percent of the Swedish population. By comparison, the EU median was 1 percent.[42]

Not only was the distribution of refugees across the continent uneven, but it was also fundamentally uneven across Swedish municipalities. Due to their relative autonomy, there were wealthy municipalities that took in hardly anyone, as well as poorer municipalities with unemployment in the double digits that received quite a lot of refugees. Several of the latter benefited economically from this reception; simultaneously, the national economy experienced unexpected growth, and the budget balance improved. Nevertheless, in October 2015 there was a breakdown of the asylum reception system, which had been tasked with guaranteeing legally secure judgments on the right of asylum, access to housing, and other necessities during the trial period. At the same time, the public sector—especially the schools and the municipal social services—faced challenges.[43] People who had fled for their lives arrived to find, in the words of a journalist, "a folkhem under liquidation."[44] Before the Swedish public, several scenes of disorder appeared: the spatial expressions of overcrowded classrooms and reception camps; an abrupt doubling of populations in small villages; lack of resources; bureaucratic confusion; for-profit companies damaging the refugee accommodations and mistreating their clients; conflicts at the accommodations (due to the mixing of refugees from antagonistic ethnic groups and the overcrowding of people with post-traumatic stress disorder); and a vast amount of volunteer and NGO aid work to bridge the gaps of municipal and the Migration Authority's refugee resettlement programs. All of this consolidated a public perception of the state not being able to control the situation, with SD giving voice to this impression of disarray.

Notably, this is where the begging question began to intersect with the refugee crisis: the increased social responsibility laid upon the municipalities (real or imagined), as well as perceptions of state authorities' inability to curtail the presence of déclassés in everyday spaces. Many of the arriving refugees were unaccompanied juvenile teenage boys, inciting moral panic regarding *skäggbarn* ("beard children," as if the teens' facial hair belied their claim to be minors), cast as the would-be rapists and harassers of Swedish girls. Based upon the weekly numbers of arriving refugees, one opinion maker made the apocalyptic prediction that this pace would increase to 500,000 refugees per year, five million in a decade, and "the downfall of the nation."[45] By September public support for SD had already swelled to 20 percent in the opinion polls.[46]

Parallel to these collective anxieties, great changes occurred in parliament. The Christian Democrats' new leader, Ebba Busch Thor, aiming to model the party after U.S. Republicans, took steps to destabilize the Alliance's relationship to the government and SD. This began on October 9, with the party breaking the December Agreement to allow the minority coalition of SAP and EP to govern.[47] Significantly, Busch had, just the day before, cowritten an article urging the government to permit municipalities to legislate begging-free zones. With that said, the argument followed the Swedish ideology script, insisting that this legislation would be implemented out of concern for the poor: "There is no solution, no future, and no dignity in begging. But there is a future for the Eastern European Roma in their home-countries by lifting them out of poverty and vulnerability. It is a time-consuming process from bottom-up, but this is also its strength. We cannot start this process in Sweden on behalf of [others], but we can facilitate the onset of their journey."[48] Ten days later the Moderates presented a proposition along similar lines, in this case citing the need to hinder "order disturbances."[49] At this point three parties had sounded calls to criminalize begging, albeit to different degrees.

What's more, following the minority government's official fall from grace, the political players seized upon the opportunity that governmental instability had provided. SD now saw their chance of strategically enhancing their race war, claiming they now turned to "extra-parliamentary struggle" to build a public movement against immigration. On October 17 Kent Ekeroth spoke at a demonstration against asylum immigration (in which uniformed Nazis also participated): "For Sweden, this means our downfall [in] the short term, the end for Sweden as a nation. [You] must take to the streets, every day, every day, and show them that we do not accept this. [. . .] the Swedish people have a long fuse, they say, but when the fuse has burned completely, it explodes. And we'll show them: now it's exploding! We have no time to spare [anymore]. You are the spearhead we need to take our country back. We are the resistance movement."[50] And the lone wolves heeded the call. As we know, the "extra-parliamentary struggle" against the EU déclassés had already been carried out all over the country—now, the "resistance movement" initiated assembled attacks against refugee accommodations. A couple of hours after Ekeroth's speech, an accommodation facility was set ablaze in a neighboring municipality. Adding to the discord, Ekeroth's brother and party colleague spread maps and lists of planned accommodations on social media. An escalation of arsons against operative or planned refugee accommodation centers followed.

Significantly, the officially recognized terror attacks in Sweden skyrocketed in 2015; according to the Global Terrorism Database, from 2010 to 2015, there were forty-seven, whereas in 2015 alone there were thirty-six.[51] It's worth noting that as the frenzy of violence targeting EU déclassés, as described in chapter 3, are not included here, the majority of these registered attacks were directed at mosques and refugee accommodations and occurred after Ekeroth's speech. Incidentally, these arsons temporarily ended the day after Åkesson officially condemned arsons on October 29.[52]

In the time between Ekeroth's speech and Åkesson's condemnation, there was one fire almost every single day—in fact, during the twenty-four hours before the latter's statement, three incidents were reported.[53] The fact that no one died in these arsons is a miracle. Other actions, however, had grave consequences: five days after Ekeroth's call, a twenty-one-year-old SD-sympathizer entered a school in Trollhättan, armed with a sword, with the aim of slaying non-white children and teachers. Before being killed by the police, he murdered two people and seriously wounded two others.

THE SHIFT TO BENEVOLENT COERCION

In the wake of the conjuncture of the settlement issue, the recharged parliamentary crisis, the widespread bureaucratic turmoil of refugee reception, and the escalation of racist violence, Sweden's crisis of hegemony—the inability of the reigning fraction to govern the state via popular consent—was undeniable. These combined events were, I argue, an eruption caused by over thirty years of dismembering the welfare state apparatus and its branches, formalized through privatizations and decentralizations of the social infrastructure. Indeed, the October conjuncture epitomized the splits among the ranks of several dimensions of the overarching state apparatus, which, it must be noted, had already been in effect prior to the refugee crisis. Among schools, the railways, health care, social services, the postal service, and the housing market, havoc already reigned—all of them restructured in favor of capitalist expropriation. On top of this, there were social issues of mounting racial segregation, income gaps, division between rural and urban populations, shrinking pensions, the housing shortage, gang shootings, and the begging question—all of which were already present before the refugee crisis, with no clear guidance from authorities on how to proceed.

Prior to the 2014 election, the first paragraph of SAP's election manifesto had read, "Sweden is about to break apart."[54] Now that they were in power, the claim appeared more accurate than ever. With the reformist-Left intent on protecting an already broken system, their defense of the underfunded, contradictory, uneven folkhem model was insufficient per se. As the melancholic housing system symptomized, the status quo was not enough to preserve exceptional equality. Only an expansion, not a defense, of the current welfare systems could revive their equality ideology's popular support—an option that was pragmatically unlikely, following SAP's generational losses of working-class voters due to their continuous concessions. And now, the government could not even maintain "law and order"; it could not neutralize the fantasy of the ruination of the National Thing. To restore their legitimacy and preserve their own power, the reigning class fractions' knee-jerk reaction was to resort to coercion. Ultimately, they saw no other choice but to comply with the prescriptions of SD's counter-ideology.

The day after the Trollhättan murders, the government announced an agreement with the Alliance to revamp Sweden's refugee policy. "Necessary efforts" were needed "to secure the Swedish reception capacity of asylum-seekers" and "to curb the cost increases."[55] Efforts to crack down on the newcomers included the shortening of the processing of asylum applications, restriction of family immigration, and the introduction of *temporary* residence permits—previously, there were only permanent permits. Although they claimed these measures were only "temporary," the reigning fraction, through these changes, signaled that the situation was out of hand, and that there was in fact justification for racial anxieties. Meanwhile, the arsons escalated. Though hardly any of these cases were solved by the police, more than a hundred officers were present when, in late October, it was finally decided to tear down the settlement in Malmö. Citing an "environmental hazard" as the legal basis, the Social-Democratic City Council defended this decision:

We cannot let it be acceptable that people live in huts, in tents [where] there is no access to water, [no] access to the sewage system, to hygiene and so on. In Sweden, we have a law that says that everyone should have access to good, dignified housing—and it is not dignified to live as they do [here]. We also have a *principle of equality*, and this means that all human [beings] should be able to live in acceptable conditions, and it is not acceptable to live as they [do]. Fifty years ago, we decided here in Sweden—and this was in connection with Katarina Taikon—that it is not allowed and we will never again accept that people live like this, that people live under such conditions. Back then, we decided that the law should be the same for everyone. We cannot say today that we are going to go back in time to fifty years ago and say that it is allowed for people to live like that.[56]

Notice that here the folkhem ideology on housing was invoked alongside a reference to Katarina Taikon, the Roma civil rights heroine in Sweden, in a bid to expel hundreds of Roma into acute homelessness (as no long-term accommodation was offered to compensate for their expulsion). Out of coercive care, in the name of Swedish exceptional equality and antiracism.

It appears as if the panicked public shift toward supporting cracking down on refugee reception allowed—or forced—the state apparatus to act against the faction of Others considered *least deserving*: the déclassés. Indeed, with the need to stringently police refugees now symbolically sanctioned by the state, homeless foreign lawbreakers could no longer go unpunished. On the day before the planned Malmö eviction, in a radio interview, Valfridsson urged the police to "take a step forward"—in other words, take action—to "help the municipalities out" and adopt a "zero-tolerance" policy against "non-allowed settlements."[57] By encouraging a creative interpretation of the Public Order Act—in effect, a legal loophole that played on the police's responsibility to *prevent* crime—Valfridsson nullified the power of Swedish legislation intended to protect evictees. Consequently, the police were free to evict settlements before they became "permanent"—at which point they invariably became the responsibility of the enforcement officer. But what of human rights advocates' insistence that Sweden is subject to legally binding conventions, and their contention that it is possible to interpret the Social Service Act as having stipulated municipal responsibility for all subjects territorially present? By way of response, Valfridsson dismissed the conventions as not part of Swedish law (although they are) by invoking the moral economy of *equality*: "Society cannot treat one group differently. We have no national guarantee of shelter. In the big towns, we are even evicting families with children who could not pay their rent without compensation." In his report, presented three months later, he elaborated: "There is a severe housing shortage in many places in the country, and there are already a number of homeless [citizens]. Regardless of the living standard at the allocated sites, it would be difficult for a municipality to justify why a certain vulnerable group would gain access to this solution, but not others."[58]

What is this, if not the fantasy of theft of Enjoyment, mobilized in support of a political objective—namely, to police the crisis? After all, it would be commonsensically wrong to give déclassés unconditional access to something Swedish residents *do not have* themselves. The logic deployed here, I argue, is rooted in the Swedish moral economy's inheritance of a melancholic exceptional-equality ideology within a neoliberalized housing system. If evicted déclassés were compensated with accommodation solutions with radically lower standards than the Swedish norm, this could lead to the acknowledged presence of apartheid-like differences in living conditions and spaces (the feared "slum communities"). Likewise, if housing instead became an unconditional right for déclassés, this would heighten the underlying political contradictions between Left and Right within the monstrous housing hybrid.

Indeed, this shift toward punishment of the poor made the Swedish ideology almost parodic in its contradictions. When, for example, one journalist pointed out the glaring discrepancy between the Swedish liberal press's condemnation of the mass evictions of Eastern European Roma in France in 2010 and their unanimous praise for the forced eviction of the Malmö settlement, one editor denied that there was any contradiction whatsoever: "It is possible to harbor compassion, to stand up for the Roma, and simultaneously state that it neither violates human rights nor free movement to evacuate the undignified and illegal settlement."[59] What's more, the editor landed a serious blow against the human rights ideology's "historical responsibility" argument by appealing to a commonsensical liberal truth: Why should Swedish law treat some Roma individuals differently from other individuals, and why should the Roma ethnicity's superficial connection to other people, places, and times affect the legal subjectivity of the EU déclassés? Here again, we see the logic of the theft of Enjoyment at work—and the demand that no one is treated "unfairly" (notwithstanding the obvious unequal social reality at hand). Other liberal columnists made use of this ideology as well, such as an *Expressen* writer, who dismissed the following critique from the UN on the Swedish state's treatment of the déclassés: "The State party should [ensure] that all individuals within its jurisdiction, including vulnerable Roma citizens of other European Union countries, enjoy equal rights without discrimination and identify ways to facilitate their access to support assistance services, including social benefits, taking into account both their de jure and de facto situation."[60] In his piece the columnist countered: "[Well,] honorable HR experts, this cannot only apply to the Roma, since then it would become ethnic discrimination against other groups. The consequence is that all EU citizens—regardless of whether they can support themselves or not—would have the right to settle not only in Sweden but in any EU country and be able to demand the entire smorgasbord of social services and benefits."[61] This postcrisis common sense having taken hold, the human rights ideology's previous strength was ultimately made impotent. While NGOs, lawyers, and human rights organizations would continue condemning the state's treatment of the déclassés in following years, hegemony's shift to coercion had rendered their truth claims "naïve moralism," not worth taking seriously. This perception was aided, of course, by Valfridsson, who used his legal expertise to show that human rights advocates' appeals to law were unrealistic. Indeed, when the police and state violated human rights, they weren't punished anyway!

As they navigated their crisis, the ruling bloc worried that their eagerness to appease the antiracist momentum had cost them the consent of the Imagined "common people." Now they redirected their anxiety at appeasing proponents of authoritarian populism. One effect of complying with the latter's radicalized common sense was the strengthening of the imagination of Swedish welfare as scarce and finite, leading to the amplification of the notion of "deservingness"—the fantasy of theft of Enjoyment included. In this way capitalism's moral precept that only working people deserve dignity became increasingly incorporated into the dominant ideology's attitudes toward not only the déclassés but also poor racial Others overall. With the introduction of temporary residence permits, the Alliance's parties welcomed this incitement for refugees to work, as the permit only lasted for three years and could be extended if one obtained steady full-time work; meanwhile, the parliamentary agreement abolished the demand for collectively agreed-upon salaries for entry-level jobs.[62] In this manner the groundwork to further declass refugees was laid, as the ruling bloc in this way expanded the diameter of the déclassé position's vortex within the Borromean welfare knot.

The "System Collapse"

The parliamentary agreement was not enough, however, to calm the political storm. Following a month of politicians from both blocs prophesying an imminent "system collapse" (a metaphor for "the downfall of the nation"), the hegemonic crisis was officially curbed on November 24 with the announcement that the government was slamming the brakes on refugee reception. In its declaration the government claimed the "refugee situation" to be "unsustainable," opting to reduce asylum numbers to the minimum the EU would permit, as well as introduce medical age assessments and ID controls on border-crossing public transport. According to a state report, these measures would "put pressure on the other EU countries to take a greater responsibility for the refugee situation"—that is, the same fantasy as the idea that banning begging would "put pressure" on the "home countries'" leaderships.[63] This break in accepting refugees was brought on by the fact that municipalities had begun to report their inability to guarantee that their reception of unaccompanied children was legally secure. Departments, meanwhile, in the words of the report, "sounded the alarm that important social functions were unable to cope with the pressure. Sweden could no longer guarantee a roof over your head for those who found their way to Sweden. For the past week, people had been forced to sleep outdoors."[64] In other words, what happens if the system doesn't work is that the refugees will become déclassés. Indeed, the government's inaction and perceived inability to do anything for the déclassés had already become a common Imaginary of the government, state, and police—institutions apparently incapable of maintaining law and order—a development attributable to the presence of settlements, as well as the anxious novelty of begging (which, to many, constituted a crime in itself). What if a large enough portion of the exceptional numbers of refugees would fall between the cracks and become difficult to find, control, and incorporate or expel—just like the few albeit incredibly visible "beggars"? With this hypothetical reasoning in mind, Löfven, during a press conference, claimed the aim of the break was to "create breathing room for Swedish asylum reception," as the EP leader standing beside him wept, feeling she had betrayed her own ideals.[65]

Because this was articulated as a matter of a Malthusian natural necessity, not political choice, Sweden's moral exceptionalism was thought to be saved—it's not that Sweden doesn't want to help, but that Sweden *can't* help. The other ideological function of these statements was to reproduce the depiction of the nation as a collective "us" of "insiders" in need of defending their "own" welfare system against "outsiders." Thinking back to Valfridsson's assertion regarding the non-right to housing, however, it becomes clear that the Real of this ideology is not a shared National Thing of Swedish welfare and care, but of a capitalist class alliance with the upper and middle positions that benefit from the hollowing out of the inherent dual welfare system. It was in this way that the fantasy of theft of Enjoyment "from below" was further dominantly verified, facilitating the perceived shared interest between the upper and middle strata against the racialized poor—and further diminishing the possibility of turning the tide toward progressive politics. What's more, a new paradox emerged: now that the reigning fraction had secured the means of hindering the growth of declassed subjects from outside, they set out to enhance the domestic production of the declassed by reducing possible ways for one to become an "insider."

Ultimately, the inability of the ruling bloc to handle the overarching contradiction of showing "tolerance" for begging and need *without* actually addressing poverty gave the predominant racist counter-ideology force. The outcomes of both the refugee crisis and the déclassés' housing question proved authoritarian populism "right." In this way the perception of the elites' anxious "political correctness" had been "confirmed"—after all, if the solution turned out to be what SD had been advocating for years, why then did the rulers act so late? Indeed, now that SD could claim that rulers had accepted their definition of societal problems, the party's support continued to rise well *after* the "refugee break," catapulting them toward the place of the second largest party. As it turned out, the crisis of hegemony was not over.

The Race to the Election and the Bottom

Abstracting the ideologies of class struggle to a Global North scale, Sweden continues to be a signifier of exceptionalism—generalized as a good object for the Left and a bad object for the Right.[66] In February 2017, for example, newly installed U.S. president Donald Trump warned his supporters: "We've got to keep our country safe. [You] look at what's happening last night in Sweden. Sweden, who would believe this?"[67] While nothing special had happened in Sweden that night, this statement symptomized the ongoing ideological project among transnational racist networks to rebrand the Sweden signifier as a cautionary tale of a country still reeling from the refugee crisis. Indeed, a retrospective article in the *New York Times* titled "The Global Machine behind the Rise of Far-Right Nationalism" demonstrates how the conceptualization of Sweden as a "failure" played a crucial function in the global counter-ideology:

> In the nationalists' message-making, Sweden has become a prime cautionary tale, dripping with schadenfreude. [. . .]
> The distorted view of Sweden pumped out by [a] disinformation machine has been used, in turn, by anti-immigrant parties in Britain, Germany, Italy and elsewhere to stir xenophobia and gin up [votes].[68]

As an interviewed researcher explains in the story, Sweden had "become an enduring centerpiece of the far-right conversation." Later in the article, a Swedish representative echoes this point: "Sweden is portrayed either as a heaven or a hell [. . .]. But conservative value-based politicians in Hungary, Poland, the United States and elsewhere would use Sweden as an example of a failed state: If you follow this path, your society will look like Sweden's."

Here, we see the ideological power that the image of Sweden holds, and that this Imaginary-Symbolic role model of equality, feminism, and antiracism made for the "perfect enemy" of a racist chauvinist counter-ideology. What's more, the Swedish reigning fraction's reactions to the events of autumn 2015 seemed to justify this narrative, with the public administration minister telling the *New York Times* that "his government had been slow to act." This statement signaled a new strategy, undertaken in order to secure their power before the approaching election in 2018, to compensate for the tolerant stance of inaction against "the beggars" with benevolent violence. For the following three years, SAP and the Moderates competed with one another to show the public that they cared about their anxieties regarding the EU déclassés, and that they were going to flex their political might—while keeping a humanitarian face, of course. Meanwhile, the deadlocks in parliament and within the parties were still not resolved, providing one realpolitikal explanation to the development of the begging question from 2016 onward.

While Valfridsson's report only contained recommendations, it generally came to function as the law. Following its publication in 2016, several municipalities canceled their former housing programs or offers of schooling and began instead to make greater use of the Public Order Act or the Swedish Environmental Code in order to tear down settlements.[69] Parallel to this, the police force and businesses "took a step forward" in chasing away déclassés from their begging spots. In fact, shopping malls and train stations hired guards, and Stockholm Public Transport announced new rules of conduct in a bid to "stop begging in commuting traffic"—prohibiting déclassés to sit on the floor, sell papers, play music, or otherwise disturb people. As the Traffic County Council explained, "The law does not allow us to ban begging. Following our order rules, we cannot target begging and say that it is not allowed. It needs to be disorderly or create *otrygghet*. That is why we use our toolbox to tackle the problem."[70]

Meanwhile, the Stockholm police, for their part, announced a campaign called A Street for Everyone, with the rather obvious (and ironic) intention of clearing déclassés off the streets. Then, when a 2014 ruling made begging permissible so long as those who did so sat down, the campaign began to depict sitting "beggars" as "obstacles for passage" for certain passengers, including the visually impaired.[71] Meanwhile, in the inner city, police initiated a reign of terror: throwing déclassés into cars and driving them to random places kilometers outside the city. According to police protocol, these acts were legitimized by the fact that begging constituted "a serious threat to public order"—that their sitting on the sidewalk was an "unnatural obstacle for individuals who are visually impaired" and made it "impossible to perform sanitary work in [a] satisfying manner."[72] Here officials followed the North American trend of avoiding engaging with notions of liberal rights to beg by framing it as a disturbance of order.[73] It was in this context, then, with begging still not officially criminalizable, that these practices were "discreetly" performed.

SAP AND UNACCEPTABLE POVERTY

In 2016 SAP introduced a new motto, "The Swedish Model shall be developed, not liquidated." This way the PR buzzword of "the Swedish Model" would represent both old-fashioned social-democratic politics and Sweden itself. In an interview that same year, SAP's public administration minister used the phraseology to *hint at* the party's readiness to "regulate" begging: "It is hardly part of the Swedish Model to solve poverty with begging," which is why "the municipalities need support from the state to handle the situation of beggars."[74] Granted, no proposal was brought forward; however, Löfven stated during Christmastime that begging had to "stop" since "it is never acceptable to have to see people get on their knees begging." At the time, such statements were dismissed by not only EP but various members of SAP too.[75] In other words, while the dominant ideology's contradiction lingered on, the SAP leadership now needed to practically circumvent it in order to appease erstwhile voters' imagined preferences. For example, in early 2017 the minister of justice presented new legislation to make it easier to evict "beggars" from unauthorized settlements on private land—to "curb" "slum communities."[76] He also acknowledged the biopolitical rationale of this measure when he reasoned, "If it gets harder to erect" settlements, "the total number of beggars will decrease and thus also the problem."

Concurrently, the party leadership launched a campaign called The Social Democrats Want to Stop Begging, a package of propositions for the party congress to make it more difficult to beg without officially prohibiting it. This was to be achieved by criminalizing the act of profiting from others' begging (a semantic variation of the Moderates' previous proposal) and changing the Public Order Act to make it possible to outlaw begging in certain zones. Even so, this was decidedly *not* a begging ban, or so claimed the minister of the interior, since "it should be possible to both give help and receive help in Sweden."[77] Notably, the proposals were put beneath the header "Together to end segregation," with the following argument to justify the party's coercive care:

> Begging is never a way out of poverty. Together, we must counteract begging and its causes. For more than 100 years Social Democrats have struggled to demolish the structures that force people to stand with cap in hand at the mercy of individual benefactors[;] instead we have built a society where everyone has equal opportunities. In today's globalised world, this political fight must continue in the EU.
>
> We will not stand idly by and see begging and homelessness normalised. Several measures need to be undertaken to eliminate the vulnerability that is characterised by begging. We must ensure that those who are begging today are offered an alternative in their home countries and tighten up and clarify Swedish legislation.[78]

Thanks to history and banal nationalism, SAP and Sweden have done their part. Because of "globalization," their only responsibility is to expel the poor bastards back home to safeguard the Imagined aesthethical order of exceptional equality, "a society where everyone has equal opportunities." Note that, to please the antiracists, the proposal included the single sentence: "Anti-Roma racism will never be accepted."[79] While the congress did not lead to any legal changes other than the ones related to evictions, the

SAP-led municipality of Eskilstuna decided in early 2018 to pave the way for the party by announcing a municipal legislation of a license system: people were to pay for applications to the police to receive a begging permit in certain zones. Although the obvious reason behind this legislation was Kafkaesque expulsion (which was later dismissed in court), City Council spokesperson Jimmy Jansson proclaimed: "Somewhere, a society must say that this is now enough. These are conditions that we would never ever accept in other contexts. Now for several years we have had a debate about this and have found that we make an exception regarding our principal stance concerning the equality of all human beings."[80] While the legislation was ruled illegal by the county court, Löfven, for his part, found the solution "interesting."[81]

What's more, during the election year the prime minister alleged that "Sweden has received too many refugees." Although there had been 163,000 asylum applications in 2015, he believed the 2017 figure—27,000—to be much too high, promising to reduce them to 13,000. The Moderates, meanwhile, considered this goal to be far too liberal.[82] Not only had the "temporary" "breathing room" of 2015 already become the norm, but even *this* was now "unsustainable" according to hegemony's newfound common sense. In its place Löfven now promised a "long-term, sustainable" refugee policy, using the exact same signifier that was popularized in discussions of the begging question.[83]

Still, SAP remained ideological enemies of SD, and complying *too* much to the latter's ideology would ultimately eliminate the reasons to vote for the former. Indeed, the newspaper *Aftonbladet* revealed that a begging legislation proposal, signed by SAP, was "aborted in panic," as SAP's coercive turn had, far from strengthening their poll numbers, won them the lowest level of support before an election in the party's history.[84] Their strategy (as one informant put it) to first "make a stand on hard issues, which people find important," and then "generate a discussion on welfare with a clear conflict between Right and Left" seemed not to pay off satisfactorily and also caused outrage among great fractions of the party.

The first steps on both the local and national levels to signal punishment of "the beggars'" deviancy was taken by the Moderates. Indeed, the municipal leadership of Vellinge was first out to recharge the strategy of bringing municipal begging prohibitions to be tried in court, by voting for local begging-free zones in early autumn 2017. A few days later the Moderates' new leader, Ulf Kristersson, who had been tasked with securing a decisive break with the liberal profile of the Reinfeldt era and returning to conservative values, announced his party's demand for a *national* begging ban. Given that the Moderates were the first party to back SD on this issue, I asked the Moderate Party's legal policy spokesperson, when I met him backstage during a radio debate, why they had changed their minds. He replied, "Before, we all believed they were only innocent moms, but now we see there's criminality out there." This answer certainly reflected the times, as a couple of months earlier the narrative of "the beggars" all being criminals had returned with a vengeance, due to ongoing revelations of Romanian and Bulgarian citizens being kidnapped and forced to beg in Sweden. Consequently, déclassés' sympathizers found themselves painted into a corner, as politicians, activists, and media voices had previously claimed rumors of organized criminality were urban legends, as exemplified by article headings from 2014–15 that read: "Organized Begging Is an Urban Legend"; "No, the Beggars Are Not Controlled by Criminal Gangs"; and "No, Begging Is Not Organized."[85] Of course, the *ideological fantasies* of the criminality of "the beggar" contained urban legends, supporting paranoid convictions of the Other's evilness. Yet to straight-out *deny* the existence of violent exploitation among the poor is also a consequence of ideological fantasies. Where proponents of the "organized begging" fantasy and its detractors differed, however, is that the former used these revelations of human trafficking as a "new" ideological rationale for outlawing begging in Sweden. The latter's position, meanwhile, had very few legal implications, since human trafficking was already criminalized—though certainly this law could be enforced more *effectively* if the authorities were willing to take a more egalitarian approach to the déclassés.

This discursive crossroads, in any case, became sanctioned as "state knowledge" when Valfridsson suddenly reappeared in the debate, more than one year after finishing his appointment. At the time an investigative program on Norwegian public television had recently exposed an urban network of Romanian citizens engaged in trafficking, drugs, prostitution, and begging. This development allowed the expert to announce he had changed his mind regarding prohibition—now he supported a national begging ban to counteract criminal exploitation, a change of heart that was nevertheless articulated through the lens of the Swedish ideology. He explained, "When one criminalizes the most vulnerable group in society, one does this to protect very vulnerable groups."[86] Two days later an editor of one of the most-read liberal papers deferred to Valfridsson's expertise, agreeing that "it's time for a begging ban," since "all experience shows that begging is destructive for all affected parties. According to Valfridsson, the conclusions from [state authorities and NGO aid organizations] are unequivocal: begging is never the way out of poverty."[87] Notably, "all experience" refers to what Valfridsson claimed in his report, which, as we know, was a reflection of his opinions, not research. It was in this way that the "criminality argument" also became available to SAP, whose minister of finance, Magdalena Andersson (who succeeded Löfven as party leader in 2021), advised the public not to give money to "beggars"; one "should know," after all, that doing so "*risks* contributing to human trafficking; we have seen horrible examples on how people are exploited."[88] Here we see the ideological primacy of the signifier of "risk." Ultimately, it never mattered whether the risky evil was "no long-term solutions" or, later, "criminal exploitation"—the objective was to urge Swedes *not to give* to begging people, based on a caring rationality.

Indeed, the actual object of desire, the spatial disappearance of "beggars," was later acknowledged by Kristersson, who proclaimed, "what is important" was whether "we should be a country where it is totally acceptable [to] beg on streets and squares."[89] Significantly, this echoes SD's populist message that what was "important" about banning begging was maintaining the moral order. Of course, this similarity was hardly coincidental, as the Moderates had half a year earlier officially broken the parliamentary taboo of not entering into a dialogue with SD. Though SAP and the latter still couldn't cooperate, the Moderates, the party of big capital, had come to realize their only chance to secure parliamentary dominance would be to let SD in from the cold. This 180-degree switch from Reinfeldt's days was facilitated by their shared historical-ideological traits—after all, SD's ideological predecessors were the members of the old reactionary Moderates' youth movement, and the Moderates' opportunism vis-à-vis fascism had a historical record.

Hegemony Turnover

On the cusp of the 2018 election, the three major parties promised fewer immigrants, stricter integration policy, and regulation of begging. Though representatives of capital and labor struggled against one another, their interests ultimately compelled them to conform to SD's agenda, thus securing and hegemonizing the latter's ideology as a dominant interpretation of the National Thing and its sense of melancholia regarding the loss of exceptional equality. Paradoxically, however, both blocs had promised *not* to seize power with SD, as SAP and the Moderates were still relying on their "idealist" and humanist little siblings to secure a majority. When the election results culminated in the greatest parliamentary turmoil in Swedish modern history, the aforestated contradiction erupted.

Although SD's support rose to above 17 percent, they did not gain second place, as had been feared. The Alliance, meanwhile, suffered a narrow defeat, losing to the Left bloc by *one* mandate. With the Alliance eager to avoid repeating their costly mistake of 2014—namely, allowing the leftist parties to overtake them by shutting out SD—the government formation process went on for 129 days. Gradually, the Christian Democrats and the Moderates became open to seizing power with SD's support, without publicly acknowledging that this would certainly entail making political promises to the latter. Consequently, when Löfven's new government was finally formed in January 2019, the tendencies of "Bonapartism" in the previous period now reached their full potential. Once again it was SD that determined politics—and since the liberal flank found it ethically unacceptable to cooperate with them, the Alliance dissolved. SAP and EP, meanwhile, were allowed to continue governing by virtue of the magnanimity—and blackmailing—of the neoliberalist Center and Liberal Parties, who let them rule on the condition that they agreed, via a signed treaty, to implement seventy-seven new reforms, including the exclusion of the Left Party from influence; the dismantling of employment security; the implementation of market rentals on new rental units; the privatization of the Public Employment Office; lower taxes; and the cancellation of aspirations to regulate profit outtakes in the welfare sector. After SAP cut this deal, in which they signed on to enact the neoliberal policies of their opponents, the "post-politicization" of Swedish politics became even more prominent. Now both parliamentary blocs were pursuing right-wing agendas with extensive working-class support, practically only divided on moral issues—in short, whether to side with SD. Therefore, logically, now was the time for the Right to whitewash SD so they would appear befitting of governmental office. First, Ebba Busch initiated official negotiations with SD; then Kristersson followed. When even the Liberal Party eventually joined them, a radical-conservative bloc was formed against a "Left-liberal" one, a development that seems to accord with fascist conspiracies of collusion between "socialists" and "liberal" "internationalists."

In a historical irony, the political defining moment that secured the Swedish folkhem ideology's hegemony in 1933 was now repeated, albeit with new power relations in favor of capital over labor: again SAP secured governmental power by cooperating with the Center Party; the latter, however, was no longer led by farmers, but rather by neoliberal capitalists' representatives, while the former lacked progressive ambitions. To add to the similarities, the Moderates are once again seeking power via radical nationalism, though this time this force was a great political movement of its own. Here we see the ways in which history has played out differently. Whereas the original folkhem hegemony project secured a cross-class alliance of the lower and middle classes against the upper stratum, contemporary Swedish ideology and hegemony became increasingly rooted in a cross-class alliance of the upper classes against the racialized poorer classes. Even if the "anti-SD" bloc held governmental power, their policies aimed to further expand the low-income sector (and thus enhance racialization processes). What's more, the year 2021, following a cross-bloc consensus, saw the "temporary" harshness of 2015's "breathing room" become permanent. The same year, when the Taliban's recapturing of Afghanistan prompted a new refugee wave, Löfven reassured the electorate that "we are never again going back to 2015."[90]

The Russian-Ukrainian war the following year constituted a somewhat tragicomic temporal detour from this development, when even SD supported refugee reception of Ukrainians (in order to cover up their pro-Putinism).[91] Crucially, the relational whiteness of the Ukrainians enabled the ruling bloc to make a distinction between *these* refugees as more deserving than the non-European ones. Indeed, when the Social-Democratic minister of labor and equality same year declared that immigrant women "should not have more children than [they] can support," it signaled that although post-exceptional-equality melancholia still prevails in the Swedish variant of the ongoing crisis of democratic capitalism, the racialization of the National Thing advances.[92]

It is not only, however, dominant leftist and right-wing parties alongside capital's spokespersons who cannot resist incorporating the fantasy of the racial Other's theft of Enjoyment as a hegemonic narrative into the ongoing reorchestration of the Swedish ideology and capitalist state economy. As the ruling bloc of hegemony also consists of the ideological apparatuses outside of the state, the media institutions (public, private, and virtual) and their interests play a crucial part in this ideological reorganization. SD knows this very well, as not only illustrated before in the global media war on the Sweden image but also exemplified by their parliamentary chief of staff's accusation of Swedish journalists for being "the enemies of the nation."[93] Since fascism hates independent public service, SD's joined forces with the privatizing Right made their counter-ideology's growing power into a threat to public service's survival. Consequently, we have witnessed the latter's successive anxious adaptation of a relativist attitude vis-à-vis fascism, racism, and discrimination and increased framing of criminality as related to immigrant heritage.[94] This development has coincided with independent right-wing editorials' adoption of SD's discourse in their legitimization of support for right-wing governmental power, *and* the ongoing "culture war" on social media.

THE RESOLUTION OF THE BEGGING QUESTION

Tellingly, it was in the midst of the government formation chaos in late 2018 that the Swedish ideology's contradiction on begging tacitly became "resolved"—not by an active political decision, but by a legal reinterpretation of the preexisting Public Order Act. On December 17 the Supreme Administrative Court ruled in favor of Vellinge's anti-panhandling legislation— thereby sanctioning Eskilstuna's model as well.[95] The clause that opened the door for this decision was the spatial aspect of the regulation: notably, it did not forbid begging throughout the municipality, but "only" within designated zones—thus, it did not formally restrict freedoms of speech and movement. What's more, the court found earlier objections to whether the presence of a few people begging could rightfully be termed a "disturbance of order" to be nonsensical; now, it was taken-for-granted that it was up to the municipalities themselves to identify what *could become* a disturbance of order. In other words, the state's shift toward policing the crisis had enabled legal interpretations that gave authorities greater leverage to suspend civil liberties in the name of maintaining order. This "apolitical" juridical work—to the collective relief of the leaderships of SAP, Moderates, Christian Democrats, and SD, conservative and social-democratic opinion makers, and probably most of the electorate—had finally neutralized the begging question, which for so long had posed a potential threat to state hegemony. Now it was possible to ban begging locally without the political need to impose prohibition via new legislation—a development that appeared to preserve the ideology of exceptional equality and spare politicians from facing their own hypocrisy. In this way the begging question was made into a legal practicality, retroactively enabling the possibility of prohibition, and the transformation of the issue from a social dilemma to a police matter was complete.

In retrospect, the begging issue's final contribution to national political intrigue in the 2010s was as a pressure tool, wielded by local Moderates against their national leadership. Roughly one year before his official compliance with SD (late 2019), Kristersson had gone as far as to promise a Holocaust survivor to never cooperate with them—his 180 degree turn from condemning to (explicitly) praising SD's policies could, namely, not be consummated *immediately* after his defeat in saving the Alliance.[96] Several local sections of his party, however, did not need the same moral incubation period, and seized municipal power by collaborating with SD. Unsurprisingly, in such cases the introduction of anti-panhandling legislation was among the first resolutions. Probably this prioritization was overdetermined by several interconnected symbolic politics: in the eyes of the public, it both signaled the Moderates' coercive turn and the power of their decision to act, daring to "do something" instead of regurgitating empty "PC talk"; it also reestablished the state's authority in punishing deviancy; and, of course, it bristled with the excitement of someone "finally" having the guts to clamp down on the Roma. Against this backdrop fourteen municipalities, by early 2020, had introduced begging regulations—some of them governed by SAP. On the other hand, more than sixty councils have voted against such proposals. With the option to regulate it, begging appeared to no longer be such a daunting problem. Nonetheless, for those intent on pursuing revenge, the alleged primary motive of protecting vulnerable people from trafficking vanished—instead the emerging rationale for criminalization was that the presence of déclassés made the public *feel* unsafe (*otrygghet*).[97] One local Moderate—who, for his part, not only sought to criminalize déclassés but also their efforts to help out with recycling—explained this otrygghet as, "One shies away from recycling" at recycling stations, and stated that "one sees loitering and misuse of public space, consolidating a feeling of lawlessness."[98] In the end the problem with begging was what I've been asserting since part 1—the anxiety of the encounter itself.

Let us return to this about-face regarding the source of begging's "evil" nature, however. This development, it must be noted, coincided with a newfound dominant national moral anxiety regarding the steady growing numbers of "gang shootings" committed by non-white déclassé Swedish youth in deprived neighborhoods in connection to the escalating war between youth networks controlling the emerging trade of narcotics.[99] Amid "feelings of lawlessness," this violence helped promote and normalize the emerging right-wing opinion that the problem of immigration was not merely one of economic costs, but also the nation's "changing *demographics*." Indeed, in 2019, by way of response to a study that concluded that the immigration of 2013–16 was not as economically disastrous as once thought,[100] one influential opinion maker wrote:

> Suddenly, beggars, mainly from Romania and Bulgaria, sat outside shops, at train stations, on streets and squares, not just in the big cities, but in almost every community. It was 2013. In a smaller urban area I often visit, which lies in what is formally defined as a thinly populated area, without train connections, there are the same kind of beggars. They are still outside [the grocery store].
>
> The large migrations of recent years can also be seen here. Previously, there were perhaps a few immigrants in this small town; now the cityscape is dominated by them. Probably because many lack jobs and therefore diddle outside. This is not something unique; all over Sweden, the population has changed. There are very few places that have not been affected. Almost everyone has seen the change with their own eyes. [. . .]
>
> It is the demographics, not the economy, that is the main reason why more and more voters in Sweden and the Western world are voting for parties that want to radically reduce immigration.[101]

As has been the perennial refrain of the last few chapters: "People believe, namely, what they see with their own eyes." What they *believe* they see, however, is conditioned by ideology via the societal Imaginary; in this way their perception is rooted in historical-geographical dialectics of racialization, as well as their unconscious anxieties and desires. While I agree with the analysis quoted above, I would rephrase "demographics" as "racist anxieties." Note, too, that the Real problem of begging—that people have to meet people begging—is acknowledged by the author. When racialized, this problem intersects with the *social* problem of "immigration": the socio-visual encounter with racial *difference* in a previously racially homogenous community (albeit a nevertheless *racial* society) readily causes anxieties regarding the Other's alterity. However, where the ideologue might find this anxiety a legitimate political problem, I submit that the actual political problem is the *legitimization* of this anxiety as a political problem.

Be that as it may, this legitimization did become hegemonic in the early 2020s, as the escalating drug-related "gang shootings" became common-sensically framed as due to the failure of "too much immigration." Indeed, the party campaigns for the national election of 2022, the theme of law and order, related to these tragedies, foreclosed all other political issues. The SAP leadership recharged their campaign strategy from last round, and therefore competed with the right-wing parties (the Center Party excluded) regarding who championed authoritarian, xeno-racist populism with a human face. All of them promised more police, harsher penalties and immigration legislation, and how to punish the racialized in deprived neighborhoods—mandatory ADHD controls of children in "vulnerable areas" (the Moderates), mandatory language test of two-year-olds with the option to forcibly take them into custody (the Liberals), and a limit to the percentage of "non-Nordic" residents in urban areas (SAP) were some of the dog whistles. Ironically, this concerted effort from the two blocs to win back the SD sympathizers only strengthened the support for fascism—for over two years, SD had stagnated in the opinion polls due to their lack of credibility regarding the handling of the COVID-19 pandemic and their associations with Kremlin. However, thanks to the combination of their frivolous promises of reducing gas prices amid the European electricity crisis with this amplified "great moving right show" (to quote Stuart Hall), during August and September 2022 SD gained another 3 percent in the election (now 20 percent) and thus dethroned the Moderates as the second biggest party in Sweden (which had not happened since 1976).[102] While the other three parties of the radical-conservative bloc scraped together less than one third of the votes, yet another Bonapartist solution was arranged, as they, with SD's blessings, could form a government formally led by Kristersson. In this way SD further secured their role as *the hegemonic force* of the reigning fraction and of Swedish politics overall—now the world's biggest party with a direct Nazi origin. During the victory rush at the party's election vigil, their prominent female influencer drunkenly exclaimed the Swedish equivalent of *sieg heil*.[103]

But what happened to "the beggars" themselves? With the revelation of COVID-19 in early 2020, national debate *temporarily* went on to discuss topics other than racial deviance. Following this intermezzo, EU déclassés appear to have been forgotten as an issue. They can still be found in the cityscapes time and again, with a majority joining poor seniors and other residents in looking for bottle deposits instead of begging. To counteract the awkward sight of people freezing to death on the streets, some municipalities outsourced their social responsibility to (underfunded) NGOs providing (too few) shelters, while towns such as Malmö incorporated temporary accommodation solutions for a wide range of homeless demographics— except the EU déclassés, that is.[104] Indeed, Amnesty International, having interviewed fifty-eight EU déclassés across the country in 2018, summarized their primary concern for members of this population in Sweden as a "lack of a secure, safe and stable place to sleep, a source of enormous stress, fear and anxiety." They cite, for example, the experiences of sixty-two-year-old Adela, who lived in a tent made of plastic sheets and blankets in a Gothenburg suburb, explaining, "Once when the police came she had shown them documentation from the hospital as proof of her serious heart condition. One of the police officers told her that she should not sleep outside and that she would die if she continued to sleep out in the cold. However, the police did not refer her to Social Services for alternative housing. Instead, they told her she should return to Romania."[105] This commonsensical procedure symptomizes the hegemonization of the third ideal type of interpreting the begging question, as presented in chapter 1: accepting "the beggars'" needs as "genuine," yet shirking personal and national responsibility for helping them, as this responsibility is framed as impossible anyway.

Through this Swedish Third Way solution to the anxiety of the begging Other, who finds themself somewhere between the binarity of "deserving" and "undeserving"—a liminality facilitated by the passage of time— the EU déclassés have become "normalized" in the Swedish urban space. Increasingly, their place there seems to rouse less and less of an emotional response—both less violence and less compassion—on the part of passersby. In this way the strategy of feeling *apathy* toward the Other's desire seems to be triumphing, as post-exceptional-equality melancholia has moved on, finding new Others to blame or defend.

As the new right-wing government was formed in 2022 upon SD's graces, among the former's concession to the latter's heart issues, a nation-wide begging ban was declared to be prepared for. One could argue that Sweden's latest decade-long begging question formally ended here, if it was not for the fact that begging had not been a national political issue for almost four years. A more fitting conclusion of the begging question's history is the justice ombudsman's critique of the police in 2019 for continually driving begging people from their preferred spots in Stockholm.[106] Eight years earlier the same ombudsman had castigated the Stockholm police for deporting begging people in 2010. In this way the decade-long begging question ended where it started, but with a new ideological direction on the part of the Swedish political formation. As David Bowie once sang:

And nothing has changed
Everything has changed[107]

The Problem

An Epitome

Let us conclude by returning to this story's introduction: the deadly beating of Gica in Huskvarna. This tragedy occurred amid the government formation crisis of 2018, only a couple of months before the court rule reintroducing explicit begging legislation. Sticking to the ideological script, Löfven suggested that the government "stop begging because that is no one's future," adding that this conclusion had been a "solidary valuation."[1] There is, of course, a kernel of truth to this moral judgment, if "stop" did not imply "criminalize." Given the context, however, the message can only be understood as a desire to foreclose the expression of something universal: after all, begging is ultimately an expression of poverty. Mediating dispossession by enclosures of resources and property, it reveals objective inequality. Begging, therefore, proves class society's existence: in a society where people are not separated from their means of subsistence, begging would not exist. Moreover, Löfven's choice of words expressed another universal phenomenon: *anxiousness* regarding both the presence and potential handling of begging. Notably, the anxiety of the begging encounter is not, *in itself*, an issue of poverty, capitalism, class society, or racism. Rather, it is an issue of what Lacan calls "the desire of the Other." This encounter with a neighbor who wants something from you is an encounter with the very existence of other minds, of their needs and wants in a reality where every being is finite and separated—yet dependent upon other beings. Because the human being is intersubjective in its unconscious, its mirroring of others is its mirroring of itself, as the subject in-itself is, in the end, an Other for-itself. Consequently, the begging encounter is an encounter with human suffering in not only an objective but also subjective sense—this ordeal takes place both in-between and within.

As we have seen, the desire to make begging vanish is an overdetermined desire, permeating class positions and identities. We find this desire reflected in the administration of political, ethical, and moral considerations. Given that it is sensed by both those who antipathize or sympathize with those begging and, of course, by the begging individuals themselves, this desire is universal. To generalize: no one wants begging. While social measures aim to neutralize the plea's ethical, political, and existential anxiety by translating it into "acceptable" expressions and curbing the number of people issuing it, the universal choice ultimately becomes how to make begging disappear: either by forcing the poor to stop begging while remaining poor or by alleviating their poverty so that they do not have to beg anymore. As history, and this story, show, the usual option has been the former route. While class society makes it impossible to give people unconditional access to their own means of survival, and elevates the rulers' ideas into common sense, I would contend that the anxiety of the encounter itself is also a determining factor. Reflecting on this book's story, one can see that the Swedish begging question was partly stalled by a perennial societal "narcissism": with very little regard to the supposed subjects of the discussion, the issue was, almost always, about one's own feelings, rationalized into societal, moral, and political value principles. While blaming this self-absorption on neoliberalism would be insufficient and nostalgically dangerous (reading the history of reactions to begging, after all, makes such pulp intellectualism fall short), the anxiety this egocentrism symptomizes, I argue, was central to the creation of a cross-class popular consensus on the necessity to remove the (perceived) cause of anxiety. And this consensus ultimately benefited the interests of the (equally anxious) reigning and hegemonic class fractions.

Setting aside the sublimations of the unconscious, another determining factor—constitutive for class society, capitalist (re)production, and contextual manifestations of anxiety for human difference—is the *dialectic of racism*. Although the begging encounter's anxiety does not fundamentally concern xenophobia or prejudice, it is no coincidence that the racial Others of various social formations have often been forced to step into an uncomfortable role: those who "cause" social anxieties. In societies where scarcity is produced and maintained, and where scarcity is a perennial risk, there always lurk fantasies of scapegoats and freeloaders—of the Other who embodies the pains of society, existence, and the human condition. While the extimate construction of the unconscious enables subjects to displace the true sources of suffering onto human targets, hierarchical societies steadily supply subjects with these sensations, while guiding them with discourses and ideologies toward becoming anchored to certain social categories. After all, the political-economic mode of production, which is based upon perpetual accumulation and the circulation of valorized labor power, demands a temporal and spatial oscillation between stability and crisis, making life more insecure than life has to be and every stranger into a potential threat to one's own security. If we bear in mind that Lacanian anxiety is "the instant when the subject is suspended" toward "something in which he will never be able to find himself again," capitalism makes this place and event constantly imminent.[2] All these forces and structures come together within the racism dialectic and are symptomized by the omnipotence of the social fantasy of the Other's theft of Enjoyment. This fantasy can, in turn, be located within the core of the dialectic of the universal and the particular.

The Particular: Strategical Universalization

The aforestated Swedish case emblemizes the ways in which the dialectic of racism finds its support in social practices, unconscious beliefs, and institutional modes of exploitation and dispossession. Perhaps one of its greatest lessons is to show how racism works beyond language and mindset: even though the debate was continuously signaling awareness of racism, anti-Roma discrimination, and desires for the opposite, the material politics nevertheless carried out repression, thus repeating Sweden's anti-Roma history. To only address racism on the level of discourse, speech, and personal values, therefore, risks vulnerability to an idealist trap if the material reality of class relations, institutional regulations, political interests, and interpersonal encounters are not taken into consideration. To paraphrase Black Power theoretician Stokely Carmichael, racism is not fundamentally about attitudes, but power. Simultaneously, the Swedish case demonstrates that ideology's contradictoriness generates political results. Although Sweden ultimately followed the universal path of punishing the poor and scapegoating the racial Other during the recharged global crisis of democratic capitalism, it did so in a peculiar way. This particularity must be understood as deriving, in part, from *beliefs* in the ideology of exceptional equality. Otherwise the repression would not have been translated into such complicated rhetorical and legal procedures; prohibition would probably have been enabled earlier; the Right would have started to cooperate with SD much earlier; and Sweden would not have accepted the EU's greatest proportion of refugees in 2015. There were, then, partial truths to this ideology of exceptionalism.

While this exposé has not denied that the content of ideology matters, it has also shown the extent to which ideological claims of values are informed by the realpolitik of the situation. Political actors navigate an ever-changing battlefield, where each chess move threatens to overturn the whole table. When there was an interest on behalf of capital and state governors to support antiracist values—because of the political composition in parliament and dominant debates in the media before 2015—there was political leverage to grant health care to the undocumented, maintain a liberal asylum policy, and decry begging prohibition as inhuman and ineffective. When this political landscape changed, capital and the dominant bloc found it in their interest to shift their values in order to save (or increase) their political power—then it became opportune to claim that a too-liberal asylum policy would disintegrate the nation, and that "beggars" needed to go back home.

In this way the ultimate winner walking out of this crisis of hegemony was, with the exception of SD, capital itself. Initially, as the racist-populist backlash would not have gained such force if it had not been fueled by anxieties stemming from neoliberal deregulations of securities and equalities, the conjuncture constituted a potential threat to capital. However, it instead became its triumph, as the ideological shift following this back-lash seriously undermined SAP's ideological dominance. Consequently, by complying with the narrative that the racial Other-in-need is a threat and not an ally, SAP's commanders lured themselves into a state of neoliberal dependency and began to encourage anxieties of theft of Enjoyment. This further betrayal of social democracy regarding working-class interests helped facilitate the loss of a shared class consciousness and the shared solidarity needed for abolishing the material base that makes the theft of Enjoyment politically relevant. One must stress that while it lies in capital's interest to flirt with fascism and racism (within fitting conditions), this dalliance on behalf of labor can only secure short-term political leverage, but never, to quote Valfridsson et al., "long-term, sustainable change" in its favor. In fact, this is increasingly the case, since the working class itself is undeniably racially mixed in contemporary Sweden, a fact that no racialist melancholia can erase.

One might, in a counterfactual sense, speculate about whether the Swed-ish begging question would have developed differently had it not inter-sected with the refugee crisis in 2015. Such speculation would be ultimately fruitless, however, as this temporal intersection was no coincidence: both its origins and outcomes were rooted in the historical-geographical devel-opment at hand and its dialectical temporal-spatial interconnection with other economic, social, political, and racial processes. However, for the sake of argument, I would guess that, if the begging question had occurred some years earlier, the political handling of the déclassés' poverty in Sweden *as such* would not have differed *that much*. Had the issue not intersected with the racist momentum of SD, maybe the *degree* of the governing of déclassés would have been less coercive, more "benevolent." After all, in retrospect, the dominant parties' strategies and ideology differed only in semantics and penal degrees to SD's. What's more, the contradictions and deadlocks within the Swedish Model's Borromean knot, the common sense of the masses, and the capitalist system would have remained the same. One mustn't forget that the (re)appearance of begging and, correspondingly, its interpretation as a moral-social problem are always symptomatic of broken-down systems of livelihood—expressing social, political, and economic disruptive change. Although the déclassés of *this* story initially fled the institutional havoc of their home countries, they encountered, and *revealed*, the institutional havocs of the Swedish institutions.

In sum, the path of the Swedish begging question was overdetermined to become solved in the way it did because of the power interests of the dominating and hegemonic classes to save their political legitimacy and power by maintaining order. However, to say that something was overdetermined does not mean it was deterministically unavoidable. History is made by people, and there were glimpses of the Real where crucial actors could have chosen other paths.

WHAT DID THE COUNTERARGUMENT LACK?

In hindsight, I see three weaknesses in the general position of those fighting for the EU déclassés' interests: one practical and two intellectual. Notably, I do not include the critique that the déclassés should have led their own struggle—given the reality of their material conditions, they did what they could with the options available to them. There were, after all, some attempts of organization, such as their refusal to leave the Malmö settlement, or the gathering of a small group of Roma who marched to Stockholm's City Hall to demand accommodation solutions.[3] While the déclassés certainly were subalternized in practice, they were nevertheless featured in myriads of news reports, radio and television programs, books, plays, films, and articles, thanks, in part, to the predominance of the Swedish ideology in the media. They were formally granted a voice in the debate, and this voice, just like the begging gesture itself, pleaded, *Please help us secure a better life.* The supposed radical statement that proclaims the exploited class must engage in its own self-advocacy holds no water here, since the "general will" of EU déclassés is in fact the general will of *everyone* being economically exploited. The EU déclassés might be "declassed," but they are nevertheless part of the proletarianized class. Helping them does not have to be philanthropy; it can be solidarity.

THE PROBLEM

In any case, what were the aforestated flaws? First, it was the widespread nonpoliticized articulation of déclassés' material interests as a matter of "human rights." As philosopher Giorgio Agamben delineates, the reason human rights cannot compensate for a lack of citizenship rights is because of the insufficiency of citizenship rights themselves. Indeed, the very concept of "citizenship" harbors the potential for its own dispensation—of the state's sovereign power to repeal rights, because of its ability to guarantee them.[4] The ultimate impotence of human rights is not their lack of implementation, but rather their replication of the distinction between "rights'" Imaginary and Real. One telling representation of this problem was the commonsensical disavowal of the demands to give the déclassés the right to housing: "Why should the Other receive something for free that isn't free?"

This brings us to the counter-ideology's second weakness: its overconfidence in the moralizing power of "the race card." Having described at great length how anti-Roma racism became articulated and mobilized into a political force, I now dare to say that, in this story, there was an overemphasis on labeling the EU déclassés, their begging, and their homelessness as a "Roma" problem, and, in doing so, well-intended people unfortunately partook in the ideological racialization of the begging question. As the Roma signifier became dominant in debating the begging question, the commonsensicality of banal nationalism helped foster a racial estrangement instead of a shared class consciousness. Notably, with the Roma narrative, human rights ideology did its very best to give "the beggar" an intelligible biography and identity, a narrative that was historically anchored and analytically accurate. In this way, however, the race signifier and its accompanying antagonistic moralities impacted Swedish common sense and the political debate in such a way that the EU déclassés effectively became alienated from being anything else than "Roma." Given the overarching political conditions, such as they were, the "victimization" narrative of the Roma locked the debate into an idealistic frenzy of values, passions, and condemnations, while the constant attention paid to whether or not "the Roma" really were "criminals" made anti-Roma folklore perennially relevant in the public (un)consciousness.

Third, and most importantly, the solidary position lacked a *political* movement that could have integrated the begging question into the conflict between labor and capital. Had this occurred, the determining political problem of begging in Sweden, the Borromean welfare knot, could have been addressed, rather than pedestrians' sentiments. In terms of parties, the ones most eager to guarantee the déclassés material social rights—EP, F!, and the Left Party—were all small parties and (with the exception of the latter) not ideologically connected enough to the class struggle. Besides, by the time the Left Party finally presented a proposal that acknowledged the déclassés as part of the working class in 2019, it was too late.[5]

Of course, all these shortcomings are interrelated, as they come from a political positionality that seeks to operate within the ongoing melancholia of left politics and theory: a melancholia directly related to the melancholies of democratic capitalism, Anglo-European whiteness, and Swedish exceptional equality. Obviously, the solution to this depression is not to anachronistically copy and paste the politics of the last century; instead melancholia needs to be transformed into grief—with the acceptance of a loss of what once was—in order to shift the focus from nostalgia to aspiration: from loss to lack. This also entails an acknowledgment on behalf of the traditional white Left in Sweden (and elsewhere) that the dialectic of racism is central to the ongoing class struggle. Likewise, it necessitates an admission on behalf of those who identify with "Good antiracist Sweden" that racism's form of reproduction is inescapably dependent upon the reproduction of capitalist class society's artificial scarcity.

I contend that a truly emancipatory politicization of the begging question would have required a solidarity based on what Žižekian scholars Ilan Kapoor and Zahi Zalloua term "universal politics": revolutionary struggles against the global omnipotent capitalist system forged on solidarity between different proletarian positions, not united in a positive shared identity, but in a negative shared experience of exploitation, dispossession, and oppression (whether by class, race, gender, sexuality, ability, or something else).[6] The theorists identify the Black Lives Matter movements as harboring such a potential after its global breakthrough in the summer of 2020. This is for several reasons: its focus on structural oppression in the form of the police force's institutionalized racist foundation; the cause's shared relatability that lent the protests cross-Atlantic appeal (in Sweden and elsewhere); and, finally, the American movement's widespread rejection of the established parties, demand to defund the police, and siding with Palestine. For all these reasons, BLM serves as a good omen—one that envisions a global solidarity of the wretched of the Earth, based on a negative universality of rejecting the status quo. Indeed, the Swedish begging question would have benefited from the mobilization of such a national movement, one that had the potential to occur in what I termed "the antiracist momentum" of 2012–15. While its remnants live on in contemporary struggles for the rights of Afro-Swedes, Swedish Sami, and more, the politics of this movement were ultimately doomed with regard to the begging question, for the same three reasons cited above. However, to conclude that these politics were not radical enough, as they neither targeted the capitalist system itself nor dared to "demand the impossible" of a global revolution that would abolish capitalism, racism, and patriarchy altogether, is a theoretical-political easy way out. While this conclusion is analytically true in an abstract sense, pragmatically, genuine mass politics first need to be grounded in something that could conceivably become commonly desirable in the immediate future—not something that appears to lead toward an uncertain, *anxiety-laden* future.[7] Meanwhile, the desirability of the quick fix of xeno-racist demagogy, the immediate closure of the borders, *appears* to be conceivable in its adherence to the status quo (even though it would not solve what it promises to solve).

At the core of this discussion lies the problem of *tactics*—how to mobilize a universal politics grounded in, to use Žižek's words, "the point of inherent exception/exclusion, the 'abject,' of the concrete positive order," "the only point of true universality," if a majority of a given political entity's exploited population doesn't sociopolitically identify with this point in the first place.[8] While this point of anxiety is universal on the level of empathetic identification (that is, the whole argument of part 1), the potentiality of a *political* identification depends upon the given social formation's class structure and its quantitative distribution; in Morales's Bolivia, Cabral's Guinea-Bissau, and Per Albin Hansson's Sweden, for example, there was a majority of the working masses who could ideologically identify with this abjection within "the concrete positive order" of the capitalist state. As regards Sweden at present, this power ratio is simply not there, due to the "labor aristocracy" positionality of the Swedish working class in the world economy, its internal racialization, and the tied interest of "insiders" in the continuation of systemic welfare duality. In the geopolitical context of capitalist core nation-states, too large of shares of the working class believe themselves to have much more to lose than "their chains," thanks to their material dependency (whether as security or privilege) on the fluctuation of financial markets.

One example of this practical-theoretical problem is outlined in an article by urban theorist Peter Marcuse, in which he divides the working class into those alienated and those deprived. The latter includes the homeless and other marginalized peoples, whereas the alienated concerns the greater mass of consumer citizens. Arguing that the Russian Revolution arose from the demands of the deprived (who were a majority back there and then), while the 1968 protests symptomized the aspirations of the alienated, Marcuse prescribes "combining the demands of the oppressed with the aspirations of the alienated."[9] If we agree to this, our problem arises when he triages the class, stipulating whose interests ought to be secured first: "Where choices must be made, the demands of the deprived are entitled to priority over the fulfillment of the aspirations of the alienated."[10] This is where the problem of racism and alterity—the fantasy of theft of Enjoyment—undoes this strategy, if taken "too literally" in a national context: if the deprived have less manpower relative to the alienated, the latter will not accept the formers' "entitled" priority—that is, if this entitlement cannot be *simultaneously* understood as an aspiration for the alienated. I admittedly do not know how to do this. All I know is that fantasies of Others' intentions and unlikeability have been far too downplayed by critical theory and egalitarian politics.[11]

All these insights lead to my "paradoxical" conclusion that Löfven's "solidary" suggestion was actually correct, if only it were taken "too literally."

What ought to have been prioritized in discussions of "the beggars" was the aim *to make begging cease to exist*. While this conclusion, at first blush, appears to accord with the Swedish ideology, said ideology *perverted* this insight, spatializing the matter into capitalist class society's tried and true method of punishing, hiding, and chasing away the impoverished. But my conclusion aspires to something different: to sublimate the overdetermined anxiety of begging into a political desire that aims to undo the anxious encounter by abolishing economic exploitation. Ultimately, the dominant desire to do away with begging is a desire shared by both the individual begging and the individual approached—no one wants it. As Žižek says, "Sometimes, alienation is like alcohol for Homer Simpson: 'the cause and solution to all life's problems!'"[12] Consequently, the only way to counteract the political alienation between the declassed and the insider working class—to enable a shared Imaginary of a common political aim for the future—is to "existentially" alienate (as in "downplay") the anxiety of the Other's desire.[13] In other words, the fantasy of theft of Enjoyment must be interpersonally neutralized, so that its libido can be politically channeled into a fruitful direction. Additionally, an envisioned solidarity between "the beggar" and the employed needs to a priori seek the abolition of begging via a *shared entitlement to the Thing*. With that said, it cannot aim to criminalize begging before it eliminates the reasons to beg—otherwise, the dominant ideology takes over, and begging continues in whatever form and place. This makes for a complicated situation, as it needs to at least *appear* that the declassed do not receive "more" entitlements than the laborer. Since ideological fantasy contains the distinction between knowledge and belief, one can "know really well" someone else needs more help than another yet nevertheless *believe* this Other gets unfair handouts at one's own expense. For this reason the strategy must conjure a vision of equal access between groups, instead of total equal distribution (ignoring fundamental differences between individuals and their needs) or total unequal distribution (overcompensating these fundamental differences so that the distribution might be commonly interpreted as unfair). Granted, such balancing might be impossible to realize—but it's worth a try.

An Epitome

As this book has relied so much on Marxian analysis, it goes without saying that the "ultimate solution" to the begging question is the *global* abolishment of capitalism and class society—racialization included. However, my empirics and conscience forbid me from stating this and not going any further. I've simply encountered too many leftists throughout these years who have invoked the grand narrative of "until the Revolution comes" in order to disavow any sense of personal or social responsibility for the begging neighbor before them. Recall that the Swedish ideology operated along similar lines, ingeniously abstracting the matter at hand into a vague utopia-cynicism that postponed "solidarity" to a distant time and place. These perspectives ignore that the entire moral problem with the begging question is the begging individuals' suffering *at the very present*. In any case, if I don't suggest any practical solutions myself, with what confidence can I stand by my critique?

What, then, is a "radical" solution that complies with my theoretical angle? To some readers' disappointment, I argue that the most realistic and radical solution would be to renew the demands of the human rights ideology. However, this time said demands must not be articulated as the universal rights of the "dispossessed," but rather the whole of the masses. Indeed, I believe the only fruitful way to overcome the theft of Enjoyment in this matter is to eschew the racial division in favor of a popular, cross-racial demand for Enjoyment of security together—that is, trying to reenact the direction of early last century's localization of the Swedish Thing in the future withheld, not ruined. Here, the great challenge is to reenact this mobilization of an ideologically cohesive working class on a national platform in the context of post-white melancholia, as Sweden's working class will never again appear to be racially homogenous. To rephrase, interpersonal alienation might be the cure instead of the disease—in this quest racial identities need to become, somehow, not (that) relevant, while *simultaneously* not reproducing "color-blind" white domination. In this regard postcolonial theorist Edward Said's motto, "Never solidarity without criticism," comes to mind.[14] To achieve such a political collective, race obviously must be acknowledged, since, as Hall and acquaintances wrote, "race is the modality in which class is lived. It is also the medium in which class relations are experienced. [This] has consequences for the *whole class*, whose relation to their conditions of existence is now systematically transformed by race. [It] also provides one of the criteria by which we measure the *adequacy* of struggle to the structures it aims to transform."[15]

The undeniable fact that class relations in Europe are experienced through race needs, however, more than to be simply "accepted." As psychoanalysis teaches us, conscious acceptance means little if unconscious and ideological practices are not broken—or, as Jameson contended, "It would be a mistake to think that anyone can ever really learn to live with" the Real, since "the retreat from it" into different forms of "intellectual comfort" is "perpetual."[16] Somehow, the antagonism of human differences needs to be, in Žižek's words, fetishistically disavowed—at least to the bearable degree of enabling a shared political-economic subjectivity that aims to eliminate artificial scarcity. As Žižek put it, one's duty to receive refugees should not be based on a glorification of them: "What if 'getting to know them' reveals that they are more or less like us—impatient, violent, demanding [and so on? Instead, we must overcome] the sentimentalism that breaks down the moment we realize that most of the refugees are not 'people like us' (not because they are foreigners, but because *we* ourselves are not 'people like us')."[17] The way the Other is "like us" is that they also fear suffering and desire pleasure, without knowing how to avoid hurting themself, and they are forced to negotiate the existence of Others: you can't live with them; you can't live without them. Trying to make the phantasmatic overcoming of the Other's fundamental humanity (their difference from their neighbor) into a political objective can only extend, and never undo, interpersonal suffering.

Thus, what is needed is not a shared "humanity" between the Swede and the EU déclassé (since their shared humanity is already a fact, and humanity's dark side is what is feared in the first place), but an acknowledged *shared interest*. This interest should empathetically build solidarity not through a perceived shared identity, but a shared material reality concerning the access to material security. In other words, what is needed is a shared *class consciousness*, which distracts anxieties related to Otherness in favor of a shared common aim. As I try to show throughout this book, the *structural position* of the EU déclassé in Swedish welfare society is a position that relates to other class positions of dispossession and repression. There is therefore an abstract potential for forging a shared class consciousness beyond the divisions of nationality, race, and employment, as the déclassé position symbolizes the potential life conditions one might face if unlucky in the Swedish capitalist system. In this way the anxiousness of the Other's theft of trygghet might be sublimated into a shared struggle to nullify this position's existence and potentiality. Today's nearest—and most commonsensical—ideology to this is human rights ideology, however flawed and isolated from politicization and class struggle it may be.

When we speak of appropriating human rights ideology for the sake of EU déclassés in Sweden, there must be an understanding of the need to counteract the division between citizenship and human rights, as well as the necessity of appealing to a shared universal need (or desire) of citizens, residents, and the nonqualified. It seems to me, therefore, that the best strategic approach to untangling the Borromean knot of Swedish welfare short-circuits is to extricate the thread of *housing*. Not only did Amnesty International's report show a great demand among déclassé respondents in their need for housing, but it has also been shown that déclassés frequently use their earnings from begging to support housing construction back home.[18] Further, at a movie screening I attended, part of a project in which EU déclassés are encouraged to make their own short films about a topic of their choosing, the popularity of the desire for housing in Sweden was striking. Notably, this aspiration aligns with the interests of the public as well, as this would radically decrease informal settlements and loitering and allow déclassés to concentrate on job searching instead of begging. Moreover, the desire for safe and secured housing is marriable with the ongoing affordable housing shortage in Sweden and, simultaneously, appeals to historical memories of the folkhem ideals of exceptional-equality housing. Indeed, the Swedish housing question has recently proved to have a "repoliticizing" potential: in the summer of 2021, the Left Party brought down the government with their opposition against the government and the Center Party's plan to legislate market rents for new rentals.[19] When the same government reformed, the proposition was abandoned, and the Left Party's popularity skyrocketed. In other words, the demand for affordable housing contains the possibility to mobilize a national class struggle such that the EU déclassés might become fellow comrades, rather than "freeloaders" benefiting "at the expense" of the "hardworking" public.

To go into detail, a specific demand to house EU déclassés' could be (more) realistically articulated as a right to high-standard accommodation for the ninety days that they have an official right to stay each time they visit Sweden, funded and run by the state (not the municipalities or civil society), in which social workers and officials are stationed to help prospective tenants start new lives in Sweden or elsewhere in the EU. But is such a proposal radical enough? First of all, it is a tangible (although not presently likely) relief to the sufferings of the here and now. While Marx advocated for an anti-capitalist revolution, he was committed enough to simultaneously support struggles for shorter working days, universal suffrage, the end of child labor and slavery, and so on. After all, a true radical cannot disavow the hardships of the present—they must resist the temptation to turn the present into the future's hostage. In other words, the class struggle must be tactical and pursued within and without the state apparatus, on both local, national, and global platforms, taking the historical-geographical and political context of each scene into account—drawing on sociologist Erik Olin Wright's thoughtful analogy of liking capitalism's totality to an ecosystem.[20] While, for example, the discourse of human rights and its global institutions have certainly contributed to the normalization of neoliberal ideology, it remains the case that, within the current phase of democratic capitalism, this discourse nevertheless harbors a radical potential.[21] Further, the suggestion to guarantee the déclassés temporary housing in Sweden is, within the contemporary ideological climate, anything but modest; as shown, such a right would undermine the dominant moral economy, which must, in any case, be changed in order to facilitate a solidarity between the lower and middle classes. This demand, accurately formulated, should reiterate what remains of the moral economy of exceptional equality in housing: that is, déclassé housing should be of an equal standard to the general norm, so that "slum communities" continue to be considered unacceptable. Finally, and most importantly: to traverse the threshold between human and citizenship rights, the demand must be issued *alongside* a demand for an unconditional right to housing for Swedish residents. What is needed, ultimately, is an ideological struggle to establish a dominant common sense proclaiming an unconditional right to housing implemented by public means.[22] In this way the theft of Enjoyment could potentially be incapacitated, allowing the Swedish public to support the "modest" demand to give déclassés "long-term, sustainable" housing options.

If there is no mobilization of a counter-ideology that reveals the gap between the "actual" and the "possible," people cannot libidinally *believe* there is a better future for them that is being withheld in the present. When the Swedish labor movements were initiated in the nineteenth century, there were the aspirations for social and political equality inspired by the promised freedoms upheld by the liberalism of the American Dream, as well as European socialists. With this in mind, democratic capitalism's relative deprivation must be transformed into class solidarity instead of interclass melancholic hostility; after all, the former was enabled by the contradictions of the bourgeois liberal ideology's promises of equality and freedom. One need only peruse the long global history of class society to see that, for many ages, fatal oppression and repression was typically met with acceptance, because it was commonly believed that nothing else was possible in one's earthly life. The exceptions to the rule have occurred when the contextual moral economy has been considered breached. It is against this backdrop that various socialists have despised begging, as the practice is interpreted as yet another acceptance of the status quo through its gesture of "subservience." However, there is no mechanical teleology assuring us that accelerating inequalities will generate revolutionary politics; the battlefield of ideology to change the moral economy, so that "the masses" are able to see the moral unacceptability of the contemporary order, is crucial to convince them that there is a viable end to artificial scarcity.

Notably, this is also why it is insufficient to suggest the déclassés themselves must *lead* their own struggle ceteris paribus. Without a feasible counter-ideology of justice that enables a class solidarity beyond their own positionality, capitalism's abjected are too busy surviving to organize themselves outside the formal economy and social communication structures. Indeed, the mission of reaching out and cultivating ideological belief cannot be understated; after all, the class consciousness required to make a noncapitalist future achievable can only come about by appealing to the lived material reality at hand. That's why "modest" policies—ones that appear to be doable on the surface yet constitute threats to the dominating class fraction's ideology—are crucial in maintaining or creating such consciousness, as Louis Althusser argues. Writing immediately after 1968, he argued from a Marxist-Leninist standpoint against the claims of "certain avant-garde theoreticians" that trade unionist struggles for "materialistic" demands are nonrevolutionary. Although Althusser believed in the need for a party to lead a political struggle to seize the state, he knew this would never come about if the conflict was not rooted in "the *economic* class struggle, that is, in the struggle for 'bread-and-butter demands.'" While trade unionism can never single-handedly conquer the capitalist state (because if so, they can only become a "loyal manager of the capitalist regime"),

> it is by way of the struggle for material demands that *the masses* can be rallied to objective actions against the capitalist system. The masses: not just the vanguard of the proletariat, not just the proletariat, but also the non-proletarian wage-workers in town and country, poor peasants, small peasants in the process of becoming proletarians, and all those, including many civil servants working in the [state apparatuses] *who are objectively victims of capitalist exploitation.*
>
> [The] masses, when they go into motion, will not accept the party's political leadership *unless* they have long since been unified and mobilized

in the struggle against *the economic exploitation* of the capitalist regime by a long, hard, heroic, tenacious, unspectacular, *trade-union* struggle for *bread-and-butter demands* on the basis of a correct line.[23]

Radical social transformation can never arise if it is not originally founded in the collective organization for "unspectacular" material struggles. Notably, the trade unionism defended here should not be literally interpreted as labor unions being the only relevant organizational form, let alone that workplaces should be the only platform for "trade unionism." As we observed in chapter 8, the déclassés' "unemployability" transformed them into a Real vis-à-vis unions, and the demand for "more jobs" is (to say the least) problematic, given the ideological position of the déclassés outlined in this book.[24] To connect to the housing struggle strategy, the historical and contemporary tenant associations are a good example of mobilizing for "bread-and-butter demands"—the demand to have somewhere safe to sleep.[25] In terms of the abject true position of universality in the contemporary political economy, the idea of the "tenant association" might become more inclusive and universal than the "trade union." Moreover, demanding shelter rather than labor has a better potential to transcend work's inherent division between deserving and undeserving poor—instead of distinguishing between who is needed and not needed for work, one highlights the distinction between who needs and does not need assistance.

The Universal: Beyond Equality and Enjoyment

As this book approaches its end, there are two remaining abstract issues that require further reflection—ones that pertain to the universal aspects of the political quest to end the necessity of both performing and encountering begging. More specifically, the first concerns the continuation of the relationship between alterity and Enjoyment; the other involves the limits of articulating the utopianist Thing "the Swedish way"—that is, toward the realization of equality.

Back in 1875 Marx critiqued the social-democratic goal of creating a society guided by equality. Rather than objecting to the moral desire, he found "equality" to be a problematic term to describe one's end goal, since he saw the concept itself as embedded in capitalist society's foundations. The concept's limitation is due to its failure, when put into practice, to account for *human difference* in capacities and needs:

> A right can by its nature only consist in the application of an equal standard, but unequal individuals (and they would not be different individuals if they were not unequal) can only be measured by the same standard if they are looked at from the same aspect, if they are grasped from one *particular* side, e.g., if in the present case they are regarded *only as workers* and nothing else is seen in them, everything else is ignored. [If] all these defects were to be avoided[,] rights would have to be unequal rather than equal. [Ultimately,] right can never rise above the economic structure of a society and its contingent cultural development.[26]

Of course, one could go on to debate on what "equality" ought to mean in the last instance: in its intended consequence (equal opportunities, equal outcomes, equal rules, similarity, or something else) or what differences it is to measure (class, gender, ability, age, race, sexuality, values, efforts, and the rest). Interestingly, in the Swedish ideological case, "equality," as we have shown, came to mean many different contradictory things—including a dangerous racial-culturalist concept of "similarity." The signifier was also employed "from one particular side" to set "an equal standard" that, in fact, enhanced inequalities. Nevertheless, something akin to the "equality" signifier is required in order to appeal to the universal of the human condition, both to garner sympathies and solidarities with the human Other and to counteract anxieties regarding the same. In other words, there is a need for an unconscious mediator between the subject and the Other, a signifier that enables the subject and Other to mirror each other as separated yet similar in their being—the nonexistent Thing "retroactively" enabling identification, communication, and ethics. Drawing from geographer Gunnar Olsson's Lacanian-influenced philosophy, we might conceptualize this signifier as =.[27]

Indeed, Marx acknowledged the necessity of some sort of equal standard in the first phases of a postcapitalist society. His proposed maxim of what should replace "equality" in communism is well known: from each according to his abilities, to each according to his needs. Unfortunately, the classical Marxist and Leninist vision of this future that eliminates the need for both equality and rights was somewhat hindered by its own conditions as a counter-ideology to the dominant ideology of capitalist society itself—in its belief in the cornucopia of Earth's resources and technological automatization. Before environmentalism, radical utopianism has generally held that *all material scarcity* can be eliminated once and for all by the upheaval of class society's artificial maintenance of it. If this would be so, there would be no need for morality, as individuals could simply grab whatever they needed, when they needed it. However, the approaching climate Armageddon forces us to seriously investigate the extent to which and, given the uneven geography of natural resources, *how* this scarcity can be overcome—including the means of achieving "even" distribution. Sadly, this debate, as crucial as it is, cannot be further explored in this book.[28]

If, in any case, scarcity is not overcome postcapitalism, and there continues to be a need for geographical and social distribution of the means of survival—which would be the case anyway during "the great transition" to another system—the problem of envy, aggression, and similarity lingers. Moreover, even if the economic problem would be surmounted, the prospect, as Erica Benner says, "of domination, whereby one party asserts the power to define another's self-image, is never wholly absent from human relationships."[29] The very relationship between child and adult is proof of this, which we, thanks to psychoanalysis, know is reflected in the relationship between one's individual and collective existence, within which one becomes a subject. In this way we have once again returned to the problem of Enjoyment—of how to counteract interhuman anxiety, hostility, and fear of the Other's desire and intentions. Even if this universal problem cannot be solely blamed upon capitalism, or likely solvable with a new mode of production, I believe this abstract problem requires further reflection from those who wish to create a genuinely free and nonhostile world—if only to come to terms with what one should (or can) *not* promise that the struggle to end all economic exploitation and repression is able to accomplish. Notably, this point mirrors Freud's reminder that psychoanalysis cannot do away with suffering; however, "much will be gained if we succeed in transforming" one's "hysterical misery into common unhappiness," so that one "will be better armed against that unhappiness."[30] While this limitation has traditionally been used as an argument for a conservative acceptance of life's injustices, it could easily be applied as a consolation that "common unhappiness" is a true universal state of mind—preferable to anxiety, certainly—and that melancholia as a libidinal structure is constitutional and beyond one's individual or collective control. That way one becomes "better armed" in the struggle for the removal of the unnecessary causes of suffering: exploitative class and social relations and their material misery. This endeavor, in turn, can only be pursued if it ultimately concerns the whole of the globe and "humanity" within it. Even if we cannot talk of an essential "humanity," we need some sort of idea of a universal unconscious structure (placed within historical-geographical specificities and alongside other theories) in order to better tackle the struggle's inescapable encounter with "irrational," "counterproductive," and unexpected social actions, reactions, and decisions.

For my own part, this book's inquiry has led me to the hypothesis that probably the greatest obstacle to abolish class society is the tendency for anxiety regarding the Other's desire: exemplified in this book as (but not limited to) racism and fear of the impoverished. However, as this book, alas, cannot delve into speculations on the theft of Enjoyment's role in Utopia, I recommend the reader consult, besides Ursula K. Le Guin's classical sci-fi novel *The Dispossessed*,[31] Fredric Jameson's thought-provoking realist-utopian manifesto *An American Utopia* for further discussion. One might not agree with his conclusions, but he takes this unconscious envy seriously, writing:

> To disprove this envy, to assure me that the Other has no more enjoyment than I do, is a barren outcome. What must instead be celebrated is enjoy-

ment itself, that it exists, and that it does not matter who has it inasmuch as no one can really have it in the first place: this is the true overcoming of envy, its elevation into a kind of religion.

[In] any case, [an] essential feature of any utopian construction or imaginative operation and too often forgotten in the conventional stereotype of utopia as an edulcorated conflict-free zone of social peace and harmony, is the necessarily antagonistic nature of individual life and experience in a classless or communist society. "Classless" in this context means the elimination of collective antagonism and thereby, inevitably, the heightening of individual ones.[32]

Of course, this must be read while concomitantly rejecting the opposite "conventional stereotype" of "human nature" as fundamentally individuated, egoistic, and aggressive. After all, that people have been able to beg for survival throughout history and space is proof of the opposite. Notably, Freud fell in this ideological trap in his (nevertheless underrated) critique of "socialism." Though he agreed with "the socialists" "that a real change in the relations of human beings to possessions would be of more help" than "any ethical commands" to curb hostility and violence, he also thought their "fresh idealistic misconception of human nature" makes utopian-communists ignore that "aggressiveness was not created by property":

In abolishing private property we deprive the human love of aggression of one of its instruments [but] we have in no way altered the differences in power and influence which are misused by aggressiveness, nor have we altered anything in its nature. [It] already shows itself in the nursery almost before property has given up its primal, anal form; it forms the basis of every relation of affection and love among [people]. It is clearly not easy for men to give up the satisfaction of this inclination to aggression. They do not feel comfortable without it.[33]

Here, Freud confuses "property" with "possessions," which are not the same thing: "private property" is a historical category that belongs to class society; "possession" is a phenomenological category that is a part of the history of humankind—beyond it, even. However, taken to its abstracted extreme, subjectivity itself, the ego-Other relationship, is a possession relationship—or, rather, *a constant compensation for the lack of a possession relationship.* What Freud calls the "primal, anal form" of aggressiveness, which forms the "basis of every relation of affection and love," is the *desire to possess* the object of one's subjectivity, the Thing; the Other. In other words, a desire to possess is inescapably embedded with aggression. "Private property," meanwhile, is so readily normalized because it allures this unconscious desire to transgress the gap between consciousness and body; body and surroundings; thought and matter; language and meaning; individual and society; interior and exterior; ego and Other. But the final reconciliation between subject and object is impossible—both regarding the Weltgeist, God, the end of all alienation in communism, and the overcoming of the extimate Real between and within human beings. This is not, of course, an endorsement of Immanuel Kant or Adam Smith, who both believed the individual mind is fundamentally *isolated* from the Other; what is true, instead, is that we are all *separated* from each other and from our own mind. Each separation is somewhat lamentable or melancholic. Yet this separation is never completed, since we continue to *depend* on each other not only to survive materially, but also to have a social consciousness at all. Each dependence is somewhat anxious and desire-laden, since "dependence" implies not only a lack of sovereignty but also the possibility of losing the object of the Other—including the loss of one's self.

This leads us back to the begging gesture's inherent ethical kernel and its unconscious expression of the Other's desire: the acknowledgment of need and dependency; the very existence of Other wills against one's own; the lack of certainty; the lack of control; the inescapability of suffering in, to paraphrase Freud, our relations to other beings. In this sense Martin Luther was right when he, on his deathbed, (ought to have) said, "We are [all] beggars."

One may wonder if this fundamental friction between and within separate beings is really a subject for politics. That depends upon the political question being asked. However, just like the finitude of resources is the origin of economy, the finitude of beings is the origin of cooperation and conflict. No one escapes suffering and pleasure, and no one escapes anxiety and desire. The desire for the elimination of suffering might ultimately be labeled a "death drive," since the final ceasing of reactions to stimuli implies the end of life itself. Nevertheless, I believe this desire is what drives all manner of politics, and it is also what we find at the heart of the begging interaction and the begging question: a desire for *something else* than what is. This yearning is universal and thus a necessary precondition for finding, together, a better future. As the characters of *The Good Person of Szechwan* conclude in Brecht's play, turning to the audience:

Ladies and gentlemen, in you we trust
There must be happy endings, must, must, must![34]

Notes

Foreword

1. Von Mahs and Mitchell, "Americanization of Homelessness?"
2. Thörn, "Soft Policies of Exclusion," 989–1008.
3. Allen, "Ambient Power," 441–55, as quoted in Thörn, "Soft Policies," 994.
4. Although it might be a common market, and while Swedish people relish their right to travel freely around Europe, to buy homes in its sunnier climes, and to see themselves as European when comparisons with, for example, the Anglo-Saxon world are made, it is unthinkable for most Swedish people—and not just those on the nationalist right—that Europe as a whole could be a common "home." Home for Swedes is Sweden. Home for Roma peoples is Romania or Bulgaria. Europeanness does not stretch so far as to allow for a common "national" identity.
5. Mitchell, *Mean Streets*.

The Problem: An Introduction

1. Martin Lindstam, "Efter dödsmisshandeln av hemlöse Gica—hovrätten fastställer tingsrättens domslut," Sveriges Television, April 5, 2019.
2. *Godmorgon, världen!*, "Hemlöse Gica trakasserades långt innan mordet i Huskvarna," Sveriges Radio, September 2, 2018; Madeleine Bäckman, "Polisens miss efter mordet på Gica—slängde bevis i container," *Göteborgs-Tidningen*, September 30, 2018.
3. Caspar Behrendt, "Minst 16 attacker mot EU-migranter," *Fria Tidningen*, February 10, 2015.
4. Linda Bergh, "Stefan Löfvens ord efter misstänkta mordet på Gica," *Göteborgs-Tidningen*, August 31, 2018.
5. Thaler and Sunstein, "Libertarian Paternalism," 175–79.
6. Barker, "Nordic Vagabonds," 120–39.
7. Jansson, "Deadly Exceptionalisms," 83–91.
8. Pred, *Even in Sweden*.
9. Hübinette and Lundström, "Three Phases of Hegemonic Whiteness," 423–37.
10. European Federation of National Organisations Working with the Homeless (FEANTSA), *Criminalising Homeless People—Banning Begging in the EU*; Helena

Löfving and Maria Blanco, "Karta: Tiggeriförbud i Europa," Sveriges Television, September 8, 2017.

11. Elisabeth Åsbrink, "Sweden Is Becoming Unbearable," *New York Times*, September 20, 2022.

12. Žižek, "Neighbors and Other Monsters."

13. Marx, *Grundrisse*, 101.

14. Hall, "Race, Articulation and Societies," 236.

15. Hall, "Race, Articulation and Societies," 236.

16. "Kommunalt tiggeriförbud i Norge," Sveriges Radio, June 10, 2014.

17. "Lagförslag om tiggeriförbud i Norge faller," Sveriges Radio, February 5, 2015.

18. Rikke Struck Westersø, "Vedtaget: Nu skal hjemløse 14 dage i fængsel for at tigge," TV 2, June 14, 2017.

19. Matilda Uusjärvi Ek, "Olagligt att hjälpa tiggare i Danmark," Sveriges Radio, July 9, 2014.

20. Uutiset, "Proposed Begging Ban Divides Opinion," July 10, 2013.

21. For the concept of banal nationalism, see Billig, *Banal Nationalism*.

22. Hall, "Race, Articulation and Societies," 234.

23. Hall et al., *Policing the Crisis*.

24. Djuve et al., *When Poverty Meets Affluence*; Amnesty International, *Sweden*.

25. Teodorescu, "Dwelling on Substandard Housing."

26. World Bank Group, *Diagnostics and Policy Advice*.

27. TT Nyhetsbyrån, "Utflyttning oroar i Östeuropa," *Sydsvenskan*, January 25, 2019.

28. Polismyndigheten Rapport, *Nationell lägesbild*, 3.

29. Ling-Vannerus, *Uppdrag om nationell samordning avseende utsatta EU/EES-medborgare som saknar uppehållsrätt i Sverige—delrapport*, 19.

30. Cabral, *Revolution in Guinea*, 48.

31. Abdullah, "Culture, Consciousness and Armed Conflict," 102.

1. Searching for Elucidations

1. Josefine Hökerberg, "Pengarna från svenska gator håller byn vid liv," *Dagens Nyheter*, March 24, 2013.

2. Kent Ekeroth, "Förbjud tiggeri i hela landet," *Svenska Dagbladet*, April 21, 2011.

3. See Hübinette and Lundström, "Three Phases of Hegemonic Whiteness."

4. Hanna Åkesson, "Novus: En majoritet vill förbjuda tiggeri i Sverige" *Omni*, March 16, 2014.

5. Beijer, *Tiggeri*.

6. I was heavily inspired by Berggren and Trägårdh, *Är svensken människa?*

2. Concrete's Historical Layers

1. Britt Peruzzi, "Polisen: Stoppa tiggare i t-banan," *Aftonbladet*, November 14, 1998.

2. Engels, *Condition of the Working Class*, 278–79.

3. Eddie Karlsson, "Tiggare kränker privatlivet," *Hela Hälsingland*, March 25, 2014.

4. Mitchell, *Mean Streets*, viii, my emphasis.

5. Marx, *Capital*, vol. 1.

6. Marx, *Capital*, 1:540.

7. Marx, *Grundrisse*, 604, emphasis in original.

8. Marx, *Economic and Philosophic Manuscripts*, 86, emphasis in original.

9. Marx, *Capital*, 1:514.

10. Geremek, *Poverty*, 228.

11. Cresswell, "The Vagrant/Vagabond," 239.

12. Levander, *Fattigt folk och tiggare*, 142.

13. See Levander, *Fattigt folk*, 149.

14. Levander, *Fattigt folk*, 146.

15. Broström, "En industriell reservarmé i välfärdsstaten."

16. Magnusson, *Håller den svenska modellen?*

17. See Dean, *Begging Questions*.

18. Beijer, *Tiggeri*.

19. See Erskine and McIntosh, "Why Begging Offends."

20. Blau, *Visible Poor*, 5.

21. Gramsci, *Selections from the Prison Notebooks*, 419.

22. Erskine and McIntosh, "Begging Offends," 27.

23. Davidsson, *Understödets rationalitet*.

24. Lars Grimlund, "Boorks utspel om tiggare får förbund att se över regler," *Dagens Nyheter*, August 17, 2015.

25. Ensamstående Pappa, "Svårt med tiggarsympatin," *Partille Tidning*, February 27, 2014.

26. Anders Cnattingius, "Tiggeriet riskerar att erodera samhällskontraktet," *Svenska Dagbladet*, August 26, 2016.

27. Hall et al., *Policing the Crisis*, 139–40.

28. Ambjörnsson, *Den skötsamme arbetaren*.

29. Paulsen, *Arbetssamhället*.

30. Socialdemokraterna, "Jobb," July 2019, https://www.socialdemokraterna.se/var-politik/a-till-o/jobb.

31. Christina Örnebjär and Birgitta Ohlsson, "Liberaler kan inte förbjuda någon att be om hjälp," *Dagens Samhälle*, September 8, 2017.

32. Anders Cnattingius and Henrik Thorsell, "Liberaler kan visst förbjuda tiggeri," *Dagens Samhälle*, September 11, 2017.

33. Blomley, "Right to Pass Freely," 331–50.

34. Hobbes, *Leviathan*, 261.

35. See Schafer, *Expressive Liberty of Beggars*.

36. Corina Heri, "Beg your Pardon!: Criminalisation of Poverty and the Human Right to Beg in Lăcătuş v. Switzerland," *Strasbourg Observers*, February 10, 2021.

37. Marx, *Capital*, 1:344.

38. Smith, *Inquiry into the Nature and Causes*, 16.

39. Johnson, *Fear of Beggars*; Himmelfarb, *Idea of Poverty*, chap. 1.

40. Johnson *Fear of Beggars*; Raphael and Mcfie, introduction.

41. Liedman, *Från Platon till Gorbatjov*, 174–76.

42. Patrik Engellau, "Min uppfattning om tiggeri," *Det Goda Samhället*, June 15, 2015.

43. Wilde, *Collected Works*, 1041.

44. See Robert Mathiasson, "Frank Baude 80 år—'Klassfrågan måste stå främst,'" *Proletären*, July 14, 2016.

45. Andreas Henriksson, "En historielektion om tiggeriet," *Dagens Samhälle*, September 12, 2015.

46. Claes Borgström, "Hur kan socialdemokrater vilja registrera fattiga?," ETC, January 3, 2017.

47. Translated quote from Andrew Brown, "Swedes Can't Go Home Again," *Foreign Policy*, September 6, 2018.

48. "Ett förbud mot tiggeri flyttar bara problemen," ETC, April 20, 2016.

49. Marx and Engels, *Communist Manifesto*, 7.

50. Stallybrass, "Marx and Heterogeneity," 82, 85.

51. Robertson, "Marxism and Anarchism," 47–59; Fanon, *Wretched of the Earth*.

52. Stewart, "Deprivation, the Roma and 'the Underclass,'" 133–56; Rorke, "No Longer and Not Yet," 89; Lewy, *Nazi Persecution of the Gypsies*, 47.

53. See Mann, *In the Long Run*.

54. See Hall et al., *Policing the Crisis*, 139f.

55. Malthus, *Principle of Population*; Himmelfarb, *Idea of Poverty*; Davidsson, *Understödets rationalitet*.

56. Johnson, *Fear of Beggars*, 125.

57. "Cannabis och kåkstäder. Hur ska vi behandla romerna?," *SVT Debatt*, February 6, 2014 (transcribed).

58. Flint and Taylor, *Political Geography*.

59. "Många vill hjälpa stans tiggare," *Landskrona Posten*, July 29, 2014.

60. Carina Stensson, "Ska tiggeri vara förbjudet?," *Svenska Dagbladet*, August 13, 2014.

61. Daniel Färm, "Nio vänsterargument mot tiggeri," Sveriges Television, April 5, 2018.

62. Flint and Taylor, *Political Geography*.

63. Vermeersch, "Reframing the Roma," 1206.

64. Elisabeth Marmorstein and Jonas Ohlin, "S vill skärpa reglerna för tiggeri," Sveriges Television, February 26, 2017.

65. Jenny Sonesson, "Hur påverkar tiggeri bilden av Sverige?," *Dagens Industri*, July 17, 2015.

66. HgF, post #9, *Flashback Forum*, April 26, 2017, 10:20, https://www.flashback.org
/t2834273.

67. Geremek, *Margins of Society*, chap. 6.

68. Erskine and McIntosh, "Why Begging Offends," 39.

69. See Selling, *Svensk antiziganism*.

70. Engellau, "Min uppfattning om tiggeri."

71. Statens Offentliga Utredningar (SOU) 2010:55, *Romers rätt*, 173.

72. Departementsserien (Ds) 2014:8. *Den mörka*, 145.

73. Edman, "Lösdrivarlagen och den samhällsfarliga lättjan."

74. Ds 2014:8, *Den mörka*, 143–49.

75. Broberg and Tydén, "Eugenics in Sweden," 77–149. The last residues of the eugenics
legislation were finally removed in 2013 when mandatory sterilization of sex change
patients was abolished.

76. Broberg and Tydén, "Eugenics in Sweden," 126.

77. Dahlberg, "Anthropometry of 'Tattare,'" 79.

78. See Ivar Arpi, "Verkligheten hann ifatt Shekarabi," *Svenska Dagbladet*, August 19, 2016;
Jonatan Lönnqvist, "Tiggarna har ett eget ansvar," *Svenska Dagbladet*, April 15, 2016.

79. SOU 2006:14, *Samernas sedvanemarker*, 145–47.

80. "Begging and Beggars," *Encyclopedia Judaica*, 2008, https://www.jewishvirtuallibrary
.org/begging-and-beggars.

81. Gilmore, *Golden Gulag*, 28.

82. Miles, *Racism after "Race Relations."*

83. See Hübinette and Lundström, "Three Phases of Hegemonic Whiteness."

84. Therborn, *Kapitalet*, 105–6.

85. SOU 2010:55, *Romers rätt*, 35–36.

86. Anders Arborelius, Per Eckerdal, Pelle Hörnmark, Daniel Norburg, Lasse Svensson,
and Karin Wiborn, "Alla goda krafter måste lösa det som tvingar människor att
tigga," *Göteborgs-Posten*, September 30, 2015.

87. Quoted in Davidsson, *Understödet*, 203.

88. Geremek. *Poverty*.

89. Johnson, *Fear of Beggars*, 24–26.

90. See Johnson, *Fear of Beggars*, 31.

91. See also Erskine and McIntosh, "Why Begging Offends," 32.

92. Geremek, *Poverty*, 38.

93. Johnson, *Fear of Beggars*, chap. 2.

94. Cavallo, *The Byzantines*, 15.

95. Richardson, "Obedient Bellies," 776.

96. Engels, *Landmarks of Scientific Socialism*, 128.

97. Benner, *Really Existing Nationalisms*, 77, 65.

98. Benner, *Really Existing Nationalisms*, 77.

3. Abjection

1. Caspar Behrendt, "Minst 16 attacker mot EU-migranter," *Fria Tidningen*, February 10, 2015.

2. Lööw, Gardell, and Dahlberg-Grundberg, *Den ensamme terroristen?*

3. Randi Mossige-Norheim, "Åtalas för attack mot tiggare," Sveriges Radio, March 25, 2015.

4. Fanny Edstam, "Hon blev attackerad av en macheteman," *Göteborgs-Tidningen*, August 8, 2015.

5. "Hotade EU-migranter tvingas gömma sig," Sveriges Radio, November 10, 2015.

6. Mimmi Epstein, "Vi vill gärna sova med tak över huvudet men vi vet inte vart vi ska ta vägen," *Vi i Vasastan*, March 4, 2016.

7. Lööw, Gardell, and Dahlberg-Grundberg, *Den ensamme terroristen?*, 127–28.

8. Gardell, *Lone Wolf Race Warriors*.

9. Lööw, Gardell, and Dahlberg-Grundberg, *Den ensamme terroristen?*, chap. 1.

10. Mathias Asplund, "Butikschef hällde vatten på tiggare," *Aftonbladet*, March 12, 2014.

11. Jakob Meijer, "Tiggare misshandlades i city," *Upsala Nya Tidning*, February 19, 2015.

12. Kenan Habul, "Jag är rädd att han ska komma tillbaka," *Aftonbladet*, May 26, 2015.

13. Daniel Olsson, "Stängd FB-grupp hyllar påkörningen," *Göteborgs-Tidningen*, May 25, 2015.

14. Staffan Lindberg, "Tiggaren George, 26, attackerades med frätande vätska," *Aftonbladet*, June 9, 2015.

15. Emma Bouvin, "16-åringar ingrep när tiggare misshandlades i Västertorp," *Dagens Nyheter*, December 20, 2015.

16. Josefin Silverberg, "'Okänd man kastade sten mot Maria: 'Jag skrek för mitt liv,'" *Aftonbladet*, September 20, 2018.

17. Per Sydvik, "Anklagade tiggare för rån—fälld själv," *Göteborgs-Posten*, January 12, 2015.

18. Cajsa Wikström, "Sweden Jails Man Who Framed Beggar for Theft," Al Jazeera, December 16, 2014.

19. Ida Persson, "Tiggare hängs ut i anonym lapp på Ica," *Aftonbladet*, April 10, 2014.

20. Karolina Skoglund, "Nej, polisen ligger inte bakom uppmaning att sluta skänka pengar till tiggare," *Metro*, March 23, 2015.

21. Fatum-Regnum, post #15817, *Flashback Forum*, March 2, 2017, 01:09, https://www.flashback.org/ t2577564p1319.

22. Gynekologstol, post #10354, *Flashback Forum*, June 6, 2016, 12:37, https://www.flashback.org/p57487257#.

23. Nordanvindarna, post #10355, *Flashback Forum*, June 6, 2016, 12:55, https://www.flashback.org/p57487257#.

24. Fatum-Regnum, post #6557, *Flashback Forum*, January 9, 2016, 02:48, https://www.flashback.org/p55955880.

25. Karin Ingströmer, "Forskare: Vi känner skuld när vi ser tiggare," Sveriges Radio, October 21, 2014.

26. Lööw, Gardell, and Dahlberg-Grundberg, *Den ensamme terroristen?*, chap. 1.

27. Lööw, Gardell, and Dahlberg-Grundberg, *Den ensamme terroristen?*, chap. 2.

28. A man who had got his asylum application rejected stole a lorry and killed five people. However, no organization, not even ISIS, claimed responsibility for the attack, which otherwise tended to be the procedure. Incidentally, one of the victims happened to be eighty-three-year-old Papuşa Ciuraru, a Holocaust survivor who begged on the street and got her leg injured. She begged on behalf of her grandchildren in Romania and used to sleep on the stairs to the Concert Hall. Emil Arvidsson, "Tiggaren Papusa, 83, ett av attackens offer," *Expressen*, April 8, 2017.

29. National Coalition for the Homeless (NCH). *Hate, Violence, and Death.*

30. Wallengren and Mellgren, "Silent Victims," 11–12.

31. Wallengren et al., *Gypsy, Go Home!*, 7.

32. Staffan Lindberg, "Polisen: Romer tvingas betala för att tigga," *Aftonbladet*, March 3, 2015; Linnéa Borgert, "Romer på Gotland samlar in pengar till flyktingar," *Aftonbladet*, October 18, 2015; Elina Pahnke, "Avhysning av romer dyrare än härbärge," *ETC*, April 12, 2016.

33. Sivanandan, "Poverty Is the New Black," 2.

34. Kent Ekeroth and Mia Danielsson, "Visumstvång behövs för att stoppa tiggare," *Svenska Dagbladet*, March 18, 2015.

35. David Baas, "Kent Ekeroth: Utvisa invandrare som 'tittar snett på svenskar,'" *Expressen*, September 28, 2018.

36. Jan Sjunnesson, "Blockera tiggarna—Reclaim the Streets," *Sjunne [dot] com*, December 28, 2015, https://sjunne.com/2015/12/28/blockera-tiggarna-reclaim-the-streets/, emphasis in original.

37. Elias Giertz, "Attackerna har fått tiggare att fly Kista," *Expressen*, August 2, 2015.

38. Gardell, *Raskrigaren*, 86.

39. "Avpixlat-skribent: Blockera tiggare," *Dagens Nyheter*, December 28, 2015.

40. Jameson, "Imaginary and Symbolic in Lacan," 385.

41. Zupančič. *Why Psychoanalysis?*, 7–8.

42. Lacan, however, repeatedly claimed his psychoanalytical theory was an "antiphilosophy."

43. Kingsbury and Pile, "Introduction."

44. Douglas. *Purity and Danger*, 35.

45. Kristeva, *Powers of Horror*.

46. Sibley, *Geographies of Exclusion*, 10.

47. Freud, *Civilization and Its Discontents*, 24.

48. See, for example, Davidson, "Displacement, Space and Dwelling."

49. Johan Westerholm, "Allt går sönder," *Ledarsidorna*, June 26, 2015.

4. Anxiety and Ethics

1. Douglas, *Purity and Danger*, 35.

2. I here use capital letters for pedagogical reasons.

3. Lacan, *Four Fundamental Concepts*, 20.

4. Lacan, *Écrits*, 214.

5. See also Anderson, *Imagined Communities*.

6. De Kesel, *Eros and Ethics*, 70.

7. Jameson, *Political Unconscious*, 274.

8. Jameson, "Imaginary and Symbolic," 384.

9. Marx, "Eighteenth Brumaire of Louis Bonaparte," 480.

10. Freud, *Three Essays on Sexuality*.

11. Freud, *Civilization and Its Discontents*, 92.

12. De Kesel, *Eros and Ethics*, 13, 19–20.

13. Lacan, *Écrits*, 80.

14. Lacan, *Écrits*, 430.

15. Kingsbury, "Extimacy of Space," 235–58.

16. Proudfoot, "Anxious Enjoyment of Poverty."

17. Lacan, *The Seminar: Object Relation*, 218.

18. See Hegel, *Science of Logic*, 121.

19. Žižek, *Sublime Object of Ideology*, 233.

20. Žižek, *Sublime Object of Ideology*, 203.

21. Bodenheimer, *Warum?*

22. Žižek, *Sublime Object of Ideology*, 202.

23. Žižek, *Sublime Object of Ideology*, 204.

24. Gaga, "This Money Begged Here"; Wagman et al., "Descriptions of Health"; Wallengren and Mellgren, "Silent Victims"; Amnesty International, *Sweden*; Wallengren, et al., *Gypsy, Go Home!*; Levy, "Homeless in 'The People's Home.'"

25. Proudfoot, "Anxious Enjoyment of Poverty," 274.

26. Freud, *Civilization and Its Discontents*, 58.

27. Adam Reuterskiöld, "DEBATT. M: Amnesty presenterar inga lösningar," *MälaröDirekt*, March 9, 2020.

28. Johan Linander, "När tiggaren är ett offer för trafficking," *Svenska Dagbladet*, June 13, 2012.

29. Vännen, "Väljer bort butiker med tiggare," *Hela Hälsingland*, November 12, 2014.

30. Geremek, *Poverty*.

31. Sveriges Radio, "Tiggare i Umeå pekas ut i film på nätet," October 13, 2014.

32. Elin Sandow, "Tjänade en miljon på tiggare i Uppsala," *Upsala Nya Tidning*, February 12, 2018.

33. Maria Ridderstedt, "Flicka tvingades tigga—insatser dröjde," Sveriges Radio, Feburary 25, 2019.

34. Žižek, *Sublime Object of Ideology*, 49.

35. Torbjörn Ingvarsson, "Tiggeri—en obehaglig förödmjukelse," *Hudiksvalls Tidning*, March 31, 2014.

36. Frida Boisen, "Lär av din egen historia innan du fnyser åt kvinnan på gatan," *Expressen*, January 6, 2016.

37. See Moi, "From Femininity to Finitude."

38. Žižek, *Ticklish Subject*, 224.

39. Engellau, "Min uppfattning om tiggeri."

40. Vännen, "Väljer bort butiker med tiggare," *Hela Hälsingland*, November 12, 2014.

41. Andreas Samuelsson, "Vi ska lära känna romerna," Sveriges Television, February 14, 2015.

42. Linda Lundqvist, "Behandla tiggande romer som vuxna människor," Sveriges Television, February 18, 2015.

43. Ann Heberlein, "Tiggarens marknad," *Fokus*, December 9, 2016.

44. Bo Rothstein, "Förslaget riktar sig mot förnedring, inte medmänsklighet," *Dagens Nyheter*, January 2, 2014; Stefan Hedlund, "Försörjning via förnedring," *Det Goda Samhället*, June 13, 2016.

45. Lacan, *Écrits*, 645–68.

46. Wallerstein, *World-Systems Analysis*.

47. Johnson, *Fear of Beggars*.

48. Lacan, *The Seminar: Ethics of Psychoanalysis*, 12.

49. Radford, "Begging Principles," 291–92.

50. Radford, "Begging Principles," 292.

51. Levinas, "Ethics and Infinity," 195–96.

52. Brecht, *Good Person of Szechwan*, 105.

53. Žižek, "Neighbors and Other Monsters," 143–44.

54. See Slavoj Žizek, "God without the Sacred: The Book of Job, the First Critique of Ideology," LIVE *from the New York Public Library*, November 9, 2010, 19.

55. Žižek, *Sublime Object of Ideology*, 32–33.

56. Žižek, *Violence*, 53–54.

57. Lacan, *The Seminar: Ethics of Psychoanalysis*, 314.

58. Andrev Walden, "När vi slutade se tiggarna," *Dagens Nyheter*, April 9, 2015, emphasis in original.

59. P. M. Nilsson, "Förbjud tiggeriet," *Dagens Industri*, May 19, 2015.

60. Svante Nycander, "Öva inte upp likgiltigheten," *Axess*, 2014.

61. Wilkinson and Pickett, *Spirit Level*.

5. Ideology

1. Jameson, "American Utopia," 311.
2. Ollman, *Dialectical Investigations*, Part II.
3. See Nilsson, "Förbjud tiggeriet."
4. Marx, *Capital*, 2:303.
5. Žižek, *Sublime Object of Ideology*, 30.
6. Žižek, *Tarrying with the Negative*, 202.
7. Žižek, *Tarrying with the Negative*, 201.
8. Svante Nycander, "Öva inte upp likgiltigheten," *Axess*, 2014.
9. "Enjoyment" is here similar to the Lacanian concept of *jouissance*, which English translators use to keep in French. For pedagogical reasons of making this book accessible for those not familiar with Lacanianism, I have chosen to strictly use "Enjoyment" or "pleasure" in its place.
10 Žižek, *Tarrying with the Negative*, 203.
11. Žižek, *Violence*, 50.
12. Žižek, *Tarrying with the Negative*, 203.
13. Žižek, *Sublime Object of Ideology*, 142.
14. Here, following Thompson, "Moral Economy," 76–136.

6. Swedish Ideology

1. Sofia Hegevall, "Reinfeldt skällde ut sd-toppen i riksdagen," *Expressen*, May 8, 2014.
2. Pär Karlsson, "Reinfeldt om tiggeriförbudet," *Aftonbladet*, August 13, 2014.
3. Anette Holmqvist, "Löfven: Fattigdom går inte att förbjuda," *Aftonbladet*, August 13, 2014.
4. Anette Holmqvist, "Stefan Löfvens nya tiggeribesked: Detta måste få ett stopp," *Aftonbladet*, December 17, 2016.
5. Pär Karlsson, "Kristersson vill göra upp med Löfven om tiggeriet," *Aftonbladet*, December 8, 2017.
6. Kerstin Holm and Anna H Svensson, "Regeringen: Ny lagstiftning för färre asylsökande," Sveriges Television, November 24, 2015.
7. Selling, *Frigörelsen*.
8. Hall et al., *Policing the Crisis*, 212–13.
9. Hall et al., *Policing the Crisis*, 154.
10. Poulantzas, "On Social Classes." Hegemonic class distinct from reigning class.
11. See Berggren and Trädgårdh, *Är svensken människa?*
12. See Lundberg and Åmark, "Social Rights and Social Security," 157–76.
13. Lundberg and Åmark, "Social Rights and Social Security," 170.
14. Lundberg and Åmark, "Social Rights and Social Security," 175.
15. Marklund and Svallfors, *Dual Welfare*.

16. Jansson, "Deadly Exceptionalisms," 86.

17. Jansson, "Deadly Exceptionalisms," 86–87, emphasis in original.

18. Erik Angner and Gustav Arrhenius, "The Swedish Exception?," *Behavioural Public Policy—Blog*, April 23, 2020, https://bppblog.com/2020/04/23/the-swedish-exception/.

19. E. Bengtsson, "Swedish *Sonderweg* in Question," 157–58.

20. Linderborg, "Socialdemokraterna skriver historia."

21. Lundberg and Åmark, "Social Rights and Social Security," 175.

22. E. Bengtsson, "Swedish *Sonderweg* in Question."

23. Hurd, *Public Spheres, Public Mores.*

24. Erik Sandberg, "Den svenska högerns segerrus när Hitler tog makten," ETC, June 28, 2021.

25. See Fredrik Hultman, "Den radikalkonservative arvtagaren," *Smedjan*, December 9, 2019.

26. Lundberg and Åmark, "Social Rights and Social Security," 171–72.

27. E. Bengtsson, "Swedish *Sonderweg* in Question," 146.

28. Therborn, *Kapitalet.*

29. J. Andersson. "Nordic Nostalgia and Nordic Light," 239.

30. OECD, "OECD Income Inequality Data Update: Sweden (January 2015)," https://www.oecd.org/sweden/oecd-Income-Inequality-Sweden.pdf.

31. Scocco, *Och några, antar jag, är ok!*, 190.

32. OECD, "Unemployment Rate (Indicator)," 2021, https://data.oecd.org/unemp/unemployment-rate.htm#indicator-chart.

33. OECD, OECD *Economic Surveys*, 47.

34. Therborn, *Kapitalet*, 52.

35. Kai-Anders Nilsson, "Lista—de har Sveriges största förmögenheter," *Expressen*, December 6, 2019; Credit Suisse Research Institute, *Global Wealth Databook 2017*, 156.

36. In the Swedish system, 4 percent of the votes in the national election (held each fourth year) are needed for a party to enter the *riksdag* (parliament).

37. Åkesson, *Det Moderna Folkhemmet.*

38. Hübinette and Lundström, "Three Phases of Hegemonic Whiteness," 430, emphasis in original.

39. Hübinette, *Adopterad.*

40. Scocco and Andersson, *900 miljarder skäl att uppskatta invandring.*

41. The profit making of militarization and wars elsewhere needs here to be treated as "exceptions" regarding the scale of "local" capitals.

42. Freja Salö, "Reinfeldt: SD ska isoleras från inflytande," SVT *Nyheter*, August 21, 2014.

43. See Mats Wingborg, "Allt hårdare villkor för thailändska bärplockare," *Dagens Arena*, September 1, 2019.

44. Aaron Israelson, "Socialdemokraterna sviker romerna," *Norran*, October 27, 2015.

45. Scocco, *Och några, antar jag, är ok!*

46. Scocco, *Och några, antar jag, är ok!*, 119.

47. See Nyberg, *Kapitalets automatik.*

48. See Althusser, *On the Reproduction of Capitalism.*

49. Pred, *Even in Sweden.*

50. Statistiska centralbyrån, "Utrikes födda i Sverige," March 25, 2021, https://www.scb
.se/hitta-statistik/sverige-i-siffror/manniskorna-i-sverige/utrikes-fodda/.

51. Therborn, *Kapitalet*, 121.

52. Gilroy, *After Empire*, 108.

53. Freud, "Mourning and Melancholia," 22.

54. Žižek, *Tarrying with the Negative*, 203.

55. Pred, *Even in Sweden.*

56. Sjöwall and Wahlöö, *Roman om ett brott.*

57. Anette Holmqvist and Erik Wiman, "SD—år för år," *Aftonbladet*, January 14, 2011.

58. Hübinette and Lundström, "Three Phases of Hegemonic Whiteness."

59. See Hall et al., *Policing the Crisis*; Gilroy, *After Empire.*

60. Streeck, *Buying Time*, preface to 2nd ed.

61. Streeck, *Buying Time*, chap. 1.

62. Streeck, *Buying Time*, chap. 1.

63. Harvey, *New Imperialism.*

64. On the role of the Americas to save democratic capitalism, see Amin, foreword, xiii.

65. See Achcar, *People Want.*

66. Nyberg, *Kapitalets automatik*, 222–23.

67. Therborn, *Kapitalet*, 34. This defunding of the welfare systems went together with the increase in millionaires and private wealth: in 2018 tax evasion was estimated at 43 billion kronor per year, and 500 billion (10 percent of GDP) was hidden in tax havens. Compare these numbers with the repeated claim that immigration "costs" Swedish state finances 39 billion kronor per year.

68. See Lundin, *Arbetsmarknadspolitik för arbetslösa mottagare.*

69. Scocco, *Och några, antar jag, är ok!*, 82, 191, 195.

70. Scocco, *Och några, antar jag, är ok!*, 208–10.

71. H. Andersson, "I väntan på klasspolitik."

72. Stig-Björn Ljunggren, "Tiggeriförbud hjälper S komma åt arbetarklassen," *Dagens Samhälle*, August 19, 2016.

7. Stance of Inaction

1. Tomas Ramberg, "Det stökiga 2010-talet," Sveriges Radio, December 31, 2019.

2. Selling, *Frigörelsen*, 167.

3. Justitieombudsmannen, "Allvarlig kritik mot Polismyndigheten i Stockholms län, som avvisat utlänningar med motiveringen att dessa ägnade sig åt tiggeri och dagdriveri," June 28, 2011, https://www.jo.se/PageFiles/1027/6340-2010.pdf.

4. Pontus Mattson, "Sala vill förbjuda tiggeri," Sveriges Radio, April 21, 2011.

5. Petter Larsson, "Tigga går bra bara du är stilla," Aftonbladet, February 25, 2014.

6. "Butiker vill ha policy för tiggare," Sydsvenskan, May 24, 2014.

7. Ekeroth, "Förbjud tiggeri i hela landet."

8. OECD, Recruiting Immigrant Workers.

9. Lova Olsson, "C: Gör det straffbart att organisera tiggeri," Svenska Dagbladet, June 11, 2012.

10. Selling, Frigörelsen, 168.

11. Examples of these debates are Stina Wirsén's Lilla hjärtat, the artworks of Makonde Linde, the redeployment of Tintin in Kongo from children's sections in public libraries, wiping out the word negerkung from the new edition of Pippi Longstocking, blackface entertainment among students, the concept of Kränkta vita män, etc.

12. Hall et al., Policing the Crisis, 154.

13. Henrietta Johansson and Angelica Lundberg, "Vittne: 'Många barn gömde sig inne på Ica,'" Expressen, December 15, 2013.

14. Niklas Orrenius, "Över tusen barn med i olaglig kartläggning," Dagens Nyheter, September 23, 2013.

15. Selling, Frigörelsen, 163.

16. Selling, Frigörelsen, 160–65.

17. Hökerberg, "Pengarna svenska gator," Dagens Nyheter, March 24, 2013.

18. See Henrik Högström, "Boende till polisen: Ta bort alla tiggare," Kvällsposten, September 17, 2014.

19. See TT Nyhetsbyrån, "Jernhusen backar om förbud mot tiggare," Sveriges Radio, November 7, 2014.

20. Ulf Stolt, "Andra gator idag," Situation Sthlm, April 2, 2015.

21. Bo Rothstein, "Därför bör vi göra det förbjudet att ge till tiggare," Dagens Nyheter, December 28, 2013.

22. Bo Rothstein, "Förslaget riktar sig mot förnedring, inte medmänsklighet," Dagens Nyheter, January 2, 2014.

23. Gustav Fridolin, "Häng ut mig på era affischer i stället," Expressen, May 14, 2014.

24. Cecilia Magnusson, "Förbjud gatutiggeriet för att minska riskerna för fattigdom," Dagens Nyheter, August 13, 2014.

25. P. Karlsson, "Reinfeldt om tiggeriförbudet."

26. Holmqvist, "Löfven."

27. Johan Delby, "Lösningen finns på tiggarnas hemmaplan," Dagens Samhälle, May 8, 2014.

28. "Öppna era hjärtan," Wikipedia, May 7, 2020, https://sv.wikipedia.org/wiki/%c3%96ppna_era_hj%c3%a4rtan.

29. SVT Pejl, "Partibytare," Sveriges Television, September 14, 2014.

30. Nyberg, *Kapitalets automatik*, 262–69.

31. SOU 2016:6, *Framtid sökes*, 14.

8. Borromean Welfare Knot

1. FEANTSA, *Criminalising Homeless People*, 4.

2. See Agamben, *Homo Sacer*.

3. Amnesty International, *Sweden*, 42.

4. Moa Höjer, "Tvingades föda i bilen—krävs på 32 000 kronor," *Norrländska Socialdemokraten*, March 30, 2015.

5. See Amnesty International, *Sweden*, 7.

6. Stadsmissioner, Räddningsmission, and Barnen, *Mellan hopp och förtvivlan*, 27.

7. See Heberlein, "Tiggarens marknad."

8. Lind and Persdotter, "Differential Deportability," 51–69.

9. Amnesty International, *Sweden*.

10. Scocco, *Och några, antar jag, är ok!*, 146–47.

11. Folkhälsomyndigheten, "Gymnasiebehörighet," March 23, 2022, https://www.folkhalsomyndigheten.se/folkhalsorapportering-statistik/tolkad-rapportering/folkhalsans-utveckling/resultat/kompetenser-kunskaper-och-utbildning/gymnasiebehorighet/.

12. See Salihu, *Tills alla dör*.

13. See Stadsmissionen, *Att vända muggen*.

14. Stadsmissionen, *Att vända muggen*, 78.

15. Amnesty International, *Sweden*, 16.

16. Lars Calmfors, "Kan vi ge tiggarna jobb?," *Svenska Dagbladet*, January 7, 2015.

17. See Robert Tedestedt, "Kampsportstjärna tiggare i Lycksele," Sveriges Television, November 11, 2014.

18. Ulrika Falk and Aaron Israelson, "Sluta ljug om romernas liv i Rumänien, Sverige," *Aftonbladet*, October 20, 2018.

19. Glenn Möllergren, "Korgbinderi räddar ingen från fattigdomen i Pauleasca," *Feministiskt Perspektiv*, June 15, 2017; Kristina Back, "Skövlas Rumäniens urskog för Ikeas möbler?," *Natursidan*, December 3, 2017.

20. One notable example of the latter case is Ruben Östlund's Palme d'Or award-winner *The Square* (2017), in which several social-realist scenes are dedicated to the anxious interaction between a "sympathetic pedestrian" and "the Roma beggars" in Stockholm.

21. Cecilia Gustavsson, "Hon lyckades få bort tiggarna från gatan," *Aftonbladet*, August 28, 2015.

22. Magda Gad and Diamant Salihu, "Lön i Sverige: 10 kr/timme," *Expressen*, November 30, 2015.

23. Scocco, *Och några, antar jag, är ok!*, 91–94.

24. "Ledare: En kålsuparteori om tiggeri," *Svenska Dagbladet*, September 17, 2015.

25. Lindbeck and Snower, *Insider-Outsider Theory*.

26. Niklas Karlsson, Johan Persson, and Erika Ullberg, "Vellinges förbud kräver att regeringen agerar," *Dagens Samhälle*, September 7, 2017.

27. Nyberg, *Kapitalets automatik*; Scocco, *Och några, antar jag, är ok!*

28. Behrang Kianzad, Karin Åberg, and Frederick Batzler, "Myndigheterna bryter mot mänskliga rättigheter," Sveriges Television, October 31, 2015.

29. SOU 1923:2, *Förslag till lag om lösdrivares behandling m.fl. författningar.*

30. Ericsson, *Svenska kommuners utestängningsstrategier mot "tattare."*

31. Selling, *Svensk antiziganism.*

32. Taikon, *Zigenare är vi.*

33. Thomas Hammarberg, "Omotiverat brutal polisauktion mot romer," *Svenska Dagbladet*, September 11, 2014.

34. Jennie Aquilonius, "Förbud eller inte förbud—det är frågan," *Amnesty Press*, October 11, 2019.

35. Mikaela Sonck, "Skolgården är ingen boplats—staden måste agera," Sveriges Television, September 30, 2016.

36. Carolin Dahlman, "Lyssna inte till vänstertokstollarna," *Kristianstadsbladet*, November 3, 2015.

37. SOU 1956:43. *Zigenarfrågan.*

38. Pred, *Even in Sweden.*

39. Sahlin, "Bostadslöshet som politiskt resultat," 62.

40. B. Bengtsson, "Bostaden som social rättighet," 49–91.

41. B. Bengtsson, "Socialbostäder och stigberoende," 39–62.

42. Nina Brevinge, "En handfull svar," *Fokus*, April 17, 2015.

43. Mitchell, *Mean Streets*, 93.

44. Grundström and Molina, "From Folkhem to Lifestyle Housing," 316–36.

45. "House of Horrors, Part 2: The Bursting of the Global Housing Bubble Is Only Halfway Through," *The Economist*, November 26, 2011.

46. Christoffer Wendick, "Kommunerna: Bostadsbristen är rekordstor," Sveriges Television, February 23, 2016.

47. Roine and Waldenström, "Wealth Concentration," 168.

48. Grundström and Molina, "Folkhem to Lifestyle Housing," 327.

49. Grundström and Molina, "Folkhem to Lifestyle Housing," 317, 323.

50. Christophers, "Monstrous Hybrid," 885.

51. See Patrik Kronqvist, "När flyktingar ställs mot medelklassen," *Expressen*, September 19, 2017.

52. "Även nöden har en lag," *Dagens Nyheter*, March 22, 2015.

53. Socialstyrelsen, *Hemlöshet 2017*.

54. See Marcuse, "Neutralizing Homelessness."

55. Daniel Swedin, "Stockholm dumpar hemlösa på landet," *Aftonbladet*, July 23, 2019.

56. Stockholms Stadsmission, "Crossroads," n.d., https://www.stadsmissionen.se/sites /default/files/2020-09/Crossroads-informationsblad-2019-engelska-Stockholm -Stadsmission.pdf.

57. Monica Saarinen, "Valfridsson: Nolltolerans mot tiggares läger," Sveriges Radio, October 31, 2015.

9. Conjuncture

1. Brevinge, "En handfull svar."

2. Interview with Sven Hovmöller, December 2017.

3. Johan Cedersjö and Adam Szoppe, "Gatutidningen Sofia Z ger miljoner till EU-migranter," Sveriges Radio, April 10, 2015.

4. Thorbjörn Spängs, "Banker nekar pengar från EU-migranter," *Dagens Nyheter*, February 17, 2015.

5. See Stolt, "Andra gator idag."

6. Sanna Wikström, "Faktum-försäljare hotade—på gatan," *Göteborgs-Tidningen*, March 11, 2015.

7. Stolt, "Andra gator idag."

8. Aaron Israelson, "Därför försvarar jag de som tigger," *Dagens Arena*, December 22, 2015.

9. Kristin Renulf, "Konflikt när tiggare återvände till Gnosjö," s v t *Nyheter*, February 12, 2015.

10. Beatrice Ask and Tomas Tobé, "Vi föreslår att organiserande av tiggeri ska kriminaliseras," *Dagens Nyheter*, April 30, 2015.

11. Nilsson, "Förbjud tiggeriet."

12. Nyberg, *Kapitalets automatik*, 262–69.

13. sou 2016:6, 47.

14. Per Gudmundson, "Lekplatsen stank av tiggarnas avföring," *Svenska Dagbladet*, October 4, 2016; Karlsson, Persson, and Ullberg, "Vellinges förbud."

15. Eric Erfors, "Avföring mitt i stan—politikerna blundar," *Expressen*, June 15, 2015.

16. Louice Tapper Florén, "Förslag: Låt ordningsvakter flytta olovliga bosättningar," *Mitt i Kungsholmen*, August 26, 2015.

17. Carl Johan von Seth, "Samhället ser men polisen tittar bort," *Dagens Nyheter*, September 25, 2015.

18. Marie Öhrström, "Upprätthåll grundlagen, skydda äganderätten," *Dagens Samhälle*, September 24, 2015.

19. Karin Lundal, "Krister Thelin: Fyrkantigt—tomten kan visst avhysas," *Dagens Samhälle*, September 29, 2015.

20. Alexandro, Ana, Constantin, Ionela, Larisa, Nelu, Nicoleta, Nicusor, Maria, and Paul, "Malmöbor, att vi bor i Sorgenfrilägret är bäst för både er och oss," *Sydsvenskan*, September 2, 2015.

21. Carina Nilsson and Niklas Karlsson, "Ni är välkomna att söka arbete och bostad," *Sydsvenskan*, September 3, 2015.

22. Eric Tagesson, "Ikea-mördaren vill avtjäna straff i Eritrea," *Aftonbladet*, May 4, 2017.

23. Herman Lindqvist, "SD-monstret är på väg att sluka oss alla," *Aftonbladet*, August 29, 2015.

24. See Rostami, "Street-Gang Violence in Sweden"; Salihu, *Tills alla dör*.

25. Ljunggren, "Tiggeriförbud hjälper S komma åt arbetarklassen."

26. Olof Svensson, Oskar Forsberg, and Sebastian Hagberg, "Mitt Europa bygger inte murar, vi hjälps åt," *Aftonbladet*, September 6, 2015.

27. Rickard Klerfors and Martin Valfridsson, "Minst 100 barn har tagits ur skolan för att resa till Sverige," *Dagens Nyheter*, June 24, 2015.

28. Åsa Regnér and Martin Valfridsson, "Skänk till organisationer på plats i hemländerna," *Dagens Nyheter*, September 11, 2015.

29. Åsa Regnér, "Frivilligorganisationerna gör mycket god nytta," *Dagens Nyheter*, September 18, 2015.

30. SOU 2016:6, 10.

31. Žižek, *Ticklish Subject*, 340.

32. Erik Helmerson, "Rätt att hjälpa hjälparna," *Dagens Nyheter*, September 12, 2015.

33. Rickard Klerfors, "Hjärta till hjärta: EU-medborgarna vill ha hjälp I hemlandet," *Dagens Arena*, June 26, 2015.

34. SOU 2016:6, 91.

35. Niklas Svensson and Hanna Jakobson, "Persson och jag delar uppfattning," *Expressen*, March 12, 2016.

36. Åsa Regnér, "EU-migranterna får det allt bättre I sina hemländer," *Expressen*, June 21, 2017; Jonathan Jeppsson, "Andersson avråder från att ge till tiggare: Kan bidra till människohandel," *Aftonbladet*, March 1, 2018.

37. Maria Ranka, Per Eriksson, Lennart Eriksson, Rickard Klerfors, and Peter Toftgård, "Hjälp tiggarna på plats I hemländerna," *Expressen*, December 1, 2015.

38. Ebba Wigerström, "Regeringens utredare om tiggeriet: 'Att kriminalisera medmänsklighet skapar ett hårdare samhälle.'" *Dagens Juridik*, May 13, 2015.

39. Rickard Klerfors, "Tiggarna vill arbeta—låt oss hjälpa dem," *Svenska Dagbladet*, March 8, 2016.

40. Kaliber, "Tiggarjobben—Företaget som försvann, del 1–2," Sveriges Radio, April 5 and May 16, 2016.

41. Scocco, *Och några, antar jag, är ok!*, 142.

42. Nyberg, *Kapitalets automatik*, 222, 226.

43. Scocco, *Och några, antar jag, är ok!*, 142.

44. Nyberg, *Kapitalets automatik*, 224–25.

45. Scocco, *Och några, antar jag, är ok!*, 137.

46. TT Nyhetsbyrån, "SD över 20 procent i ny opinionsmätning," *Aftonbladet*, September 15, 2015.

47. Julia Wågenberg and Oskar Forsberg, "Kinberg Batra: 'Överenskommelsen är upphävd,'" *Aftonbladet*, October 9, 2015.

48. Ebba Busch Thor and Annika Eclund, "Tiggeri bidrar till fattigdom," *Svenska Dagbladet*, October 8, 2015.

49. "M vill kunna förbjuda tiggeri lokalt," Sveriges Radio, October 18, 2015.

50. Lööw, Gardell, and Dahlberg-Grundberg, *Den ensamme terroristen?*, 270.

51. Global Terror Database, "Years: Between 2010 and 2015. Countries: Sweden. Incidents: 47. Incidents 2010: 3, incidents 2011: 1, incidents 2012: 2, incidents 2013: 0, incidents 2014: 5. Incidents 2015: 36," https://www.start.umd.edu/gtd/search/Results.aspx?expanded=no&search=sweden&ob=gtdid&od=desc&page=1&count=100#results-table.

52. Niklas Svahn, "Åkesson om bränderna: 'Ni attackerar samhället,'" *Aftonbladet*, October 29, 2015. The arsons began again in early November and continued into December, although they occurred less often.

53. Gustaf Tronarp and Victor Lindbom, "Flyktingboende utsatt för brandattack," *Aftonbladet*, October 29, 2015.

54. Markus Ljungholm, "Löfven: Sverige håller på att gå sönder," Sveriges Television, September 2, 2014.

55. SOU 2017:12, *Att ta emot människor på flykt—Sverige hösten 2015*, 100.

56. Persdotter, "Free to Move Along," 157, emphasis added.

57. Monica Saarinen, "Valfridsson: Nolltolerans mot tiggares läger," Sveriges Radio, October 31, 2015.

58. SOU 2016:6, 6, 70.

59. Heidi Avellan, "Ingen mänsklig rätt att bo I Malmö," *Sydsvenskan*, November 4, 2015.

60. International Covenant on Civil and Political Rights, "Concluding Observations on the Seventh Periodic Report of Sweden," April 28, 2016, https://www.ecoi.net/en/file/local/1024626/1930_1467815033_g1608783.pdf.

61. Eric Erfors, "Lita inte på all kritik från FN," *Expressen*, March 31, 2016.

62. Nyberg, *Kapitalets automatik*, 226.

63. SOU 2017:12, 302.

64. SOU 2017:12, 302.

65. Holm and Svensson, "Regeringen."

66. With the notable exception of the corona governance.

67. Sewell Chan, "'Last Night in Sweden': Trump's Remark Baffles a Nation," *New York Times*, February 19, 2017.

68. Jo Becker, "The Global Machine behind the Rise of Far-Right Nationalism," *New York Times*, August 10, 2019.

69. See Ivan Loftrup-Ericson and Emilia Halling, "Flera kommuner stänger boenden för EU-migranter," Sveriges Television, April 27, 2016; Mikael Leijon, "Luleå kommun ändrar strategi mot migranter," *Norrbottens-Kuriren*, September 16, 2016; Anne-Li Lehnberg, "Omstridd regeringsrapport används mot EU-migranter," *Flamman*, May 19, 2016; Daniel Wikdahl, "Nya riktlinjer för EU-migranter," Sveriges Television, October 29, 2016.

70. Johanna Senneby, "Nu ska M sätta stopp för obehag I t-banan," *Dagens Arena*, April 20, 2016.

71. Ossi Carp, "Poliskampanj mot sittande tiggare," *Dagens Nyheter*, May 9, 2016.

72. Amnesty International, *Sweden*, 48.

73. Mitchell, *Mean Streets*; Blomley, "Right to Pass Freely."

74. "Regeringen överväger att införa tiggeriförbud," *Dagens Nyheter*, August 18, 2016.

75. See Ann-Sofie Hermansson, "Tiggeriförbud är inget för Socialdemokraterna," *Dagens Nyheter*, January 4, 2017.

76. Hans Olsson, "Ministern hoppas minska antalet tiggare med ny lag," *Dagens Nyheter*, February 27, 2017.

77. Marmorstein and Ohlin, "S vill skärpa reglerna för tiggeri."

78. Socialdemokraterna, "Trygghet i en ny tid: Kongress 2017 Göteborg 8–12 april—Political guidelines," 2017, 12, https://www.socialdemokraterna.se/download/18
.12ce554f16be946d04640bb5/1568881616693/security-in-a-new-era---political
-guidelines_2017.pdf.

79. Socialdemokraterna i en ny tid, "Trygghet," 13.

80. Mitchell, *Mean Streets*, 103.

81. TT Nyhetsbyrån, "Löfven: Eskilstunas tiggeribeslut intressant," *Aftonbladet*, June 14, 2018.

82. Scocco, *Och några, antar jag, är ok!*, 145.

83. Hedda Berglund and Kerstin Holm, "S vill ha fortsatt restriktiv migrationspolitik," *svt Nyheter*, May 5, 2018.

84. Anette Holmqvist and Pär Karlsson, "Uppgifter: S tiggeriförslag panikstoppas," *Aftonbladet*, May 25, 2018.

85. Anders Lindberg, "Organiserat tiggeri är en råtta i pizzan," *Aftonbladet*, May 20, 2015; Clara Guibourg, "Nej, tiggarna styrs inte av kriminella ligor," *Metro*, August 28, 2014; Stefan Lisinski, "Nej, tiggeriet är inte organiserat," *Dagens Nyheter*, April 30, 2015.

86. Karina Segura Moberg, "Tidigare tiggerisamordnaren Martin Valfridsson: 'Inför ett förbud,'" Sveriges Television, April 27, 2017.

87. Anna Dahlberg, "Dags att införa ett tiggeriförbud," *Expressen*, April 29, 2017.

88. Jonathan Jeppsson, "Andersson avråder från att ge till tiggare: Kan bidra till människohandel," *Aftonbladet*, March 1, 2018, my emphasis.

89. Olof Svensson, "Moderaterna vill ha nationellt förbud mot tiggeri," *Aftonbladet*, September 5, 2017.

90. Patrik Dahlin, "Löfven: 'Vi ska aldrig tillbaka till 2015,'" *Omni*, August 18, 2021.

91. Regarding SD's relations to Russia, see Åsbrink, "Sweden Is Becoming Unbearable"; Richard Aschberg, Lisa Röstlund, and Mattias Sandberg, "SD-topp: Ekeroth är destruktiv för partiet," *Aftonbladet*, September 27, 2016.

92. Anna Sjögren, "Ministern: Man ska inte skaffa fler barn än man kan försörja," *Aftonbladet*, May 28, 2022.

93. Kulturnyheterna, "SD-politiker kallar journalister för 'nationens fiender,'" *SVT Nyheter*, April 20, 2016.

94. See Catomeris, *Människovärdet!*

95. Högsta Förvaltningsdomstolen, "HFD 2018 ref. 75: Förutsättningarna för att en kommun ska få reglera tiggeri genom lokala ordningsföreskrifter," December 17, 2018, https://www.domstol.se/globalassets/filer/domstol/hogstaforvaltningsdomstolen /avgoranden-2008-2018/2018/hfd-2018-ref.-75.pdf.

96. Susanne Sjöstedt, "Det går inte att lita på den där mannen," *Värmlands Folkblad*, July 6, 2022.

97. Oskar Brusén, "Danderyd tredje kommunen i länet att införa tiggeriförbud," Sveriges Television, October 15, 2019; Karin Thurfjell and Johan Pehrson, "Lidingö inför tiggeriförbud—först i Stockholms län," *Svenska Dagbladet*, November 9, 2019.

98. Reuterskiöld, "DEBATT."

99. Rostami, "Street-Gang Violence in Sweden"; Salihu, *Tills alla dör*.

100. Joakim Ruist, "Sammanfattning: Global migration—orsaker och konsekvenser," *Studieförbundet Näringsliv och Samhälle*, 2019, https://snsse.cdn.triggerfish.cloud /uploads/2020/02/global-migration--orsaker-och-konsekvenser-sammanfattning .pdf.

101. Ivar Arpi, "Migrationen förändrar hela Sverige i grunden," *Svenska Dagbladet*, June 10, 2019.

102. Hall, "The Great Moving Right Show."

103. Åsbrink, "Sweden Is Becoming Unbearable." The Swedish direct translation of *sieg heil* is "hell seger" (hail to victory). To be correct, what the profile did actually say was, "Hel . . . g, seger. This is a *segerhelg* [victory weekend]." As the word *helg* means "weekend," she managed to turn *hell* into *helg* before finishing the phrase. However, a fluent Swedish-speaking person would never say *helg seger* as this is grammatically absurd.

104. Amnesty International, *Sweden*, 25.

105. Amnesty International, *Sweden*, 23.

106. "JO kritiserar Polismyndigheten—förde systematiskt bort tiggande kvinna," *Dagens Nyheter*, October 23, 2020.

107. David Bowie, "Sunday," track 1 on *Heathen*, ISO Records, 2002, compact disc. Written by David Bowie. Lyrics © Tintoretto Music, Warner Chappell Music, Inc.

The Problem: An Epitome

1. Bergh, "Stefan Löfvens ord."

2. Lacan, *The Seminar: Object Relation*, 218.

3. Malin Bennet, "Romsk nationaldag—önskan om camping," SVT *Nyheter*, April 10, 2015.

4. Agamben, *Homo Sacer*, 126–35.

5. Jonas Sjöstedt, Jens Holm, Birger Lahti, Maj Karlsson, Karin Rågsjö, Mia Sydow Mölleby, Linda Westerlund, and Christina Höj Larsen, "Utsatta EU-medborgare: Motion till riksdagen 2019/20:2578," Sveriges Riksdag.

6. Kapoor and Zalloua, *Universal Politics*.

7. To exaggerate my point: the Baader-Meinhof Group, for example, never received popular support.

8. Žižek, *Ticklish Subject*, 224.

9. Marcuse, "From Critical Urban Theory," 192.

10. Marcuse, "From Critical Urban Theory," 190.

11. Obviously, universal politics need to be global in subject formation and struggle, and if the political platform were global, the distribution of deprived and alienated would be alternated. However, this book concerns contemporary Sweden, thus what could be done at *that* scale to facilitate the ethico-political identification with the déclassés.

12. Žižek, *Against the Double Blackmail*, 75.

13. See Žižek, "Neighbors and Other Monsters."

14. Said, *Representations of the Intellectual*, 31.

15. Hall et al., *Policing the Crisis*, 386–87, emphasis in original.

16. Jameson, *Political Unconscious*, 274.

17. Žižek, *Against the Double Blackmail*, 71, emphasis in original.

18. See Teodorescu and Molina, "Roma Street-Workers in Uppsala," 1–26.

19. Jennifer Snårbacka, "Stefan Löfven avgår som statsminister," *Expressen*, June 28, 2021.

20. Erik Olin Wright, "How to Be an Anticapitalist Today," *Jacobin*, February 12, 2015.

21. See Whyte, *Morals of the Market*. For a thoughtful example, see Carmalt, "Human Rights, Care Ethics, Universal Norms."

22. As Swedish history shows us, such an example of common sense is not impossible to imagine: in 1966, another era of housing shortages, the SAP prime minister lost face during a journalist's interrogation when he could not give a satisfactory answer

as to what a young housing-seeking couple should do to expect to remain in the housing queue (see Anders Björkman, "Åke Ortmark skrämde makten—förändrade intervjuerna i tv," *Expressen*, October 19, 2018).

23. Althusser, *On the Reproduction of Capitalism*, emphasis in original.

24. It is also not a "long-term, sustainable" solution to believe more work would solve poverty in the long run. Namely, ever since the postwar productivity explosion turned into the chronic overcapacity of manufacturing, and the constant decline of real productivity rates since the 1980s intersected with the greatest worldwide subsumption of people into the capitalist workforce (an expansion of 75 percent, or 1.5 billion people since 1980), the problem is not unemployment but structural *underemployment* (Benanav, *Automation and the Future of Work*). The viable solution to this structural issue would be to make sure people work less by sharing the labor that actually remains, while radically increasing wages so that people can live on their salaries—a solution that the capitalist class will never accept voluntarily.

25. See Rolf, "Union for Tenants."

26. Marx, "Critique of the Gotha Programme," 1031, emphasis in original.

27. See Olsson, *Abysmal*.

28. See, however, Holgersen, *Krisernas tid*.

29. Benner, *Really Existing Nationalisms*, 77.

30. Freud and Breuer, *Studies on Hysteria*, 305.

31. Le Guin, *The Dispossessed*.

32. Jameson, "American Utopia," 88–89, 63.

33. Freud, *Civilization and Its Discontents*, 60–61.

34. Brecht, *Good Person of Szechwan*, 109.

Bibliography

Abdullah, Ibrahim. "Culture, Consciousness and Armed Conflict: Cabral's Déclassé/ (Lumpenproletariat?) in the Era of Globalization." *African Identities* 4, no. 1 (2006): 99–112.

Achcar, Gilbert. *The People Want: A Radical Exploration of the Arab Uprising.* Berkeley: University of California Press, 2013.

Agamben, Giorgio. *Homo Sacer: Sovereign Power and Bare Life.* Translated by Daniel Heller-Roazen. Stanford: Stanford University Press, 1998.

Åkesson, Jimmie. *Det Moderna Folkhemmet.* Sölvesborg: Asp & Lycke, 2018.

Allen, John. "Ambient Power: Berlin's Potsdamer Platz and the Seductive Logic of Public Spaces." *Urban Studies* 43 (2006): 441–55.

Althusser, Louis. *On the Reproduction of Capitalism: Ideology and Ideological State Apparatuses.* London: Verso, 2014.

Ambjörnsson, Ronny. *Den skötsamme arbetaren: Idéer och ideal i ett norrländskt sågverkssamhälle, 1880–1930.* Stockholm: Carlssons Bokförlag, 2017.

Amin, Samir. Foreword to *Rethinking Unequal Exchange: The Global Integration of Nursing Labour Markets,* edited by Salimah Valiani, xi–xvi. Toronto: University of Toronto Press, 2018.

Amnesty International. *Sweden: A Cold Welcome—Human Rights of Roma and Other 'Vulnerable EU Citizens' at Risk.* London: Amnesty International, 2018.

Anderson, Benedict. *Imagined Communities: Reflections on the Origin and Spread of Nationalism.* London: Verso, 2006.

Andersson, Hampus. "I väntan på klasspolitik: En klassmedveten befolkning utan representation." In *Klass i Sverige: Ojämlikheten, makten och politiken i det 21: A århundradet,* edited by Daniel Suhonen, Göran Therborn, and Jesper Weithz, 53–82. Lund: Arkiv förlag, 2021.

Andersson, Jenny. "Nordic Nostalgia and Nordic Light: The Swedish Model as Utopia, 1930–2007." *Scandinavian Journal of History* 34 no. 3 (2009): 229–45.

Barker, Vanessa. "Nordic Vagabonds: The Roma and the Logic of Benevolent Violence in the Swedish Welfare State." *European Journal of Criminology* 14, no. 1 (2017): 120–39.

Beijer, Ulla. *Tiggeri: Ett nygammalt fenomen.* Stockholm: Forsknings-och utvecklingsenheten, Socialtjänstförvaltningen, 1999.

Benanav, Aaron. *Automation and the Future of Work*. London: Verso, 2020.

Bengtsson, Bo. "Bostaden som social rättighet. Den generella bostadspolitikens logik." In *Den nya bostadspolitiken*, edited by Anders Lindbom, 49–91. Umeå: Boréa, 2001.

———. "Socialbostäder och stigberoende: Varför har vi inte 'social housing' i Sverige?" In *Den motspänstiga akademikern: Festskrift till Ingrid Sahlin*, edited by Björn Andersson, Frida Petersson, and Anette Skårner, 39–62. Malmö: Egalité, 2017.

Bengtsson, Erik. "The Swedish *Sonderweg* in Question: Democratization and Inequality in Comparative Perspective, c. 1750–1920." *Past & Present* 244, no. 1 (2019): 123–61.

Benner, Erica. *Really Existing Nationalisms: A Post-Communist View from Marx and Engels*. London: Verso, 2018.

Berggren, Henrik, and Lars Trägårdh. *Är svensken människa? Gemenskap och oberoende i det moderna Sverige*. Stockholm: Norstedts, 2006.

Billig, Michael. *Banal Nationalism*. London: SAGE, 1995.

Blau, Joel. *The Visible Poor: Homelessness in the US*. New York: Oxford University Press, 1992.

Blomley, Nicholas, "The Right to Pass Freely: Circulation, Begging, and the Bounded Self." *Social & Legal Studies* 19, no. 3 (2010): 331–50.

Bodenheimer, Aron R. *Warum? Von der Obszönität des Fragens*. Ditzingen: Reclam, 1986.

Brecht, Bertolt. *The Good Person of Szechwan*. London: Eyre Methuen, 1974.

Broberg, Gunnar, and Mattias Tydén. "Eugenics in Sweden: Efficient Care." In *Eugenics and the Welfare State: Sterilization Policy in Denmark, Sweden, Norway, and Finland*, edited by Gunnar Broberg and Nils Roll-Hansen, 77–149. East Lansing: Michigan State University Press, 1996.

Broström, Lovisa. "En industriell reservarmé i välfärdsstaten. Arbetslösa socialhjälpstagare i Sverige 1913–2012." PhD diss., University of Gothenburg, 2015.

Cabral, Amílcar. *Revolution in Guinea: An African People's Struggle*. London: Stage One, 1974.

Carmalt, Jean Connolly. "Human Rights, Care Ethics and Situated Universal Norms." *Antipode* 43, no. 2 (2011): 296–325.

Catomeris, Christian. *Människovärdet!* Stockholm: Carlssons bokförlag, 2022.

Cavallo, Guglielmo, ed. *The Byzantines*. Chicago: University of Chicago Press, 1997.

Christophers, Brett. "A Monstrous Hybrid: The Political Economy of Housing in Early Twenty-First Century Sweden." *New Political Economy* 18, no. 6 (2013): 885–911.

Credit Suisse Research Institute. *Global Wealth Databook 2017*. Zurich: Credit Suisse, 2017.

Cresswell, Tim. "The Vagrant/Vagabond: The Curious Career of a Mobile Subject." In *Geographies of Mobilities: Practices, Spaces, Subjects*, edited by Tim Cresswell and Peter Merriman, 239–54. Farnham: Ashgate, 2011.

Dahlberg, Gunnar. "Anthropometry of 'Tattare,' a Special Group of Vagabonds in Sweden." *Uppsala Läkareförenings Förhandlingar*, n.s., 50 (1944): 69–79.

Davidson, Mark. "Displacement, Space and Dwelling: Placing Gentrification Debate." *Ethics, Place & Environment* 12, no. 2 (2009): 219–34.

Davidsson, Tobias. *Understödets rationalitet: En genealogisk studie av arbetslinjen under kapitalismen*. Malmö: Egalité, 2015.

Dean, Hartley, ed. *Begging Questions: Street-Level Economic Activity and Social Policy Failure*. Bristol: Policy Press, 1999.

De Kesel, Marc. *Eros and Ethics: Reading Jacques Lacan's Seminar VII*. Albany: State University of New York Press, 2009.

Departementsserien (Ds) 2014:8. *Den mörka och okända historien: Vitbok om övergrepp och kränkningar av romer under 1900-talet*. Stockholm: Arbetsmarknadsdepartementet.

Djuve, Anne Britt, Jon Horgen Friberg, Guri Tyldum, and Huafeng Zhang. *When Poverty Meets Affluence: Migrants from Romania on the Streets of the Scandinavian Capitals*. Copenhagen: Rockwool Fonden, 2015.

Douglas, Mary. *Purity and Danger: An Analysis of the Concepts of Pollution and Taboo*. London: Ark Paperbacks, 1984.

Edman, Johan. "Lösdrivarlagen och den samhällsfarliga lättjan." In *Villkorandets politik: Fattigdomens premisser och samhällets åtgärder—då och nu*, edited by Hans Swärd and Marie-Anne Egerö, 131–43. Malmö: Egalité, 2008.

Engels, Friedrich. *The Condition of the Working Class in England in 1844*. New York: Cambridge University Press, 2010.

———. *Landmarks of Scientific Socialism: Anti-Duerhing*. New York: Cosimo Classics, 2008.

Ericsson, Martin. *Svenska kommuners utestängningsstrategier mot "tattare," 1880–1924*. Stockholm: Arbetsmarknadsdepartementet.

Erskine, Angus, and Ian McIntosh. "Why Begging Offends: Historical Perspectives and Continuities." In *Begging Questions: Street-Level Economic Activity and Social Policy Failure*, edited by Hartley Dean, 27–42. Bristol: Policy Press, 1999.

European Federation of National Organisations Working with the Homeless (FEANTSA). *Criminalising Homeless People—Banning Begging in the EU*. Brussels, 2015.

Fanon, Frantz. *The Wretched of the Earth*. New York: Grove Press, 2005.

Flint, Colin, and Peter J. Taylor. *Political Geography: World-Economy, Nation-State and Locality*. New York: Routledge, 2018.

Freud, Sigmund. *Civilization and Its Discontents*. New York: W. W. Norton, 1962.

———. "Mourning and Melancholia." In *On Freud's "Mourning and Melancholia,"* edited by Leticia Glocer Fiorini, Thierry Bokanowski, and Sergio Lewkowicz, 19–34. London: Karnac, 2009.

———. *Three Essays on the Theory of Sexuality: The 1905 Edition*. London: Verso, 2017.

Freud, Sigmund, and Josef Breuer. *Studies on Hysteria*. New York: Basic Books, 1957.

Gaga, Filip Daniel. "'This Money Begged Here Is Paid with Blood': A Qualitative Study of the Romanian Beggars' Perceptions on Their Health Status before and during Begging, and Their Health Maintaining Strategies in Uppsala, Sweden." Master's thesis, Uppsala University, 2015.

Gardell, Mattias. *Lone Wolf Race Warriors and White Genocide*. Cambridge: Cambridge University Press, 2021.

———. *Raskrigaren: Seriemördaren Peter Mangs*. Stockholm: Leopard förlag, 2016.

Geremek, Bronisław. *The Margins of Society in Late Medieval Paris*. Cambridge: Cambridge University Press, 1987.

———. *Poverty: A History*. Oxford: Blackwell, 1997.

Gilmore, Ruth W. *Golden Gulag*. Berkeley: University of California Press, 2007.

Gilroy, Paul. *After Empire: Melancholia and Convivial Culture*. Abingdon: Routledge, 2004.

Gramsci, Antonio. *Selections from the Prison Notebooks*. New York: International, 1992.

Grundström, Karin, and Irene Molina. "From Folkhem to Lifestyle Housing in Sweden: Segregation and Urban Form, 1930s–2010s." *International Journal of Housing Policy* 16, no. 3 (2016): 316–36.

Hall, Stuart. "The Great Moving Right Show." *Marxism Today* 23, no. 1 (1979): 14–20.

———. "Race, Articulation and Societies Structured in Dominance." In *Selected Writings on Race and Difference*, edited by Paul Gilroy and Ruth Wilson Gilmore, 195–245. Durham NC: Duke University Press, 2021.

Hall, Stuart, Chas Critcher, Tony Jefferson, John Clarke, and Brian Roberts. *Policing the Crisis: Mugging, the State and Law and Order*. Basingstoke: Palgrave Macmillan, 2013.

Harvey, David. *The New Imperialism*. Oxford: Oxford University Press, 2005.

Hegel, Georg Wilhelm Friedrich. *Science of Logic*. London: Routledge, 2014.

Himmelfarb, Gertrude. *The Idea of Poverty: England in the Early Industrial Age*. London: Faber, 1984.

Hobbes, Thomas. *Leviathan*. London: Penguin Books, 1988.

Holgersen, Ståle. *Krisernas tid: Ekologi och ekonomi under kapitalismen*. Göteborg: Daidalos, 2022.

Hübinette, Tobias. *Adopterad: En bok om Sveriges sista rasdebatt*. Stockholm: Verbal förlag, 2021.

Hübinette, Tobias, and Catrin Lundström. "Three Phases of Hegemonic Whiteness: Understanding Racial Temporalities in Sweden." *Social Identities* 20, no. 6 (2014): 423–37.

Hurd, Madeleine. *Public Spheres, Public Mores, and Democracy: Hamburg and Stockholm, 1870–1914*. Ann Arbor: University of Michigan Press, 2000.

Jameson, Fredric. "An American Utopia." In *An American Utopia: Dual Power and the Universal Army*, edited by Slavoj Žižek, 1–96. London: Verso, 2016.

———. "Imaginary and Symbolic in Lacan: Marxism, Psychoanalytic Criticism, and the Problem of the Subject." *Yale French Studies*, no. 55/56 (1977): 338–95.

———. *The Political Unconscious: Narrative as a Socially Symbolic Act*. Abingdon: Routledge, 2013.

Jansson, David. "Deadly Exceptionalisms, or, Would You Rather Be Crushed by a Moral Superpower or a Military Superpower?" *Political Geography* 64 (2018): 83–91.

Johnson, Kelly. *The Fear of Beggars: Stewardship and Poverty in Christian Ethics*. Grand Rapids MI: Wm. B. Eerdmans, 2007.

Kapoor, Ilan, and Zahi Zalloua. *Universal Politics*. New York: Oxford University Press, 2021.

Kingsbury, Paul. "The Extimacy of Space." *Social & Cultural Geography* 8, no. 2 (2007): 235–58.

Kingsbury, Paul, and Steve Pile (2016). "Introduction: The Unconscious, Transference, Drives, Repetition and Other Things Tied to Geography." In *Psychoanalytic Geographies*, edited by Paul Kingsbury and Steve Pile, 25–62. Farnham: Ashgate, 2014.

Kristeva, Julia. *Powers of Horror: An Essay on Abjection*. New York: Columbia University Press, 1982.

Lacan, Jacques. *Écrits: The First Complete Edition in English*. New York: W. W. Norton, 2006.

———. *The Four Fundamental Concepts of Psycho-Analysis*. London: Karnac, 2004.

———. *The Seminar of Jacques Lacan. Book IV: The Object Relation*. Edited by Jacques-Alain Miller. Translated by A. R. Price. Cambridge: Polity, 2021.

———. *The Seminar of Jacques Lacan. Book VII: The Ethics of Psychoanalysis, 1959–1960*. Edited by Jacques-Alain Miller. Translated with notes by Dennis Porter. London: Routledge, 1992.

Le Guin, Ursula K. *The Dispossessed*. New York: Harper & Row, 1974.

Levander, Lars. *Fattigt folk och tiggare*. Stockholm: Gidlund, 1974.

Levinas, Emmanuel. "Ethics and Infinity." *CrossCurrents* 34, no. 2 (1984): 191–203.

Levy, Joshua. "Homeless in 'The People's Home': Exploring the Experiences of 'Vulnerable EU Citizens' in Stockholm, Sweden." PhD diss., Stockholm University, 2022.

Lewy, Guenter. *The Nazi Persecution of the Gypsies*. New York: Oxford University Press, 2000.

Liedman, Sven-Eric. *Från Platon till Gorbatjov*. Stockholm: Bonniers, 1989.

Lind, Jacob, and Maria Persdotter. "Differential Deportability and Contradictions of a Territorialised Right to Education: A Perspective from Sweden." *Movements* 3, no. 1 (2017): 51–69.

Lindbeck, Assar, and Dennis J. Snower. *The Insider-Outsider Theory of Employment and Unemployment*. Cambridge: MIT Press, 1988.

Linderborg, Åsa. "Socialdemokraterna skriver historia: Historieskrivning som ideologisk maktresurs, 1892–2000," PhD diss., Uppsala University, 2001.

Ling-Vannerus, Claes. *Uppdrag om nationell samordning avseende utsatta EU/EES-medborgare som saknar uppehållsrätt i Sverige—delrapport*. Stockholm: Länsstyrelsen, 2018.

Lundberg, Urban, and Klas Åmark. "Social Rights and Social Security: The Swedish Welfare State, 1900–2000." *Scandinavian Journal of History* 26, no. 3 (2001): 157–76.

Lundin, Martin. *Arbetsmarknadspolitik för arbetslösa mottagare av försörjningsstöd (IFAU rapport 2018:12)*. Uppsala: Institute for Evaluation of Labour Market and Education Policy, 2018.

Lööw, Heléne, Mattias Gardell, and Michael Dahlberg-Grundberg. *Den ensamme terroristen? Om lone wolves, näthat och brinnande flyktingförläggningar*. Stockholm: Ordfront, 2017.

Magnusson, Lars. *Håller den svenska modellen? Arbete och välfärd i en global värld*. Stockholm: Norstedts Akademiska Förlag, 2006.

Malthus, Thomas R. *An Essay on the Principle of Population and Other Writings*. London: Penguin Books, 2015.

Mann, Geoff. *In the Long Run We Are All Dead: Keynesianism, Political Economy, and Revolution*. London: Verso, 2017.

Marcuse, Peter. "From Critical Urban Theory to the Right to the City." *City* 13, no. 2–3 (2009): 185–97.

——. "Neutralizing Homelessness." *Socialist Review* 18, no. 1 (1988): 69–96.

Marklund, Staffan, and Stefan Svallfors. *Dual Welfare: Segmentation and Work Enforcement in the Swedish Welfare System*. Research Reports from the Department of Sociology, University of Umeå, 1987.

Marx, Karl. *Capital: A Critique of Political Economy*. Vol. 1. London: Penguin Books, 1992.

——. *Capital: A Critique of Political Economy*. Vol. 2. London: Penguin Books, 1992.

——. "Critique of the Gotha Programme." In *The Political Writings*, edited by David Fernbach, 1023–43. London: Verso, 2019.

——. *Economic and Philosophic Manuscripts of 1844*. Amherst NY: Prometheus Books, 1988.

——. "The Eighteenth Brumaire of Louis Bonaparte." In *The Political Writings*, edited by David Fernbach, 477–583. London: Verso, 2019.

——. *Grundrisse: Foundations of the Critique of Political Economy*. New York: Random House, 1973.

Marx, Karl, and Friedrich Engels. *The Communist Manifesto*. London: Penguin, 1967.

Miles, Robert. *Racism after "Race Relations."* London: Routledge, 1993.

Mitchell, Don. *Mean Streets: Homelessness, Public Space, and the Limits of Capital*. Athens: University of Georgia Press, 2020.

Moi, Toril. "From Femininity to Finitude: Freud, Lacan, and Feminism, Again." *Signs: Journal of Women in Culture and Society* 29, no. 3 (2004): 841–78.

National Coalition for the Homeless (NCH). *Hate, Violence, and Death on Main Street USA: A Report on Hate Crimes and Violence against People Experiencing Homelessness 2008*. August 2009. https://nationalhomeless.org/publications/hatecrimes/hate_report _2008.pdf.

Nyberg, Mikael. *Kapitalets automatik: Mänskliga robotar och systematisk dumhet*. Stockholm: Verbal Förlag, 2020.

OECD (Organization for Economic Co-operation and Development). OECD *Economic Surveys: Sweden 2019—Overview*. Paris: OECD, 2019.

——. *Recruiting Immigrant Workers: Sweden 2011*. Paris: OECD, 2011.

Ollman, Bertell. *Dialectical Investigations*. New York: Routledge, 1993.

Olsson, Gunnar. *Abysmal: A Critique of Cartographic Reason*. Chicago: University of Chicago Press, 2010.

Paulsen, Roland. *Arbetssamhället: Hur arbetet överlevde teknologin*. Malmö: Gleerups, 2010.

Persdotter, Maria. "Free to Move Along: On the Urbanisation of Cross-Border Mobility Controls—A Case of Roma 'EU déclassés' in Malmö, Sweden." PhD diss., Malmö University, 2019.

Polismyndigheten Rapport. *Nationell lägesbild: Brottslighet med koppling till tiggeri och utsatta EU-medborgare i Sverige*. Stockholm: Polismyndigheten, Nationella operativa avdelningen, 2015.

Poulantzas, Nicos. "On Social Classes." In *The Poulantzas Reader: Marxism, Law and the State*, edited by James Martin. London: Verso, 2008.

Pred, Allan. *Even in Sweden: Racialized Spaces and the Popular Geographical Imagination*. Berkeley: University of California Press, 2000.

Proudfoot, Jesse. "The Anxious Enjoyment of Poverty: Drug Addiction, Panhandling, and the Spaces of Psychoanalysis." PhD diss., Simon Fraser University, 2011.

Radford, Colin. "Begging Principles: The Big Issue." *Journal of Applied Philosophy* 18, no. 3 (2001): 287–96.

Raphael, David Daiches, and Alec Lawrence Mcfie. Introduction to *The Theory of Moral Sentiments*, edited by Adam Smith. Indianapolis: Liberty Fund, 1984.

Richardson, Seth. "Obedient Bellies: Hunger and Food Security in Ancient Mesopotamia." *Journal of the Economic and Social History of the Orient* 59, no. 6 (2016): 750–79.

Robertson, Ann. "Marxism and Anarchism: The Philosophical Roots of the Marx-Bakunin Conflict." *What's Next? Marxist Discussion Journal* 27 (2003): 47–59.

Roine, Jesper, and Daniel Waldenström. "Wealth Concentration over the Path of Development: Sweden, 1873–2006." *Scandinavian Journal of Economics* 111 (2009): 168.

Rolf, Hannes. "A Union for Tenants: Tenant Militancy in Gothenburg as a Historical Example." *Radical Housing Journal* 3, no. 1 (2021): 167–86.

Rorke, Bernard. "No Longer and Not Yet: Between Exclusion and Emancipation." In *Roma Diplomacy*, edited by Valeriu Nicolae and Hannah Slavik, 87–102. New York: International Debate Education Association, 2007.

Rostami, Amir. "Street-Gang Violence in Sweden Is a Growing Concern." *Sociologisk forskning* 54, no. 4 (2017): 365–68.

Sahlin, Ingrid. "Bostadslöshet som politiskt resultat." *Fronesis* 42–43 (2013): 53–64.

Said, Edward W. *Representations of the Intellectual: The 1993 Reith Lectures*. New York: Vintage Books, 1996.

Salihu, Diamant. *Tills alla dör*. Stockholm: Mondial, 2022.

Schafer, Arthur. *The Expressive Liberty of Beggars: Why It Matters to Them, and to Us.* Ottawa: Canadian Centre for Policy Alternatives, 2007.

Scocco, Sandro. *Och några, antar jag, är ok! Varför nationalistiska vänstern är en åter-vändsgränd och nationalistiska högerns ärende inte är främlingsfientlighet.* Stockholm: Bokförlaget Atlas, 2019.

Scocco, Sandro, and Lars Fredrik Andersson. *900 miljarder skäl att uppskatta invandring: En analys av invandringens effekter på de offentliga finanserna i Sverige 1950–2014.* Stockholm: Arena Idé, 2015.

Selling, Jan. *Frigörelsen: Romers och resandes emancipation i Sverige och andra länder.* Stockholm: Carlssons, 2020.

———. *Svensk antiziganism: Fördomens kontinuitet och förändringens förutsättningar.* Ormaryd: Östkultur, 2014.

Sibley, David. *Geographies of Exclusion: Society and Difference in the West.* Abingdon: Routledge, 1995.

Sivanandan, Ambalavaner. "Poverty Is the New Black." *Race & Class* 43, no. 2 (2001): 1–5.

Sjöwall, Maj, and Per Wahlöö. *Roman om ett brott.* Stockholm: Norstedts Pocket, 2005.

Smith, Adam. *An Inquiry into the Nature and Causes of the Wealth of Nations.* MεταLibri Digital Library, 2007.

Socialstyrelsen. *Hemlöshet 2017—Omfattning och karaktär.* Stockholm: Socialstyrelsen, 2017.

Stadsmissionen. *Att vända muggen: Insatser, idéer och inspiration för att se EU-medborgare som resurs.* Stockholm: Stadsmissionen, 2016.

Stallybrass, Peter. "Marx and Heterogeneity: Thinking the Lumpenproletariat." *Representations* 31 (1990): 69–95.

Statens Offentliga Utredningar (SOU). 1923:2. *Förslag till lag om lösdrivares behandling m.fl. författningar—Del V av Fattigvårdslagstiftningskommitténs betänkanden.* Stockholm: Socialdepartementet.

———. 1956:43. *Zigenarfrågan. Betänkande avgivet av 1954 års zigenarutredning.* Stockholm: Socialdepartementet.

———. 2006:14. *Samernas sedvanemarker: Betänkande av Gränsdragningskommissionen för renskötselområdet.* Stockholm: Kulturdepartementet.

———. 2010:55 *Romers rätt: En strategi för romer i Sverige. Betänkande av Delegationen för romska frågor.* Stockholm: Kulturdepartementet.

———. 2016:6. *Framtid sökes: Slutredovisning från den nationella samordnaren för utsatta EU-medborgare.* Stockholm: Socialdepartementet.

———. 2016:78. *Ordning och reda i välfärden: Betänkande av välfärdsutredningen.* Stockholm: Finansdepartementet.

———. 2017:12. *Att ta emot människor på flykt—Sverige hösten 2015: Betänkande av Utredningen om migrationsmottagandet 2015.* Stockholm: Justitiedepartementet.

Stewart, Michael. "Deprivation, the Roma and 'the Underclass.'" In *Postsocialism: Ideals, Ideologies and Practices in Eurasia,* edited by Chris Hann, 133–56. Abingdon: Routledge, 2002.

Streeck, Wolfgang. *Buying Time: The Delayed Crisis of Democratic Capitalism.* London: Verso, 2017.

Sveriges Stadsmissioner, Göteborgs Räddningsmission, and Rädda Barnen (Save the Children Sweden). *Mellan hopp och förtvivlan: En lägesrapport om minderåriga EU-medborgare i utsatthet.* Stockholm: Rädda Barnen, 2016.

Taikon, Katarina. *Zigenare är vi.* Stockholm: Tiden, 1967.

Teodorescu, Dominic. "Dwelling on Substandard Housing: A Multi-Site Contextualisation of Housing Deprivation among Romanian Roma." PhD diss., Uppsala University, 2019.

Teodorescu, Dominic, and Irene Molina. "Roma Street-Workers in Uppsala: Racialised Poverty and Super Precarious Housing Conditions in Romania and Sweden." *International Journal of Housing Policy* 21, no. 3 (2021, first published 2020): 1–26.

Thaler, Richard, and Cass Sunstein. "Libertarian Paternalism." *American Economic Review* 93 (2003): 175–79.

Therborn, Göran. *Kapitalet, överheten och alla vi andra: Klassamhället i Sverige—det rådande och det kommande.* Lund: Arkiv förlag, 2018.

Thompson, E. P. "The Moral Economy of the English Crowd in the Eighteenth Century." *Past & Present* 50 (1971): 76–136.

Thörn, Catharina. "Soft Policies of Exclusion: Entrepreneurial Strategies of Ambience and Control of Public Space in Gothenburg, Sweden." *Urban Geography* 32 (2011): 989–1008.

Vermeersch, Peter. "Reframing the Roma: EU Initiatives and the Politics of Reinterpretation." *Journal of Ethnic and Migration Studies* 38, no. 8 (2012): 1195–212.

von Mahs, Jürgen, and Don Mitchell, eds. "The Americanization of Homelessness?" *Urban Geography* 32, no. 7 (2011).

Wagman, Petra, Anita Björklund, Ann Johansson, and Sofi Fristedt. "Descriptions of Health by EU Citizens Begging Abroad." *Society, Health & Vulnerability* 8, no. 1 (2017): 1–6.

Wallengren, Simon, Erik Hansson, Adriana Holmberg Milea, Albert Dandos, and Christian Tigerblad. *Gypsy, Go Home! Hate Crime against Roma EU-Migrants Who Make a Living on the Streets of Malmö, Sweden. An Intermediary Report.* Malmö: Skåne Stadsmission and Civil Right Defenders, 2019.

Wallengren, Simon, and Caroline Mellgren. "Silent Victims in the Public Eye: Socially Vulnerable EU Citizens' Exposure to Crime and Its Consequences." *Journal of Interpersonal Violence* 36, no. 3–4 (2021, first published 2018): 1–23.

Wallerstein, Immanuel. *World-Systems Analysis: An Introduction.* Durham NC: Duke University Press, 2004.

Whyte, Jessica. *The Morals of the Market: Human Rights and the Rise of Neoliberalism*. London: Verso, 2019.

Wilde, Oscar. *Collected Works of Oscar Wilde: The Plays, the Poems, the Stories and the Essays Including De Profundis*. Ware, UK: Wordsworth Editions, 1997.

Wilkinson, Richard, and Kate Pickett. *The Spirit Level: Why Equality Is Better for Everyone*. London: Penguin, 2010.

World Bank Group. *Diagnostics and Policy Advice for Supporting Roma Inclusion in Romania*. Washington DC: World Bank, 2014.

Žižek, Slavoj. *Against the Double Blackmail: Refugees, Terror and Other Troubles with the Neighbours*. London: Penguin, 2016.

———. "Neighbors and Other Monsters: A Plea for Ethical Violence." In *The Neighbor: Three Inquiries in Political Theology*, edited by Slavoj Žižek, Eric L. Santner, and Kenneth Reinhard, 134–90. Chicago: University of Chicago Press, 2005.

———. *The Sublime Object of Ideology*. London: Verso, 2008.

———. *Tarrying with the Negative: Kant, Hegel, and the Critique of Ideology*. Durham NC: Duke University Press, 1993.

———. *The Ticklish Subject: The Absent Centre of Political Ontology*. London: Verso, 2000.

———. *Violence: Six Sideways Reflections*. London: Profile Books, 2009.

Zupančič, Alenka. *Why Psychoanalysis? Three Interventions*. Copenhagen: NSU Press, 2014.

Bibliography

Index

abject, 87, 90–91, 111, 118, 173, 277, 285–86
abjection, 86–94, 96, 115, 144, 219, 222,
    278. *See also* ideology: racism as;
    lumpenproletariat; racialization
accumulation by dispossession, 35,
    182–84
activity and passivity, 39–40, 43, 66, 144,
    187–88. *See also* deservingness
aesthethics, 55, 91, 148, 162, 256
Agamben, Giorgio, 275
Åkesson, Jimmie, 170, 245–46
alienation, 46, 48, 91, 180, 275; Marxist,
    53, 278–79, 280, 291, 313n11; philosoph-
    ical, 102, 112–13, 116, 134, 142, 144, 148,
    279, 280, 291
Allemansrätten, 227
Alliance, 167, 169, 176–77, 183–84, 188, 191,
    196, 197–98, 200, 211–13, 223, 244, 247,
    250–51, 260–61, 264
Althusser, Louis, 138, 285–86
Amnesty International, 192, 203–4, 207–
    8, 218, 267, 282
Andersson, Magdalena, 259
antipathy, 23–24, 77–78, 81–83, 109–15,
    119–20, 139, 170, 194
antiracism, 171–73, 189–94, 227, 236, 248,
    250, 254, 256, 272, 274–77
anti-Semitism, 14, 61, 88, 115, 146, 164
apathy, 109, 116, 120, 123, 215, 268
arsons, 71–73, 74, 176, 217, 245–46, 247,
    310n52

artificial scarcity, 69, 79, 141, 147, 181, 200,
    271, 276, 281, 285

bad object, 78, 89–91, 98, 110, 253
Black Lives Matter, 276–77
Blomley, Nicholas, 44–45
Bowie, David, 268
Brecht, Bertold, 129, 292
Bulgaria, xiii, xvi, 2, 12–13, 16, 114, 173,
    183, 186, 238, 265, 293n4
Busch Thor, Ebba, 244, 261

Cabral, Amílcar, 12, 15–17, 49, 90, 278
capital, xi, 16, 33–35, 40, 65, 140, 154, 180–
    83, 221–22; hegemonic fraction of,
    156–59, 181, 198, 213, 231, 260–62, 272–
    73, 314n24; logic of, xvi, 33–35, 38, 41–
    43, 53, 61–63, 117, 134, 140, 149, 158–59,
    172–73, 175, 215, 222–23, 272–73, 287;
    Swedish, 3–4, 37, 154–55, 163, 166–67,
    170, 172–73, 198, 213–15, 220, 222–23,
    231, 241–42, 252, 260–62, 272–73
caring rationality, 236–42, 259
Carmichael, Stokely, 272
Ceaușescu, Nicolae, 14, 209
Center Party, 165–66, 167, 189, 198, 228,
    261, 283
Christian Democrats, xiii–xiv, 51, 53, 153,
    167, 197–98, 244, 260, 263
Christianity, 51, 64–66, 121, 237. *See also*
    religion

gang shootings, 205, 235, 246, 265–66,

Germany, xi, 49, 57, 60, 61, 62, 87, 146, 164–65, 167, 243, 253

Gica (Gheorghe Hortolomei-Lupu), 1–2, 13, 88, 269

Gilmore, Ruth Wilson, 61

Gilroy, Paul, 177

good object, 89–91, 143, 214, 253

Gramsci, Antonio, 12, 39, 41, 136

Great Britain, 50, 57, 167, 253

guilt, sense of, 105, 118–21, 124, 128–29. *See also* superego

Hall, Stuart, 7, 10, 12, 156, 182, 184, 190, 266, 281

Hansson, Per Albin, 47, 54, 59, 170, 278

Harvey, David, 33, 182

Heart to Heart (Hjärta till hjärta), 237, 241, 242

Hegel, Georg Wilhelm Friedrich, 103, 117, 135

hegemony: crisis of, 10–11, 78–79, 154–59, 179, 181, 186, 197–99, 222, 232–36, 240–52; of the state, 154–59, 164–66, 199, 205, 215, 232–36, 243–52, 261–63, 274. *See also* capital: hegemonic fraction of; class struggle; democratic capitalism; ideology

Hobbes, Thomas, 44

Holocaust, 14, 59, 174, 191; survivor of, 174, 264, 299n28

Hortolomei-Lupu, Gheorghe. *See* Gica (Gheorghe Hortolomei-Lupu)

"the human," 116–18, 141–42, 144–45, 149, 271, 287. *See also* empathy; Real

human rights, 4, 13, 30, 44–45, 122, 192–93, 199, 202, 203–4, 207, 216–19, 225, 236, 237, 249–50, 275, 280, 282, 283

ideology: counter-ideology, 147–48, 156–58, 167–68, 280–86, 288; counter-

ideology of human rights and anti-racism, 156, 189–93, 216–18, 227, 236–37, 250, 274–77, 280; counter-ideology of SD, 5, 23–24, 50–51, 79, 82–86, 154, 156–57, 170, 179–80, 182, 184–85, 195, 198, 213, 232, 236, 244–45, 247, 252–54, 259–60, 262–63, 266–67, 273; dominant, 42, 136, 139–42, 147–49, 154, 156, 158–59, 166, 168, 175, 182, 184, 200–201, 213, 219, 221, 227, 237, 242, 250, 255, 266–67, 279, 288; racism as, 7, 24, 56–60, 61–62, 93, 110–11, 115, 139, 144–47, 149, 159, 170–73, 176–77, 179, 181–82, 184, 205, 213, 217, 225, 252–54, 262–63, 266–67, 270–73, 275, 277; through the unconscious, 91, 93, 96–97, 116, 130, 133–39, 141–49, 177–82, 271–72, 279, 281

Imaginary, 52, 95, 98–102, 109, 112, 117–18, 135–37, 141, 143, 173, 175, 182, 200, 251, 254, 265, 275, 279

income security principle, 37, 164, 205

industrial reserve army, 34, 37, 212

insider-outsider theory, 212–16, 252, 278. *See also* neoliberalism

ISIS (Islamic State of Iraq and Syria), 79, 230, 299n28

Jameson, Fredric, 86, 96, 97, 135, 281, 289–90

Jesus Christ, 64–65

jouissance, 302n9. *See also* theft of Enjoyment

justice ombudsman, 187, 200, 268

Kant, Immanuel, 117, 125, 126, 127, 129, 291

Keynesianism, 3, 37–38, 166, 174, 180

Kjellén, Rudolf, 165

Klein, Melanie, 89, 98, 99

Kristersson, Ulf, 153, 258, 259, 261, 264, 267

Kristeva, Julia, 87–88

190, 214, 220, 224, 234–35, 252, 262, 265–66, 275, 278, 280. *See also* dialectic: of racism; ideology: racism as

Real, 95–97, 99–104, 107–8, 110, 112, 116–18, 124, 130, 132, 135–36, 137–39, 141–42, 146–47, 149, 155, 158, 159, 173, 175, 201–2, 215, 222, 240, 252, 266, 274–75, 281, 286, 291

Red-Green government, 188, 199, 200, 233, 252, 260–61

refugees: accommodations for, 71, 73–74, 176, 204, 224–25, 244–45; "crisis" of, xiii, 4, 10–11, 71, 83, 154, 156, 185, 196, 213, 224, 227, 242, 243–52, 253, 273

reigning fraction, 157–59, 184–85, 189–91, 193, 195–97, 214, 216, 236, 242, 246–47, 250–54, 267, 270. *See also* hegemony; ruling bloc

Reinfeldt, Fredrik, 153, 167, 173, 196–97, 258

religion, 51, 61, 64–66, 140–41, 290. *See also* Christianity

revolution, 49, 163, 276–90

right of residence, in the EU, 4, 13, 81, 201, 202, 204, 207–8, 211

Roma: in Romania, 1, 13–15, 23, 54, 192, 210, 299n28; Swedish, 16, 27, 58–60, 63–64, 79–80, 81, 156, 191, 193, 216–18, 220; Swedish civil right movement of, 191, 193, 217

Romania, xiii, xvi, 1, 2, 12–15, 16, 23, 38, 52, 54, 114, 116, 173, 183, 186, 192, 210, 237, 238, 241, 265, 267, 293n4, 299n28

ruling bloc, 10–11, 156, 236, 250–52, 262–63. *See also* reigning fraction

Said, Edward, 280

Sami, 60–61, 62, 171, 277

Scocco, Sandro, 168, 174, 184

Simpson, Homer, 279

Sivanandan, Ambalavaner, 82

Smith, Adam, 45–46, 50, 291

social contract, 28–32, 37, 41

social Darwinism, 46, 59–60

social democracy, 8, 10, 42, 47–48, 54, 133, 153, 162–69, 174, 182, 213, 246–47, 255–56, 263, 273, 286

socialism, 3, 14, 43, 46–49, 53, 140–41, 146–47, 164–65, 170, 182, 219, 284, 290

solidarity, 3, 23, 54, 108, 147, 240, 269, 273, 276–81, 287; with EU déclassés, 122, 189, 192, 214–15, 218, 274, 276, 279, 283–85; national, 42, 119, 133, 140, 145, 147–49, 170, 205–6, 237; white, 171–75, 177, 236; of the working class, 47–48, 141, 205, 273, 276–77, 284–85

Sorgenfri settlement, 232–34, 247–49, 274

Streeck, Wolfgang, 180–81, 222

superego, 124, 126, 127. *See also* guilt

Sweden image, xvii, 3, 55, 162, 171–72, 177, 253–54; Sweden's self-image, xiv–xv, 4, 24, 54–55, 163, 176–77, 193, 262

Swedish ideology, 3, 139–40, 159, 164, 166, 170, 193–96, 198–99, 210, 219, 233, 236–37, 244, 249, 259, 261–62, 271, 274, 279–80. *See also* exceptional equality; ideology: dominant

Swedish Model, 161–63, 174, 200–201, 204–16, 224, 255, 273

Symbolic, 88, 95–102, 109, 117–18, 124, 130, 131–32, 135–36, 141, 146, 148, 173, 192, 200–201, 254

sympathy, xiii–iv, 28, 82, 94, 100, 108, 109, 118–34, 141, 194–95, 215, 270, 306n20

Taikon, Katarina, 217, 247–48

tattare, 59–60

terrorism, 71–75, 154, 176, 186, 190, 216, 245, 310n51; jihadist-Salafist, 79, 92, 186, 230, 299. *See also* lone wolf terrorism

theft of Enjoyment, 7, 144–45, 148–49, 155, 164, 167, 170, 172–73, 178, 181, 200,

In the Cultural Geographies + Rewriting the Earth series

Topoi/Graphein: Mapping the Middle in Spatial Thought
Christian Abrahamsson
Foreword by Gunnar Olsson

Negative Geographies: Exploring the Politics of Limits
Edited by David Bissell, Mitch Rose, and Paul Harrison

Animated Lands: Studies in Territoriology
Andrea Mubi Brighenti and Mattias Kärrholm

Mapping Beyond Measure: Art, Cartography, and the Space of Global Modernity
Simon Ferdinand

The Begging Question: Sweden's Social Responses to the Roma Destitute
Erik Hansson
Foreword by Don Mitchell

Psychoanalysis and the GlObal
Edited and with an introduction by Ilan Kapoor

A Place More Void
Edited by Paul Kingsbury and Anna J. Secor

Arkography: A Grand Tour through the Taken-for-Granted
Gunnar Olsson

A Different "Trek": Radical Geographies of "Deep Space Nine"
David K. Seitz

To order or obtain more information on these or other University of Nebraska Press titles, visit nebraskapress.unl.edu.

CPSIA information can be obtained
at www.ICGtesting.com
Printed in the USA
LVHW041618200323
742025LV00001B/80